Teaching Learners of English in Mainstream Classrooms (K–8)

One Class, Many Paths

Linda New Levine

Mary Lou McCloskey

Boston   New York   San Francisco
Mexico City   Montreal   Toronto   London   Madrid   Munich   Paris
Hong Kong   Singapore   Tokyo   Cape Town   Sydney

Executive Editor: Aurora Martínez Ramos
Editorial Assistant: Kara Kikel
Executive Marketing Manager: Krista Clark
Production Editor: Mary Beth Finch
Editorial Production Service: Nesbitt Graphics, Inc.
Composition Buyer: Linda Cox
Manufacturing Buyer: Linda Morris
Electronic Composition: Nesbitt Graphics, Inc.
Interior Design: Nesbitt Graphics, Inc./adaptation
Photo Researcher: Annie Pickert
Cover Administrator: Elena Sidorova

For related titles and support materials, visit our online catalog at www.pearsonhighered.com.

Between the time web site information is gathered and then published, it is not unusual for some sites to have closed. Also, the transcription of URLs can result in typographical errors. The publisher would appreciate notification where these errors occur so that they may be corrected in subsequent editions.

Library of Congress Cataloging-in-Publication Data

Levine, Linda New.
   Teaching learners of English in mainstream classrooms (K-8): one class, many paths/Linda New Levine, Mary Lou McCloskey.
      p. cm.
   Includes bibliographical references and index.
   ISBN 0-205-41059-6
   1. English language–Study and teaching (Elementary)–Foreign speakers. 2. English language–Study and teaching (Middle school)–Foreign speakers. 3. Second language acquisition. I. McCloskey, Mary Lou. II. Title.

PE1128.A2L39 2009
372.65′21–dc22

2008022082

Printed in the United States.

10 9 8 7 6 5 4 3 2 1   12 11 10 09 08

Photo Credits: p. 3: Ruth Jenkinson/Dorling Kindersley Media Library; pp. 21, 32: Robert Harbison; pp. 28, 188, 206, 253: Lindfors Photography; pp. 31, 34: Courtesy of Mary Lou McCloskey; p. 37: David Mager/Pearson Learning Photo Studio; p. 48: Bob Daemmrich Photography; p. 50: Krista Greco/Merrill Education; p. 52: Tony Freeman/PhotoEdit; p. 73: Pearson Learning Photo Studio; p. 96: Karen Mancinelli/Pearson Learning Photo Studio; p. 107: Michael Newman/PhotoEdit; p. 133: Photodisc/Getty Images; p. 166: Paul Almasy/Corbis; pp. 171, 211: Ellen B. Senisi/The Image Works; p. 191: GeoStock/Photodisc/Getty Images.

Text Credits appear on page xvi, which constitutes an extension of the copyright page.

Allyn & Bacon
is an imprint of

www.pearsonhighered.com

ISBN 10: 0-205-41059-6
ISBN 13: 978-0-205-41059-0

About the Authors

Linda New Levine is a consultant for ESL and EFL programs for school-age children. She has assisted in the development of English language programs for successful academic content learning in countries in the Middle East, Africa, and Asia, and for school districts and professional organizations within the U.S. In addition, she works with mainstream classroom teachers for differentiation of teaching and learning in the content areas and for the development of literacy for ELLs in English language classrooms K through 12.

Dr. Levine has worked as an ESL teacher and a staff development facilitator in the Bedford, New York, school district, and as an Assistant Professor at Teachers College, Columbia University.

She has taught EFL in the Philippines with the Peace Corps and in the People's Republic of China as a Fulbright professor. In addition, she has worked with faculties and ministries of education in Egypt to implement English as a Foreign Language programs in elementary schools throughout the country and to improve the supervisory skills of school supervisors. As part of a design team for USAID, Dr. Levine evaluated language programs in Egypt and designed a format for future funding in that region. She currently consults for the Center for Applied Linguistics.

Dr. Levine is the Home Room columnist for TESOL's Essential Teacher. Among her publications is the recent *Helping English Language Learners Succeed in Pre-K-Elementary Schools* (2006) with Jan Lacina and Patience Sowa (TESOL International).

Dr. Levine holds a Masters in TESOL and a PhD in Applied Linguistics from New York University.

Mary Lou McCloskey, former President of Teachers of English to Speakers of Other Languages, is Director of Teacher Education and Curriculum Development for Educo in Atlanta. As a consultant and author in the field of English language education, she has worked with teachers, teacher educators, and departments and ministries of education on 5 continents and in 35 of the 50 United States.

Dr. McCloskey has taught in undergraduate and graduate programs at Emory University, Georgia State University, and the University of Memphis. The author and co-author of many journal articles, chapters, and professional texts for educators (including *Integrating English* (1988), *Teaching English as a Foreign Language in the Primary School* (2006), and *Leadership Skills for English Language Educators* (2007)), she has also developed six programs for English learners, including *On Our Way to English* (2004); *Visions: Language, Literature, Content; Voices in Literature* (2008); *Teaching Language, Literature and Culture* (1995); and was consulting author and ESOL specialist for the 2008 *McDougal Littell Language Arts, Grades 5–12* (2008). For the past three summers, Dr. McCloskey has worked as a teacher educator in the Teaching Tolerance Through English program conducted for middle school teachers and learners from countries throughout Central Europe. Her current project is an anthology of contemporary U.S. literature for teens learning English as a foreign language worldwide.

Dr. McCloskey, who holds an MS degree from Syracuse University and a PhD from Georgia State University, considers her most important qualification her years of experience with English learners from many cultures, at levels from preschool through graduate education.

Contents

Preface   xii

Chapter 1   Language Acquisition and Language Learning in the Classroom   1

What Do We Know About First Language Acquisition?   3
Language Acquisition Is Universal   3
Language Acquisition Is Natural   3
Language Acquisition Does Not Require Instruction   4

What Is the Nature of the First Language Environment?   5
Children Are Immersed in Language   6
Language Is Highly Contextualized   6
Language Is a Tool for Purposeful Use   6
Children Are Physically Active While Acquiring Language   6
Acquisition Occurs Within a Social Environment   7
Children Choose Those Aspects of Language That They Wish to Acquire   7
Language Acquisition Is Emotionally Embedded   8
Language Acquisition Is an Integrated Learning Experience   8

How Is Learning a Second Language in the Classroom Different from Acquiring a First Language?   9
The Acquisition-Learning Hypothesis   9
The Natural Order Hypothesis   10
The Input Hypothesis   10
The Affective Filter Hypothesis   10
The Monitor Hypothesis   11
The Interactionist Position   11

What Are Factors Affecting Acquisition?   12
Limited Language Input   12
Classroom Organization   12
High Content and Language Load   13
Academic Language and Social Language   14
Negative Bias   15
Cognition, Age, and Social and Cultural Differences   15
Error Correction   16
Culture Shock   17

What Strategies Do ELLs Use to Acquire Languages?   17

What Can ELLs Tell Us About Positive Classroom Environments and Learning Experiences?   19

ELLs Are Active Acquirers of Language Throughout Their School Years   19

ELLs Seek to Find Meaning in All of Their Learning Experiences   19

ELLs Seek to Use Language for Purposeful Activity Even Though They May Have Limited Skills in English   20

ELLs Profit from Physical Activity   20

ELLs Are Social Beings in Any Language   20

ELLs Choose Which Aspects of Language to Learn   20

ELLs Respond to an Emotionally Positive Classroom Environment   20

ELLs Respond to Interesting Content Information   21

Questions for Reflection   21

Activities for Further Learning   22

Suggested Reading   23

Web Sites for Further Learning   23

References   24

Chapter 2   Principles of Integrated Language Teaching and Learning   26

Activity-Based Language Teaching and Learning   27

Principle 1 Active Engagement   27

Principle 2 Cultural Relevance   28

Principle 3 Collaboration   29

Principle 4 Learning Strategies   29

Communicative Teaching and Learning   30

Principle 5 Comprehensible Input with Scaffolding   30

Principle 6 Prior Knowledge   32

Principle 7 Content Integration   34

Principle 8 Differentiation   36

Principle 9 Clear, Appropriate Goals and Feedback   37

Questions for Reflection   40

Activities for Further Learning   40

Suggested Reading   41

Web Sites for Further Learning   41

References   42

Chapter 3   Reaching Out to Home and Community   44

Teachers as Cultural Mediators   45

How Do Teachers Connect to the Homes and Families of Their Students?   48

How Can the School Community Support the Education of English Language Learners?   51

How Can the Community Outside the School Support the Education of ELLs?   52

Questions for Reflection   56

Activities for Further Learning   56

Suggested Reading   57

Web Sites for Further Learning   58

References   58

Chapter 4   Classroom Management for Integrated Language Learning   60

First Things First: Feeling Ready to Learn   61
  Provisioning   61
  Gathering Information   61

Organizing the Physical Environment to Promote Language Learning   63
  Furniture Is Important   63
  Public Areas   64
  Private Space   65

Organizing the Classroom Social Environment to Promote
Language Learning   67
  Social Integration   67
  Presentation Formats   67
  Grouping   68
  Matching Learning Styles   68

Organizing Instruction to Promote Language Learning   72
  The Cognitive Academic Language Learning Approach (CALLA)   74
  Sheltered Instruction   76
    Preparation for Instruction   77
    Instruction   77
    Review/Assessment   78
  Cooperative Learning   79
    Basic Principles   79
    Teambuilding   80
    Management   81
    The Will and the Skill to Cooperate   81
  Problem-Based Learning   81
  Project Learning   83
  Differentiated Instruction (DI)   85

Questions for Reflection   86

Activities for Further Learning   87

Suggested Reading   88

Web Sites for Further Learning   89

References   89

Chapter 5   Strategies for Oral Language Development   92

Conditions for Oral Language Learning   93

Academic Language Learning   94
Culturally Diverse Language Patterns   96

Oral Language Development   97

Stages of Oral Language Development   98
Pre-production   99
Early Production (TESOL Level 1)   102
Speech Emergence (TESOL Level 2)   104
Intermediate Fluency (TESOL Levels 3, 4, and 5)   104

Teacher Tools for Oral Language Development   105
Clarity Tools   106
Clear Speech   106
Explanatory Devices   108
Cognitive Empathy   109
Giving Directions and Stating Reasons for Learning   109
Question and Response Tools   110
Sticking with Your Students   110
Wait Time   111
Interactional Structures   112
Scaffolding Oral Language Development   113
Collaborative Dialogues   118
Instructional Conversations   119

Assessing Oral Language Development   119

Questions for Reflection   122

Activities for Further Learning   122

Suggested Reading   123

Web Sites for Further Learning   124

References   124

Chapter 6   Oral Language Development in the Content Classroom   126

Content Learning and Oral Language Development   127
Language Arts   127
Storytelling   127
Reader's Theatre   130
Social Studies   130
Oral Language and the Textbook   131
Oral History   132
Dialogues   134
Math   134
Factors Affecting Achievement   135
Instructional Techniques for Math Class   136

Science   140

    Factors Affecting Achievement   141

    Instructional Techniques for Science Class   142

Oral Language Development Every Which Way   144

    Songs and Chants/Poetry and Rap   144

    Role Plays, RAFTS, and Simulations   147

    WebQuests   148

Listening In While Not Tuning Out   149

    Sound Discrimination   149

    Listening for Understanding   151

Assessing Listening and Speaking Skills in the Content Classroom   155

Questions for Reflection   155

Activities for Further Learning   156

Suggested Reading   157

Web Sites for Further Learning   157

References   158

Chapter 7   Developing Literacy with English Learners: Focus on Reading   160

What Is Literacy?   162

    Top-Down Approaches   163

    Bottom-Up Approaches   164

    Integrated Approaches   164

    ELLs Developing Literacy Require Special Instruction   165

What Is Unique About English Language Learners Who Are Developing Literacy?   165

    What ELLs Bring   166

    What ELLs Need   168

The Language/Literacy Matrix   172

What Tools and Strategies Can We Provide to Help ELLs Develop Literacy?   173

    21 Strategies to Support ELL Reading Development   174

Issues in Literacy Development with Older English Learners   190

    What Are Our Recommendations for These Older Learners?   192

Assessing ELL Literacy Development   193

    Standardized Reading Achievement Tests   194

    English Language Proficiency Tests   194

    Holistic Measures of Literacy Development   194

    Reading Skills Tests   195

Questions for Reflection   197

Activities for Further Learning   197

Suggested Reading   198

Web Sites for Further Learning   199

References   200

Chapter 8   Developing Literacy with English Learners: Focus on Writing   203

Why Teach Writing with English Learners?   206

How Does Writing Develop with ELLs?   206

Connecting Writing to Active, Communicative Language
Teaching and Learning   207

Challenges of Teaching Writing to English Learners   209

Developing a Writing Environment   209

Getting Started: Interactive Writing   210

Scaffolding Learners Through the Writing Process   214
Steps in the Writing Process   214
The Shared Writing Process   216

Assessing Writing   221
Mini-Lessons and Checklists   221
Determining Goals: Standards for ELL Writing   222

Questions for Reflection   225

Activities for Further Learning   226

Suggested Reading   227

Web Sites for Further Learning   227

References   229

Chapter 9   Structuring and Planning Content-Language Integrated Lessons   230

Lesson Characteristics That Support Learning   231
Teacher-Directed Instruction   231
Heterogeneous Grouping   232
Appropriate Content   233
Attention to Language   233
Supported Practice   234
Corrective Feedback   234

A Lesson Format for Integrated Learning   234

Into the Lesson: Defining Objectives, Activating, and
Preparing for Learning   235
Defining Content Objectives   235
Defining Language Objectives   237
Defining Learning Strategy Objectives   239

Performance Indicators   240

Activating Prior or Current Knowledge   242

Through the Lesson: Input for Active Understanding, Vocabulary Development, and Practical Purpose   245

Vocabulary Learning   245

Language and Content Input   248

Guided Practice   250

Beyond the Lesson: Providing Reasons for Further Communication   254

Independent Practice   254

Summarizing   256

Assessment   257

Questions for Reflection   258

Activities for Further Learning   258

Suggested Reading   259

Web Sites for Further Learning   260

References   260

Chapter 10   Assessment Tools for the Integrated Classroom   263

What Is Assessment?   264

Standardized Testing   264

Classroom-Based Assessment   264

Program Evaluation   264

Different Types of Assessment   265

What Are the Fundamental Principles of Classroom-Based Assessment for ELLs?   266

Conduct a Fair, Reliable, and Valid Assessment   266

Inform Teaching and Improve Learning   268

Use Multiple Sources of Information   270

Use Familiar Instructional Techniques   270

What Are the Critical Factors Affecting Assessment of ELLs?   273

Formative versus Summative Assessment   273

Formative Assessment   276

Cultural Issues in Testing   277

Language versus Content   278

What Are Examples of Authentic, Performance-Based Classroom Assessment?   278

Performance-Based Assessment (PBA)   279

Self-Assessment   279

Visible Criteria   283

Rubrics   284

How Do Standards Affect Classroom Assessment?   286

Questions for Reflection   293

Activities for Further Learning   293

Suggested Reading   294

Web Sites for Further Learning   295

References   295

Chapter 11   Putting It All Together Thematically: Developing Content-Based Thematic Units   297

What Is Thematic Instruction?   298
  Criteria for Thematic Instruction   299

Why Teach Thematically?   301

How Are Thematic Units Structured?   303
  Concrete to Abstract   303
  Low to High Cognitive Levels   305
  Simple to Complex Content Structures   305

What About Standards in a Thematic Unit?   308

Organizing Content Curriculum in a Thematic Unit   312

Organizing Language Curriculum in a Thematic Unit   316

How Can Learning Strategies Be Incorporated into Thematic Instruction?   318

A Last Word   319

Questions for Reflection   320

Activities for Further Learning   320

Suggested Reading   321

Web Sites for Further Learning   322

References   323

Appendix A Fairy Tales: A Thematic Unit for Grades K Through 3   324

Appendix B Ocean Connections: A Thematic Unit for Grades 4 Through 8   337

Glossary   356

Index   362

Preface

We have written this text to provide guidance to classroom teachers from grades K through 8 who find that their classes are increasingly including children who are learning English. We understand the challenges you face. We have worked in those classrooms and with those children ourselves. We hope to help you understand critical aspects of language development, the ways in which culture affects learning, and approaches and strategies for teaching English and content-area subjects to your English language learners. At the same time, we'll provide you with ideas for classroom management and suggest strategies that will enable you to challenge learners at many levels to grow and develop.

Who Are English Language Learners?

First, a quick word about terminology. Many terms have been used for students who are learning English. For many years, the legal U.S. government term for students who were served in special programs for language learners was Limited English Proficient (LEP). Other terms that have been used are English as a second language (ESL) students (even though English may be the third or fourth language these youngsters are learning), or English Language (EL) students. We have chosen to use the term English Language Learners (ELLs) for the purposes of this book, as we think it is both positive and descriptive. Likewise, classes for ELLs have many terms: ESL classes, English for Speakers of Other Languages (ESOL) classes, and English Language Development (ELD) classes are among them. In our book, we have described programs for ELLs as either English as a Second Language (ESL) programs or English Language Development (ELD) programs.

ELLs comprise a large and growing population of children in our schools. The growth of the ELL population from the 1995 to 1996 school years to the 2005 to 2006 school years was more than 57 percent. At this same time, growth in the total school enrollment was fairly flat. ELLs represented 10 percent of the total school population in 2005 to 2006, with an enrollment of more than five million students. Twelve states saw the greatest change during this 10-year period, with a growth of more than 200 percent in their ELL populations: Nevada, Colorado, Georgia, North Carolina, South Carolina, Tennessee, Alabama, Kentucky, Indiana, Nebraska, New Hampshire, and Arkansas (National Clearinghouse for English Language Acquisition and Language Instruction).

The ELL school population includes the children of immigrants, although they themselves are not all immigrants. Three-quarters of ELLs were born in the U.S. And they are, for the most part, poor. One in four school-age, low-income children under the age of 18 is an English language learner (Capps, Fix, Murray, Ost, Passel, & Herwantoro, 2005).

Although their numbers are growing, the level of academic achievement among ELLs, measured as a subgroup, is lower than that of proficient English-speaking learners. This is an obvious, natural result of the fact that they are learning a new language. Students classified as LEP (Limited English Proficient) do not meet state norms for reading in English according to reports from 41 state education agencies (Kindler,

2002). ELLs also score below their classmates on standardized tests of math (Moss & Puma, 1995), and are deemed to have lower academic abilities and be placed in lower ability groups than native English speakers (President's Advisory Commission on Educational Excellence for Hispanic Americans, 2003).

In spite of these commonalities, immigrant ELLs are a diverse group. Some of them come to school as excellent readers and writers in their first languages. Others are illiterate in any language. Some ELLs start school in kindergarten while others walk through our doors in adolescence as first-time students. Middle and high school age ELLs are most likely to have missed years of schooling and thus have significant gaps in their education (Ruiz-de-Velasco & Fix, 2000). Some ELLs come from countries with an alphabet system similar to that of English, such as Spanish and Haitian Creole. Others come with language skills from a widely different reading-writing system, such as Arabic or Chinese.

Many ELLs have been born and raised in the U.S. but speak a language other than English at home. They may have no preschool experience, or they may have acquired some pre-literacy skills and language in day care, preschool programs, or from older siblings. They may come from highly literate homes or from homes where there are no magazines and newspapers, and parents cannot read at all. ELLs born in the U.S. are as diverse as those who immigrate here.

In addition to language proficiency, other factors put ELLs at risk for educational failure: economic circumstances, trauma of war or dislocation, race, educational environment, geographic location, immigration status, health, family structure, age, learning disabilities, cultural bias, and many others (Christian, 2006).

All of them have come to us, their teachers, to help them find the promise that education can bring to their young lives. We greet them with the preparation of our college degrees, inservice education, and teaching experiences, the support of our colleagues, and the personal motivations that color all that we do.

Language and Cultural Diversity in the Classroom

The most important items children bring with them to school are their cultures and their languages. We need to learn all we can about the languages and cultures of our students in order to prevent the kinds of miscommunication that can occur when cultures clash. Children coming from countries with very formal schooling will be confused with the informal style of some elementary classrooms. Children who have been taught to be self-reliant at home will not respond to dependence upon the teacher. Children whose cultures emphasize cooperative work styles will feel isolated working alone at a single desk. Children with holistic learning styles will not respond quickly to linear thinking. Children from countries where same-sex groupings are common will be embarrassed working in girl-boy partnerships. Effective teachers are aware of children's cultural histories, life experiences, and learning strengths, and work to learn what else they need to know. They use this information to tailor the curriculum and their instructional strategies to the child. In close collaboration with colleagues, teachers create learning environments that promote success for their students.

ELLs in our classrooms can help us to create a positive cultural climate there as a result of the interactions they have with us, their teachers, and the experiences we create to help them learn. The kind of teacher we need to be for these ELLs is the kind of teacher most students want—a teacher who is caring. We need to be the teacher who takes the time to listen to students and answer their questions, who takes the time to prepare lessons thoughtfully and to ensure student interest. We need to be the teacher who provides a safe classroom environment for students—one where all will feel comfortable participating and where no one is fearful of ridicule. We need to be the teacher who is patient when ELLs are struggling with the burdens of a new language and culture, and feeling lost in a country where friends may be far away. We need to be the teacher who is knowledgeable and comfortable with diverse cultures, and sensitive to the needs of young people.

Whole School Involvement

Teachers within a school community are responsible for all learners within that community. For too long, teachers closed the doors of their classrooms and individually worked with their own students. We need to open our doors and talk about "our" students. We need the collective intelligence of all of our colleagues to teach all of the students in school today. We can't do it alone any more because the problems are too great and the stakes are too high.

Racism, low student expectations, discrimination, rigid school structures, cultural mismatch, and disrespect for linguistic diversity are some of the issues that cause school communities to be less than optimal for all learners (Nieto, 2003).

Because racism and discrimination are deadly to students' self-esteem and ability to achieve at a high level, we need to eradicate all vestiges of them from our schools. We value schools that search for and maintain a diverse, highly qualified teaching staff. Schools that discourage discrimination often include the study of racism and the study of differences as part of the curriculum. These schools cannot condone an attitude that allows some students to be viewed as "slow" or deficient because of linguistic differences. Teachers working in these schools know that although their ELLs can't produce a five-page academic essay today, they will in time. They just need to learn how.

There are structural factors in schools that encourage failure for ELLs. Tracking, standardized testing, teaching with rigid and traditional pedagogy, and maintaining isolation from the rest of the school community (Nieto, 2003) are some factors that need to be reconsidered. Schools that promote multicultural learning are those that encourage the integration of all learners through collaborative projects involving teachers planning together to create interdisciplinary learning units with a focus on community problems. Parent and community involvement are encouraged in these schools, flexible grouping procedures are used, classroom-based assessment is given a high priority, and teachers use innovative instructional strategies in an effort to help all children achieve.

We believe culture is a powerful curriculum source for students at all grade levels. We have seen teachers use culture as a stepping stone to student involvement in learning. The sharing of culture is compelling to all students. By integrating culture into the curriculum, we are likely to engage the attention and interest of English and non-English speaking students alike. In addition, we convey the clear message that we respect the cultures and traditions of our students.

Respect for the language skills of our students is often overlooked in North American classrooms, where English-speaking students are struggling to learn a foreign language while multi-lingual students are not encouraged to display their language abilities. Respect for the languages of our students begins with respect for their names. Students deserve to have their names used and pronounced correctly. The use of the native language as a tool for learning in the classroom is another area where teachers convey respect for ELLs and their cultures. Learning a little of our students' languages helps us to be aware of how difficult language learning is and creates a comfort level in the classroom when we attempt to make our students feel more accepted by speaking a few words of Chinese, Spanish, or Arabic.

Our Purpose and Beliefs

Throughout this book you will discover the underlying belief systems that drive us. We believe, firstly, that all children can learn to a high level. We believe children in schools are capable of learning more than one language and can use their languages to learn content courses even to the high standards that our schools demand. We believe all children are entitled to a challenging, innovative, and intellectually rigorous curriculum. In the classroom vignettes we have included at the beginning of most chapters, we have tried to provide models of best practices that we have compiled from the many great teachers we have worked with over the years. Unless we have included citations, the names of teachers, students, and schools we have used are pseudonyms.

We believe language acquisition is an innate ability of children everywhere, and this ability is honed through interactions with knowledgeable teachers and peers. We believe the community of learners in a school and within the larger community outside of school is important to the learning process. Most importantly, we believe the teacher is the critical factor in every classroom. What we do and say, the decisions we make, affect the learning environment for our students. We support the notion of the teacher as a critical thinker—one who arranges, changes, and modifies the curriculum in ways that will support the learning and emotional needs of all students.

It has taken us many years to accumulate the beliefs, concepts, and strategies described in this text. Simply reading about them won't help you to grow and develop as an effective teacher of diverse learners. You will need to question them, experiment with them, ask your colleagues about them, and, finally, test them out in your own classrooms. We believe that teachers need to develop a philosophy of education and a system of educational practice that works for them. It is helpful to take courses and attend workshops, but in the final analysis, these ideas and theories must be developed within the confines of our daily classroom practice. When teachers approach education in this way, they continue to grow and develop professionally throughout their careers.

Acknowledgments

We wish to thank our colleagues who reviewed the manuscript for this text: Katie Bell, Central Elementary School; Clara Lee Brown, the University of Tennessee, Knoxville; Dorothy Valcarcel Craig, Middle Tennessee State University; Emily Morgan, Fairmont Junior High School; Mary A. Phillips, Title III Program Specialist in ESOL, Georgia; Adrean Rivers-Horan, Remington Elementary School; and Sharon Ulanoff, California State University, Los Angeles.

We have learned much for this book from our colleagues (both cited and uncited) who shared with us their ideas and concerns, and who welcomed us into their classrooms to observe and learn; we are grateful to all of them. We thank our careful editors and assistants at Allyn & Bacon, who worked collaboratively to help us create the best book possible; we thank Prabha Varma for her careful assistance with manuscript preparation; and we marvel at the patience and support that Mike Levine and Joel Reed showed throughout the writing process.

References

Capps, R., Fix, M., Murray, J., Ost, J., Passel, P. S., & Herwantoro, S. (2005). The new demography of America's schools: Immigration and the No Child Left Behind Act. http://www.urban.org/uploadPDF/311230_new_demography.pdf.

Christian, D. (2006). Introduction. In F. Genesee, K. Lindholm-Leary, W. M. Saunders, & D. Christian (Eds.), *Educating English language learners: A synthesis of research evidence.* NY: Cambridge University Press.

Kindler, A. L. (2002). Survey of the states' limited English proficient students and available educational programs and services: 2000–2001 summary report. Washington, DC: National Clearinghouse for English Language Acquisition and Language Instruction Educational Programs.

Moss, M. & Puma, M. (1995). Prospects: The congressionally mandated study of educational growth and opportunity: Language minority and English language learners. Washington, DC: U.S. Department of Education.

National Clearinghouse for English Language Acquisition & Language Instruction Educational Programs. http://www.ncela.gwu.edu/policy/states/reports/statedata/2005LEP/GrowingLEP_0506.pdf

Nieto, S. (2003). *Affirming diversity: The sociopolitical context of multicultural education* (4th ed.). NY: Longman.

President's Advisory Commission on Educational Excellence for Hispanic Americans. (2003). From risk to opportunity: Fulfilling the educational needs of Hispanic Americans in the 21st century. Washington, DC.

Ruiz-de-Velasco, J. & Fix, M. (2000). Overlooked and underserved: Immigrant students in U. S. secondary schools. Washington, DC: The Urban Institute.

Text Credits:
Table 2.3 "Including Language and Content-Learning Goals" (p. 35), and **Table 7.1** "The Language/ Literacy Matrix" (p. 172) from pp. U148 and T23 of Freeman, et al., *On Our Way to English Teacher's Guide, Grades 2* and 3 respectively; **Table 7.4** "Sound-Symbol Transfer" (p. 178) from Morganthaler, *On Our Way to English Teacher's Resource Guide of Language Transfer Issues for English Language Learners;* all copyright ©2004 Harcourt Achieve Inc., adapted and reprinted by permission of the publisher. **Figure 4.4** "Range of Contextual Support and Degree of Cognitive Involvement in Communication Activities" (p. 74) from p. 57, *Negotiating Identities: Education for Empowerment in a Diverse Society,* by Jim Cummins, copyright ©1996. Used with permission of the California Association for Bilingual Education. **Table 5.1** "Language Development Stages" (pp. 100–101) adapted with permission from Grognet, A., Jameson, J., Franco, L., & Derrick-Mescua, M. (2000). *Enhancing English Language Learning in Elementary Classrooms: Study Guide* (p. 43). Washington, DC, and McHenry, IL: Center for Applied Linguistics and Delta Systems. **Table 5.4** "Student Oral Language Observation Matrix (SOLOM)" (pp. 120-121) from California Department of Education, Sacramento (2007). San Jose Unified School District. Cycle chart (p. 129) and **Figure 7.1** (p. 161) from *A Pocketful of Opossums* by Patricia Almada, copyright ©2004 Rigby/Harcourt Achieve Inc., adapted and reprinted by permission of the publisher. **Table 8.3** "WIDA English Language Proficiency Standards: Language of Social Studies" (p. 222) ©2004, 2007 Board of Regents of the University of Wisconsin System. **Table 9.2** "Bloom's Taxonomy of Thinking Levels" (p. 238) adapted from Zainuddin, H., Yahya, N., Morales-Jones, C., & Ariza, E., pp 257–258, *Fundamentals of Teaching Eng. to Spkrs. of Other Languages in K–12 Mainstream Classrooms* copyright ©2002 Kendall/Hunt. **Table 11.1** "Learning Activities on This Hierarchy Proceed from a Low Cognitive Level to Higher Cognitive Levels" (p. 306) excerpted from Ch. 4 (Levine), "Outline of Topics and Skills Covered in Teaching ESL K–12" p. 65, in *English as a Second Language Teacher Resource Handbook,* copyright ©1995 Sage Publications Inc. **Table 11.2** "Mohan Suggests Using These General Procedures for Organizing Information in Thematic Units" (p. 307) from Mohan, *Language and Content* (1986) used with permission of the author. **Table 2.4** "PreK–12 English Language Proficiency Standards in the Core Content Areas" (p. 38), **Table 2.5** "Mathematics Rubric Using Standard 3" (p. 38), **Table 10.18** "Shelly's Science Lesson Objectives" (p. 292) from Lacinda, et al., *Helping English Language Learners Succeed in PreK–Elementary Schools,* **Table 11.3** "ESL Standards for PreK–12 Students (Abridged)" (pp. 310–311), **Table 11.4** "The Performance Indicators Differentiate Listening Skill Levels for Language Proficiency While Maintaining Similar Science Content" (p. 312), and **Table 11.5** "The Performance Indicators Differentiate Speaking Skill Levels for Language Proficiency While Maintaining Similar Social Studies Content" (p. 313), all reprinted with permission of Teachers of English to Speakers of Other Languages, Inc. (TESOL, 2006).

CHAPTER 1

Language Acquisition and Language Learning in the Classroom

Children's language development is wonderful, novel, creative, and awe inspiring. Children speak in order to tell us stories:

Adult: *What did you do yesterday at school?*

Leslie: *I listened to a story. Was a horse. And roses maked him sneeze. And his nose itched and his eyes itched. Sumpin' else. I had . . . uh I haved . . . a had a motorcycle and I sit down and thinking what I was doing and lookin' at all those kids and teacher goed by and she didn't ask me anything.*

Adult: *What might she have asked you?*

Leslie: *How come you're sittin' here? (Weeks, 1979, p. 71)*

They speak to amuse us:

Child: *(Sitting close to the teacher during Rug Time, an opening activity.) Hot. (Touches the microphone.)*

Teacher: *It's not hot. It's not hot. It's a microphone.*

Child: *(Takes the teacher's hand and places it on the microphone.) See hot?*

Teacher: *Cold. It's cold.*

Child: *See. Hot.*

Teacher: *No, it's not hot. It's cold.*

Child: *Ahm, hot.*

Teacher: *No, it's not hot (Urzua, 1981, p. 56).*

They sometimes speak to resist us:

Child: *Nobody don't like me.*

Mother: *No, say "nobody likes me."*

Child: *Nobody don't like me (eight repetitions of this dialogue).*

Mother: *Now listen carefully; say "nobody likes me."*

Child: *Oh! Nobody don't likes me (McNeill, 1975, p. 27).*

And they often speak to help themselves learn:

Wally: *The big rug is the giant's castle. The small one is Jack's house.*

Eddie: *Both rugs are the same.*

Wally: *They can't be the same. Watch me. I'll walk around the rug. Now watch—walk, walk, walk, walk, walk, walk, walk, walk, walk—count all these walks. Okay. Now count the other rug. Walk, walk, walk, walk, walk. See? That one has more walks.*

Eddie: *No fair. You cheated. You walked faster.*

Wally: *I don't have to walk. I can just look.*

Eddie: *I can look too. But you have to measure it. You need a ruler. About 600 inches or feet.*

Wally: *We have a ruler.*

Eddie: *Not that one. Not the short kind. You have to use the long kind that gets rolled up in a box.*

Wally: *Use people. People's bodies. Lying down in a row.*

Eddie: *That's a great idea. I never even thought of that (Paley, 1981, pp. 13–14).*

Developing and using language to promote learning is the focus of this book. We will describe the classroom conditions and teacher behaviors that promote language development and academic achievement for **English language learners (ELLs)** in grades K through 8. If you are a teacher with ELLs in your classroom, you have the double task of teaching those children content learning and the language they need to understand, speak, read, and write about that content. This is an exciting and challenging task.

In order to help us understand the kinds of classrooms we need to create for our English language learners, it's important to understand how languages are acquired. Although this discussion is limited, it will highlight the essential information you need to know.

What do we know about first language acquisition?

- What is the nature of the first language environment?
- How is learning a second language in the classroom different from the experience of acquiring the first language?
- What strategies do ELLs use to acquire languages?
- What can ELLs tell us about positive classroom environments and learning experiences?

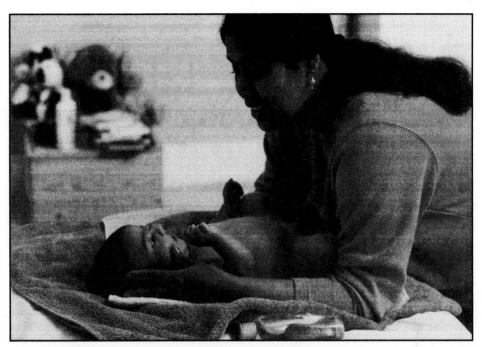

Parents the World Over "Talk" to Their Infant Children

What Do We Know About First Language Acquisition?

- First language acquisition is universal.
- First language acquisition is natural.
- First language acquisition does not require instruction.

Language Acquisition Is Universal

The birth of a child is a joyous event in all cultures of the world. Even so, parents worry about their newborns. They worry the child will be born healthy and with all fingers and toes intact, and whether their children will see, hear, and function normally. It is very rare, however, for a parent to worry about whether a child will learn to talk. We all assume our children will learn to speak a language even though we may wonder if they will learn to read. Language acquisition is universal in all cultures of the world. All children with normal or near-normal mental and physical abilities learn to speak a language.

Although children in various parts of the world are spoken to in a variety of diverse languages, children within those language communities are able to acquire languages that many adult speakers in the United States find to be difficult. In addition, children accomplish much of their learning at an age when their cognitive abilities are not yet fully developed.

Language Acquisition Is Natural

Human beings are born with the biological predisposition to acquire languages. Children begin to create the language they hear around them by completing the brain's innate blueprint for language learning with the specifics of the language or languages they hear at home.

Innate language theorists such as Noam Chomsky have speculated children are born with mechanisms that predispose them to learn language systems (1957, 1975). Chomsky believes the human brain contains the basic structures for all rule-governed, human languages. As evidence of this, he notes all languages contain components in common, such as categories of word classes, hierarchical structure, and linearity. He calls this innate device the *language acquisition device* (LAD) and proposes it contains a "universal grammar" that enables all children to analyze the language spoken to them and construct grammatical rules for that language.

The process through which children create languages is one of hypothesis testing. Children generate rules based upon the language input of the community: for example, the word "dat" refers to objects distant from the child, whereas "dis" refers to objects close by. In time, these rules are refined until, around the age of ten, most children have created the basic grammars of their first languages.

Children learn the language of the community around them. Those who live in multilanguage communities will sort through those languages and learn each in the specific context where it is used. For example, one author lived in a small town in the Philippines on the northern coast of Mindanao. The children of the town spoke Visayan with Christian shopkeepers, Maranao with Muslim schoolmates, and Tagalog and English with their teachers in school.

Children are known to create their own languages in order to communicate with others. The ten-year-old son of one author moved to the Peoples' Republic of China with his parents for a year's teaching assignment. Shortly after arrival in the country, the boy was observed playing ball with Japanese, Chinese, and American children of the University faculty. None of the children spoke the others' languages as yet. But in order to play baseball, the children began to create a language mix from words used by each of them. They used Japanese for the word "throw," English for "catch," and Chinese words for "you" and "run." In the absence of a common language, children will create one because it is natural for human beings to communicate with language (Figure 1.1).

Judy Shepard-Kegl attests to the instinctive quality of language acquisition in her description of a group of deaf children in Nicaragua in 1985. These youngsters had developed a sign language of their own. The language system was so complete it functioned as well as American Sign Language and was compiled into a dictionary (Piper, 1998). Plantation workers in Hawaii often did not speak a language in common and had difficulty communicating with one another. Their children, however, created a complete language system of their own.

Language Acquisition Does Not Require Instruction

If we taught children to speak, they'd never learn.

Holt, *How Children Fail*, 1964

It was once believed children acquired languages because they listened to and repeated the language of their parents. Imitation was seen as a form of tutoring for young children. We now know this behaviorist perspective is too simplistic an explanation for a complex and creative learning process. Children rarely repeat exactly what their parents say and often say things they have never heard said around them.

Even in the second language classroom, the creativity of children is apparent. When Marisol, (a ten-year-old student recently arrived in the U.S. from Spain) raised her hand in class, we were surprised because the child spoke very little English and had never volunteered to speak. When called upon, she asked "Me go peepee?" Marisol was ignoring the structured lessons of the language classroom in order to create her own language

Figure 1.1 Children Often Acquire New Languages because of a Need to Communicate During Play with Children Who Don't Speak the Same Language.

system. She substituted "Me" for the first person pronoun "I" and simply used intonation for the request form. She was highly communicative and creative but could not be said to be imitating her teacher or any of her fourth grade classmates.

In addition to not instructing their children in language, parents rarely make overt corrections of children's language. Instead, parents usually respond to the substance of their children's talk and ignore the grammar. One author watched two-year-old Anthony coloring with his mom (Levine, 1981). Anthony held up a crayon and his mother said, "That's yellow." Anthony then jumped up and said, "I get red." His mother responded with, "You want to get the red? Show Mommy the red if you're gonna get it. What's red? It's like the red light. That's the same color as the red light when Mommy's gotta stop the car."

Anthony's mother did not correct her child's grammar but responded to the topic of the conversation and used it as an opportunity to expand the child's utterance into a grammatical sentence: "You want to get the red?" She then continued to model a variety of other sentence forms all related to the subject of the red crayon. Her conversation doesn't resemble what we usually think of as language teaching but her language input to her child is important to his growing language system. The next section explores first language acquisition more thoroughly.

What Is the Nature of the First Language Environment?

- Children are immersed in language.
- Language is used in context—for example, in real-life situations—in order to help children attach meaning to words.

- Language is a tool that is used to fulfill a variety of purposes and functions such as socializing, controlling, satisfying needs, imagining, reporting, and reasoning.
- Children are physically active while learning.
- Language acquisition occurs within a social environment.
- Children choose those topics and aspects of language that they wish to acquire.
- Language acquisition is emotionally embedded.
- Language acquisition is an integrated learning experience.

Video Exercise

First Language Development

Go to MyEducationLab, select the topic **Oral Language Development**, and watch the video entitled "**First Language Development**" to observe a communicative interaction between a mother and her child. Complete the questions that accompany it. You may print your work or have it transmitted to your professor as necessary.

Children Are Immersed in Language

As we saw in the conversation with Anthony and his mom, parents immerse their children in a "veritable language bath" (Lindfors, 1987). Parents of newborns begin speaking to their infants in the delivery room. They continue the conversation with questions, exclamations, and commentary even though their babies are unlikely to answer a single question for at least two years. The lack of a child's response doesn't deter parents one bit. They keep on talking to their babies and attempt to engage the developing attention spans of their children for increasingly longer periods of time.

Language Is Highly Contextualized

The language that parents and other family members use is thought to be helpful to language acquisition because it is highly contextualized. Contextualized language is accompanied by many visual cues as to its meaning. For example, pointing to a dog is one way to identify the meaning of the word "dog." Caretakers use gestures such as pointing, touching, and making facial expressions to convey meaning to young children. They almost always speak about topics that young children are attending to at the moment of the utterance. Children can easily attach meaning to the language they hear because parents and family members are intent on helping their children understand their language. Children, then, acquire language within a context of use. They learn to ask for milk by pointing to the milk and approximating the "m" sound. They get picked up by raising their arms and saying "up." They play with the doors on the cabinets and learn how to open and close them while also learning the words "open" and "close."

Language Is a Tool for Purposeful Use

For children, language is a tool used to satisfy a purpose. Language helps children to get what they want, enables them to interact with other people, and allows them to report, have fun, imagine, and learn more about the world around them.

Children use language tools initially to satisfy their personal needs: "Want milk!" They quickly learn to use language as a tool for controlling others: "Gimme dat." Informing and identifying objects is part of early language development: "Dat a doggy." Later, children develop these functions in more complex ways and add others as required. Imaginative play produces language such as: "You be the mommy and I be the daddy." Children's curiosity prompts them to ask "Why?" and is the precursor to higher-level reasoning skills.

Children Are Physically Active While Acquiring Language

The child acquiring a first language is physically very active in exploring the environment. Sucking, crawling, dropping, and throwing are learning activities for young children. Jean Piaget, a Swiss psychologist, explained how the physical activity of young children contributed greatly to the developmental stages of a child's conceptual growth. Children progress through several stages of development and capability, finally culminating in a stage called "formal operations." In the early stages of language growth, the sensory-motor stage, children acquire knowledge by touching, grasping, looking at, and manipulating the objects around them (Labinowicz, 1980).

When children are not permitted to engage in active play, the cognitive and language losses that result are tragic. We have heard of these results in children who are confined to their cribs in orphanages and are unable to move outside of a small space. Depression and retardation are some of the consequences of a lack of physical, active play in young children.

Active movement has been found to be central to learning. There seems to be a neurological basis to learning that occurs in activity-based environments. The cerebella system, which controls motor activity, is one of the first parts of the brain to mature and has been found to be central in the formation of memory, attention, and spatial perception. In other words, the same part of the brain that controls movement also processes and promotes learning (Jensen, 1998). It is highly likely that environment plays an important part in determining the cognitive and linguistic maturity of children. Active play is a critical element of a child's environment.

Acquisition Occurs Within a Social Environment

The environment of a child acquiring language is a predominantly social environment. Young children need caretakers for a long time. While parents are caring for their young children, they are also talking and playing with them. Daily activities such as feeding, bathing, and dressing take on the nature of games as parents encourage children to eat ("Open wide. Here comes the airplane!") or to cooperate while putting on socks and shoes ("This little piggy went to market, this little piggy stayed home").

Parents interact with children in a cycle of speech that is geared to the child's level of understanding. Most caregivers modify their speech in ways to help children understand the language. In English, for example, parents will eliminate pronouns ("Come to Mommy"), use redundancy ("You want the red? What's the red, honey?"), use diminutives ("See the doggy?"), simplify the topic and the length of the sentence, and exaggerate intonation in order to engage a baby's attention (Snow, 1977). Although other cultures may customize caretaker language in different ways, all cultures modify language for children to enable babies to understand and grasp meaning from the interactions they have with other children and adults (Figure 1.2). This customizing of language is finely tuned to the baby's beginning speech comprehension. The bond of love and trust between the parent and child ensures parents will continue to speak to children and children will continue to take risks to develop linguistically even after the age of three, when basic communication has been established.

Children Choose Those Aspects of Language That They Wish to Acquire

The young child's language environment is one where the child chooses the language topic. Children decide what is interesting to them and parents begin to talk about those interests. For example, in an interaction between Anthony and his mother (to whom we were introduced earlier in this chapter), Anthony sat at a table coloring while his mother watched. The two of them talked about the colors. At one point, Anthony shifted his gaze from the coloring book to a truck on the toy shelf. His mother immediately changed the topic of the conversation to the truck and engaged Anthony in talking about it. Children direct the nature of their own language

Figure 1.2 Parents Modify Their Speech in Response to a Child's Linguistic Proficiency.

learning by choosing which grammar elements to focus on, deciding which words to learn, and even choosing the topics of the conversations they have with their caregivers (Levine, 1981).

Language Acquisition Is Emotionally Embedded

The language acquisition environment is an emotional environment for children. The bond of love and trust between parents and children is the major impetus to the continuing conversations that occur for years between them. Recent brain research (Jenson, 1998) tells us that the emotional overlay to language learning has a neurological basis. Results from research that was begun in the mid-1980s upset our notions of the rational mind and the separation of emotion and reasoning. Emotions drive attention, create their own memory pathways, and create meaning. Although the amygdala, an almond-shaped organ in the central brain, seems highly involved in emotional thought, the expression circuitry of emotion is widely distributed in the brain. In fact, when the frontal lobe of the brain is destroyed through accident, human performance on intelligence tests drops very little. Removal of the amygdala, however, is extremely harmful; it destroys the capacity for decision making, creativity, humor, imagination, altruism, and love (Jensen, 1998, pp. 73–75). It appears emotions are critical to all learning experiences and the formation of memory.

Language Acquisition Is an Integrated Learning Experience

The language environment of the young child is one where language is not separated from learning about the way the world operates. Although schools find it helpful to separate the math class from the social studies class, the learning of a young child is integrated. Children don't learn about the parts of language as described in a grammar book. They are completely uninterested in the names of word classes and verb tenses. Rather, children acquire language as a holistic experience while playing with objects and people around them. One-year-olds enjoy dropping objects into containers and spilling them out again (in and out). Two-year-olds explore every object in their environment while asking "What's dat?" Eight-year-olds are captivated by the world of nature and enjoy learning information about animals and their habitats. These children will often report on their learning using the language of a biological scientist.

How Is Learning a Second Language in the Classroom Different from Acquiring a First Language?

In our work with **English as a second language (ESL)** programs in the public schools, we have encouraged teachers to use children's natural, innate language-acquisition mechanisms in order to be successful language learners of English. In doing so, we acknowledge our belief in language acquisition driven by innate mechanisms interacting with the language-learning environment. Other factors driving language acquisition have equal importance, in our view, in content classrooms. The interaction between speaker-hearers is highly influential in the acquisition and learning of academic language; thus we value the interactionist position as well. Explanations for both positions follow.

Stephen Krashen (Krashen & Terrell, 1983) was an early proponent of the innatist position as described by Chomsky, and extended Chomsky's theory to second language acquisition research. Krashen believed that children learning the English language constructed their own grammars through a process of hypothesis testing, thus creating grammatical rules for the new language in a way similar to that of first language acquisition. Krashen explained the path of second language acquisition as a "natural approach," and has developed five hypotheses that have had an impact on classroom instruction of English language learners: the acquisition-learning hypothesis, the natural order hypothesis, the input hypothesis, the affective filter hypothesis, and the monitor hypothesis.

The Acquisition-Learning Hypothesis

The distinction between acquisition and learning is a critical one for classroom teachers. Krashen and Terrell (1983) define **acquisition** as "developing ability in a language by using it in natural communicative situations" (p. 18). When children play softball together on the playground or chat in the school cafeteria, acquisition may be coming into play. ELLs pay little attention to grammatical forms and instead concentrate on understanding and communicating meaningful messages. Language **learning,** however, requires "having a conscious knowledge about grammar" (p. 18). When learning about a language, children are taught word forms, suffixes and prefixes, spelling regularities, mechanics, and other aspects of a formal language system. Most learning about languages occurs in classrooms but it is possible for classrooms to foster acquisition as well. Krashen's emphasis on the acquisition-learning distinction is not merely one of environment, however. The claim is that "the learner actually processes and stores language differently under the two conditions. Acquisition leads to subconscious internalization of language structures and rules while learning leads to conscious learning" (Piper, 1998, p. 112).

Krashen believes children acquire their first language and "most probably, second languages as well." He says adults can also acquire languages although "they do not usually do it quite as well as children." Both learning and acquisition are important in classroom language development, but Krashen feels "Language acquisition is the central, most important means for gaining linguistic skills even for an adult" (Krashen

& Terrell, 1983, p. 18). Intuitively, the acquisition-learning distinction has appeal to teachers who have worked with ELLs. We recognize that students will not be effective or efficient learners when the focus of instruction is placed on rote repetition and grammar drills. Instead, effective teachers focus on meaningful communication related to purposeful content-learning activities.

The Natural Order Hypothesis

The natural order hypothesis claims that learners acquire language rules in a predictable order. This claim is based upon morpheme studies of second language acquirers (Dulay & Burt, 1974). Some of these structures, such as the progressive –*ing* ending and the plural, were shown to be acquired early in the grammars of both children and language-learning adults. Other structures, such as the regular past, the third person singular –*s,* and the possessive -*s* were acquired relatively late. This order prevailed when learners were acquiring (not learning) languages and focusing on meaning rather than form. Later work on the natural order hypothesis indicates that structures in a learner's first language may influence the order of morphemes acquired in the second language (McLaughlin, 1987). In spite of the evidence to indicate a natural order in the acquisition of morphemes, teachers do not base their language curriculums on this order and Krashen would not recommend that they do so. The reason is that language is acquired most efficiently in an environment of natural conversation that responds to children's interests and is structured for their understanding.

The Input Hypothesis

Language input in the form of oral language or reading is of primary importance for progress in the target language. Krashen asserts that the best input (*i*) is language that is understood by the learner but is a little beyond the learner's current understanding or competence (*i* + 1). The role of the teacher then is to provide abundant input to learners and to do so in ways that will help students understand the meaning of the communication. By providing a here-and-now context, instruction becomes **comprehensible input** and helps ELLs to negotiate the meaning of increasingly more complex structures and thus continue the acquisition process. Krashen considers comprehensible input the "most important part of any language teaching program" (Krashen & Terrell, 1983, p. 55). Teachers' experiences and classroom practice support the input hypothesis.

The Affective Filter Hypothesis

There are social and emotional variables that affect language acquisition. Those learners in a low-anxiety environment with motivation and good self-esteem have a lower **affective filter** and are more open to the input of others. This openness allows the learner to interact easily with proficient speakers and receive increasingly larger amounts of comprehensible input. Because acquisition proceeds under these conditions, it is important teachers don't force ELLs to speak, thus creating a high-anxiety situation. Many children spend time in a **silent period** during which they attempt to understand the input around them and then choose to speak when they are ready. The silent period of some ELLs can be lengthy depending on the personality of the student. Silence does not indicate acquisition is not taking place, however. Many ELLs begin to speak rather fluently at the end of their silent periods.

The Monitor Hypothesis

Krashen & Terrell (1983) assert acquisition is primary to language development. As such, there is little emphasis on formal rules. When writing, however, ELLs are able to reflect upon the formal rules of language (if they know them), spend sufficient time in following those rules, and focus on the form of the language. This reflection process devoted to form is called the **monitor,** an internal grammatical editor that is called into play as students learn the formal structure and requirements of a language.

Krashen has had a major influence on the teaching and learning of second languages. He has been influential in showing teachers the importance of comprehensible input for oral and written language, the existence of the silent period, and the need for a low anxiety classroom. These ideas in connection with techniques developed to increase academic competency in language have changed the nature of language classrooms.

The Interactionist Position

While acknowledging the importance of comprehensible input in language acquisition, interactionists stress the need for language interaction among speaker-hearers in order to promote language acquisition and language learning (Long & Porter, 1985; Swain, 1985; Pica, Lincoln-Porter, Paninos, & Linnell, 1996; Izumi & Bigelow, 2000; Klingner & Vaughn, 2000). Small-group work in classrooms between native speakers (NS) and ELLs or among pairs of native speakers has shown increased motivation and initiative among learners. Students produce more language in these conditions and are less anxious about their language usage (Long & Porter, 1985). Indeed, small groups of students, engaged in two-way tasks that require exchange of previously unknown information, engage in a higher quantity of language practice, produce a broader range of language functions, greater grammatical accuracy, frequent corrections, and more negotiation of meaning than those classes that are conducted by a teacher (Long & Porter, 1985).

Negotiation of meaning is crucial to effective interaction in classrooms in that it significantly aids the development of second language acquisition (Long & Porter, 1985). Negotiation of meaning occurs as learners receive comprehensible input and/or feedback on prior utterances. This input serves as data that enable learners to construct grammars while modifying and adjusting their language output, thus expanding their language development (Pica et al, 1996). Modified output results from signals from other speakers that communication has not been achieved; for example, open-ended questions such as "Glass? What about glass?" Requests such as these tend to generate modification in ELL language output that is more comprehensible and grammatically on target. Izumi and Bigelow (2000, p. 239) found that "extended opportunities to produce output and receive relevant input were found to be crucial in improving learners' use of the grammatical structure."

Even when the members of the small groups are language learners themselves, negotiation of meaning occurs that promotes language learning. "Teachers can be confident that the interaction can assist second language learning whether the source of that interaction is a NS [native speaker] or another learner" (Pica et al., 1996, p. 80). Klingner & Vaughn (2000) demonstrated negotiation of meaning among small groups of bilingual fifth graders using a collaborative reading strategy (CRS). Interactions among the ELLs in their study led to semi-structured vocabulary practice, negotiation of the meaning of text, and progress toward both language and content-learning goals.

It is clear that both innatist and interactionist theories have contributed to the nature of classroom instruction today. Teachers who "think language" while teaching content area objectives, and who provide effective small-group work experiences with abundant comprehensible input in a low-anxiety environment, will be effective in enabling ELLs to both acquire and learn language. In spite of the gains made in helping teachers to create classrooms that take advantage of the brain's ability to acquire languages, there are still major differences in the first and second language experience. Table 1.1 illustrates some of the differences in the two environments.

What Are Factors Affecting Acquisition?

Classroom language learning is very different from home language acquisition. There are factors in the nature of classroom instruction that affect second-language acquisition and ultimately, academic achievement, and are important for all teachers to understand.

Limited Language Input

Classrooms contain many children and this may lead to limited language input to the learner. The ratio of speaker-hearer is increased from a one-on-one situation to a thirty-to-one situation. Without careful planning, children's language needs for abundant input cannot easily be addressed by the teacher. Whereas a child is immersed in language while acquiring a first language, many students are rarely spoken to in schools at all (Harklau, 1994, 2000). As children proceed through the grades, comprehensible input is reduced. Without abundant input of meaningful language, ELLs will not acquire language efficiently or quickly.

The emotional attachments that occur between parents and their children are not easily replicated in classroom experiences either. After elementary school, teacher interactions with students become more formal. Lectures increase and circle time decreases. These distinctions may lead to a classroom environment where ELLs are spoken to infrequently and receive little emotional support. Teachers who recognize the necessity for emotionally rich, input-abundant environments will need to restructure the typical classroom situation in order for children to acquire language more efficiently.

Classroom Organization

The way in which we organize our classroom has an impact on the amount of language learned. With all the demands of the content classroom, math, social studies, science, and language arts teachers may report little time to teach to the specific language-learning needs of one or two children. Teachers tend to feel guilty about not spending enough time alone with ELLs to help them develop language skills. Teacher-centered, frontal teaching styles lead to more limited interaction between teacher and student and between student and student. There are times when this organizational style is necessary, for example when viewing a movie, listening to a speaker, or viewing a demonstration. But frontal teaching is only one of many classroom organizational patterns.

When we realize teachers are not the only speakers of the language within a class, we can begin to understand how other students can be used to facilitate the language development of their peers. Classrooms that differentiate instruction through activities, projects, and group work are more easily able to manage the needs of a wide variety of learners. Because language acquisition occurs in a social environment, student-centered classrooms place the focus on activities that are multilayered, allowing for diverse kinds of learning and permitting children at all levels to integrate themselves within the classroom learning community. When ELLs are given purposeful opportunities to communicate about topics interesting to them, language acquisition is facilitated

Table 1.1 Language-Learning Environments

	L1 Acquisition Environment	L2 Classroom Learning Environment
Opportunities for Interaction	• Constant and continuous. • Focus on meaningful communication. • Proceeds from gestural responses to one-word utterances to phrases to sentence forms. • Interaction promotes cognitive growth.	• May be limited by large classes and restricted opportunities for interaction. • Teacher-directed lessons. • Limited time available for language practice. • Unmovable furniture. • May be few opportunities for language interaction outside the classroom.
Language Input	• Abundant and frequent: teacher to student ratio often 1 to 1. • Simplified syntax. • Highly redundant. • Well formed. • Semantically concrete.	• May be limited in transmission-type classrooms. • May not be at each student's level of ability. • May be limited by lack of exposure to target language in the community.
Language Context	• Focused on the here and now. • Highly meaningful to the child. • Context provides the meaning for most utterances.	• May be removed from the here and now, and focused on course book content. • May be limited by lack of pictorial resources, gestural cues, and explanatory devices.
Topic Selection	• Learner initiates the topic. • Adults adjust language topics to those that capture the child's interest. • Focus on communication of meaning.	• Topics are decided by curriculum or textbook, not by the learners.
Language Output	• Output is abundant after a long, initial, silent period. • Output is used for hypothesis testing and patterning. • Characterized by grammatical errors initially but still communicative. • "Authentic."	• May be extremely limited. • Speech may be delayed for several years. • Large classes with full group instruction limit opportunities for output. • Output errors are discouraged. • Output opportunities may not be "authentic."
Love and Trust (Affective Environment)	• Language is acquired in a highly trusting environment. • High expectation of success. • Affective environment mediates the risk of language acquisition and motivates the speech act.	• Trust does not occur naturally in the classroom but must be created. • Affective environment depends on the skills of the individual teacher and the school setting. • Highly authoritarian classrooms may increase anxiety of learners and decrease language growth.

High Content and Language Load

Language acquisition and content learning are difficult and demanding tasks. Content mandates now require students to learn content information and develop communication skills at increasingly higher standards. ELLs may not be able to read the textbook or easily comprehend teacher lectures or classroom discussions. But teachers expect all students will become able to use language in complex ways and to pursue further learning. Teaching content in a way that supports the learner's efforts promotes both content learning and language acquisition. Differentiation of objectives, activities, and assessments helps ELLs to cope with the heavy language and content load of the typical classroom.

Language learning is a highly complex activity. Acquiring a language means acquiring the following:

- **Phonemes:** speech sounds that make a difference in meaning between words (such as pin/pen)
- **Phonology:** rules governing the sound system of English, including sound-symbol relationships, intonational variations, stress, pitch, and juncture
- **Morphemes:** a word or part of a word conveying a grammatical or lexical meaning (such as the *–ed* ending turning a present tense verb into the past tense)
- **Morphology:** the system dealing with the structure or form of words (want, wanted, wanting, unwanted)
- **Syntax:** the system describing the way in which words, oral or written, combine into sentences; grammar
- **Lexicon:** the vocabulary of the language
- **Semantics:** the meaning underlying a word, phrase, or sentence
- **Pragmatics:** the conversational rules guiding the use of language in a social situation. These rules change as a variety of social factors change: context, age, purpose, etc.

All of the above can be acquired by ELLs in meaningful, communicative classrooms. But they will also need to learn aspects of language to extend their communication into academic discourse. Aspects of syntax, for example, can be acquired but certain grammatical constructions that are rarely used in oral language can only be learned through classroom instruction.

In addition to the systems of language and its various components, speakers of a language are able to adjust their language usage between formal and informal usage and use all four language skills: listening, speaking, reading, and writing in complex ways and for a variety of purposes. Academic **registers** and formal written **discourse** are examples of language requiring classroom instruction and learning.

Teachers assist ELLs the most in the early stages of language acquisition by helping them comprehend the language of the classroom and giving them time to attempt to make themselves understood. As ELLs feel more comfortable with and begin to use the language, we provide more opportunities for formal language learning and higher-level thinking and problem solving.

Academic Language and Social Language

In addition to the aspects of language mentioned earlier, the language of school is different from the social language used by students in the cafeteria or the playground. Cummins (1980) describes social language (Basic Interpersonal Communication Skills or **BICS**) as language occurring within a **context-embedded** social environment. It is more easily understood because the speaker uses the context of the situation, gestures, and facial expressions to promote comprehension. This form of language is acquired by ELLs within two years of schooling in an English-speaking environment. Academic or school language (Cognitive Academic Language Proficiency or **CALP**) is the language of the textbook and is **context reduced.** Learners will not be able to learn the verb forms, transitional and cohesion devices, and specific lexicon of this language register unless they receive targeted instruction. The amount of time required to reach grade level competency in academic context-reduced language is between five to seven years (Collier, 1989).

Video Exercise

Language Environments— Early Childhood

Go to MyEducationLab, select the topic **Second Language Acquisition**, and watch the video entitled "**Language Environments—Early Childhood**" to observe photos of a typical early childhood classroom. Complete the questions that accompany it. You may print your work or have it transmitted to your professor as necessary.

The distinction between social and academic language is an important one for teachers to understand. ELLs who speak social language are sometimes viewed as competent speakers of English. When they are slow to make academic progress, the delay may be ascribed to learning deficits in the students. However, there is no relationship between academic achievement and social language. Unless students master academic language, including reading and writing, they will not achieve academically. When we involve students in appropriate grade level content curriculum and support learning with context, we are helping ELLs acquire and learn the language necessary to be successful in school.

Negative Bias

Although no one expects a young child to use language well, older students are expected to know languages. When children in school classrooms cannot use the language of their peers, they are viewed as non-knowers by the school community. These negative opinions can affect the child by slowing the pace of language development. Rather than viewing the child as deficient or culturally deprived, we need to examine the school systems in which many of our children are failing. The native language abilities of ELLs are underutilized in many schools. The cultural backgrounds of our students are not always viewed as a resource by the school community. Recognition of our common immigrant past is a useful way of promoting better learning by integrating student experiences and cultures into the curriculum, the classroom instruction, and the educational experience in general.

Cognition, Age, and Social and Cultural Differences

School-age children don't always receive the abundant language input that very young children do when acquiring their first languages. But the cognitive level of school-age children is much higher than that of an infant. Thus, higher cognitive abilities can facilitate language-learning experiences in school. If the ELL has already acquired a first language and can read and write in that first language, the transition to a second language will be much smoother and more efficient. The ability to read in one language is an asset when learning to read in another. Aspects of reading transfer from language to language. For example, literate ELLs expect to retrieve meaning from the printed page and use strategies to find and retain information. Those who are writers in their first language can use writing as an aid to language learning, taking notes, and collecting vocabulary lists. The learning strategies used in first language schooling also transfer to the second language classroom. ELLs can use dictionaries, memorize vocabulary, compare grammatical rules, and focus on areas of the language that are problematic. Higher cognitive functioning is an asset to the older, literate, and educated ELL.

Under-schooled ELLs are lacking in the first language academic skills that promote learning of a second language. These children are usually placed in age-appropriate grade levels even though they may have had limited or no prior schooling. Age level placement of these children is appropriate and desirable for affective and emotional reasons but the learning curve for these youngsters is very steep and the challenges for their teachers are great. For children such as these, the entire school community is needed to plan a comprehensive educational program and carry it out.

The different social and cultural contexts of school are more difficult for older learners in general. As children advance through the grades, they may feel ostracized from social groups and friends. Newly-arrived students will not understand the cultural and social patterns of American adolescents. At times, the demands of school may be at odds with the demands of home and family. Older ELLs, for example, may be expected to earn money to help the family, which detracts from time spent studying. Isolation and loneliness can deter the progress of language development. The older ELL has less time overall to achieve language equality with peers in the classroom and older learners face higher expectations. For these reasons, many older ELLs are frustrated in their language-learning attempts.

Error Correction

Error correction of ELLs is problematical. Parents of very young children generally do not correct the grammar of their children's utterances. They concentrate instead on the meaning of the utterance. When Anthony tells his Mom "Here pot," she corrects him by saying "No, that's a scoop" and ignores the fact that his sentence lacks a verb form. Instead she models a fully correct sentence form, "That's a scoop."

In school, however, teachers are torn by their desire to correct an ELL's incorrect grammar and an unwillingness to embarrass the student. Teachers might take a cue from Anthony's mom who responded to her son's utterances with grammatically correct, expanded sentences.

> **Student:** *It go down.*
>
> **Teacher:** *Yes, the metal sank in the water.*

Errors are best dealt with on a case-by-case basis—adapting our responses to the context of the utterance, the content requirements, as well as students' age, level, and need.

Oral language errors are frequently made because speaking gives little time to think about the grammar being used. The intent of the utterance is on conveying meaning to the hearer, and the speaker is not focusing on accuracy. For this reason, it is good policy for the teacher to respond to the meaning of the statement rather than to the speaker's grammar. Teachers can respond, however, by providing good modeling of an expanded grammatical utterance. When Marisol asked "Me go pee pee?" we restated her request and responded to it at the same time. "You want to go to the bathroom? Yes, go right ahead." This response is similar to the responses of caretakers to children's first language grammatical errors. The correct modeling provides the ELL with the grammatical information at the moment when it is needed.

Some oral errors in young ELLs are developmental. Native-English speakers aged five to seven often make similar errors. The overgeneralization of the past tense *–ed* ending (e.g., "bringed") and the addition of the *–s* plural (e.g., "mans") are two examples. These errors will correct themselves as students grow and receive more input.

Older English learners need to develop oral accuracy quickly in order to be successful both academically and socially. For this reason, older learners may be ready to focus on accuracy in their oral language and may be grateful for feedback or lessons about frequent errors. Older learners are embarrassed by speech errors and they will want to learn how to avoid them. In addition, errors that are not corrected tend to **fossilize**, persist in speech and become impervious to change (Selinker, 1972). Teachers can attend to these errors in sensitive ways. For example, if a teacher notices that students are having trouble with subject-verb agreement, she might develop a task in which learners use language frames to answer questions about a picture. For example, she might use a picture of family members making tamales (from *Making Tamales* by Carmen Lomas Garza in McCloskey & Stack, 1996, p. 136). Learners use a variety of verbs (wear, wrap, stand, sit, and play) to describe the picture in the present and past tense with different persons and numbers, and receive specific feedback on how they use the language.

Errors that persist past the beginning stages of language acquisition are best dealt with in writing. Written errors can be responded to more analytically. Teachers can take note of constant errors and focus on these in small group mini-lessons.

Culture Shock

One factor that affects almost all newly arrived ELLs is culture shock. Culture shock occurs when the ELL begins to be aware of the mismatch between the second-culture and first culture expectations. The identity of the individual is disrupted when old ways of thinking, feeling, and communicating are not available or severely taxed by the new culture. The result is a feeling of resentment at the new culture, anger, loneliness, frustration, profound sadness, and, occasionally, physical illness.

There are four stages of culture shock universally acknowledged. Brown (1992) describes the first stage as a time of excitement. The ELL feels euphoric about the new culture and is excited by all the new experiences in the surroundings. The second stage occurs as the learner experiences more differences between the first and second culture. ELLs feel uncomfortable in their new surroundings where everything is difficult and frustrating. During this stage, learners will cling to other students from their culture or those who speak the same language for a respite from the frustrations and unpleasant associations of the new culture. This stage is the most difficult for children in our schools. They will often be absent or tune out instruction if they are in class. The teacher will notice work is not completed and many times classroom disruptions occur as anger mounts. It is important to provide comfort in the form of a buddy who speaks the same language, if possible, or at least an accommodating friend. The third stage of culture shock may last for a long time. The ELL has made some gradual progress to adapting to the new culture but not all problems have been solved. Some feelings of empathy for others in the second culture begin to develop at this time. Children who are accepted into peer groups in school are better able to pass through this phase of culture shock than those who are isolated from other students. The fourth stage of culture shock occurs when ELLs acculturate into the new culture or adapt themselves to the new culture without completely assimilating.

Christine Igoa (1995) helped her students to adapt to the new culture academically, psychologically, and culturally. The result was that many of her students were able to reach this fourth stage of culture shock—recovery. "If the new immigrant child can get over the emotional hurdle of accepting the new culture without rejecting his or her home culture, if the child can free himself or herself from the emotional burdens of loneliness, isolation, fear of ridicule, helplessness, and anxiety, it then becomes very easy to reach and teach the child" (Igoa, 1995, p. 146). Table 1.2 highlights some of the factors affecting language development in positive and negative ways in school.

What Strategies Do ELLs Use to Acquire Languages?

Children use problem-solving strategies in order to acquire and learn languages. Teachers who are aware of these processes can accelerate the language-acquisition process through support of these strategies, which fall into two broad categories: learning strategies and communication strategies. Language-learning strategies are "the conscious thoughts and behaviors used by learners with the explicit goal of improving their knowledge and understanding of the target language" (Cohen, 1998, p. 68). Communication strategies are used "to encode and express meaning in order to communicate in a language" (Piper, 1998, p. 106). Children use similar strategies in both first language and second language acquisition environments. Some of these strategies lead children to create incorrect utterances in the new language. Rather than view these

Table 1.2 Factors Affecting Language Development

	Positive Effects	**Negative Effects**
Language Input	Student peers can help ELLs to acquire language even if the teacher is occupied elsewhere.	Language delays will occur without sufficient comprehensible input.
Classroom Organization	Differentiated, student-centered classrooms promote language and content learning.	Teacher-centered frontal instruction limits the interactive possibilities of classrooms.
High Content and Language Load	ELLs are held to a high standard by teacher and community expectations.	The heavy load can be overwhelming for ELLs unless the content is differentiated.
Academic vs. Social Language	ELLs are capable of acquiring a variety of language registers.	Academic language takes a long time to acquire/learn but is essential for academic achievement.
Negative Bias	ELLs bring diverse cultural and social perspectives to our classrooms.	ELLs are viewed negatively because they cannot speak English even though they may speak other languages.
Cognition, Age, Social, and Cultural Factors	Older ELLs bring literacy skills and prior education to help them acquire the language.	Older ELLs have less time to be successful students and may be isolated socially and culturally from their peers.
Error Correction	Errors are sometimes an indication of language growth. Teachers can use errors as opportunities to model correct grammar.	Public correction of errors is embarrassing to students.
Culture Shock	At first, ELLs will be euphoric about the new language and culture.	ELLs will experience an emotional roller coaster during the first three stages of culture shock.

as errors, we can recognize them as the result of the ELL generating hypotheses about the new language and testing those hypotheses in their communication.

Learning strategies are general cognitive strategies such as memorization, generalization, and inference. Learners use these strategies to gain meaning from oral language words and structures, and then remember them for later use. Communication strategies include **overgeneralization,** language **transfer,** and avoidance or **simplification.** What are these strategies and how do they assist acquisition?

Overgeneralization occurs when ELLs perceive patterns of language usage, generate a rule from many examples heard in the environment, and use the rule in a speaker-listener conversation. On occasion, the rule may be incorrect or partially correct. For example, when children perceive the –ed ending of English verbs, they often attach the ending to irregular verbs in incorrect ways: "runned," "bringed," and so on. The -s plural may be added to generate "sheeps" and "deers." This strategy occurs in both first and second language acquisition. As we hear students use these over-generalized rule forms, we realize they have made important learning gains. In time, with more opportunities for meaningful input of the irregular forms, ELLs will acquire accurate grammar.

Language transfer is a communication strategy whereby ELLs use rules from their home languages to understand and speak the new language. Spanish-speaking children use language transfer when they place adjectives after nouns when speaking English (truck big). ELLs use transfer in a positive way when they anticipate the new language will contain similar structures to the home language. Thus, learners will anticipate that English contains noun and verb forms because Spanish contains these forms. When the new language contains forms such as articles that don't exist in the target language (e.g., Chinese), students tend to eliminate those forms in their earliest utterances.

ELLs use a simplification or avoidance communication strategy when they avoid speaking about complex topics, avoid using full grammatical utterances, or avoid using word forms that they do not yet know. Young ELLs, responding to questions such as "How old are you?" use a simplification strategy by responding simply "ten." The learner answers the question very simply, and thus continues the conversation, which may in turn lead to additional meaningful input. Simplification is more easily used by younger learners than by older students. Classroom conversations may require older ELLs to speak about complex topics even though they are not yet capable of doing so in grammatically correct forms. Teachers can encourage simplification as a strategy by providing a variety of formats for responding to teacher questions such as signal responses, written responses, or group responses.

ELLs who actively use learning and communication strategies are more successful as language learners and acquirers. Teachers who encourage and teach strategy use are providing children with the tools they need to learn and acquire language while also learning classroom content.

What Can ELLs Tell Us about Positive Classroom Environments and Learning Experiences?

In order to answer this question, let's compare the similarities between the optimal language-learning classroom and the first language environment as described earlier in this chapter.

ELLs Are Active Acquirers of Language Throughout Their School Years

Pronunciation and intonation are readily acquired by young learners of a language who receive adequate language input. Complex grammar and an increased vocabulary load can be acquired most efficiently by children of ten or eleven who are already literate in a first language. Although different language skills are more easily learned at different ages, children are capable of acquiring native-like proficiency in multiple languages provided they receive sufficient comprehensible input in the new language.

ELLs Seek to Find Meaning in All of Their Learning Experiences

Krashen & Terrell (1983) described comprehensible input as a necessary prerequisite to language acquisition. In order for acquirers to make progress in the language, they need to understand input, either speech or written text, which is a little more complex than language that they are currently able to produce ($i + 1$). Krashen believed providing optimal input could be easy. "It may be that all the teacher need do is make sure the students understand what is being said or what they are reading" (1983, p. 19).

The Russian psychologist Vygotsky, writing at the beginning of the twentieth century, spoke of the importance of the social context of learning. Vygotsky (1962) described a **zone of proximal development** wherein children are enabled to learn or solve problems beyond their actual developmental level. Teachers, parents, and knowledgeable peers can provide the assistance that learners need to comprehend and learn at higher levels. This assistance is now referred to as **scaffolding.** In the area of language learning, teachers modify the input to students through joint activities that help them comprehend and develop concepts in ways they would not be able to do on their own. The nature of this work is collaborative and not directive. It is an interactive approach to teaching that supports learning through meaningful conversations, adjustments, and supports such as charts, the chalkboard, pictures, physical gestures, physical models, graphic organizers, cues, diagrams, audio-visual materials, highlighting, and restating in simpler language.

ELLs Seek to Use Language for Purposeful Activity Even Though They May Have Limited Skills in English

Teachers can create purposes for using language to increase student motivation. Games, group projects, crafts, experiments, peer pairing, drama, role play, presentations, and music are some of the ways to create purposeful activities for learning and acquiring English.

ELLs Profit from Physical Activity

Even in large classrooms of children, teachers can create brief moments of controlled activity that will promote interaction, provide for variety, and increase language acquisition through opportunities to listen and talk, and read or write about the target content.

ELLs Are Social Beings in Any Language

The language classroom is one where children must participate by both listening and speaking. Silent classrooms do not produce language learners. Vygotsky emphasized the role of the environment in language acquisition. He wrote of language acquisition as a social construct requiring adults and other children to help learners develop language and concepts. Initially, children may produce limited amounts of English, but gradually they increase their ability to comprehend and speak through the interactions of caring and knowledgeable teachers, adults, and friends.

ELLs Choose Which Aspects of Language to Learn

Provided they are given adequate amounts of comprehensible input, children will acquire those aspects of language that they wish to use or need for their own purposes. The target vocabulary of the content classroom must be available and accessible to learners in order for them to acquire academic language. Songs, chants, tapes, video, the computer, and other children's voices can be used in addition to the teacher as sources of comprehensible input in the classroom.

ELLs Respond to an Emotionally Positive Classroom Environment

In the 1950s and 1960s, a humanist orientation to education led to improvements in the learning experiences of many students. Psychologists stressed the importance of a nonthreatening environment to enable students to be risk takers. Since that time, teachers are more aware of student-centered and student-initiated approaches to learning that more closely resemble the first language acquisition experience. Recent work on the brain suggests the optimal environment for many kinds of learning includes some cognitive challenge as a motivation to learn, but not high stress (Jenson, 1998). This tells us that ELLs need to be cognitively challenged in our classrooms. Too often in the past, these children were not included in classroom

Interesting Content-Related Experiences Provide Excellent Language-Learning Opportunities

activities because they couldn't speak the language. We have learned children will never speak English if they are not included in the instructional conversations of our classrooms.

ELLs Respond to Interesting Content Information

Just as the first language experience is an integrated one, children also respond more eagerly to second-language learning when interesting topics are taught through the new language. Many teachers today attempt to make connections for their students between what they already know and what they are going to learn. Teachers who help students make connections between what is already known and understood in the past and what is currently being learned in the present increase their students' participation and motivation for learning. Planting seeds, reading familiar fairy tales, describing the rain cycle, or conducting a science experiment with dependent and independent variables are some examples of how to integrate English language learning into the content of the school learning experience.

No matter what the age of our students, we need to create classroom environments that will help ELLs acquire and learn the language of school. School language is necessary for successful achievement, and the skills required (listening with comprehension, speaking clearly and specifically, reading and writing academic text) are difficult to acquire. The process takes many years. It's time to begin.

Questions for Reflection

1. Why will children learning a second language in school find that task so difficult when we know that all children learn their first languages with almost no effort?
2. Of all the factors affecting acquisition in classrooms, which ones do you feel are the most difficult to overcome? Why?

3. What suggestions would you give to a new teacher in your school who is trying to create effective classroom experiences for new English language learners?

Activities for Further Learning

1. We have seen language input is critical to language development. Discuss this notion with your classmates. Cite opportunities for language input in a primary classroom, an elementary classroom, and a middle-school classroom. What obstacles do you foresee in providing sufficient input for ELLs? What are some practical suggestions for overcoming these obstacles?
2. Observe two young children at play for fifteen minutes. Take notes on the language used by the children during your observation. Bring your notes to class and compare with your colleagues. What have you discovered about the children's language? What verb tenses are used? What question words? Do the children use many nouns and adjectives? Does the type of play change the nature of the language?
3. With your classmates, use your observation notes to design an activity for ELLs in the classroom that can be accomplished with similar, simple language items. Create a different activity for older learners.
4. Design a content-based card game for children that helps them to learn the following English verbs: "pick up," "put down," "take," "give."
5. Interview a person who has learned English while attending a public school in the United States. Ask questions as to the effect of the following on his/her language development: age, home language, the classroom environment, the teacher, friends and social group, error correction, and literacy in the first language. Be prepared to describe the positive and negative effects of the factors on your interviewee.
6. Look at Table 1.2 and consider how each of the language development factors will affect the organization of your classroom and the way in which you instruct children. Consider an elementary classroom and a middle-school classroom. How would the grade level differences lead to a change in your classroom organization and instruction?
7. Krashen's definition of comprehensible input and Vygotsky's zone of proximal development are similar notions. They presuppose a teacher or knowledgeable peer can assist in language development. Describe how these notions could be practically implemented in a classroom.
8. Cummins's definition of social language (BICS) and academic language (CALP) are useful in helping teachers understand different registers of English. Identify examples of social and academic language that might be encountered in a classroom. Provide examples of ways to scaffold the academic language so ELLs can understand it.

PEARSON myeducationlab *Where the Classroom Comes to Life* is a collection of online tools for your success in this course, your licensure exams, and your teaching career. Go to www.myeducationlab .com to utilize these extensive resources including videos from real classrooms, Praxis and licensure preparation, a lesson plan builder, and materials to help you in your teaching career.

Suggested Reading

Cowley, G. (1997). The language explosion. In *Newsweek Special Edition: Your child*: 16–22. This is an informative and easy-to-read description of the first language acquisition process.

Cummins, J. (1992). Language proficiency, bilingualism, and academic achievement. In P. A. Richard-Amato and M. A. Snow (Eds.), *The multicultural classroom: Readings for content area teachers*. NY: Longman. In this classic article, Cummins defines context-reduced academic language and offers implications for both teaching and testing.

Cummins, J. (1996). *Negotiating identities: Education for empowerment in a diverse society*. Ontario, CA: California Association for Bilingual Education. Here, Cummins proposes a framework for analyzing the patterns of educational outcome observed in different world contexts. It is argued that students in subordinated groups will succeed academically only to the extent that patterns of interaction in school challenge and reverse those of society at large that subordinate some communities.

Cummins, J. (2000). *Language, power, and pedagogy: Bilingual children in the crossfire*. Clevedon [England]; Buffalo [NY]: Multilingual Matters. Cummins's latest effort to inform practice with theory and enable theory to be informed by practice. He searches here for coherence through an integrated interdisciplinary perspective that brings disparate fields into dialogue with each other.

Dudley-Marling, C. & Searle, D. (1991). *When students have time to talk: Creating contexts for learning language*. Portsmouth, NH: Heinemann. An academic but readable text describing both first-language acquisition in home and at school. Topics include strategic approaches for teaching language, encouraging extended conversations, using language for a variety of purposes and audiences. There is also a chapter about second language learners and their unique learning needs.

Heath, S. B. (1992). Sociocultural contexts of language development: Implications for the classroom. In P. A. Richard-Amato and M. A. Snow (Eds.), *The multicultural classroom: Readings for content area teachers*. NY: Longman. Heath discusses the role of home and family in the development of literacy skills for language minority students. She presents examples from major language groups on the differences between language usage in the home and mainstream language usage of the school. She argues success in school depends on a wide range of oral and written language usage.

Krashen, S. D. (2003). *Explorations in language acquisition and use: The Taipei lectures*. Portsmouth, NH: Heinemann.

Krashen, S. D. & Terrell, T. D. (1983). *The natural approach: Language acquisition in the classroom,* San Francisco, CA: The Alemany Press. Krashen's classic explanation of natural language learning coupled with ideas for incorporating this approach in schools.

Lightbown, P. & Spada, N. M. (2006). *How languages are learned* (3rd ed.). Oxford, UK: Oxford University Press. This clear and useful text explains language theory with the teacher in mind.

Scarcella, R. (1992). Providing culturally sensitive feedback. In P. A. Richard-Amato and M. A. Snow (Eds.), *The multicultural classroom: Readings for content area teachers*. NY: Longman. This article provides many examples of the kinds of cross-cultural differences learners will encounter in our schools and communities. Scarcella offers ideas for giving helpful feedback to students in order to minimize cultural differences.

Web Sites for Further Learning

Chomsky. This site explains Noam Chomsky's theories relating to innate language mechanisms. Retrieved May 2, 2008.

http://www.sk.com.br/sk-chom.html

Piaget. This site provides an explanation of the major contributions of Jean Piaget to our understanding of how young children learn. Retrieved May 2, 2008.

http://www.sk.com.br/sk-piage.html

Steven Krashen's Theory of Second Language Acquisition. This site gives a clear explanation of the processes involved in second and foreign language acquisition and learning. Definitions of important terms are included. Retrieved May 2, 2008.

http://www.sk.com.br/sk-krash.html

Summary of Stephen Krashen's Principles and Practice in Second Language Acquisition by Reid Wilson. This brief article explains Krashen's learning/acquisition distinctions. It also reviews five hypotheses explaining second language acquisition. Retrieved May 2, 2008.

http://www.languageimpact.com/articles/rw/krashenbk.htm

Vygotsky. This site briefly explains the thinking of the Russian psychologist who helped us to understand children's learning processes. Retrieved May 2, 2008.

http://www.sk.com.br/sk-vygot.html

References

Brown, H. D. (1992). Sociocultural factors in teaching language minority students. In P. A. Richard-Amato and M. A. Snow (Eds.), *The multicultural classroom: Readings for content-area teachers.* NY: Longman.

Chomsky, N. (1957). *Syntactic structures.* The Hague: Mouton.

Chomsky, N. (1975). *Reflections on language.* NY: Pantheon.

Cohen, A. D. (1998). *Strategies in learning and using a second language.* London, UK: Longman.

Collier, V. (1989). How long? A synthesis of research in academic achievement in a second language. *TESOL Quarterly, 23*: 509–531.

Cummins, J. (1980). The construct of language proficiency in bilingual education. In J. E. Alatis (Ed.), *Georgetown University roundtable on languages and linguistics* (pp. 76–93). Washington, DC: Georgetown University Press.

Dulay, H. & Burt, M. (1974). Natural sequences in child second language acquisition. *Language Learning 24*: 37–53.

Garza, C. L. (1987). *Making tamales.* San Francisco, CA: Children's Book Press.

Harklau, L. (1994). ESL and mainstream classes: Contrasting second language learning contexts. *TESOL Quarterly, 28*: 241–272.

Harklau, L. (2000). From the "good kids" to the "worst": Representations of English language learners across educational settings. *TESOL Quarterly, 34*(1): 35–67.

Holt, J. (1964). *How children fail.* NY: Dell Publishing.

Igoa, Christine. (1995). *The inner world of the immigrant child.* Mahwah, NJ: Lawrence Erlbaum.

Izumi, S. & Bigelow, M. (2000). Does output promote noticing and second language acquisition? *TESOL Quarterly, 34*(2): 239–278.

Jensen, E. (1998). *Teaching with the brain in mind.* Alexandria, VA: ASCD.

Klingner, J. K. & Vaughn, S. (2000). The helping behaviors of fifth graders while using collaborative strategic reading during ESL content classes. *TESOL Quarterly, 34*(1): 69–98.

Krashen, S. D. & Terrell, T. D. (1983). *The natural approach: Language acquisition in the classroom.* San Francisco, CA: The Alemany Press.

Labinowicz, E. (1980). *The Piaget primer: Thinking, learning, teaching.* Reading, MA: Addison-Wesley.

Levine, L. N. (1981). Mother-child communication and the acquisition of deixis. Unpublished doctoral dissertation, NY University, NY.

Lindfors, J. W. (1987). *Children's language and learning.* Upper Saddle River, NJ: Merrill/Prentice Hall.

Long, M. & Porter, P. (1985). Group work, interlanguage talk, and second language acquisition. *TESOL Quarterly, 19*: 207–227.

McCloskey, M. L. & Stack, L. (1996). *Voices in Literature: An anthology for middle/high school ESOL* (Bronze). Boston, MA: Heinle and Heinle.

McLaughlin, B. (1987). *Theories of second language acquisition.* London, UK: Edward Arnold.

McNeill, D. (1975). The contribution of experience. In S. Rogers (Ed.), *Children and language: Readings in early language and socialization.* London, UK: Oxford University Press.

Paley, V. (1981). *Wally's stories.* Cambridge, MA: Harvard University Press.

Pica, T., Lincoln-Porter, F., Paninos, D., & Linnell, J. (1996). Language learner's interaction: How does it address the input, output, and feedback needs of L2 learners? *TESOL Quarterly, 30*(1): 59–84.

Piper, T. (1998). *Language and learning: The home and school years.* Upper Saddle River, NJ: Prentice Hall.

Selinker, L. (1972). Interlanguage. *International Review of Applied Linguistics, 10*: 209–231.

Snow, C. E. (1977). Mothers' speech research: From input to interaction. In C. E. Snow and C. A. Ferguson (Eds.), *Talking to children: Language input and acquisition.* NY: Cambridge University Press.

Swain, M. (1985). Communicative competence: Some roles of comprehensible input and comprehensible output in its development. In S. M. Gass and C. G. Madden (Eds.), *Input in second language acquisition* (pp. 235–253). Rowley, MA: Newbury House.

Urzua, C. (1981). *Talking purposefully.* MD: Institute of Modern Languages, Inc.

Vygotsky, L. S. (1962). *Thought and language.* Cambridge, MA: MIT Press.

Weeks, T. E. (1979). *Born to talk.* Rowley, MA: Newbury House.

CHAPTER 2

Principles of Integrated Language Teaching and Learning

Though we still have far to go toward a thorough understanding of language development, and language teaching and learning, the teaching profession has a rich body of research upon which to base our instructional decisions. Teachers need to understand and be able to articulate the principles that underlie their teaching, and these principles should be based on sound research about how language is learned and what works best in supporting language development in the classroom. The principles that teachers hold not only make a difference regarding how and how well they teach; they also make teachers more able to learn from observation of their learners and from reflection on their own teaching.

What are the principles of integrated language teaching and learning?

- What principles can we draw from research about language learning and teaching?
- What are strategies and practices that exemplify research-based principles?

In this chapter, we outline nine principles that apply our best understandings of research on both effective teaching and learning for school-age learners and specific knowledge about how language is most efficiently acquired and best taught. We have named our model the **Activity-Based Communicative Teaching and Learning** Model (or the **ABC Model**). The nine principles are organized along two dimensions: Activity-Based Teaching and Learning, and Communicative Teaching and Learning.

Activity-Based Teaching and Learning focuses on what learners bring to the classroom and the active role that learners play in the language acquisition process. Research on learning and memory (Sprenger, 1999), on language acquisition and language learning (Cameron, 2001), and on the functions of the brain (Genesee, 2000) show us that English language learners in elementary and middle school are *not* passive recipients of learning. Rather, they are actively constructing **schema** (organizational structures of language and content) and meaning. Thus, all teaching—even direct teaching—must be planned so that learners play active roles as they learn. Four of the ABC Principles describe how classroom instruction can be planned and conducted to promote active student roles in learning.

Communicative Teaching and Learning focuses on the importance of authentic, comprehensible communication in the learning of language. For teaching and learning to be effective and efficient, language must be used in ways that clearly convey meaning and have communicative purpose. Five of the ABC Principles fall along this dimension and outline how our instruction must include communicative elements.

These two dimensions and nine principles are designed as guidelines for organizing and planning instruction for classrooms in which language develops as quickly and smoothly as possible. Though there is necessarily some overlap among the nine Activity-Based and Communicative Principles, we have found each to provide unique guidelines and organization for planning and evaluating the instruction of English language learners and we apply them in the aspects of instruction detailed throughout the book. In the following paragraphs, we introduce each principle, provide a brief theoretical/research foundation, and give an example of each. These examples offer snapshots of the principles in action in the classroom in various content areas at various grade levels. Though we work to cover the range of learners in grades K through 8, we encourage readers, as they study the principles, to transform these examples by thinking about how each might be adapted and revised to best depict their own current or potential teaching situations.

Activity-Based Language Teaching and Learning

Principle 1 Active Engagement

Learners play enjoyable, engaging, active roles in the learning experience. Language and literacy development is facilitated by a comfortable atmosphere; not only one that values, encourages, and celebrates efforts, but one that also provides the appropriate level of challenge to motivate and engage learners (Jensen, 1998; Sprenger, 1999; Krashen, 2003). When **active engagement** is practiced, language is learned while doing something with it, not just learning it. Language is best viewed as a verb (language as something to use and do) than as a noun (language as a content to be learned). K through 8 learners develop language and literacy best first by using language as a tool for creating and sharing meanings (Vygotsky, 1986); and later, as they are developmentally ready, by studying language structures and features as they are needed and used in authentic contexts (Lightbown & Spada, 2006).

Active Engagement in Practice

To help his multicultural, multilingual third-grade students "use" language authentically in studying the food pyramid, Ted Burch had his students keep a written and/or pictorial food diary, then use word source tools (such as a picture dictionary, bilingual dictionary, or Internet search) to list in English the foods they eat. Next, the third-graders made word cards of the foods and taught their classmates and teacher names of unfamiliar foods from the various cultures represented in the class. As a final step, they classified all the foods they'd eaten two ways: by geography on a map of the world and by placing word and picture cards next to the appropriate category on a large food pyramid.

Language Is First Used as a Tool to Communicate Meaning While Engaging Actively in Learning Experiences

Principle 2 Cultural Relevance

Classrooms respect and incorporate the cultures of learners in the classroom while helping them to understand the new culture of the community, the school, and the classroom. Teachers play the most important role in determining the quality and quantity of participation of ELs in their classrooms. When teachers develop a climate of trust, understand children's social and cultural needs, and model for the rest of the class how they, too, can include English learners in classroom conversations and activities as important members of the classroom learning communities, ELs' active involvement in the classroom and their learning show improvement (Yoon, 2007).

Research has also led to a wide consensus concerning the value of parental involvement in students' school achievement and social development (Cummins, 1986; Delpit, 1995), and in literacy development in particular (Bronfenbrenner, 1975; Tizard, Schofield, & Hewison, 1982; Heath, 1983; Snow, Burns, & Griffin, 1998; Reese, Garnier,

---

Cultural Relevance in Practice

Lydia Achebe knows that her first graders want to see themselves in the books that they read, and sees how they appreciate when their home cultures are viewed in a positive light. She works closely with the school library media specialist, who tries to acquire texts from and about the cultures of children in the school. When a new student arrived who was from the Ndebele region of South Africa, the teacher and media specialist found the delightful book, *My Painted House, My Friendly Chicken, and Me,* with text by Maya Angelou and photographs by Margaret Courtney-Clarke (1994). All the class enjoyed looking at a globe and discussing the path the new student took to come to the U.S. from Southern Africa. They shared the book as a read-aloud several times, compared and contrasted schools and homes in different places where they had lived, and then painted their own pictures using elements of the bright designs of the Ndebele.

Collaboration in Practice

When Kamal Gebril's fifth-grade class studied ancient Egypt, collaboration among peers included a simple "elbow buddy" or "pair-share" activity, in which partners restate to one another something they have learned about burial practices in the time of the pharaohs. Collaboration between teacher and learners included a shared writing activity in which students, after studying pictures in David Macaulay's classic book, *Pyramid* (1975), described and illustrated the process of building a pyramid. Kamal was careful to include discussion of contemporary Egypt as well, describing such family customs as visiting ancient monuments, and traveling outside the city on special holidays to visit graves of their forebears and having a family picnic. The assignment was extended to collaboration between school and home when children took home pictures they'd drawn and stories they'd written about customs of ancient and modern Egypt. First they read the story in English to family members and then they retold the story in the home language. A final collaboration at the end of the unit was a "numbered heads" review of what they'd learned. In this strategy, children, in groups of about four, are each given a number. Kamal asks a question and the groups put their "heads together" to find the answer. Then a number is chosen randomly and the child with that number gives the group's response. Even newcomers are able to participate meaningfully and actively in the review due to the coaching and support of their peers to prepare them to answer the questions.

Gallimore, & Goldenberg, 2000). Creating a culturally responsive and **culturally relevant** classroom goes beyond "parental involvement" and requires thoughtfulness and effort on the part of teachers to learn about students' cultures from students, families, community members, and library and Internet resources; to value and include what learners bring to the classroom from their cultures; and to take into account the different world views represented in the classroom. It requires an understanding of culture deeper than viewing the "exotic" differences between cultures, or focusing on holidays, foods, and customs. Instead, it integrates a multicultural perspective on the daily life of the classroom (Derman-Sparks, 1989).

Principle 3 Collaboration

Learners develop and practice language in collaboration with one another and with teachers. As language is a tool for meaning-making, and communication and thinking are developed through using language to accomplish things (Vygotsky, 1986), and as learning cooperatively has been shown to be effective at improving learning (Kessler, 1991; Slavin, 1995), so instruction should be organized to facilitate interaction and collaboration. Learning should provide two-way experiences through which learners solve problems, negotiate meaning, and demonstrate what they have learned.

Principle 4 Learning Strategies

Learners use a variety of language and learning strategies to expand learning beyond the classroom and to become independent, lifelong learners. **Learning strategies** (also called learner strategies) (Chamot & O'Malley, 1996; Nunan, 1996; Oxford, 1996; Lessard-Clouston, 1997) are steps taken by learners to enhance their learning and develop their language competence. These strategies can be observable behaviors, steps, or techniques, such as **SQ3R (Survey, Question, Read, Recite, Review),** a reading strategy, or nonobservable thoughts or mental practices, such as visualization or positive thinking. Although learners do use strategies unconsciously, the focus in teaching learning strategies is to bring them to the learners' attention and make them

Learning Strategies in Practice

To help her eighth-graders become more independent in learning new vocabulary, Lenore Duink first used modeling, supported practice, and independent practice to develop learners' ability to ask questions when they don't understand—teaching them polite phrases for asking a teacher, peer, or other person appropriately for repetition, clarification, or explanation of vocabulary. Then she taught her students various ways to support their vocabulary learning, including making **word squares** (see Table 2.1 for an example), sorting terms into categories, visualizing meanings, practicing with a peer, drawing pictures, composing and singing songs with new terms, highlighting verb endings, listening for words on the radio and TV, using mnemonic devices, and finding ways to put new terms to use in conversations both in the classroom and beyond.

consciously part of the learners' repertoire. Learning strategies allow learners to control and direct their own learning. These strategies also expand the role of language teachers beyond teaching language to that of helping learners develop their own strategies. They are generally oriented toward solving problems and can involve many aspects of language to be learned beyond the cognitive.

Communicative Teaching and Learning

Principle 5 Comprehensible Input with Scaffolding

Teachers provide rich input with appropriate context and support, to make that input comprehensible to learners, and appropriately and increasingly more challenging. English learners can't learn from language they don't understand. **Comprehensible input** is a term first used by Steven Krashen (2003) that refers to language used by teachers and others in ways that English learners can understand as their language ability is developing. It ties back to Vygotsky's (1986) thinking about the social nature of learning. Oral and written input from teachers can be adapted to convey meaning to language learners at various

Table 2.1 Word Square Graphic Organizer

Mammal	
Definition a type of vertebrate **Translation in my language (Spanish)** mamífero	**Characteristics** • warm blooded • produces milk • young are born alive • have hair • are vertebrates • have lungs to breathe air
Examples • human • monkey	**Non-examples** • rooster • fish

A Scaffold Is a Metaphor for the Way Teachers Provide Support for Language Learners as They Acquire English

**Video
Exercise**

**Peers Provide
Scaffolding for
Language Learning**

Go to MyEducationLab,
select the topic
Comprehensible Input,
and watch the video
entitled "**Peers Provide
Scaffolding for Language
Learning**" to observe a
teacher guide an older
child to share a book with
a younger one, who uses
the first language they
share (Hmong) to provide
comprehensible input.
Answer the questions that
accompany the video. You
may print your work or
have it transmitted to your
professor as necessary.

levels and to be more understandable in a variety of ways. To make learners better understand oral language in the classroom, teachers make sure they face students when they speak (so that students can watch their mouths and facial expressions), speak slowly, and articulate clearly (so that students can hear the separate words), and increase **wait time** (the time after a question is asked before a student or students are asked to respond). To improve the comprehensibility of written input, teachers choose texts with rich graphic elements and teach students how to understand and use these graphics; teach learners to use a variety of print and online sources to find word meanings,

Figure 2.1 Rosa's Personal Dictionary

MY DICTIONARY.
ROSA   A

antilope · antílope
  animal like a deer
abandon   abandono
  stop helping, leave alone
anticipate anticipe
  feel before it happens
aware   enterado
  know about
                      tonto
airhead cabeza buscadora
  dumb person.

Comprehensible Input with Scaffolding in Practice

When Jim Stalzer's sixth-grade class was studying the life cycle in science, he invited an ornithologist to come to speak to the class on the life cycle of birds. Jim wanted to make sure that all the students in his class, including newcomers who were beginning learners of English, could enjoy the visit. After the ornithologist accepted his invitation, Jim asked him for a short set of terms that he could pre-teach before the visit, and also supplied the speaker with a short list of suggestions (much like the ones in Table 2.2 for oral language input) that might help him to be more easily understood in the multilingual, multicultural classroom. He also pre-taught some of the terms to the newcomers and helped them practice questions to ask the guest.

---

pronunciations, and examples of use; teach learners to organize and keep their own vocabulary notebooks or personal dictionaries (see example in Figure 2.1); provide alternate texts when texts are clearly beyond student comprehension; and use a variety of strategies to help students access texts that are near their instructional level. Table 2.2 suggests means to increase comprehensible input both orally and in writing. Strategies and techniques in Chapter 5, Oral Language Development, and in Chapters 7 and 8 on reading and writing will expand on these ideas to add to your repertoire of tools to support English learners by helping them to understand the language of your classroom.

Principle 6 Prior Knowledge

Teachers help learners use their prior knowledge of language, content, and the world to develop new language and increase learning. If we already know a lot about a topic—global warming, for example—we will find television programs, lectures, or written materials on global warming much easier to follow. If a student has learned a lot about a topic in his home language, it's easier to develop new language about that topic. **Prior knowledge** or background knowledge is key to comprehension for all learners (Marzano et al.,

An Ornithologist Engages Learners in a Dialogue About Birds

Table 2.2 Scaffolding Instructional Language

Adaptations to Make Oral Language Input Comprehensible	Adaptations and Resources to Make Written Language Input More Comprehensible

• Select topics that are familiar to learners and/or make connections between learners' prior knowledge and information they will read.
 	
• Check comprehension often (use signals, cards, choral responses, questions, slates). When learners don't understand, demonstrate, explain, or rephrase.
 	
• Use translation when this is the most efficient way to convey meanings of new words.
 	
• Adapt language of input to help learners understand:
  • Face students.
  • Speak slowly (but naturally) and articulate clearly.
  • Pause frequently and increase wait time.
  • Use gestures, mime, facial expressions, pictures, props, and real objects to enhance meaning.
  • Model, and provide student models of language to be used.
  • Monitor use of idioms and figurative language and explain them when needed.
  • Use more direct sentence structures, articulate carefully, adjust vocabulary.
  • Point out key ideas and vocabulary.
  • Use terms consistently; avoid overuse of synonyms for key terms.
	• Select topics that are familiar to learners and make connections between learners' prior knowledge and information they will read.
	
	• Use pictures, maps, graphic organizers.
	
	• Pre-teach and reinforce key vocabulary.
	
	• Use, and teach learners to use dictionaries and other word sources: picture dictionaries, learner dictionaries, translation dictionaries, word source software.
	
	• Teach learners to find and use picture, translation, and dictionary resources on the Web.
	
	• Provide alternate texts at appropriate levels.
	
	• Teach learners to select texts at appropriate reading/language levels.
	
	• Assign key selections from texts when entire text is out of reach.
	
	• Use audio texts.
	
	• Include reference links (to pronunciation, translation, pictures, background, etc.) in digital texts (McCloskey & Thrush, 2005).
	
	• Use scaffolding strategies to support reading (e.g., reciprocal teaching, shared reading, guided reading).

2004), but it is of particular importance for English learners. If learners are less familiar with a topic and structures of the oral discussion or written text, they will have more difficulty with comprehension (Carrell & Eisterhold, 1988). Language difficulty increases with cognitive difficulty, unfamiliarity, and lack of context. So, when developing language with English learners, teachers must work to *start where students are*. Starting where students are includes finding out what students already know about a new topic and helping them to make connections between what they already know and what they are learning. It includes making connections between learners' cultures and cultural knowledge and the new culture of the school and the community. It also may include, at beginning levels, selecting topics that learners are likely to have familiarity with, providing necessary background information on new topics in home languages, pre-teaching key vocabulary to expand background knowledge before studying a topic, and/or English, helping learners make connections between what they know about language in their home language (L1) to uses of this knowledge in English (L2). It also might include providing background information in L1 before proceeding to study a theme or topic in L2. In a bilingual classroom, content could be taught in two languages.

Prior Knowledge in Practice

Liz Bigler is introducing a lesson to her fourth-graders on Rosa Parks and the Montgomery bus boycott. She wants her beginning learners to understand the meaning of the word "fair" that is key to understanding the motivation for the boycott. She takes a bag of pennies and gives them out to a group of students. Three students get 10 pennies. The fourth gets 1. The children look puzzled, and Liz explains to them (with repetition, rephrasing, and gestures) that this is an example of something that is "not fair." The students then proceed with their Total Physical Response (TPR) lesson, which includes acting out the boycott as the teacher tells the story. (See Bigler, 2006, for a complete description of this lesson.)

In a monolingual classroom teachers might, for example, have learners read or listen to a home language summary of a text before they will be reading it in English.

Video Exercise

An Active, Interactive Science Vocabulary Review

Go to MyEducationLab, select the topic **Academic Language Development**, and watch the video entitled "**An Active, Interactive Science Vocabulary Review**" to watch a teacher use slates in a formative review of science vocabulary in a middle school classroom. Complete the questions that accompany it. You may print your work or have it transmitted to your professor as necessary.

Principle 7 Content Integration

Language learning is integrated with meaningful, relevant, and useful content—generally the same academic content and higher-order thinking skills that are appropriate for the age and grade of learners. Teaching language along with age-appropriate academic content has several advantages: it is efficient, because two goals—acquisition of language and content learning—are accomplished at once. It is effective first because language is learned better when learners are doing something purposeful and important to them—and learning the content for their grade level is very important. It is also necessary because learners can't afford to take a year or two off from content learning while they develop language—they'll only end up further behind their peers. Content-based language learning can happen in a variety of settings: in a pull-out English Language Development (ELD) class (also

Children Reenact the Story of Rosa Parks and the Montgomery Bus Boycott

---

Content Integration in Practice

Julia Raca teaches in a multicultural, multilingual second grade with several English learners at different levels. She wants to make sure that everyone benefits from her science curriculum, including the new arrivals in her classroom, and so she includes both language objectives and science objectives in all her lesson plans. (See Table 2.3.) When she teaches her "How Things Work" unit, her goals include students' understandings about tools, machines, and magnets, but she adds to these language goals including key vocabulary, giving instructions, and using verbs in the command form and future tense form. Julia starred objectives that she thought were appropriate for newcomers to achieve and others she expected them to work toward.

---

called an ESL class), in which the teacher introduces content through integrated themes (this is often used with newcomers/ beginners); in a special section of a content class with a grade level teacher with training in teaching ELD, who teaches the content using approaches that make the content comprehensible to language learners and promote language development (this is sometimes done in middle and high schools with significant numbers of English learners); or in grade level classes that include both English proficient learners and English language learners, and in which teachers have training to attend to both content and language needs of learners, and to differentiate instruction to include learners at different language and learning levels. These integrated models are used because research findings have shown that they are the most effective at both language learning and content learning for English learners (Cummins, 1986; Thomas & Collier, 2003). Teachers can differentiate through adapting the language, content, process, or product in classrooms (Tomlinson, 1999).

Table 2.3 Including Language and Content-Learning Goals

Content Goals	Language Goals
• Learners name uses of various machines and explain/demonstrate how they work.*	**Key Vocabulary** Pound, hammer, build, birdhouse, tools, magnet, pick up, pin, . . .*
• Learners identify certain machines and their parts.	**Grammar** • Future tense with "going to." • Helping verb "can/can't." Commands.*
• Learners demonstrate an understanding of magnetic force.	**Comprehension** • Visualizes information from text and charts. **Literacy** • Uses alphabet to find information.* **Writing** • Labels a diagram.

*Objectives appropriate for newcomers.

Source: Adapted from Freeman, D., Freeman, Y., Garcia, A. C., Gottlieb, M., McCloskey, M.L., Stack, L., & Silva, C. (2003).

Differentiation in Practice

Marie Matluck wanted to address a variety of learning styles while helping her kindergarteners learn letter names and sounds, so she provided opportunities for learners to learn these by differentiating the process—involving children in looking at pictures, singing, building with blocks, teaching one another, searching for letters in the environment outside schools, drawing letters and words that included the sounds of the letters, visualizing—making "mind pictures" associating letters with key words, and making letter shapes with their bodies. She sometimes gave learners choices as to which activities they used to practice their skills. With sounds that are used in both English and students' home languages, Marie provided pictures of key words that begin with the letter in both languages, to take advantage of what children already knew and enhance transfer of learning from one language to another (Figure 2.2).

Principle 8 Differentiation

Learning activities accommodate different language, literacy, and cognitive levels and incorporate many dimensions of learning: different learning styles, intelligences, and preferences. All learners are not the same: they have different native intelligence, learned intelligence, learning styles, and preferences. Including English learners in a grade-level classroom expands the differences by adding different language backgrounds, educational levels, cultural experiences, experiences of culture change, and sometimes the trauma of war, famine, or poverty. When learners are limited in their comprehension of English, providing input through other means—pictures, gestures, sounds, movement, graphics—helps provide them with the "hook" they need to be included in the classroom conversation. Effective **differentiation** to include English learners involves expanding the dimensions of learning across different learning styles—verbal, auditory, kinesthetic; and different intelligences. Gardner's (1983, 1996) categories of intelligences include: linguistic (language, e.g., writer), logical-mathematical (e.g., mathematician or engineer), musical (guitarist), bodily-kinesthetic intelligence (athlete, dancer), spatial intelligence (artist, designer), interpersonal intelligence (counselor, politician), intrapersonal intelligence (philosopher), and naturalist (oceanographer). Teachers differentiate the language they use and introduce in the classroom, the content they use, the classroom processes, the products that learners are asked to produce, and the assessment of those products.

Figure 2.2 "Lion" / "León" Is a Key Word That Begins with the Same Letter in Both English and Spanish.

Good Teaching Involves Making Assessment an Integral
Part of Every Lesson

Principle 9 Clear, Appropriate Goals and Feedback

Teachers set and communicate attainable goals for learners and provide students with appropriate and consistent feedback on their progress in attaining these goals. Setting clear goals helps both teachers and learners have a much greater chance to attain those goals. Goals begin our curriculum, inform our curriculum, and new, more advanced goals are the outcome of our curriculum. As John Dewey once said, "Arriving at one goal is the starting point to another."

We want English learners to attain the same high goals as their English-proficient peers, but to do this we must set the right goals—goals that comprise the next step forward for individual learners. Learners want to do well, and will do much better when they understand what is expected of them and when our expectations are appropriate. We must establish clear language and content goals for learners and provide learners with feedback on their progress toward those goals. We can also, in developmentally appropriate ways, encourage learners to begin to evaluate their own progress toward accomplishing goals to help them become independent, self-motivated learners.

Clear, Appropriate Goals and Feedback in Practice

Scott Kessler teaches a seventh-grade mathematics class that includes seven early and late intermediate learners of English. His aim is to make the content of mathematics comprehensible to English learners in his class, and to do this he works to set incremental goals toward full achievement of content and language goals. He's consulted the TESOL Standards and his own state standards, and adapted the following rubric to use with his learners in a unit on decimals and measurement of central tendencies (mean, mode, median) in the domain of listening. His rubric is shown in Table 2.5.

Table 2.4 PreK–12 English Language Proficiency Standards in the Core Content Areas (TESOL, 2006)

....

Standard 1	English language learners communicate for *social, intercultural,* and *instructional* purposes within the school setting.
Standard 2	English language learners communicate information, ideas, and concepts necessary for academic success in the area of *language arts.*
Standard 3	English language learners communicate information, ideas, and concepts necessary for academic success in the area of *mathematics.*
Standard 4	English language learners communicate information, ideas, and concepts necessary for academic success in the area of *science.*
Standard 5	English language learners communicate information, ideas, and concepts necessary for academic success in the area of *social studies.*

We must determine intermediary steps toward grade-level standards that are attainable at learners' language level. The professional organization, Teachers of English to Speakers of Other Languages (TESOL) has recently published a revision of its standards for school-age learners of English (TESOL, 2006). The new volume, *PreK–12 English Language Proficiency Standards in the Core Content Areas,* outlines standards for teaching English learners the language they need to develop

Table 2.5 Mathematics Rubric Using Standard 3 (TESOL, 2006)

....

Language Domain	Topic: Measures of Central Tendency				
	Level 1 **Starting Up**	**Level 2** **Beginning**	**Level 3** **Developing**	**Level 4** **Expanding**	**Level 5** **Bridging To**
Listening	Match proportional representation of objects with oral directions and illustrations (e.g., percent, fractions, or decimals; "Which ___ shows ___?") Identify language associated with measures of central tendency displayed visually (e.g., range, the distance from one place to another).	Follow multi-step directions to identify proportional representation in graphs Depict graphically examples of measures of central tendency based on oral directions.	Match examples of uses of proportion with oral descriptions (e.g., interest or taxes; "If . . . then . . .") Select appropriate measures of central tendency based on visual and oral descriptions of real-life situations.	Analyze and apply the use of proportion from oral word problems. Make estimates based on measures of central tendency from oral scenarios.	Evaluate ways of using proportion to solve grade-level oral word problems. Make inferences about uses of measures of central tendency from oral scenarios of grade-level materials.

Table 2.6 Nine Principles of ABC Language Teaching and Learning

Activity-Based	Communicative
1. *Active Engagement.* Learners play enjoyable, engaging, active roles in the learning experience.	5. *Comprehensible Input with Scaffolding.* Teachers provide rich input with appropriate context and support to make that input comprehensible to learners, and appropriately and increasingly more challenging.
2. *Cultural Relevance.* Classrooms respect and incorporate the cultures of the learners and their families in the classroom while helping them to understand the new culture of the community, the school, and the classroom.	6. *Prior Knowledge.* Teachers help learners use their prior knowledge of language, content, and the world to develop new language and increase knowledge.
3. *Collaboration.* Learners develop and practice language in collaboration with one another and with teachers.	7. *Content Integration.* Language learning is integrated with meaningful, relevant, and useful content, generally the same academic content that is appropriate for the age and grade of learners.
4. *Learning Strategies.* Learners use a variety of learning strategies to maximize learning in the classroom, to expand their learning beyond the classroom, and to become independent, lifelong learners.	8. *Differentiation.* Learning activities accommodate different language and literacy and cognitive levels, and incorporate many dimensions of learning—different learning styles, intelligences, and preferences.
	9. *Clear, Appropriate Goals and Feedback.* Teachers set and communicate clear attainable goals to learners and provide students with appropriate and consistent feedback on their progress in attaining these goals.

essential content concepts. The general standards are included on Table 2.4. The standards document offers specifics on expectations for language arts, science, math, and social studies learners at five levels of English language proficiency, across the domains of listening, speaking, reading, and writing, for grade level clusters PreK–K, 1–3, 4–5, 6–8, and 9–12. Many states and districts have determined their own standards for English learners and selected instruments to assess their achievement.

But good assessment goes far beyond summative tests at the beginning or end of the year. Good assessment includes multiple assessments. Good teaching includes assessment as an integral part of every lesson so that children and teachers can clearly see the progress they are making. Teachers may assess in many ways that range from informal to formal: by asking questions to individuals, groups, and the whole class; by having learners give signs or signals; by having learners demonstrate their understanding with responses on slates; by giving a group quiz; by having learners score themselves along a rubric or on a checklist; by keeping checklists of learner accomplishments; by writing portfolios; by using state and national English language assessment instruments; and, when learners are ready, by giving district, state, and national criterion-referenced or standardized tests designed for all learners.

We've now outlined nine principles included in two dimensions—principles that we hope will guide you toward supporting the learning of English language learners in your setting. Table 2.6 summarizes these principles for your review. The following chapters will show these principles at work in various aspects of your instructional program for English language learners: in organizing your classroom, teaching oral language, reading, writing, assessing, and putting it all together through content-based learning.

Questions for Reflection

1. How is what a teacher believes about teaching reflected in how that teacher performs in the classroom?
2. What do you believe is important to best promote learning for all learners? What do you believe is important for enhancing the academic language of English language learners in particular?
3. Reflect on your own experiences of studying a new language. Were you successful? What was most helpful? What was least helpful? What classroom principle and characteristics promoted your learning? Compare and contrast these principles with the ones outlined in this chapter.
4. Which of the principles outlined do you think is the most important, in your view? Why? Did any principle surprise you? How?

Activities for Further Learning

1. Each "principle in practice" in this chapter describes teaching English learners in a particular grade-level classroom. Rewrite one of these vignettes to describe how this principle in practice might be changed to meet the needs of students at a different grade level.
2. Develop a lesson for a grade level that you teach or may teach. Focus your lesson on meeting one or more of the principles named in order to include learners of English. Exchange lessons with a partner and discuss how you have succeeded in teaching according to the principles and how you might take the lesson even further in that direction.
3. Observe an English learner in a content classroom over several days. Note what the student is doing, saying, and attending to during your observation. Does that learner seem to comprehend the language and expectations of the classroom? What does the learner seem to comprehend? What evidence from your observation indicates that the learner comprehends? What does the learner not seem to understand? What evidence from your observation indicates that the learner does not comprehend?
4. If a new student entered your class from a culture with which you were unfamiliar, outline preparation and processes that you might use to provide cultural relevance for that student in your classroom.
5. Interview two adults who learned English after starting school. Ask your interviewees about their educational history and experiences as early, intermediate, and advanced learners. Ask about the difficulties they faced and what people, processes, materials, or strategies they feel helped them to learn English. How do these connect with the principles in this chapter?
6. Visit a church, community center, farmers' market, place of worship, or other location frequented by members of language minority groups in your area and where another language or languages are often spoken. Spend some time listening and observing. Reflect: What does it feel like to be the one who does not understand? If you can, begin a conversation with some individuals. Ask them

how people in their community go about learning English and about challenges they face. Ask them what they wish for their children.

7. Choose a language that you don't know much about and that is spoken by one of your students/potential students. Visit the Ilovelanguages web site (www.ilovelanguages.com). Search for information on the language you selected. See how much you can learn about that language in 20 to 30 minutes—just a little about pronunciation, writing system, grammar, vocabulary, related languages, and so on. What might speakers of that language find difficult when learning English? What connections to English might you capitalize upon?

8. Visit the Safe Schools Coalition web site on guidelines for avoiding bias in school curriculum materials (http://www.safeschoolscoalition.org/identifyingbias .html). Use their criterion to review your textbooks and/or materials that you are using or considering using in a future unit or theme.

myeducationlab Where the Classroom Comes to Life   is a collection of online tools for your success in this course, your licensure exams, and your teaching career. Go to www.myeducationlab .com to utilize these extensive resources including videos from real classrooms, Praxis and licensure preparation, a lesson plan builder, and materials to help you in your teaching career.

Suggested Reading

Ariza, E. N. W. (2006). *Not for ESOL teachers: What every classroom teacher needs to know about the linguistically, culturally, and ethnically diverse student.* Boston, MA: Allyn & Bacon. Teachers of diverse learners are offered essential concepts for fully including those English learners in the mainstream classroom. Using many examples in the voices of students and teachers, Ariza considers the classroom settings, learning about cultures, specific information about cultural groups, language acquisition, and learning English through academic content, assessment, and connecting to the community.

Brown, H. D. (2000). *Teaching by principles: An interactive approach to language pedagogy* (2nd ed.). Upper Saddle River, NJ: Pearson ESL. This popular methodology text surveys a variety of language teaching options grounded in accepted principles of language learning and teaching.

Gibbons, P. (2002). *Scaffolding language, scaffolding learning: Teaching second language learners in the mainstream classroom.* Portsmouth, NH: Heinemann. Gibbons introduces the theory behind second-language learning in readable language, and provides concrete classroom examples of applications, along with classroom activities to implement to help English learners speak, listen, read, and write.

King-Shaver, B. & Hunter, A. (2003). *Differentiated instruction in the English classroom: Content, process, product, and assessment.* Portsmouth, NH: Heinemann. The authors clearly and concisely explain differentiation as a way of thinking about the classroom and a strategy for improving teaching. They provide both the rationale for differentiating and descriptions of differentiated teaching in the English classroom through modifications in learning content, learning process, and learning products and assessment.

Li, X. & Zhang, M. (2004). Why Mei still cannot read and what can be done. *Journal of Adolescent & Adult Literacy 48*:2. This case study explores the educational factors that failed a 14-year-old sixth grader from China, and how schools can prevent such students from failing in school.

Web Sites for Further Learning

ESL Infusion: Practices for English Language Learners. Gersten, R. & Baker, S. (May, 2001). National Institute for Urban School Improvment. Retrieved May 2, 2008.

http://www.urbanschools.org/pdf/ts_eng.pdf?v_document_name=Topical%
20summaries%20English

iLoveLanguages, by Tyler Chambers (2006), is a comprehensive catalog of language-related
Internet resources, including information about languages, online language lessons,
translation dictionaries, and so on. Retrieved May 2, 2008.

http://www.ilovelanguages.com/

National Council of Teachers of English (NCTE). NCTE has collected resources for teachers
of English language learners at elementary and secondary levels. Retrieved May 2, 2008.

http://www.ncte.org/collections/elemell

http://www.ncte.org/collections/secell

Northwest Regional Education Laboratory. This group, one of 13 national resource labora-
tories, has developed a number of resources and training programs for teachers of
English learners—many of them available for free. One of their key themes is equity.
Retrieved May 2, 2008.

http://www.nwrel.org/free/

Safe Schools Coalition. The safe schools coalition offers guidelines on identifying bias in
school materials relating to stereotypes of ethnicity, home language, religion, race,
disabilities, occupation, and so on. Retrieved May 2, 2008.

http://www.safeschoolscoalition.org/identifyingbias.html

Teachers of English to Speakers of Other Languages, Inc. (TESOL) is an international professional organization whose mission is to ensure excellence in English language
teaching to speakers of other languages. TESOL's Core Values include professionalism
in language education, individual language rights, accessible, high-quality language
education, collaboration in a global community, interaction of research and reflective
practice for educational improvement, and respect for diversity and multiculturalism.
TESOL has Interest Sections (membership groups) for elementary, secondary, and
bilingual teachers, where you can network, find resources, and learn about teaching.
Retrieved May 2, 2008.

http://www.tesol.org

http://www.tesol.org/s_tesol/sec_document.asp?CID=709&DID= 6065
(Intro to TESOL)

References

Angelou, M. (Photographs by Margaret Courtney-Clarke) (1994). *My painted house, my friendly chicken, and me.* NY: Clarkson Potter.

Bigler, L. (2006, March). Using TPR to illuminate stories: Reenacting the Rosa Parks bus protest. *TESOL in Elementary Education Interest Section Newsletter, 28:* 1, Alexandria, VA: TESOL. Retrieved May 2, 2008. http://www.tesol.org/s_tesol/sec_issue.asp?nid= 2842&iid=5649&sid=1

Bronfenbrenner, U. (1975). Is early intervention effective? In U. Bronfenbrenner, (Ed.), *Influences on human development.* Hinsdale, IL: Dryden Press.

Cameron, L. (2001). *Teaching languages to young learners.* NY: Cambridge University Press.

Carrell, P. L. & Eisterhold, J. C. (1988). Schema theory and ESL reading pedagogy. In Patricia L. Carrel, Joanne Devine, and David E. Eskey (Eds.), *Interactive approaches to second language reading* (pp. 73–92). NY: Cambridge University Press.

Chamot, A. & O'Malley, M. (1996). Implementing the cognitive academic language learning approach (CALLA). In R. Oxford (Ed.), *Language learning strategies around the world: Cross-cultural perspectives* (pp. 167–173). Honolulu: University of Hawaii, Second Language Teaching and Curriculum Centre.

Cummins, J. (1986). Empowering minority students: A framework for intervention. *Harvard Educational Review, 56*(1): 18–36.

Delpit, L. (1995). *Other people's children: Cultural conflict in the classroom.* NY: New Press.

Derman-Sparks, L. & the Antibias Curriculum Task Force. (1989). *Anti-bias curriculum: Tools for empowering young children.* Washington, DC: National Association for the Education of Young Children.

Freeman, D., Freeman, Y., Garcia, A. C., Gottlieb, M., McCloskey, M. L., Stack, L., & Silva, C. (2003). *On our way to English, K–5.* Austin, TX: Rigby/Harcourt Achieve.

Gardner, H. (1983). *Frames of mind.* NY: Basic Books.

Gardner, H. (1996, Apr.). Multiple intelligences: Myths and messages. *International Schools Journal, 15*(2): 8–22.

Genesee, F. (2000). Brain Research: Implications for Second Language Learning. University of California, Santa Cruz: Center for Research on Education, Diversity & Excellence Occasional Reports. ERIC Paper 00 12. Retrieved May 2, 2008. http://pegasus.cc.ucf.edu/~gurney/BrainLearning.doc

Heath, S. (1983). *Ways with words: Language, life and work in communities and classrooms.* Cambridge, UK: Cambridge University Press.

Jensen, E. (1998). *Teaching with the brain in mind.* Alexandria, VA: ASCD.

Kessler, C. (1991). *Cooperative language learning: A teacher's resource book.* Englewood, NJ: PrenticeHall.

Krashen, S. (2003). *Explorations in language acquisition and use.* Portsmouth, NH: Heinemann.

Lessard-Clouston, M. (1997). Language Learning Strategies: An Overview for L2 Teachers. *The Internet TESL Journal,* Vol. III, No. 12, December 1997. Retrieved May 2, 2008. http://iteslj.org/Articles/Lessard-Clouston-Strategy.html

Lightbown, P. M. & Spada, N. (2006). *How languages are learned* (3rd ed.). Oxford: Oxford.

Macaulay, D. (1975). *Pyramid.* Boston, MA: Houghton Mifflin.

Marzano, R., Pickering, D. J., & Pollock, J. E. (2004). *Classroom instruction that works: Research-based strategies for increasing student achievement.* Alexandria, VA: ASCD.

McCloskey, M. L. & Thrush, E. (2005). Building a reading scaffold with WebTexts. *Essential Teacher, 2*(4): 48–51.

Nunan, D. (1996). Learner strategy training in the classroom: An action research study. *TESOL Journal, 6*(1): 35–41.

Oxford, R. (Ed.). (1996). *Language learning strategies around the world: Cross-cultural perspectives.* Honolulu: University of Hawaii, Second Language Teaching and Curriculum Centre.

Reese, L., Garnier, H., Gallimore, R., & Goldenberg, C. (2000). Longitudinal analysis of the antecedents of emergent Spanish literacy and middle-school English reading achievement of Spanish-speaking students. *American Educational Research Journal, 37*(3): 633–662 (Autumn, 2000).

Slavin, R. E. (1995). *Cooperative learning: Theory, research, and practice* (2nd ed.). Boston, MA: Allyn & Bacon.

Snow, C. E., Burns, S. M., & Griffin, P. (Eds.). (1998.) *Preventing reading difficulties in young children.* Washington, DC: National Academy Press.

Sprenger, M. (1999). *Learning and memory: The brain in action.* Alexandria, VA: ASCD.

TESOL (2006) *PreK–12 English language proficiency standards in the core content areas.* Alexandria, VA: TESOL.

Thomas, W. P. & Collier, V. P. (2003). *What we know about effective instructional approaches for language minority learners.* Arlington, VA: Educational Research Service.

Tizard, J., Schofield, W., & Hewison, J. (1982). Collaboration between teacher and parents in assisting children's reading. *British Journal of Educational Psychology, 52*(1): 1–15.

Tomlinson, C. (1999). *The differentiated classroom: Responding to the needs of all learners.* Alexandria, VA: ASCD.

Vygotsky, L. S. (1986). *Thought and language.* NY: Wiley.

Yoon, B. (2007). Offering or limiting opportunities: Teachers' role and approaches to English-language learners' participation in literacy activities. *The Reading Teacher 61*(3): 216–225.

●●●

CHAPTER 3

Reaching Out to Home and Community

Lynn King is a kindergarten teacher at an elementary school in Florida. Pelican Bay Elementary is located in an agricultural area and many of the students come from migratory families. Lynn's classroom of eighteen children contains twelve children who are English language learners.

Although Lynn has been at Pelican Bay for ten years, she is constantly learning about the cultures of the children in her classroom. She recently recalled a parent conference with the father of one of her students, a child who was having difficulty conforming to classroom rules and routines. Lynn suggested to Miguel's father (through an interpreter) that she could send home a note when Miguel has had a bad day at school, so that he would be able to follow through at home.

"What can I do to him at home?" the father asked.

"Well," Lynn responded, "you might take away one of his toys for a day or two."

"He doesn't have any toys," the father replied.

"Then don't let him watch TV for a while," Lynn said.

"The TV has been broken for a long time and I don't have the money to get it repaired," the father said. "Miguel never watches TV."

"Okay, then don't let him ride his bike."

"He doesn't have a bike either, Miss King."

Lynn was running out of ideas but she finally said, "Then don't let him go outside to play."

The father explained patiently, "We don't have any air conditioning in our house and it's very hot. The kids have to play outside because it's too hot for them to stay inside."

Lynn told us this story because for her it was a turning point in her role as a teacher of migrant students. Lynn realized that she needed to learn more about the cultures of her students and to become a cultural mediator for them.

How do teachers make connections among their students, their families, the school, and the community?

●●●

- How do teachers become cultural mediators?
- How do teachers connect to the homes and families of their students?
- How can the school community support the education of English language learners?
- How can the community outside the school support the education of ELLs?

Teachers as Cultural Mediators

Lynn King's determination to become a **cultural mediator** for her students led her to start exploring the notion of culture and what it meant to her and to her students. Nieto and Bode (2007, p. 171) defines **culture** as "the values, traditions, world view, and social and political relationships created, shared, and transformed by a group of people bound together by a common history, geographic location, language, social class, religion, or other shared identity."

For Lynn, multiculturalism has begun to mean more than celebrating food, holidays, and clothing. Miguel's father taught her that family relationships, communication styles, values, and attitudes are also components of culture. Acquiring the skills, attitudes and knowledge to enable her to effectively communicate and interact with individuals from other cultures would be an ongoing process that would engage her cognitively, affectively, and behaviorally during the rest of her teaching career.

As Nieto's definition indicates, culture is not a monolithic, stagnant concept. Nor are individuals from a common culture homogeneous. Culture is fluid, ever changing, and non-deterministic. It consists of regularities in the experiences of individuals living in the world and in the schema of those people who share in those regularities. Culture is the summary of those regularities (Atkinson, 1999).

Teachers who are cultural mediators act as translators of culture, guides to the invisible patterns that connect groups of people. Lynn's European American middle class experiences do not prepare her well for teaching young migrant Mexican children of agricultural workers in the citrus industry of south Florida. Lynn has resolved to explore the links between language, literacy, and culture and to change her instructional practices both in and out of the classroom in order to be a strong advocate for the children under her care.

Lynn is learning different ways of dealing with her students and with their families. She is learning to acknowledge the differences that her students bring with them to school. This includes differences in their genders, races, social classes, family structures, school experiences, religions, learning styles, and languages. She is learning that these differences affect the way that her students learn. And finally, she is learning that accepting their differences also means making provisions for them in her instructional program (Nieto & Bode, 2007).

Teachers like Lynn develop the attributes that enable them to create effective learning environments for multicultural children. Some of the skills developed by multicultural teachers include the following (Education 173 Online):

- *Understanding* how culture affects the teaching/learning process.
- *Exploring* one's own cultural perspective.
- *Helping students expand their knowledge* of their own culture and develop an appreciation for differences in others.
- *Creating an atmosphere* in the classroom in which cultural differences are respected and explored.
- *Communicating that all cultures* have their own integrity, validity, and coherence.
- *Drawing upon the cultural experiences* of children and parents, and including this authentic, relevant perspective in the curriculum.
- *Adapting instructional practices* to accommodate varied learning styles, building on students' strengths, and avoiding judgments that might negatively impact the achievement gains of students.

Gay (2000) has a similar outline of the roles and responsibilities of the teacher as a cultural mediator. These roles define teachers as the following:

Cultural organizers: creating a variety of learning environments in the classroom to reflect the styles and preferences of the learners.

Cultural mediators: honoring other cultures, clarifying new cultural concepts, combating prejudice, talking about cultural differences.

Orchestrators of social contracts: helping children adapt to the culture of the classroom while creating a classroom culture that is compatible to the learners.

Culturally mediated instruction may provide the best learning conditions for all learners because it reduces student frustrations in the classroom and therefore limits the amount of unacceptable behavior occurring there (Hollins, 1996). Culturally mediated classrooms accomplish this by encouraging multiple viewpoints among learners. Instruction is based upon students' prior knowledge. Learning experiences are created that are highly relevant to the learners and differentiated for their language proficiencies. Teachers allow for diverse ways of knowing and learning, and multiple possibilities for sharing knowledge and representing an understanding of the content.

Such changes are not easy to accomplish. North American classrooms are not traditionally structured to accommodate diversity. The lowering of cognitive challenge during instruction, the focus on basic skill development, and the limited exposure to sophisticated narrative structures in texts are some of the accommodations made for English language learners by teachers who have had little training in or experience with cultural diversity. ELLs in their classes may be called on less frequently, not encouraged to elaborate on their responses, and not challenged to develop higher-order thinking skills. They are rewarded for being "nice" but not expected to learn at a high level.

Some consequences of cultural illiteracy on the part of teachers are reported in a study by Willett (1995) of three first graders, the children of Chinese families enrolled in an English dominant classroom. The children (a boy and two girls) experienced differential access to achievement because of the socialization style of the classroom. The two girls were seated together and worked cooperatively throughout the year on their phonics workbooks. They were quiet and busy, supported each other in their learning goals, and appealed to other girls in the class to help them on occasion. The lone boy, Xavier, was seated apart from the girls and was not allowed to get out of his seat to solicit their help. In addition, the boys in the classroom were competitive rather than cooperative with each other and would not provide any help on the phonics seatwork. Xavier had to rely on the teacher for help far more often than the girls did. He came to be viewed as needy, while the girls, who were seen as independent workers, held a higher status in the class. Eventually, Xavier was taken out of the classroom for extra help in an **English language development (ELD)** workbook, further reducing his status in the class. Although he scored the same as the two girls on the Bilingual Syntax Measure at the end of the school year, he was retained in the ELD class but the girls were not.

Why did the girls succeed while Xavier was deemed less successful? All of the children benefited by the routine nature of the task—completing pages in a phonics workbook—that was repetitive in its structure. But the girls had the additional assistance of a collaborative relationship and a cooperative learning environment. This greatly increased their confidence as learners and earned them esteem in the status hierarchy of the classroom.

What could a cultural mediator have done to change the outcome for these children? The teacher could have tried some of the following techniques:

- Created a safe environment by reducing competition and encouraging all of the children to negotiate meaning with their peers.
- Encouraged children to use their native languages in class when seeking help with content learning.
- Talked to students about their learning and asked them to think of ways to help develop academic competency.

- Encouraged children to use social interaction as a means of summarizing, organizing, brainstorming, and reflecting upon new learning.
- Talked to parents about their child's learning style and reactions to the classroom.

Indeed, changes in the organization of the classroom have dramatic effects on learners of every age. The Center for Research on Education Diversity and Excellence or CREDE (2001) recommends principles for organizing a classroom for all at-risk learners. The CREDE principles call for:

1. *Joint Productive Activity:* This principle echoes the thinking of Vygotsky (1978) that learning occurs when an adult or expert peer assists a learner to higher achievement levels by working together toward a common goal or product. Through a focused activity, teacher and learner create a common culture grounded in the learning experience, even though they do not share the same home culture. When Shelly Sanders, a fifth-grade teacher at a migrant school in Florida, works in the school garden with the fifth-grade garden club, she is engaged in the kind of Joint Productive Activity that helps these children make the connections between their migrant agricultural experiences and their school science learning.

2. *Challenging Activities:* ELLs are able to learn at a high level when their teachers believe in their abilities and view them as "knowers" rather than as having a deficit. Xavier's experiences in first grade phonics occurred not because he was unable to learn phonics, but because his teachers did not believe that he could, and did not structure the classroom to facilitate his learning.

    Children in classrooms today must be challenged to learn to high standards and supported in their achievement of those standards by carefully crafted lessons that build incrementally on a foundation of student success.

3. *Instructional Conversation:* Group discussions are usually not helpful to ELLs in mainstream classrooms. ELLs may lag behind the other students in their comprehension of the language that swirls around them. They feel disconnected from the group and hesitant to participate. The instructional conversation, however, can be an excellent technique for including all learners toward a learning goal.

    The instructional conversation requires a classroom arrangement that accommodates a teacher meeting with a small group of students. They might be talking at a lab table in biology or meeting for a guided-reading session or working on a social studies project in the corner of the room. The teacher has a clear learning goal in mind and encourages all of the students to express their views and justify them. The teacher assists by questioning, restating, probing, encouraging, and praising. The students do most of the talking in these conversations and the teacher does a great deal of listening. The end of the conversation yields a resulting product: an oral summary, a listing of procedures, or a resolution of a problem.

4. *Language Development:* One of the most important changes in a content teacher's instructional load is the inclusion of language objectives in the content lesson plan. Purposeful instruction in the language of the academic content is required for students to learn at a high level. ELLs cannot be successful in math class without specific knowledge of the vocabulary and syntax of math. By incorporating academic language learning into classroom content, teachers further mediate for these students through the unknown culture of the classroom.

5. *Contextualization:* Classroom learning reflects the experiences and skills of the home and the community when teachers contextualize their instruction. In contextualized classrooms, activities derive from the experiences of the

Instructional Conversations Provide Excellent Opportunities for Students to Learn Academic Language

learners. They reflect community norms and make connections between the home and the school. Doing community-based learning activities in middle school, encouraging parent participation in literacy workshops, sending home books on tape for shared reading, growing vegetables in a school garden, and teaching cellular structure by decorating cookies are all examples of learning activities based upon student preferences and knowledge.

Richard Albaugh's fourth-grade students wrote their best essays of the school year when he asked them to write about "The Day the Crops Failed." His students, children of migrant agricultural workers, related to the freeze that killed the crops upon which their families' livelihood depended. They wrote and rewrote and delighted in reading their stories to multiple audiences. Their teacher had contextualized his writing instruction to facilitate his students' best efforts.

How Do Teachers Connect to the Homes and Families of Their Students?

Why is it important that teachers reach out to parents? The answer is unequivocal. There is a strong link between parent involvement and children's success in school. The research is clear and abundant on the effects: higher grades and test scores, better attendance, fewer special education placements, higher graduation rates, and greater enrollment and completion of postsecondary education (Bennett, 2004). Additional evidence indicates that school morale, teacher morale, teacher satisfaction, and school reputation all improve in districts with high parental involvement in education (CCSSO, 2006).

Studies show that student achievement grows in relation to the amount and duration of family involvement in the school. When low-income parents participate extensively in the school community, they see their children's test scores rise to the level of middle-class children and the teachers' expectations rise for those students (Bennett, 2004).

Teachers and school administrators rank strong parenting roles in children's learning as the highest priority issue in education policy (Harris & Associates, 1993), and the lack of parent involvement as the biggest obstacle to school reform (Finn & Rebarber, 1992).

And yet, actual parent involvement in most schools is low. This is especially true in low-income communities and in schools with high ELL populations. As of 1997, only 18 percent of high-poverty school districts reported any efforts in their schools to involve

Video Exercise

Embracing Home Experiences of Culturally Diverse Students

Go to MyEducationLab, select the topic **Diversity**, and watch the video entitled "**Embracing Home Experiences of Culturally Diverse Students**" to listen to teachers describe the ways in which home experiences prepare children for school. Complete the questions that accompany it. You may print your work or have it transmitted to your professor as necessary.

parents in their children's education (U.S. Department of Education, 1997), and the great majority of teachers in those districts blamed academic failure on home and family life (U.S. Department of Education, 2001). This trend, happily, appears to be changing in that more recent data indicate increased involvement of parents and increased attendance at meetings for the general population of students. (Child Trends Data Bank, http://www.childtrendsdatabank.org/indicators/39ParentalInvolvementinSchool .cfm)

Individual teachers can make great differences with the children and families in their own classrooms. They can make the connections that count by viewing the linguistically and culturally diverse households of their students as repositories of "funds of knowledge" that can enrich classroom learning (Moll, Amanti, Neff, & González, 1992).

Teachers who seek to connect with the families of their students create a welcoming environment in the classroom. In addition to organizing the classroom and adjusting instructional practices, teachers who are cultural mediators seek to understand the hopes and concerns of families through the following strategies:

- Finding opportunities to talk to parents informally.
- Sending newsletters home with information about classroom events (translated in the language of the family).
- Using e-mail and the telephone to inform parents of student success stories.
- Conducting home visits to learn more about families and their cultures.
- Inviting parents to volunteer in the classroom.
- Hosting family nights at school to showcase student accomplishment, to introduce parents to new concepts such as bedtime reading, to inform parents of school activities, or to explain the school's report card.
- Researching the cultural backgrounds of families.
- Visiting local community centers and neighborhoods to learn more about community resources and norms.

The traditional parent-teacher conference is the most likely place for parents and teachers to start a relationship. Teachers who are aware of a parent's limited language skills in English make sure that the school will provide appropriate translators for the conference. On occasion, schools have been forced to use children as translators, especially in the case of uncommon languages with few adult translators available. For the most part, this is not a desirable practice. Using children in a translation role diminishes the role of the parent and interferes with adult communication.

Teachers with strong communication skills are more effective at developing relationships with parents. They consider the following activities to be essential to their role as an effective parent partner:

- *Prepare in advance for the conference.* Collect student work samples and have a clear notion of what essential information is to be communicated and what information is to be learned from the parent.
- *Monitor nonverbal signals.* These convey a great deal to others, including notions of respect. Being on time, using eye contact, nodding while listening, and using peer-to-peer seating arrangements are techniques that send positive signals to parents.
- *Convey an attitude of acceptance, care, and concern* for the parents and their child. Sharing success stories with parents will help to send these messages.
- *Listen to parents.* Let them tell their story and listen for the content and the level of feeling behind the words. Restate what you have heard and allow the parent to confirm your understanding.
- *Use open-ended questions* to learn more about the family and the child. For example, "Tell me what Irina is like at home" or "What does she enjoy doing with the family?"
- *Avoid placing blame on the family or making judgments about the family.*

Relationship Building Between the Parents and the Teacher Can Begin at the Parent Conference

The interventions and strategies mentioned above presuppose that the family is emotionally and culturally ready to relate to the school and cooperate in their child's education. There is a prevailing notion that parents of English language learners are not interested in assisting their children's school achievement because, statistically, their involvement with the school community is low. Teachers can be frustrated by families that make conference appointments and then don't show up, or by parents who arrive late without any explanation. One author's experience with one such family required the help of the bilingual social worker in the district. We discovered a mother threatening suicide and a father who was physically abusive. This family was in need of extensive intervention. Their concerns were not at the level of school achievement. We learned that sometimes teachers need to be detectives to unearth information that can help us to advocate for our students.

There are other reasons for this lack of engagement, however. One explanation relates to the differences between Latin American and U.S. schools. In Latin American schools with large classes, teachers often administer "pass/fail" grades. Parents assume that, if a child has passed the grade, everything is fine. But U.S. schools are increasingly slow to retain or fail ELLs; therefore, passing from one grade to the next is not a signal that all is well.

Another explanation arises from the fact that many Asian and Latino families see the teacher as an education expert. Families from these cultures are not expected to offer opinions to the teacher or make suggestions. However, studies indicate (Goldenberg, 1987), and it has been our experience, that when families are given specific tasks to perform at home, they are willing to comply. For example, when parents in one author's classroom were asked to listen to children's books on tape and co-read with their children as a homework assignment, all of the parents accomplished this task and signed off daily on the worksheet that they had done so. Parents of our middle-school students were eager to pick their children up from school so that the students could attend after-school tutoring sessions.

Non-English families are hesitant to participate in school events when their English skills are poor and the school has limited bilingual staff. Parents and teachers both are uncomfortable in these situations and communication difficulties impede a partnership between the two.

Video Exercise

School Support for Culturally Diverse Students and Families

Go to MyEducationLab, select the topic **Diversity**, and watch the video entitled "**School Support for Culturally Diverse Students and Families**" to listen to an expert description of one of a teacher's roles in a culturally diverse classroom. Complete the questions that accompany it. You may print your work or have it transmitted to your professor as necessary.

In addition to the barriers mentioned above, many newly arrived parents are not ready to take on responsibilities at school because they are still adjusting to a different culture. As parents proceed through various stages of adjustment, they are ready for different kinds of school involvement.

1. *Arrival/Survival Stage:* As new arrivals, parents need a basic school orientation and information about the school community. It is most helpful to give this information in the native language and in a face-to-face meeting. At this point, parents' interest in school is high but their participation may be limited.
2. *Culture Shock:* Parental energies are drained during this emotionally difficult period. Schools and teachers can support families by linking them to networks of other parents, initiating personal contact, minimizing demands on their time, and keeping lines of communication open.
3. *Coping:* When parents have had time to become familiar with the new culture and begin to accept the cultural system, they may be ready to participate in school activities related to their children, assist in specific tasks to help learning at home, and participate in teacher-parent communication.
4. *Acculturation:* In this final stage, parents feel comfortable in the culture. At this point they can be encouraged to participate in more school activities, including leadership roles and mentoring for other parents. Opportunities for wider community involvement are appropriate at this stage (Violand-Sanchez, Hutton, & Ware, 1991).

How Can the School Community Support the Education of English Language Learners?

There has been a great deal of research in the past fifteen years on parent involvement and family-school partnerships. A framework for six different kinds of involvement has been developed to describe the range and complexity of these partnerships (Epstein, Sanders, Simon, Salinas, Jansorn, & Van Voorhis, 2002). Table 3.1 identifies the types of involvement, indicates what schools can do to assist at each stage, and suggests possible practices at each stage.

Of the six main types of school involvement in Table 3.1, the first three are the most common in schools:

- Parent as audience
- Parent as home tutor
- Parent as program supporter

This was found to be true for groups of Anglo, African American and Latino parents (Chavkin & Wiliams, 1993). The last three are less frequent:

- Parent as co-learner
- Parent as decision maker
- Parent as advocate

Part of the reason may lie in the fact that these roles are non-traditional for all parents. Even for parents who are interested in school involvement, the last three categories require a commitment from the school and the community in order for this kind of involvement to occur.

Students Succeed Best When Parents Support Their Children's Education

How Can the Community Outside the School Support the Education of ELLs?

Fellsmere Elementary School on Florida's east coast is a migrant school within an agricultural county devoted to growing citrus crops. The school is comprised of over 90 percent bilingual students, many of whom are the children of migrant citrus workers. Fellsmere has teamed with the wider community around the school to promote the health and welfare of the children in the school and their families.

The migrant specialist at the school worked with community health organizations to provide a medical clinic for families in the town. Migrant funding was obtained from Title I federal funds to create new Pre-K classes for all of the four-year-olds in the community. The companies hiring migrant workers provided low-cost housing for its workers. The Catholic churches in the surrounding community began a fundraising drive to enlarge the local church in order to include a learning center for instruction in language and computer technology, and to provide a community center. Other local groups stocked pantries with non-perishable foods for those in need.

The school also reaches out to parents and reflects their cultural styles. There is a uniform dress code at the school with clothing sold at WalMart at reasonable prices. The PTA is 100 percent bilingual. The school hosts at least one family night per month with time for socializing, food, a presentation of school literacy events, and occasional presentations of literacy techniques that parents can use to encourage reading in the home.

Positive neighborhood environments such as the Fellsmere example have an effect on the academic achievement of children in that community (Ainsworth, 2002; Crowder, & South, 2003; Fischer & Kmec, 2004). One of the authors saw the effects of community involvement in the support that community volunteers gave to an after-school homework club in a suburban New York school. Meeting twice a week for an hour per session, community members and teachers at the school provided personal, up-close help to ELLs struggling with homework demands. It didn't take long for teachers to begin reporting changes in classroom achievement as a result of the homework club.

Formal, after-school programs of all kinds—Boys' and Girls' Clubs, sports teams, game activities, and so on—have shown a positive effect in the form of increased achievement gains for ELL students. The "protective" function of the formal activity is greatest for students who have no structured activities in their lives and for those students whose parents don't yet speak English (Cosden, Morrison, Albanese, & Macias, 2001). It remains unclear as to why sports teams might affect achievement gains. But for children who only speak English in school, there may be

Table 3.1 School, Family, and Community Partnerships

Type of Involvement	Schools and Teachers Can:	Suggested Practices
Type 1 Parenting	Support parents in the maintenance of a home environment and parenting practices conducive to academic achievement.	• Inform parents of necessary school supplies. • Encourage parents to read from native language children's literature at bedtime. • Suggest appropriate amounts of sleep for the age of the child. • Discuss the school lunch and invite parents' comments on its appropriateness for their child. • If necessary, talk about climate changes and the clothing required. • Suggest a quiet study area at home stocked with resources for learning. • Encourage parents to praise their children's accomplishments. • Provide guidance on developmentally appropriate family activities. • Provide guidance on appropriate disciplinary practices. • Develop teen parenting programs.
Type 2 Communicating	Establish ongoing procedures for communication from school to home and home to school.	• Conduct at least two parent conferences per year. • Provide translations for oral and written communication as needed (determine literacy levels in the home). • Send home notices of classroom events. • Alert parents by telephone, e-mail, or in person of their child's successes. • Alert parents to important school-wide events such as school picnics, shows, music concerts, etc. • Alert parents to problems with behavior or academics, and ask for their suggestions and assistance. • Make home visits. • Maintain a parent-friendly office. • Post welcome signs in all languages spoken in the school. • Link new families with mentors. • Coordinate school tours and orientation for new families. • Hire a family coordinator/liaison.

(Continued)

Table 3.1 School, Family, and Community Partnerships   *(Continued)*

Type of Involvement	Schools and Teachers Can:	Suggested Practices
Type 3 Volunteering	Recruit and organize parent help and support in the school and classroom.	• Survey family and community members for prospective volunteers. • Provide access to ELD programs for parents at night. • Set up networks of ELL parents with addresses and phone numbers. • Invite parents to assist in a classroom project, activity, or field trip. • Invite parents to share a special skill with the children in the classroom. • Invite parents to share stories, photos, and artifacts from their culture. • Host an orientation program to prepare volunteers. • Help volunteers feel welcome and show appreciation for their efforts. • Announce volunteer activities throughout the year. • Provide volunteer information packets. • Develop a volunteer data base and directory.
Type 4 Learning at Home	Provide information and ideas as to how parents can help their children with homework and other curriculum-related activities.	• Encourage parents to review finished homework each night. • Encourage parents to ask their children to explain topics studied in the classroom. • Set out expectations for school behavior and learning. • Assign specific tasks for parents to assist their children in learning, e.g., play with math fact cards, listen to the child read, share the contents of a child's journal, or learning log. • Encourage parents to talk to their children about their school experiences and peer relationships. • Establish evening workshops to teach parents how to interpret a report card, read aloud to children, and establish appropriate disciplinary practices. • Offer opportunities for parents and children to learn together. • Encourage parents to explain to their children the importance of education in life.
Type 5 Decision Making	Include parents in school decision making and develop parent leaders.	• Encourage ELL parents to attend PTA meetings. • Develop networks of parents to work with teachers on school-related projects such as advisory councils. • Encourage involvement from every segment of the school community.

Table 3.1 School, Family, and Community Partnerships *(Continued)*

Type of Involvement	Schools and Teachers Can:	Suggested Practices
Type 5 Decision Making (continued)	Include parents in school decision making and develop parent leaders.	• Provide classes for parents on topics of interest to them as parents and school partners. • Develop a Parent Resource Center with books, multilingual videos, CDs, and other material to support parent leadership.
Type 6 Collaborating with the Community	Identify and integrate resources from the community to strengthen school programs, family practices, and student achievement.	• Provide parents with information on community organizations that provide health, recreation, and social support for families. • Invite community groups and industries to partner with the school for information sharing, grant assistance, developing laboratories for improved technology, scholarships, and internships in local business. • Provide opportunities for staff, families, and community members to learn together. • Bring together families, schools, and community organizations for mutual benefit. • Develop schools as community learning centers.

Adapted from Epstein, Sanders, Simon, Salinas, Jansorn, & Van Voorhis, 2002, p. 3, and from Carter, 2003.

Video Exercise

Community Support for Culturally Diverse Students and Families

Go to MyEducationLab, select the topic **Diversity**, and watch the video entitled "Community Support for Culturally Diverse Students and Families" to listen to an expert describe how community members can impact young language learners. Complete the questions that accompany it. You may print your work or have it transmitted to your professor as necessary.

an increase in overall language competency that results from speaking English in a variety of settings.

Individual school districts throughout the U.S. have made concerted efforts toward connecting their schools to parents and the local community. One of these is the Anoka-Hennepin Independent School District in Minnesota. Anoka-Hennepin was awarded the 2005 Partnership District award from Johns Hopkins University to recognize the long standing commitment and sustainable systemic approach to partnering family, school, and community.

A visit to the Anoka-Hennepin Parent Involvement web site (http://www.anoka .k12.mn.us/education/dept/dept.php?sectiondid+10792) indicates the commitment this district has made to family involvement. The program began in the 1992 to 1993 school year when community education teamed with K–12 education to develop the Parent Involvement Program. Joyce Epstein's model (see Web Sites for Further Learning at the end of the chapter) was selected to provide a research framework for the program. Funding was obtained for sixteen separate projects and for training parent groups.

In the 2004 to 2005 school year, 9,000 parents and community members volunteered in the district. Halfway through the 2005 to 2006 year, 80,000 hours had been volunteered with a monetary value of $1,405,478. Forty-three of the district schools work in partnership with parents and community members, and sponsor volunteer programs.

In the spring of 2006, eighteen workshops were offered to parents and community members. The workshops ranged from two-hour sessions to twelve-hour workshops and presented a diverse array of offerings:

• Raising Your Child's Self-Esteem
• Unlocking Teen Conversations
• How to Chill Out and Be a Cool Parent
• Eating Disorders

- Recognizing Illicit Drugs
- Understanding the New Brain
- Parenting on Purpose
- What Girls Need/What Boys Need
- Life as a Stepparent

The district has a Parent Legislative Council and has developed a Parent Resource Center equipped with books, videos, audiotapes, and CDs available to parents. The Resource Center also offers resources for parent leaders to assist organizations in the district, such as the PTA, PTO, Booster Clubs, and advisory panels. The resources and contact people available help parent leadership with skill-training, giving information on nonprofit management, publishing a monthly publication, and dispersing seventeen documents crucial for nonprofit management. Parents have access to a Parent Organization Directory and a Citizen Involvement Handbook.

With strong leadership, necessary resources and conditions that foster collaborative relationships among the school, families, and the community, school districts can be assured that all students will have the support they need to achieve at a high level.

Questions for Reflection

1. Lynn King began this chapter with a resolve to become a cultural mediator for her students. In what ways will Lynn have to change her traditional role as a classroom teacher? What specific skills and knowledge will Lynn have to acquire? Do you think this kind of change is necessary for all K–12 teachers in North American schools?
2. In what specific ways must a teacher relate differently to parents of language-learning students? Is the time and effort justified in a teacher's busy day? Give reasons for your answer.
3. Schools with large populations of language-learning children are often understaffed, crowded, and lacking in resources. In what ways could parent involvement change that situation?

Activities for Further Learning

1. Re-read the vignette regarding Lynn King and the parent of the unruly boy. Identify areas of cultural confusion in the conversation. Next, indicate in what ways Lynn could have resolved the situation in a more culturally sensitive way.
2. Teachers have always had a mandate to connect to parents in order to report on student progress. This chapter suggests that teachers and schools must do a great deal more for ELLs and their parents. Prioritize the suggestions made for teachers and schools in their connections to parents of ELLs. Provide a rationale for your work.
3. Read Chapter 4 of *The Inner World of the Immigrant Child* by Christina Igoa (Lawrence Erlbaum Associates, 1995). This chapter entitled "Cultural/Academic/Psychological Interventions" deals with balancing three aspects of the whole child. After reading about the CAP Intervention, list the teacher strategies that a teacher of ELLs might use to help immigrant children achieve happiness and be successful in school.
4. Imagine that you are preparing for a teacher conference with the parent of a Latino student who has been in the U.S. for a year. Your student is creating

minor behavior problems in the classroom, has not made any friends and is not motivated to work hard academically. Work with a partner to write and perform a role-play in which you attempt to establish a relationship with the parent, convey unpleasant information, and encourage the parent to assist you in the education of the child.

5. Visit a local school that has ELL students among the school population. Look for evidence that the school is:

- Creating a family-friendly environment
- Building a support infrastructure
- Encouraging and supporting family involvement
- Developing family-friendly communication
- Supporting educational opportunities for families
- Creating family-school partnerships

6. Design a classroom that is both "student friendly" and "family friendly." Create a floor plan and describe the way that the room organization, the objects, pictures, and realia contribute to a "culturally friendly" learning environment.

7. Visit the following Education World web site: http://www.education-world .com/a_curr/curr200.shtml and read the article entitled "A Dozen Activities to Promote Parent Involvement!" For each of the activities mentioned, indicate how that activity could be changed to become appropriate for parents of ELLs.

8. Do research about your local community to determine if local organizations or businesses are in partnership with the schools in that community. After determining the level of involvement, research Joyce Epstein's model to create a list of "Next Steps" for the school district and the community in their progress toward creating a school, family, and community partnership.

myeducationlab <small>PEARSON</small> <small>Where the Classroom Comes to Life</small> is a collection of online tools for your success in this course, your licensure exams, and your teaching career. Go to www.myeducationlab .com to utilize these extensive resources including videos from real classrooms, Praxis and licensure preparation, a lesson plan builder, and materials to help you in your teaching career.

Suggested Reading

Epstein, J., Sanders, M. G., Simon, B. S., Salinas, K. C., Jansorn, N. R., Van Voorhis, F. L., (2002). *School, Family, and Community Partnerships: Your Handbook for Action* (2nd ed.). Thousand Oaks, CA: Corwin Press. This is a very comprehensive volume containing action steps for community partnerships with the school as a focus. It can be ordered from the Johns Hopkins web site publication list A: http://www.csos.jhu.edu/P2000/center.htm

Igoa, C. (1995) *The inner world of the immigrant child.* Mahwah, NJ: Lawrence Erlbaum Associates. Igoa's work is unique in that it communicates to teachers the affective dimensions of immigrant children's experiences in a new culture and the impact of those experiences on academic achievement.

Nieto, S. & Bode, P. (2007) *Affirming diversity: The sociopolitical context of multicultural education* (5th ed.). Boston, MA: Allyn & Bacon. Nieto explains how personal, social, political, cultural, and educational factors interact to affect educational achievement of language-learning students. She provides a research-based rationale for multicultural education.

Web Sites for Further Learning

Building Partnerships with Parents. Search at the web site for this report from Harcourt which itemizes areas for teachers to consider when developing relationships with parents. It is not specifically directed toward ELL parents. Retrieved May 2, 2008.

http://harcourtassessment.com/NR/rdonlyres/73E53CF9-64D8-4459-8B11-6BCE9E2668CB/0/Building_Partnerships_with_Parents.pdf

Center on Schools, Families, and Community Partnerships. This site is the base for Parent Involvement networks. It contains publication lists with a wealth of information. Retrieved May 2, 2008.

http://www.csos.jhu.edu/P2000/center.htm

Center on Schools, Families and Community Partnerships. This is a PowerPoint presentation containing the outlines of Epstein's model for parental involvement. There are specific suggestions for achievement gains in the content areas. Retrieved May 2, 2008.

www.bocyf.org/epstein_presentation.pdf

Connecting Families to Schools. This is a 2004 research-based paper listing important strategies related to family-school-community involvement and indicating studies related to the effectiveness of those strategies. Retrieved May 2, 2008.

http://www.ncscatfordham.org/binarydata/files/PARENT.doc

Educating Our Children Together. A sourcebook for effective family-school-community partnerships. The book contains eight strategies with many suggestions for enacting them. Retrieved May 2, 2008.

www.directionservice.org/cadre/EducatingOurChildren_01.cfm

Education World. This site has links to a great deal of material. A search of "Parent Involvement" yielded more than 300 sites with practical information for teachers, schools, and community partners. Retrieved May 2, 2008.

http://www.educationworld.com

Parent Involvement at Select Ready Schools. Council of Chief State School Officers (CCSSO), 2006. Retrieved May 2, 2008.

http://www.ccsso.org/content/pdfs/Parent_Involvement_at_Ready_Schools.pdf

The Laboratory for Student Success. Tellez and Waxman describe the kinds of educational practices that lead to success in their article entitled "Quality Teachers for English Language Learners" (2005). Retrieved May 2, 2008.

http://www.temple.edu/lss/pdf/ReviewoftheResearchTellezWaxman.pdf

References

Ainsworth, J. W. (2002). Why does it take a village? The mediation of neighborhood effects on educational achievement. *Social Forces, 81*(1): 117–152.

Atkinson, D. (1999).TESOL and culture. *TESOL Quarterly, 33* (4).

Bennett, E. (2004). *Connecting families to schools: Why parents and community engagement improves school and student performance.* NY: Fordham University, the National Center for Schools and Communities.

Carter, S. (2003). Educating our children together: A sourcebook for effective family-school-community partnerships. Consortium for Alternative Dispute Resolution in Special Education (CADRE) and New York State Education Department Office of Vocational and Educational Services for Individuals with Disabilities (VESID). Washington, DC: U.S. Office of Special Education Programs. Retrieved May 2, 2008. www.directionservice.org/cadre/EducatingOurChildren_01.cfm

Center for Research on Education Diversity & Excellence (2001). *Standards and Indicators.* Retrieved May 2, 2008. http://crede.berkeley.edu/products/print/occreports/g1.html

Child Trends Data Bank. Parent involvement in schools. Retrieved May 2, 2008. http://www.childtrendsdatabank.org/indicators/39ParentalInvolvementinSchools.cfm

Chavkin, N. & Williams, D. (1993). Minority parents and the elementary school: Attitudes and practices. In N. Chavkin (Ed.), *Families and schools in a pluralistic society* (pp. 73–83). Albany, NY: State University of New York Press.

Cosden, M., Morrison, G., Albanese A. L., & Macias, S. (2001). When homework is not homework: After school programs for homework assistance. *Educational Psychologist, 36*(3): 211–221.

Council of Chief State School Officers (CCSSO) (2006). Parent involvement at select ready schools. Council of Chief State School Officers (CCSSO), 2006. Retrieved May 2, 2008 from http://www.ccsso.org/content/pdfs/Parent_Involvement_at_Ready_Schools.pdf

Crowder, K. & South, S. J. (2003). Neighborhood distress and school dropout: The variable significance of community context. *Social Science Research, 32*(4): 659–698.

Education 173 Online. Diversity in Today's Schools, online lecture 5. University of CA at Irvine. Retrieved May 2, 2008 from http://pact.gse.uci.edu/ed173online/notes/173unit5.html

Epstein, J., Sanders, M. G., Simon, B. S., Salinas, K. C., Jansorn, N. R., Van Voorhis, F. L. (2002). *School, family, and community partnerships: Your handbook for action* (2nd ed.). Thousand Oaks, CA: Corwin Press.

Finn, C. E. & Rebarber T. (Eds.). (1992). Education reform in the '90s. NY: MacMillan.

Fischer, M. J. & Kmec, J. A. (2004). Neighborhood socioeconomic conditions as moderators of family resource transmission: High school completion among at-risk youth. *Sociological Perspectives, 47*(4): 507–527.

Gay, G. (2000). *Culturally responsive teaching: Theory, research, and practice.* NY: Teachers College Press.

Goldenberg, C. (1987). Low-income Hispanic parents' contributions to their first grade children's word-recognition skills. *Anthropology and Education Quarterly,* 18: 149–179.

Harris and Associates. (1993). *The American teacher: Teachers respond to President Clinton's education proposals.* The Metropolitan Life Survey. NY: MetLife. (ERIC Document Reproduction Service No. ED358082).

Hollins, E. R. (1996). *Culture in school learning: Revealing the deep meaning.* Mahwah, NJ: Lawrence Erlbaum Associates.

Moll, L. C., Amanti, C., Neff, D., & González, N. (1992). Funds of knowledge for teaching: Using a qualitative approach to connect homes and classrooms. *Theory Into Practice, 31*(2): 132–141.

Nieto, S. & Bode, P. (2007). *Affirming diversity: The sociopolitical context of multicultural education* (5th ed.). Boston, MA: Allyn & Bacon.

U.S. Department of Education (2001). National Center for Education Statistics. Efforts by public K–8 schools to involve parents in children's education: NCES 2001–676, by Xianglei Chen. Public Officer: Kathryn Chandler. Washington, DC.

U.S. Department of Education (1997). Overcoming barriers to family involvement in Title I schools. Report to Congress. (ERIC Document Reproduction Service No. ED407483).

Violand-Sanchez, E., Hutton, C. P., & Ware, H. W. (1991). *Fostering home-school cooperation: Involving language minority families as partners in education.* National Clearinghouse for Bilingual Education.

Vygotsky, L. S. (1978). *Mind and society.* Cambridge, MA: Harvard University Press.

Willett, J. (1995). Becoming first graders in an L2: An ethnographic study of L2 socialization. *TESOL Quarterly, 29*(3): 473–503.

CHAPTER 4

Classroom Management for Integrated Language Learning

Mary Le's fifth grade class of mixed language speaking students has been studying a math unit on ratio and proportion. Mary wants the students to have hands-on practice with the language and the concepts of the unit. Today she has divided her 28 students into seven groups of four and divided the roles among the students to ensure that all will participate equally. Mary's students are working with dry red beans, lima beans and black-eyed peas—grouping the beans to reflect the math salad recipes she has created for them. Mary has demonstrated that each salad has all three types of beans and she has presented several salad recipes on the overhead projector, modeling the language and the strategies to use when solving the problems.

> **Ms. Le:** *This salad contains twelve beans. Half of the beans are red. How will we find out the number of red beans? Talk to your buddy.*

After the students have had a chance to discuss the problem, Mary asks one pair of students to tell the answer and how they arrived at the answer. Mary also illustrates the problem on the blackboard.

> **Ms. Le:** *Lima beans make up one fourth of the salad. How many lima beans are there? Talk to your buddy.*

After solving several problems in this manner, Mary gives red beans to one student in each group, lima beans to another and black-eyed peas to another. She explains that the student with the red beans is responsible for determining the correct number of red beans in the salad. The fourth student in each group is the recorder of the math solutions. While the students are working on their problems, Mary plans to float around the room listening to the language used and observing the social and learning strategies of her students. In the middle of the math activity, the principal arrives at Mary's door to introduce a new student recently arrived from Central America. Mary greets her new student and prepares a desk for the child to work, including pencils and a notebook. She then introduces the new student to a group involved in bean problems. She has chosen this group because the records indicate that the student is a Spanish-speaker and she knows that two students in the group can speak Spanish. (She knows that she needs to check because some students from Central and South America may not speak Spanish or Portuguese, but one of a number of indigenous languages.) She asks one of the students to work as a buddy with the new child, explaining the math problem she is working on and engaging the new student in helping to find the solution to the problem. Mary makes a mental note to assess the new student's math skills at a later time and to ascertain information about prior schooling from the front office at the end of the school day.

How do teachers manage mixed language classrooms to promote efficient language and content learning?

- What must teachers consider when a new language learner enters the classroom?
- How can we organize the physical environment to promote language learning?
- How can we organize the social environment to promote language learning?
- How can we organize instruction to promote learning?

First Things First: Feeling Ready to Learn

When English language learners arrive in a classroom, our first concern is to make sure that they feel safe and welcome in the class. English language learners (ELLs) come from a variety of places, some of them war torn and dangerous. Many of them want to be in our schools but others regret that their parents have taken them away from familiar family and friends. Usually, we know very little about our students when they first appear. But we know one thing—all of them are uncomfortable in this new environment and are anxious about how they will adapt to it.

We greet our new comers with a smiling face and a welcoming classroom. We are aware that even though our students cannot yet speak English, they can interpret our facial gestures.

Provisioning

What else can we do to make ELLs feel comfortable? A clear sign of welcome is to have a desk ready in advance for your new student. Learn how to pronounce the student's name correctly. Put a name tag on the desk with the student's name written in both the home language (if the student comes from a country that uses a different spelling or writing system) and in English. If the child arrives with no materials, find pencils and paper in the classroom to provision the new learner. Sit your new student near a friendly buddy—if possible, one who speaks the same language. The buddy system is useful to help new English language learners feel that they are not alone when they leave for the school cafeteria, the bathroom, the playground, or the bus to go home. Help the buddy to know that the new student will depend on their directions, and show the buddy ways to use gestures to communicate. We can do this best by modeling those gestures.

Gathering Information

As soon as possible after a new arrival, find out the information you'll need to teach the new ELL well. Some important things to learn are the following:

- Basic information
- Previous schooling
- Cultural information

Basic information includes the child's name with correct spelling and pronunciation, native country and language, address, guardians or parents, telephone number, English speaking contacts and emergency contacts, and health history. It's important to know how children will arrive and depart from school—on the bus or with a parent—so that you can direct them safely at the end of the day. Find out, too, if your student is an immigrant, a refugee, or a migrant. Immigrants are permanent or semi-permanent residents who have voluntarily entered the U.S. either on a documented or undocumented basis. Refugees may have been moved because of upheaval in their countries of origin. Sometimes refugees have been moved several times and may have stopped in semi-permanent camps along the way. Migrants move in and out or around the country following seasonal work opportunities.

Often, translators are available to help when parents first enroll their ELL children in school. Take advantage of this opportunity to find out as much as possible about students' school history. Be sure to find out what language(s) students speak and to ask how many days a year students went to school—not just how many years.

Previous schooling records are occasionally delayed and sometimes never arrive at all. When they do, they are usually in the child's home language. You will need translation help in some cases, as well as help in interpreting the meaning of terminology used in various other countries. (Note: Many schools, districts, and states have support resources to help you with this. There are also online support services available, such as the TransAct multilingual library of forms at www.transact.com.) Take note of the days present and absent, and the accumulated amount of instruction the child has received. This information will be important in preparing a plan of instruction for your student. Those children who have received instruction continuously in their countries of origin will understand how school functions, will have acquired literacy skills, and will be able to adapt to the classroom more easily. Those children who have received little instruction previously or whose instruction has been interrupted by war, sickness, migrant status, and other events will not have the skills expected of their peers. Some of these children are not able to use a pencil or a pair of scissors. They will not be able to quickly adapt to the transitions of the classroom or find ways to help themselves learn. The learning plan for these children will be very different from the plan of a child with first language literacy and education.

Learning about ELLs' cultures is helpful for developing relationships with the child and avoiding miscommunication. It is also helpful in planning for their instruction. A child's culture includes the values, traditions, social and political relationships, and worldview shared by the child's family. The family culture is cemented by its shared history, geographic location, language, social class, and/or religion (Nieto & Bode, 2007). Culture determines many aspects of our personalities and ways of dealing with the world. Within some cultures, children should rarely speak to adults unless asked to do so. These children, who remain silent in the classroom, will be waiting for us to invite them into the classroom conversation, whereas others will jump into the mix without raising their hands. Some cultures teach children not to look at adults and are often misunderstood by European American teachers who require eye contact with students. In some cultures, touching on the head is disrespectful and boy-girl groupings intolerable. We have taught children who laugh when embarrassed, respond poorly to praise, and view time far more fluidly than European Americans. Some of our students stand very close to us, refer to us as "teacher," and put their arms around our shoulders; others stand at a distance and never make physical contact. The more we learn about the cultures of our students, the better we are able to develop comfortable relationships with them.

Organizing the Physical Environment to Promote Language Learning

Effective teachers plan carefully for the furniture, materials, and wall spaces in their classrooms. The physical environment can be structured in ways that limit our teaching choices and our ability to promote interaction, or it can contribute to learning efficiency and ease of socialization throughout the school day. If we use all the flexibility we can find or create, we can use the physical classroom to have a positive impact on instruction.

Furniture Is Important

Furniture structures much of what we do in classrooms. We realized how closely furniture defined classroom activities when we observed schools in rural areas of Egypt, China, and the Philippines. There the furniture consisted of heavy wooden benches shared by two or three students. The desk tops were clean but rough and the children could not easily get up and move around the room. The culture of those classrooms did not value movement by the students and so the furniture was appropriate to the educational philosophy of the school. Instead, children worked together constantly. This was easy to do because of the close proximity of two or three classmates at all times. Individualized work assignments were not valued in these cultures and instead, children were encouraged to collaborate on their learning.

In schools in the U.S. in the last century, chairs and desks were sometimes bolted to the floor. This made group work very difficult and led teachers to rely mostly on individualized assignments for learners. Once again, the approach to learning was dictated by the constraints of the furniture.

We like furniture that allows teachers to create flexible groupings for students and have seen great variation in furniture arrangements in classrooms (Figure 4.1). Tom Silverman, a fourth grade teacher, likes to place his students in a large U shape on days when he is showing a film or preparing for student presentations. The U shape allows all students to see and hear without obstruction. Other days, Tom places his students into groups of two. This is an organization that allows two students to work individually

Figure 4.1 Furniture Arrangement Differs as Instructional Goals Change

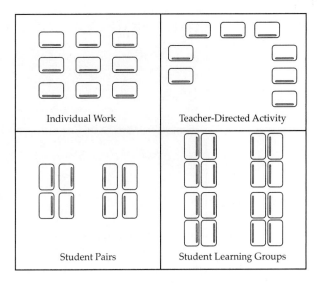

Individual Work

Teacher-Directed Activity

Student Pairs

Student Learning Groups

but still have access to a buddy whom they can call on for help. Many times, Tom places four students together into a learning group. This arrangement allows him to use cooperative learning, encourages group work, and promotes collaboration. During testing sessions, Tom resorts to the traditional pattern of rows of individual desks to provide privacy and security for the test results.

Sheila Arnow, a middle-school teacher, also likes the versatility that moveable furniture gives her, but she has very little time between class changes to move all the furniture herself. She has devised a system of symbols; each symbol designates a classroom arrangement. When Sheila's students enter the room, they look to the chalkboard for the symbol of the day and immediately begin to arrange the desks into the appropriate placement. Sheila finds that this technique is efficient and saves time. Her students have been taught to help with furniture placement quickly and quietly before beginning the lesson of the day. Sheila uses a U shape arrangement, double desks, grouped desks, and individual desks. These arrangements meet most of her classroom needs.

Anita Brisken has enough space in her second grade classroom for a very flexible furniture arrangement. For small-group and individual activities, her learners sit at tables. For teacher-directed activities, they have tiered benches in a semi-circle. In that setting, all the children can see and hear well, and the teacher can easily monitor comprehension and participation.

Public Areas

Every classroom has public areas that all students share. One of these areas is the chalkboard (or whiteboard) where daily objectives and agendas are located (Figure 4.2). Students need to be aware of the purposes of board information and the information needs to be accessible to all learners in the class. We like to designate one area of the board as a daily calendar. We noticed that Cheryl Boynton does the same thing in her fifth grade class. Cheryl's students look at the left side of the board daily to discover what they will do that day and the order in which each event will occur. Some of Cheryl's students who are new to literacy are able to comprehend the information because Cheryl writes her daily agenda using rebus pictures as clues to the activities. Cheryl draws a book for the language arts period, a math symbol for the transition to

Figure 4.2 The Chalkboard or Bulletin Board Is an Important Communication Tool
••

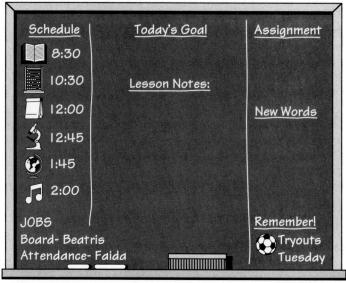

Video Exercise

Organizing Your Classroom for Language Development

Go to MyEducationLab, select the topic **Comprehensible Input,** and watch the video entitled "**Organizing Your Classroom for Language Development**" to hear a second grade teacher describe the physical arrangement of her classroom. Complete the questions that accompany it. You may print your work or have it transmitted to your professor as necessary.

math class, a musical note, paintbrush, or soccer ball for the "special" of the day and so on. The children in her class feel secure in knowing what will happen in the classroom that day; and they feel valued by their teacher because she includes all of her students in her preparation by differentiating her communication.

The bulletin boards inside and outside the classroom are public spaces that communicate needed information to students and to the school community. We have seen teachers use these boards to celebrate the successes of their students. Here is where we honor the best efforts of learners: the stories, tests, artwork, or projects that show academic achievement. Some of our ELLs will not have access to these celebrations unless we value their writing in their home languages and provide opportunities for them to be publicly successful.

Sharon Medford uses her bulletin boards to display information that students need to learn in her sixth grade social studies classes. Sharon turns her bulletin boards into "word walls" that contain the vocabulary of the content unit under study. By keeping the words on display, Sharon has the opportunity to point to the words as she is talking about them and also to encourage students to use these words in oral discussions and in writing. The word wall gives language learners a better opportunity to be surrounded by the language of instruction.

Anne Marie Rice, a third grade teacher, displays the language of mathematics on her bulletin board. Anne Marie groups math function words pertaining to addition, subtraction, multiplication, and division around the symbol for each function (as shown in Figure 4.3). Her students are better able to solve word problems because they can refer to the vocabulary that signals the math function needed for the solution. This is one way that teachers can provide context for needed academic information.

Private Space

At times, we need to provide private space for students in our classrooms. Christine Igoa (1995) discovered that her students' desks began to mirror her own when the

Figure 4.3 Math Function Words

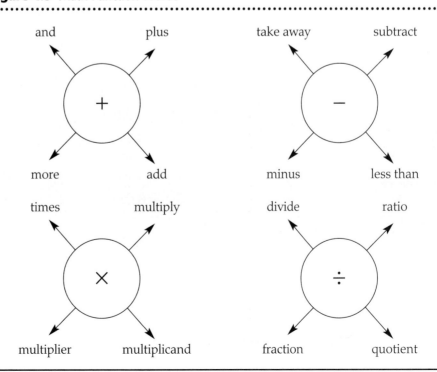

children began to bring meaningful symbols from home to decorate their desks. Just as the teacher's desk contained a flower, a pencil holder, and other personal mementoes, the children brought artifacts related to their homes and their cultures. Igoa found that the children took comfort in being near reminders of their culture and were better able to focus on their work as a result.

You may want other areas of your classroom to function as personal space and to double as spaces for individual tasks students engage in while you work with small groups. Bill Harris, a second grade teacher, was quite skilled as a carpenter and built a reading loft for his students. The soft carpet and throw pillows provided a comfortable spot for reading quietly, writing in a journal, or working with a buddy. A computer center/listening center with headphones helps teachers to provide learners with materials chosen for their levels for independent learning times. For those learners who are overwhelmed listening to a new language, a quiet reading spot could provide a restful time-out area.

No matter how you decide to organize your classroom, try to place ELLs in seats close to the area where most announcements and instruction take place. Our goal must be to integrate our ELLs into the work of the classroom as quickly and as easily as possible. We want to send the message that "What we are doing is important. You can do it. I will not give up on you." The arrangement of furniture can help us to communicate those messages.

Table 4.1 Community-Building Activities

Name	Purpose	Description
Ball Toss	Greeting	Students stand in a circle greeting one another by name: "Good morning Jack!" and then tossing a foam ball. Each student responds to the greeting and tosses the ball to another until all students have been greeted.
People Bingo	Get acquainted	Students circulate, searching for a person described in a box on a Bingo grid. Descriptions vary. For example: "Speaks another language, Roller blades every day," etc.
Structured Interview	Get acquainted	Teacher gives each student a list of questions to ask others in the class. Students are paired and rotate.
Birthday Line Up	Get acquainted	Teacher calls students to come to the front of the class and form a line beginning with students born in January. Students can arrange themselves in correct birthday order by asking each other: "When were you born?"
Guess the Fib	Get acquainted	Students tell three facts about themselves, one of which is a fib. The class guesses which one is the fib.
Class Calendar	Affirmation	Birthdays and perhaps one other important event are included on the calendar for each student. The special days are celebrated with interviews, favorite games played, favorite song played, memories of proudest moments, etc.
Spotlight (Seigle & Macklem, 1993)	Affirmation	A different child each day is called upon by the teacher to sit in the Spotlight. Other students take turns offering complements by identifying specific examples: "I like the way you always offer to help me with my math problems."

Organizing the Classroom Social Environment to Promote Language Learning

In the same way that teachers plan carefully for the physical environment of the classroom, they also plan for the social environment. Because much language learning occurs in social environments, our interactions with our students and their interactions with each other can affect learning efficiency. Let's consider some of the components of a classroom's social environment.

Social Integration

Activity-based communicative language learning requires active engagement and collaboration among ELLs. Integrating children physically in the classroom helps to promote active engagement. But, we also need to integrate them socially into the classroom community in order to encourage collaboration and promote academic achievement. Children need to feel safe in our schools, and they need to feel accepted socially before they will be ready to tackle the difficult job of learning in a new language. We can help to socialize ELLs in classrooms by including them in classroom activities enjoyed by English-speaking students and providing support for them to succeed. Assign jobs to a new student and an English-speaking buddy to accomplish together. Watering plants, cleaning the board, and delivering messages are some of these classroom tasks. Routines are another way to integrate ELLs. Activities such as distributing materials, collecting papers, transitioning, lining up for outdoor activities, hanging up coats, finishing the lunch count, and beginning the morning's activities can be ritualized in order to help children adapt to a routine, patterned behavior. In this way, they can understand, anticipate, and begin to participate in these activities.

We think it is useful to use classmates to help socialize ELLs. Ask your students to teach playground games, hopscotch, jump rope, ball games, hand-clapping routines, and the fundamentals of baseball and basketball to the ELLs in your classroom. Children enjoy taking on these instructional roles, and the roles provide needed language input to ELLs outside the classroom. Most importantly, however, they engage new learners in play with English-speaking classmates, an important first step to making a friend.

Community building can be accomplished through teacher-structured activities that help learners learn more about each other (see Table 4.1 for examples). Some teachers devise information surveys that require students to ask one another about hobbies, pets, favorite sports, and games. The more students know about each other, the more they will be willing to help each other learn.

Older ELLs may have a more difficult time fitting into the social life of the classroom. Adolescents form tight peer groups and are wary of others who look different and speak imperfectly. Group projects and cooperative learning provide excellent ways for a teacher to integrate ELLs into middle school and high school classrooms. Making expectations clear that everyone is to be included in your class, teaching learners specific behaviors for welcoming new students, and helping the new learners to learn to function in the class are also very important (Paley, 1993).

Presentation Formats

The social organization of our lessons will be more or less successful depending on how well they match the needs of the learners. We have choices to make when structuring new input. We can choose formal presentations, such as lectures, or informal presentations, such as role plays, interviews, and group inquiry. Some world cultures value the role of the teacher to a high degree and children from those cultures may not realize that informal group work is a learning opportunity. They will be culturally acclimated to learn only from the teacher in a lecture format. Unfortunately, lecture format is a difficult presentation style for language acquisition. Cultural relevance, a principal of the Activity-Based Communicative Teaching and Learning or ABC Model discussed in Chapter 2, reminds us to teach ELLs to adapt to the culture of the school as we also attempt to incorporate student cultures into the classroom.

Grouping

We also have choices of whole-class, small-group, or individual formats for learning. There are cultural determinants for these choices as well. Whole-class formats can put a heavy comprehension load on ELLs unless the oral language input is scaffolded by the teacher. Gauging their level of comprehension is difficult in these situations. Many listeners "tune out" when the listening burden becomes too heavy. Individualized formats are problematical when language learners need help in accomplishing tasks. If the teacher is not available, the learner has nowhere to go for assistance.

Buddy-group and small-group formats are supportive of ELLs if planned carefully. We need to take the learner's gender, personality, language level, and educational level into account to make good matches for successful group work. These matches are more difficult to accomplish at the middle-school level. Unless the teacher has created a culture of cooperation and collaboration in the classroom, students may balk at working with a non-English speaker. We would hope to avoid this kind of rejection of any youngster by teaching our students to work together from day one and sometimes including group support in the grading system. In a classroom of diverse learners, a variety of presentation and grouping methods will best match the needs of the all learners. Gibbons (2002, pp. 20–28) identifies the following conditions in Table 4.2 for supporting ELLs during group work.

Matching Learning Styles

Teaching would be a lot easier if our students were cut out with cookie cutters—each one an exact duplicate of the other. If this were the case, we could simply find the one instructional practice that best fits and use that practice consistently day after day. In our experience, however, our students were wonderfully surprising and diverse. There were no two alike. They provided us with challenges and issues that continually required us to develop professionally and personally. Because our students and yours are children who learn in many different ways, we must ensure that our instruction includes a variety of learning experiences that will appeal to each of them. Every child can learn but they don't all learn the same way. Finding the learning styles of our students is like turning on the magic switch that enhances learning.

Khan was one English language learner who had us stumped for a while. Although he was a precocious leader of the other children and obviously curious, he could not learn to read. Many of our strategies failed until Khan reached the third grade and encountered a learning unit on animals. We discovered that Khan was an encyclopedia of knowledge about animals. He watched the Discovery Channel daily and remembered large amounts of factual information that he heard there about animals, their habitats, and their behaviors. We used that information to find colorful, fact-filled CD-ROMs about strange animals: spiders, wolves, and snakes. We sat with Khan as the CD-ROM read to him about the animals, then we read aloud with him, and eventually, Khan began to read too. His world opened up that year as he quickly found his place among the grade-level readers in his class. For Khan, the combination of the colorful photos, his personal interest, the computer, and the auditory accompaniment on the CD-ROM was the key that eased him into reading.

Learning through multiple modalities has been shown to enhance long-term learning (Wolfe, 2001). Promoting visual, auditory, and kinesthetic experiences related

Table 4.2 Effective Strategies for Successful Group Work

Essential Condition	Support Elements
1. Provide clear and explicit directions.	Directions that are explained with clear contextual clues, modeling, pointing and gestures, written explanations, and picture clues.
2. Make talk a required part of the activity.	Students report to each other, to the teacher, or to other groups of children as part of the learning experience.
3. Group work has a clear outcome.	Something happens as a result of the group work. Information is shared or a problem is solved. The results are written or read.
4. The group work is cognitively appropriate.	The task is one that is cognitively challenging, requiring learners to think in order to accomplish the outcome.
5. The task involves content and language learning.	Language-learning objectives are aligned with grade-appropriate content-learning objectives.
6. All children are involved in the group.	Each child is assigned a task within the group in order to ensure that all learners are involved. Examples include timekeeper, manager, encourager, checker, recorder, and reporter.
7. Children are taught how to accomplish group work.	Develop group rules collaboratively with the entire class. Before beginning, post rules and ask students to retell group procedures before each group experience.
8. Provide enough time for learning and language to develop.	Group work cannot be rushed. Recall the rules, state the purpose of the work, check for understanding, monitor the groups, and require summarization either orally or in writing.

to content and language objectives ensures that neural pathways in the brain will be activated and that new ones will begin to form. The visual components of memory are especially robust. Long-term memory for vocabulary, for example, can be greatly increased by associating words with pictures. Associating visual mapping with sounds and music activates all systems in the brain—those associated with patterns, emotions, sounds, images, and language. These multiple modalities enhance the ability of the brain to recall the information perhaps because information is not stored in only one area but in networks throughout the brain. Multiple pathways of neurons efficiently store and retrieve the networks of information.

ELLs from diverse ethnic communities and cultures will display strikingly different learning styles from each other. We noticed these differences with children at very young ages, as we observed their reactions to varying kinds of learning experiences: song and dance, artwork, projects, individual assignments, group role plays, or memorization tasks. Styles and preferences became apparent. As we noted these differences, it became easier to group ELLs in mixed modality groups or to pair them with buddies of a similar modality. Our strategy of using a variety of learning experiences was designed not only to captivate a diverse group of learners but also to enable all children in the classroom to develop capability in an increasingly wider range of learning styles. So even though some of our Japanese students preferred not to speak aloud or participate in singing at first, we helped them with these skills, knowing that they are useful for language development. Even though our Guatemalan learners preferred to work in small groups with similar students, we supported their attempts to work in-dividually as well, knowing that they would be tested in this way.

The learning styles that students bring to our classrooms are often culturally de-termined. Individuals living within a culture and a family unit will develop learning styles that are congruent with others in their culture. ELLs who find themselves in North American schools will attempt to learn via the learning styles dominant in their home cultures. After years in North American schools, however, they tend to use learning styles of the mainstream students in their classrooms as well.

Americans value individualism. They tend to raise their children with strategies of self-reliance. As an indication of this, nursery schools and kindergartens typically teach North American children to dress themselves by placing their coats on the floor with the collar facing them, inserting both arms into the sleeves, and flipping the coat overhead in one motion. Other cultures, such as the Chinese, value cooperation rather than individualism. In Chinese nursery schools, children are paired when it's time to put on coats. One child holds the coat for his partner to put on and the partner does the same. Our European American students learn quite early to tie their shoes and eat by themselves. But Colombian parents that we spoke to did all these things for their children. As a result, their children had more dependence upon their families but that dependence led to strong bonding within the family unit.

Through many experiences such as these, children become predisposed to learn in generally similar ways. These culturally determined learning styles are modes of orga-nizing, classifying, and assimilating information, and are unique to cultural groups. Thus, Mexican-American and Chinese-American parents generally enculturate their children in a **field sensitive style** while European-American parents tend to use a **field independent style** with their children. This generalization is just that—a gener-alization. It is not meant to indicate that every person within a culture exhibits a similar learning style but rather that each culture has a tendency toward one style over another competing style. The terms *field sensitive* (or *field dependent*) and *field independent* were first defined by Witkin, Dyk, Faterson, Goodenough, and Karp (1962) in their work on perception. Field sensitive learners tend to perceive the organization of the field as a whole rather than its parts, while field independent learners perceive discrete items as separate from the organized field. Field independent learners are often referred to as **analytical learners,** while the field sensitive learners are termed **global learners.**

As a result, children respond differently to a wide range of cognitive and affective learning conditions. Field sensitive/global learners prefer to learn within a social environ-ment, helping and assisting others to reach a common goal and emphasizing the main idea of the topic—the "big picture." They tend to avoid analysis of words, sentences, and grammar rules. They enjoy using compensation strategies such as hypothesizing, the use of synonyms and paraphrase (Scarcella & Oxford, 1992). These learners are sensitive to the feelings and opinions of others and welcome guidance and demonstration from the teacher. They understand best when new concepts are presented in a humanized story format and when the curriculum is relevant to their personal interests and experiences (Cox & Ramirez, 1981). Students from Puerto Rican, Caribbean, Chinese, Greek, Latino, and many African societies, among others, tend to be field sensitive.

Field independent/analytic learners enjoy working within an individualistic and competitive environment. They restrict their interactions with and dependence on the teacher, preferring to work out problems on their own. They prefer to focus on gram-matical details, and enjoy analyzing language. They learn inductively, preferring to start with multiple examples and discrete facts and intuiting the principles and rules. They tend to work in a step by step, linear fashion focusing on details (Cox & Ramirez, 1981). European, Canadian, and U.S. cultures are field independent for the most part.

Teachers dominant in one learning style tend to teach to that style and value learners whose styles are congruent with their own. Greater intellectual ability tends to be ascribed to learners whose style matches our own. We have difficulty

Table 4.3 Characteristics of Learner Styles

Field Sensitive/Global	Field Independent/Analytical
• enjoys working with others to achieve a common goal	• enjoys working independently
• assists others and is sensitive to their feelings	• competes with others
• seeks guidance and direction from the teacher	• interacts with the teacher only when necessary
• learns concepts more easily in a humanized story format	• prefers to learn specific details
• functions well when curriculum is adapted to personal interests and experiences	• pays little attention to the social environment of learning
• prefers communicative activities	• prefers to concentrate on grammatical rules
• processes the whole picture	• processes the separate pieces
• processes simultaneously	• processes sequentially
• seeks patterns	• seeks parts

understanding the value of different paths to learning unless we have walked along those paths ourselves. Many grade-level teachers in North American schools are field independent, analytic learners. Many ELLs are field sensitive, global learners. It's important to know how to expand our teaching structures so that a mismatch does not occur between a teaching style and a learning style.

Knowing that learning styles are teachable, we have opportunities for expanding the learning potential of all of our students. Activity-based communicative language learning emphasizes that ELLs use a variety of learning strategies to maximize learning in the classroom and to become independent learners. We can assist ELLs in that goal by teaching and supporting learning strategies for both global and analytical learning. Variety ensures that all learners will be welcome in the instructional conversation. Table 4.3 provides a brief description of these two styles, while Table 4.4 indicates teacher behaviors that promote learning for each.

In addition to field sensitive/independent and global/analytical styles, other learning style categories affect the teaching/learning situation. More complex but more specific frameworks include Bernice McCarthy's 4MAT System (1987) and Gardner's Multiple Intelligences (1983) frameworks. Most useful for classroom teachers, however, are the visual, auditory, and kinesthetic styles exhibited by learners. Every individual has one of these as a primary learning mode, although many learners use a combination of all three.

Approximately 40 percent of school-age students are visual learners. They recall most easily information they have seen or read. They benefit from diagrams, charts, pictures, films, and written directions. Another 20 to 30 percent rely on an auditory learning style. These learners attend well to traditional lecture-style instruction. They benefit from discussions, verbal directions, text read aloud, and nuanced teacher speech inflections. Tactile/Kinesthetic learners learn best through a hands-on approach. They enjoy actively exploring, touching, and feeling the materials around them. These learners benefit from writing, using manipulatives in math class, drama, dance, lab activities, and field trips (Carbo, Dunn, & Dunn, 1986).

Most young children come to school as kinesthetic learners in kindergarten and then, after two or three years, become adept at visual learning. Some children,

Table 4.4 Teaching Suggestions for Learning Style

Field Sensitive/Global	Field Independent/Analytical
• Give objectives in advance and incorporate short-term goals.	• Outline step-by-step procedures.
• Use visuals and graphic organizers, advance organizers, outlines, and study guides.	• List the known facts.
• Highlight the patterns.	• Allow written answers to oral questions.
• Use Think/Pair/Share in group discussions and presentations; encourage brainstorming.	• Provide wait time for oral responses.
• Base instruction on student interests and experiences.	• Encourage students to make guesses from known information.
• Use personal anecdotes to humanize instruction and include fantasy and mental imagery.	• Develop students' curiosity and encourage questions.
• Provide teacher modeling and guidance.	• Limit teacher explanations.
• Provide teacher reinforcement, interaction, and feedback.	• Use inquiry, discovery, and Socratic questioning.
• Use a deductive approach (rules first, followed by examples).	• Use an inductive approach (examples first, followed by student determined rules).
• Encourage cooperation and collaboration.	• Provide competition.
• Include group projects, peer tutoring, and cooperative learning.	• Allow for independent projects.
• Provide group rewards.	• Provide individual rewards.

particularly girls, become auditory learners in late elementary school. However, many students, boys in particular, retain their kinesthetic/tactile learning style all of their lives (Dunn & Dunn, 1993).

Traditional teaching in North American classrooms stresses the auditory modality as a preferred teaching/learning style. Teachers' use of this style prevails from late elementary through university education. ELLs, even those with a preferred auditory modality, will be at a disadvantage in classrooms where auditory, lecture-style teaching predominates. ELLs and many other learners benefit from a classroom where a variety of teaching and learning styles are available.

Organizing Instruction to Promote Language Learning

Even in schools where English Language Development (ELD) teachers are available, ELLs spend most of their day with their classroom teacher. It is no longer possible to think of these learners as someone else's students. They are "our" students. We don't have the luxury of waiting until they learn English to instruct them. We need to teach

Sorting Tasks Are Appealing to Kinesthetic Learners

them now, and we need to find ways to ensure that they will continue to learn while English-proficient students in our classrooms are thriving as well.

Given the external and internal pressures on teachers, Cummins (1984, 1996, 2000) has provided educators with a theoretical framework to explain the dimensions relevant to the relationship between language proficiency and educational achievement in the classroom. The two dimensions displayed in Figure 4.4 are continuums. One is a continuum relating to a range of contextual support found within the learning situation for expressing and receiving meaning. The context-embedded extreme of the continuum allows for the ELL to actively negotiate meaning with a speaker-hearer, indicate a lack of communication, ask questions to enhance clarity, use facial gestures, and utilize a range of behaviors that occur in face-to-face communication to enhance meaning. The other extreme, "content-reduced," relies on "linguistic cues to meaning" with no contextual support. The context-reduced situation thus requires higher-level knowledge of the language for communication to be successful (Cummins, 1984, 1996, 2000).

The second dimension in Cummins's theoretical framework consists of language tasks and activities that are **cognitively demanding/undemanding.** Those tasks termed "undemanding" are ones in which the "language tools have become largely automatized (mastered) and thus require little active cognitive involvement for appropriate performance" (Cummins, 1996, p. 57). Quadrants A and C represent undemanding tasks. Quadrants B and D represent tasks and activities requiring active cognitive involvement for successful completion. Many classroom tasks, such as presenting an oral report, writing an essay, or taking a standardized test, are cognitively-demanding. Thus, quadrants B and D represent cognitively demanding classrooms. Quadrant B describes a classroom where tasks are cognitively demanding but teachers provide the contextual supports to aid ELLs in achieving success. These are the classrooms we describe as effective classrooms for English language learners.

With the increasing number of English language learners entering our schools, we have seen the development of a variety of approaches for organizing the classroom to promote better learning for all students. These approaches are developed to make content information more accessible for ELLs (more context-embedded), sometimes through the teacher's presentation techniques, the use of content as a vehicle for learning, grouping techniques, and/or the organization of the curriculum. The following approaches structure classrooms in ways to promote learning for all. It will be seen that there is overlap in the

Figure 4.4 Range of Contextual Support and Degree of Cognitive Involvement in Communication Activities

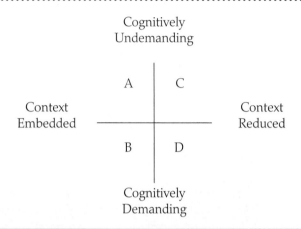

Source: California Association for Bilingual Education, 1996.

techniques and strategies used in many of these approaches and that overlap represents the best practice for all learners. We will describe these approaches briefly. In order to fully implement them, however, teachers should be aware that specialized training programs are the best way to gain thorough knowledge of any of them. The approaches are:

- The Cognitive Academic Language Learning Approach (CALLA)
- Sheltered Instruction: Specifically Designed Academic Instruction in English (SDAIE) and Sheltered Instruction Observation Protocol (SIOP)
- Cooperative Learning
- Problem-based Learning
- Project Learning
- Differentiated Instruction

The Cognitive Academic Language Learning Approach (CALLA)

CALLA is an instructional approach that integrates academic language development with content-area instruction and learning strategies. It requires thoughtful planning on the part of the teacher in an effort to teach the essential elements of the approach, as well as determine how individual ELLs will receive and act upon the instruction.

CALLA is used solely for content instruction. It can be used by ESL teachers, bilingual teachers, content area teachers, and elementary or secondary teachers. In any instructional setting where CALLA is used, teachers must first be familiar with and select appropriate content topics and concepts for the unit or the lesson. In addition, academic language skills and functions required to perform a specific content area task are itemized. CALLA instructional planning includes the following five steps (Chamot & O'Malley, 1994):

1. Preparation
2. Presentation
3. Practice
4. Evaluation
5. Expansion

CALLA specifies that teachers select and teach learning strategies that are appropriate for tasks in different phases of the lesson. For example, in the *preparation* phase, when students are uncovering their prior learning, an appropriate learning strategy to teach is brainstorming. In the *presentation* phase, selective attention is needed for attending to

A Classroom Picture of a CALLA Lesson

Sandy Chu teaches a thematic unit entitled "Life on Earth" to her class of multilingual sixth graders. The unit is essentially a science unit but Sandy also incorporates reading in the science fiction genre—a subject she knows will interest her students.

In the initial stages of the unit, she leads the students in the preparation phase with a challenging question. Sandy presents a rock and a plant to the class, divides students into work groups, and asks them "Which of these objects is alive and why?" Sandy requires that the students list reasons for their answers that they will share with the larger group. The group-work activity provides an opportunity for Sandy to encourage her students to develop the CALLA social strategy of cooperation. She provides lists of encouraging phrases and asks that each student use at least one of them during their discussions.

The reasons given by the students lead them into the presentation phase of the lesson, a reading on the characteristics of living things. Here, Sandy will focus on the CALLA reading skill of selective attention. She asks students to search for six characteristics of living things in the article, and to confirm or add to the lists that they have developed in their work groups. For those students requiring help with the reading, Sandy assigns buddy pairs to read aloud to one another.

In the practice phase of the lesson, Sandy pairs her students to work at the computer creating a table that will describe the characteristics of living things and provide examples of those characteristics from the plant and animal kingdoms. Here, Sandy will teach a CALLA grouping strategy—showing her students how to classify and organize the new information.

For the evaluation of this lesson, Sandy will ask students to include the information on the tables they have made in two summary paragraphs describing the characteristics of living things and provide appropriate examples. In addition to displaying model sample paragraphs, Sandy also asks students to self-assess their written paragraphs by sharing a writing rubric appropriate to the task.

In the extension phase of the lesson, Sandy will introduce a science fiction reading that describes an alien from another planet. Students will be asked to determine if the alien is alive by using the characteristics they have learned. The CALLA cognitive strategy of deduction is appropriate to this phase of the lesson as Sandy encourages students to apply scientific characteristics to a fictionalized character.

new information either orally or in print. The *practice* phase is a good time to teach cooperation strategies needed for group work. The *evaluation* phase lends itself to teaching students strategies for self-evaluation. And the *expansion* phase is the time when students use higher-order thinking and reflection skills in order to evaluate their learning in light of prior knowledge. A short summary of each phase of a CALLA lesson follows.

In the *preparation* phase of CALLA, teachers assess students' prior knowledge and experience with the curriculum concepts. CALLA suggests an exploration of ELLs' cultural, experiential, and educational background through a search of school records, talking with parents, discussion with colleagues, and sharing students' previous experiences through genuine conversation. Activities to help ELLs activate their own prior knowledge include brainstorming, using graphic organizers, doing hands-on activities, using manipulatives, holding teacher demonstrations, showing videos and films, and going on field trips (Chamot & O'Malley, 1994). In many cases, ELLs have had no prior experience with content concepts; in this case, teachers plan concrete experiences designed to build prior knowledge for future learning.

The *preparation* phase is also where the teacher provides an overview of the content topic and explicitly communicates learning objectives. Many teachers preview and teach new vocabulary at this point while others prefer to wait until information is shared in the next phase of the instructional sequence.

The *presentation* phase of the lesson is where the teacher introduces new information, skills, and learning strategies to students. CALLA recommends that teachers use variety in their presentations in order to appeal to a range of learning styles. Questioning is encouraged during this phase, including questions to clarify understanding and to answer higher-level comprehension questions.

The *practice* phase of the lesson is student-centered. Here, ELLs engage in hands-on exploration and practice of the new skills, strategies, and content; identify new vocabulary; and expand their language skills through interaction with other students in a group setting.

The *evaluation* phase is specifically designed to teach ELLs self-evaluation strategies in order to help them determine the effectiveness of their own learning efforts and lead them to become self-regulated learners. These activities can be either cooperative or individual.

The purpose of the *expansion* phase of CALLA is to help ELLs integrate their new learning into existing schema or conceptual frameworks. Here, teacher-led discussion encourages ELLs to use higher-order thinking skills for purposes such as determining the importance of the content information, relating it to a student's prior knowledge, and understanding applications of that learning to the world outside the classroom and to a student's individual life in particular.

The CALLA approach is notable for helping teachers to plan for and structure appropriate learning strategies in their content lesson plans. ELLs in particular are in need of learning strategy instruction. ELLs learning in a new language, and attempting to comprehend complex content knowledge and vocabulary require skill in a variety of cognitive, metacognitive, and social/affective strategies in order to be successful. The CALLA approach can be incorporated into any teacher's lesson planning.

Sheltered Instruction

Sheltered instruction (SI) promotes the use of second language acquisition strategies while teaching content-area instruction. It is typically used for ELLs who have achieved some aural-oral competency in English. The term *sheltered* refers to the assistance learners receive in the form of visuals, modified texts and assignments, scaffolding techniques, and attention to academic language development (Echevarria & Graves, 1998; Echevarria, Vogt, & Short, 2003). Sheltered instruction can be found in a variety of educational program designs. It may be part of an ELD or bilingual program or it may be part of a secondary content course, such as a sheltered algebra course. Teachers using sheltered instruction include ELD and bilingual teachers, grade level elementary teachers and secondary level content teachers. The one thing they all have in common is their interest in promoting content area learning for all students while developing the academic language skills of English language learners.

The underlying theoretical basis of sheltered instruction is the notion that languages are acquired through meaningful use and interaction. The social, collaborative nature of learning as described by Vygotsky (1962), the emphasis on comprehensible input (Krashen & Terrell, 1983), the use of scaffolding techniques, and the integration of the four language skills (listening, speaking, reading, and writing) for the learning of school content are integral to this method of instruction.

Sheltered instruction is sometimes referred to as **Specially Designed Academic Instruction in English** or **SDAIE** (California State Department of Education, 1994). This program model has been used to promote cognitively demanding, grade-appropriate content curriculum for language learners who have an intermediate or advanced level of language proficiency. It has been particularly successful in addressing the needs of secondary-level learners of English, students who have little time to catch up with their peers in content learning. In a sustained professional development effort, sheltered teachers are taught to operationalize SDAIE through an observational protocol called the **Sheltered Instruction Observation Protocol (SIOP)** (Echevarria, Vogt, & Short, 2003). The SIOP model spells out those features of sheltered instruction that can enhance content learning and expand a teacher's educational practice. The model specifies 30 observable classroom behaviors grouped into three major categories:

- Preparation
- Instruction
- Review/Assessment

We will briefly discuss the characteristics of sheltered instruction specified in SIOP.

Preparation for Instruction.   Sheltered instruction begins with clearly defined *content* and *language objectives* that focus on age-appropriate content concepts. Planning for instruction also includes the gathering of a wide variety of supplementary materials, sometimes called **explanatory devices,** which are used to promote clarity and meaning. Examples include visuals, graphs, charts, models, realia, and so on. It is at this time that teachers think of ways of adapting the content to ELLs. This could mean using a text outline or study guide, a graphic organizer, highlighting, or tape recording the text and occasionally rewriting the text to shorten sentences or eliminate nonessential information. Meaningful activities are planned to assist learners in integrating the concepts of the lesson with language practice in listening, speaking, reading, and writing. Examples of these include role plays, surveys, and presentations.

Instruction.   During instruction, SIOP focuses on six areas that are considered essential. The first is *building a background* for learning. Building a background involves activating what students already know about the topic and explicitly linking the new topic to student background and to past learning experiences. At this time, target vocabulary is introduced using redundancy through oral repetitions, writing, and highlighting.

The second area of instruction involves the delivery of *comprehensible input.* Teachers moderate their speech to a slower rate for beginning learners. They enunciate clearly and use simple sentence structures. They explain academic tasks clearly and use a variety of techniques all dedicated to helping learners understand the content: demonstrations, gestures, body language, modeling, hands-on activities, and oral and written directions.

The third area to consider in sheltered instruction is the use of *learning strategies.* In order to promote higher-level thinking skills and to teach ELLs how to be effective learners, opportunities for strategy use are built into each lesson. Scaffolding techniques, both oral and procedural, are used to support understanding during instruction; a variety of question types, especially those that promote higher-order thinking, are also used.

The fourth area of instruction concerns the *interaction* opportunities in the lesson. The sheltered lesson encourages ELLs to interact with the teacher and with peers concerning the lesson concepts. Grouping configurations are designed to support both language and content objectives. Teachers use wait time to allow enough time for ELLs to respond, and structures are used to help them clarify key concepts in the first language with their teachers, peers, or through the use of the text.

The fifth area of instruction is *practice/application.* Sheltered teachers use hands-on materials whenever possible for guided practice of the new concepts. These manipulatives may be sorted, observed, created, or arranged but they are to be used to help ELLs apply content and language knowledge. In other words, ELLs are to be doing something with the new content and using the four language skills of listening, speaking, reading, and writing as they learn.

The sixth area of instruction to consider is that of *lesson delivery.* During this phase of instruction, both content and language objectives are clearly supported by the structure of the lesson. ELLs are engaged 90 to 100 percent of the time, and the lesson is paced appropriately to the age and level of the learners.

A Classroom Picture of Sheltered Instruction

Helen Fields is a fifth grade teacher with a mixed language classroom. She is teaching an economics unit based upon the district curriculum. Helen has scheduled one month to teach the unit. She has structured her lessons to include content, language, and learning strategy objectives. In the following example, Helen has grouped her culturally and linguistically diverse students into heterogeneous groups of four. Each student has been assigned a state of the U.S. and must determine the major products of that state. This information will be used later when students learn economic principles such as supply and demand, and scarcity.

Helen has given each student an illustrated map of the United States showing the products produced by each state. There is an explanation key at the bottom of the map. Helen wants the students to work in small groups in order to interpret the product key and construct a model of each of the products in a student's state. Helen has collected art materials, fabric, popsicle sticks, and other materials to help students construct their products. After the products are made, Helen wants each student to report briefly to the entire class on the products produced in that student's state and then summarize their report in writing in their learning logs.

Helen begins her directions by checking the understanding of her students regarding their state assignments. When she is sure that students know their assigned states, can recognize their names when spoken, and locate them on the map, she begins to focus on the target vocabulary in the map key. Helen tells the students to work in their groups to identify all of the items in the map key and informs them that they will be assessed with **Numbered Heads Together.** Numbered Heads is one of the cooperative learning structures that Helen uses routinely to promote active learning among all of her students.

Helen assigns each small group a number from one to four and indicates that she will check their understanding by spinning for one of these numbers. As Helen poses a question, each group is responsible for "putting their heads together" to come up with the answer and ensure that all students in the group know that answer. When Helen spins a number, students with that number are required to answer.

As Helen floats around the classroom listening to the groups work, she is aware that some students are translating for their peers. Helen feels that judicious use of the target language helps solve many comprehension problems. During her comprehension check, however, the students will use English to explain each of the vocabulary items.

Helen next shows the students the various materials to use to construct a model of each of the products in the map key. She has constructed a few models herself to show the students what she wants them to do. While the students work, Helen has a chance to speak to her language-learning students and model the language she wants them to use when describing their products. She uses questioning techniques that are targeted to differing student language proficiencies to begin her dialogues.

Tell me about your product.

Is your product grown or manufactured?

What is your product used for?

Where is your product produced (grown, manufactured, mined, raised)?

Was your product produced (grown, etc.) in Illinois or in Georgia?

Review/Assessment.   In this last phase, teachers provide for active summarizing of the target vocabulary and the key concepts of the lesson. ELLs are given feedback on their learning and the teacher conducts an assessment of student comprehension of lesson objectives. The assessment need not be on paper and pencil, but might consist of group responses, spot checking, and asking many questions on the same topic to all learners throughout the lesson.

In this classroom snapshot, we can see many examples that are described in SIOP. Ms. Fields has targeted the language necessary to teach the content objectives, and included the use of passive voice constructions and content-specific vocabulary in her learning objectives. She has used a variety of techniques to teach target vocabulary (e.g., peer group, map pictures, and models) and used oral scaffolding and differentiated questioning to help ELLs report on their state products. The grouping configurations provide further support for learners' comprehension and the Numbered Heads Together technique used to check comprehension ensures that all students help each other. The students have opportunities to work hands-on with manipulatives and the later reporting session will integrate the use of all four language skills.

Cooperative Learning

In both sheltered instruction and CALLA, group work is used to provide support for language learners. A specific kind of group work, **cooperative learning** can be used in mixed language classrooms to promote the kinds of collaborative social environments so conducive to content and language-learning students. Peregoy and Boyle (2004, p. 89) define cooperative learning as "an instructional organization strategy in which students work collaboratively in small groups to achieve academic and social learning goals." It may be that a cooperative structure is more supportive than the traditional competitive structure of classrooms for the current school population. The increase in racial and ethnic diversity in our school systems is a major reason why many large urban schools have invested heavily in professional development in cooperative learning. Another reason is that cooperative learning has been shown to promote higher achievement across all grade levels and all subjects for both minority and majority students (Johnson, Maruyama, Johnson, Nelson, & Skon 1981; Slavin, 1983; Kagan, 1994).

Cooperative learning is a particularly valuable organizational structure for language learners in that input to the learner is made comprehensible by team members, thus increasing the probability of improving language skills as well as of learning new content. The interaction required for cooperative learning not only increases the comprehensibility of the input but also increases the quality and quantity of language production. Through the collaborative negotiation process, one student's language production becomes the comprehensible input for another (Kagan, 1990). Thus, both language and content are understood and practiced simultaneously.

The strength of cooperative learning over group work rests on the method's basic principles, which Kagan (1994) cites as the following:

- Simultaneous interaction
- Positive interdependence
- Individual accountability
- Equal participation

Basic Principles. Cooperative learning involves *simultaneous interaction*. Traditional classroom structures require that the teacher ask a question, wait for a student to respond, and then ask another question. The process takes a long time and, in a class of 30 students, this means that each student might be actively involved with learning for less than a minute. Language-learning students will rarely volunteer to respond to a teacher's question and may be left out of the conversation entirely. But cooperative learning classrooms involve all students simultaneously in discussion of the content concepts, thus maximizing active learning involvement.

Positive interdependence occurs when the gains of one member of a group are also seen as gains by all the members of a group. The stronger the positive interdependence, the more encouragement and tutoring is given to the lower achieving members of the group. Thus, if each member of the group must perform well to receive an award (above 80 percent, for example), then group members are motivated to make sure that all learners can achieve at that level. This kind of group support is most helpful to language learners and low-achieving students. Not only do they receive tutoring help from their peers but the group structure creates a cooperative rather than competitive learning environment, possibly better suited to the learning styles of these students. Positive interdependence can be achieved by structuring the task or by establishing rewards. Teachers create task structures like **Jigsaw** that lead to positive interdependence when they divide the information among group members, require a team product, limit the available resources (e.g., scissors, textbooks), or make a rule that no group member can proceed to the next step or station until all group members have completed the task. Rewards can determine positive interdependence by using the lowest score on the quiz as the group score, using the group average as a group score, or selecting at random only one test from each group as the group score.

Another way that cooperative learning is different from group work is the principle of *individual accountability*. This principle is important to prevent what Kagan (1994) calls a "freerider." This is an individual who lets others in the group do the work while accepting the reward or grade. Each member of the group must be accountable for his or her own contribution for achievement gains to occur. Teachers structure tasks that ensure individual accountability when they make each student in the group responsible for one portion of the project. When group grades are averaged, each student in the group is made aware of the grades so that all know the contributions of each group member. In the Numbered Heads Together technique used by Helen Fields, students were responsible for answering on their own when their numbers were called. In the division of information Jigsaw, each student is responsible for becoming an expert in one area of knowledge and then teaching that information to others in the group. When cooperative activities require group roles such as recorder, reporter, illustrator, time keeper, manager, reader, and so on, care should be taken to assign roles based on the level of language required for the role. The reader, for example, should have competency in reading while the reporter must be able to speak in English with notes or a graphic organizer as support. Even though the roles are differentiated, all students are required to perform a role for the benefit of the group effort. In these ways we can ensure that all students in the group are participating and contributing fully.

Equal participation is critical in groups containing language learners, otherwise those who speak the language imperfectly will be dominated by their English-speaking peers and low-language-proficient students will be passed over by high-proficiency members of the group. Even in the case of buddy pairs, we can not always be sure that there is equal participation (i.e., 50 percent) between the pairs. Buddy talk is an example of group work, not cooperative learning. To create equal participation between the pairs, we can use a cooperative learning structure called Timed-Pair-Share (Kagan, 1994). Partner A is called on to speak for a specified period of time, then partner B has a turn for the same amount of time. This simple structure provides for simultaneous interaction and equal participation. It gives language learners the rare gift of uninterrupted speaking time, time to talk about a content concept, solve a problem, or express an opinion.

Teambuilding.   Cooperative learning teachers create teams rather than groups. Cooperative teams maximize heterogeneity. They mix achievers of all levels, genders, and ethnic and linguistic diversity. Teams build bonds of support through teambuilding activities and endure over an extended period of time. It's possible to create teams by chance, but more often they are carefully planned by teachers to distribute differences evenly throughout all groups and to separate learners who are too friendly, too dependent, or too volatile from each other. Kagan (1994) suggests changing teams after five to six weeks. This amount of time allows strong bonds to develop that promote learning. Changing teams after this period of time gives all team members the chance to practice their new social and language skills with other class members.

Management. Cooperative learning classrooms require a teacher skilled in classroom management and students who have been taught to respond to the management tools used to keep learning progressing efficiently. A great deal of modeling is used to teach students to modulate their voices, respond to an attention signal, and monitor time. Cooperative-learning structures, such as Timed-Pair-Share and Jigsaw, are taught so that students can use them in a variety of content areas. Cooperatively determined class rules help determine responsibilities for individuals as well as teams. Efficient methods of distributing and collecting materials are also incorporated into the teacher's management system. Although few teachers use cooperative learning 100 percent of the time, those teachers who are adept at these management tools tend to use aspects of cooperative learning frequently. The group organization and management structures promote a more collaborative and efficient learning environment.

The Will and the Skill to Cooperate. Teachers in classrooms of diverse learners quickly learn that they need to spend time creating a cohesive classroom environment—building the will to cooperate. Cooperative learning provides the structures to teach children how to work together with people from very different backgrounds. Team-building and classbuilding structures are aimed at creating a positive team identity and promoting respect and trust among group members. In this context, maximum learning can occur for all students. (See Table 4.5 for five examples of cooperative learning structures.)

Teambuilding structures are devoted to getting acquainted activities, creating a team identity and team puzzles, projects and problems. Classbuilding activities involve the creation of class goals and rules, building a class identity, valuing differences, and providing mutual support (Kagan, 1994). Time spent on these kinds of activities pays off eventually when the diverse classroom unites into a supportive classroom.

The skill to cooperate does not come easily and naturally to children. We were not surprised to discover that the graduate school business programs attended by our own children included classes devoted to building skills in teamwork. These skills are essential in the business world as well as in the medical and legal communities. Most career paths require workers to cooperate and collaborate with others. The skills for efficient cooperative work need to be taught and learned. Our students need to learn how to listen to each other, resolve conflicts, persuade and encourage each other. Cooperative learning, as opposed to group work, incorporates the learning of social skills. Teachers use modeling, role-playing, reinforcement, and self-assessment as some of the ways to teach specific social skills during cooperative content lessons.

Problem-Based Learning

In a local eighth grade science class, students are learning to raise tilapia as part of an "Adventures in Aquaculture" thematic unit ("Gifford students," 2003). Mrs. Zielske, their teacher, has incorporated into the unit a wide range of activities:

- Testing water samples
- Charting growth rates
- Weighing and measuring the fish
- Solving a problem (Why were the fish swimming into the drain and getting trapped there?)
- Taking a field trip to Sea World
- Reading a nautical novel

Video Exercise
Cooperative Learning for All Students

Go to MyEducationLab, select the topic **Comprehensible Input**, and watch the video entitled "**Cooperative Learning for All Students**" to observe a classroom involved in cooperative learning in math class. Complete the questions that accompany it. You may print your work or have it transmitted to your professor as necessary.

Table 4.5 Five Cooperative Learning Structures

Stand and Deliver	Pose a question or a topic to the class. Ask students to *think* about their answer to this question or their reactions to the topic. Wait for 5 to 7 seconds or longer while students "think." Next, ask students to stand up and find a Buddy (*pair*) and talk about their answers or reactions. Finally, after several minutes of sharing, ask students to *share* their responses with the entire class. The brief opportunity to stand allows students some freedom of movement after sitting for long periods and provides more opportunities for buddy pairing.
Numbered Heads Together	This versatile activity can be used effectively for both memory-level and higher-order thinking activities. Instead of answering questions, learners can brainstorm ideas, solve a problem, draw a diagram, invent a product, etc. Place students in groups of four by numbering off from 1 to 4. (If groups have 5, two students take turns as one number; if groups have 3, one student has two numbers). The teacher (or a student, after students have learned the strategy well) asks a question about the reading and gives a time limit. Students take a few minutes to "put their heads together" to find and agree on an answer. (This may include looking up the page citation in the text.) Teacher calls a number to designate which student will answer for the team. Students with that number give their groups' answers (verbally, on paper, or on the board). Teacher gives feedback as appropriate; teams may receive points for correct answers, creative answers, correct spelling, etc.
Round Robin or Roundtable	This activity is useful for brainstorming, writing, and reviewing concepts and vocabulary learned. *Oral version:* divide the students into groups of 3 or 4. Write the topic on the board (e.g., "The Life Cycle of the Whale"). The first student names a stage in the life cycle. The next student adds to the description but cannot repeat something already said. Students continue to add responses until the teacher calls time (three to five minutes). The teacher asks one student from each group to summarize the group's work. Students are asked not to repeat an answer already stated by another group. The teacher charts each group's answers on the board or chart paper. In Roundtable (the written version), students pass around a sheet of paper and each student adds their contributions. Alternatively, place papers with questions on desks and have groups of students rotate from station to station answering the questions/ prompts. Create a class summary as above.
Carousel Brainstorming; Carousel Reports	This is an efficient way to do either brainstorming or oral reports. Students all have a chance to present and discuss their work and discuss it with teacher and peers in a short amount of time. Arrange chart paper or notebook paper in four (or more) parts of the room. On the charts, write a series of questions to preview/review content that learners read and study. Form groups of about four students (one group per chart). Assign each group a chart. Give each group a different colored marker. Groups review their question and discuss their answers. Then one person writes the group's response. After five to ten minutes (or time needed), each group rotates to the next station. Students review questions and the answers other groups have given. They put a check by each answer they agree with, comment on answers they don't agree with, and add their own new answers. Finally, groups share the information on their last chart with the rest of the class.
Line-Ups	This activity provides for authentic use of language learned, repeated practice of structures being studied, along with opportunities to move around and interact. Have learners line up in order along some continuum, e.g., day and month of their birth, alphabetical or numerical order, etc. Teach the language they will need to determine the order, e.g., what month and day were you born? What number do you have? (In this case, students can interact but cannot show the number or words they have been given.)

- Making metric measurements
- Growing vegetables hydroponically
- Hosting a fish fry

The aquaculture unit is an example of **Problem-Based Learning.** Creative teachers such as Mrs. Zielske are providing meaningful learning for their students by basing the curriculum on solving real-life problems facing our community and our world. Mrs. Zielske presented her students with the following problem:

> You are a consultant with the Florida department of Fish and Wildlife. You have been asked to find a solution to the problem that Florida's rivers are not suitable to raising food fish.

Examples of problems used in intermediate and middle-school classrooms include the protection of natural habitats, the allocation of scarce water resources, the homeless, highway congestion, and the effects of global warming. Even young children can be involved in problem-based learning when the problems affect them. We used this model to involve our students in designing the new playground for our school. Others have attempted to change the food offerings at lunchtime, find transportation for a field trip, or save a favorite tree from the saw mill.

The nature of the problems used for problem-based learning is that they are complex and require students to delve into inquiry, information gathering, and reflection. These problems have no simple solutions and thus encourage students to take on the active role of problem solvers.

Because many of our strongest neural networks are formed by experience (Wolfe, 2001), problem-based learning leads to long-term retention of information as well as fostering skills of critical thinking and problem solving. Students are empowered by their ability to directly affect outcomes in the world around them, and ELLs increase their language growth by the collaborative nature of the learning experiences. The popularity of this system has led to many books and Internet sites offering suggestions for curricula at all grade levels (see Delisle, 1997; Brandt, 1998; Torp & Sage, 1998; Center for Problem-Based Learning, 1993–2008).

Project Learning

Our most memorable learning experiences relate to the projects of our childhood. Who could forget the three-dimensional map of Europe stuck to the dining room table with flour and water paste, and dripping with water colors? These experiences stay in our memories because they engage learners in ways that simply listening cannot. Projects also offer many possibilities for ELLs to become involved in classroom learning because they enable learners to acquire and share information in ways other than the traditional text book reading or report writing experiences that new English speakers find so difficult.

Student choice in **project learning** empowers and motivates learners as they exert more control over their learning experiences. Some teachers use the **Multiple Intelligences** (Gardner, 1983) framework to provide variety and choice for student projects. Examples of reading projects might include:

Kinesthetic

- Construct a scene from the novel you read.
- Create a life-like model of the story's hero.
- Create a three-dimensional model of the story's setting.

Verbal/Linguistic

- Choose one character from the book and create a series of letters written by the character during a difficult period of time.
- Choose one event in the novel and write the scene as a TV soap opera script.
- Write a newspaper article describing the most exciting event in the novel.

Intrapersonal

- Choose one character in the story and show in what ways you and the character are alike. You may show the similarities through writing, drawing, or other appropriate means.
- Write a diary as if you were the main character of the story. Talk about your feelings as the events unfold.
- Express your reactions to the story—your feelings and responses—through music, art, or poetry.

Logical/Sequential

- Create a graphic organizer that visually shows the plot development of the story.
- Create a game board that represents the story's development.
- Create a series of puzzles or brain teasers about the major characters in the story.

Rhythmic

- Write a rap or song for the major character to sing.
- Create a mime dance to illustrate the major conflicts in the novel.
- Choose songs that represent the conflicts of the major characters in the book.

Visual

- Create a comic book representation of the story.
- Design a collage to represent the major character in the story.
- Take photographs of scenes that represent the setting of the story and create a collage with them.

Interpersonal

- Work with a friend to create a problem-mediation session between you and a major character in the book. Provide helpful alternatives to the character's problems.
- Work with a friend to role-play one of the events in the story in a way that makes sense to readers today.
- Work with a friend to interview class members on their reactions to the story and report to the class.

Naturalist

- Collect leaves, rocks, flowers, trees, and animal products that represent the setting of the story.
- Create a tape with sounds heard in the natural world to play while reading an outdoor scene of the novel.
- Identify the main character with a signature flower, plant, tree, and animal, and explain your choices.

Projects, to be successful, must be closely related to learning objectives and serve to increase student understanding of the content concepts. Wolfe (2001) gives an example of an interesting and engaging project in a California school that did not meet these criteria. Students were studying their state's history and were asked to build a replica of an early mission out of sugar cubes. The students enjoyed the project but it taught them nothing about the impact of the missions on California history or the contributions of the people who built them.

Linda Karl and Ray Kropp (Rutherford, 1998) designed a multidisciplinary math and English project for their students in Oaklawn, Illinois, titled the "Invention Convention." The project required students to identify a difficult task and create an invention that would make the task simpler. In the course of the unit, students:

- Created a scale drawing of the invention
- Developed a scale model of the invention
- Wrote a description including any math or physics formulas
- Described the benefits of the invention
- Designed a newspaper/magazine ad
- Created a TV commercial
- Wrote a feature article for the newspaper
- Prepared an outline and a five-minute speech to be presented in class

The many and diverse tasks required for this project called several skills into play—especially the language skills of listening, speaking, reading, and writing. At the same time, students had several choices concerning the nature of their invention and their depiction of it. Course objectives were also directly related to the tasks required for the project. Every student could find a task suited to learning style and interest in this stimulating and valuable project.

Differentiated Instruction (DI)

Differentiated instruction (DI) is an alternative for heterogeneous classes that provides multiple avenues of learning and different challenges to different students. Teachers learn to recognize the differences, and then plan and deliver instruction according to learner needs. It requires flexibility and trust on the part of teachers. It helps teachers to focus not on what they *teach*, but on what their students *learn*. Those who have described Differentiated Instruction (Tomlinson, 1999; King-Shaver & Hunter, 2003), recommend four different areas of possible modification of instruction:

1. *Content:* What a student is to learn. Although we have clear standards and content for our curriculum, it is so full that we must make choices regarding what should be and is taught.
2. *Process:* How the student is to learn the content. Students can learn by speaking, listening, reading, writing, and doing. They can learn alone or together, they can work independently or with the teacher.
3. *Product:* How the student is to display what they have learned. Learners can show what they have achieved in different ways—orally, in writing, through a variety of projects, through a test, or by demonstration.
4. *Assessment:* How the teacher evaluates the learner's product. Teachers can choose to evaluate different components of the same assignment with the same objective, or to use a different rubric.

We suggest that teachers need to consider a fifth area when their classes include ELLs—*language* or the language level of oral instruction and of the materials used. Teachers can vary the language level of instruction and the language mode (oral, written, audio recording, role play, debate, etc.). They can even choose to use materials and/or instruction in learners' home languages when advisable and possible.

Teachers can make choices among these areas based on learners' interests, readiness, or learning styles. The result is that all students participate in work that respects

Figure 4.5 About Me Blank Worksheet

···

About Me

Name _____ I like to be called _____

My favorite things to do are:

I speak this language (these languages): _____

My pet peeve (something that really annoys me): _____

My favorite book: _____

My favorite music or musician: _____

My favorite movie or game: _____

My favorite subject in school: _____

The hardest subject for me: _____

A goal I have is to: _____

In the summer, I like to: _____

Note: This inventory may need to be administered orally and/or made available in home languages for beginning learners. Younger learners might answer by drawing pictures. Older, more proficient learners might interview one another.

their interests and capabilities. The classroom is flexible—from grouping, to instruction style, to tasks, and assessment, all instruction is connected and intertwined (Tomlinson, 1999).

To implement DI, teachers need to have strategies for getting to know their students: their interests (determined by interviews and forms, such as the "About Me" form in Figure 4.5); their learning styles (determined by observations and interviews with families); their language levels in whatever languages they use and are learning (determined by records, entry assessment, and ongoing class performance and test scores); and their academic levels (determined by records, test scores, and classroom performance).

A one-size-fits-all delivery system isn't optimal for any classroom, and isn't possible for a classroom with many differences in language, academic or learning levels, and cultural backgrounds. The instructional approaches described here offer valid and appropriate alternatives.

Questions for Reflection

···

1. Planning for classroom management and for instruction of language-learning youngsters is a complex task. As a teacher, your classroom will include monolingual English speakers in addition to language learners. How well will the above suggestions work with English-dominant students? Where will you have to add to these suggestions or modify them?

A Classroom Picture of Differentiated Instruction

Gabriela Kallal teaches eighth grade language arts in a multicultural, multilingual class room that includes five learners of English and two students designated as having special needs. A special education teacher is available in her class five periods per week to assist her. To implement differentiated instruction in her class, Gabriela has reviewed records and assessed interests, language levels, content levels, learning styles, and learning preferences of her learners. She includes ongoing assessment as part of her learning and keeps a roster nearby with key information about her learners that she can use in instructional decisions. One day in October, her students are studying a unit on character and point of view, reading two selections about Harriet Tubman: one from a biography by Ann Petry (1996) and the other a letter by Frederick Douglass (2001). Gabriela chooses to work with her class in four groups to use different processes for reading the text. On this day, the following activities are taking place:

1. An advanced group, after reading the text independently, works in the library with the support of a media specialist to research the Philadelphia Vigilance Committee and prepares to report to the class.

2. A group of English language learners first works with Gabriela. She discusses background vocabulary and introduces them to the story of Harriet Tubman and the Underground Railroad through viewing a series of paintings of Tubman's life by Jacob Lawrence (1993). Then she extends their understanding of the Underground Railroad by helping them use an interactive web site (http://www.nationalgeographic.com/features/99/railroad/). Finally, the group works independently, listening to an audio recording of the Douglass letter three times, each time for a different purpose: first time, listen for specific information; second time, list challenging terms; and third time, read along with the text.

3. A group of students, after exploring the Underground Railroad web site on their own, works with the teacher as she introduces a reciprocal teaching strategy for reading the text. Pairs will take turns reading a paragraph and questioning their partners, asking questions to summarize, clarify, identify details, and predict what will happen next.

4. A fourth group of students with special needs works with the special education teacher. This teacher has learners "read" the art first, trying to make guesses about what the story will entail. Next she helps learners with background information about Harriet Tubman and the Underground Railroad, and finally she works with learners to help them understand a targeted passage in the Percy selection that presents the essence of Harriet Tubman's mission.

2. The social environment of the classroom can help or hinder learning. How will language learners from different cultures change that environment? In what ways will their presence add to or detract from the classroom environment?

3. A basic premise of the organizing tools discussed in this chapter (CALLA, sheltered instruction, cooperative learning, problem-based and project learning, and Differentiated Instruction) is that language learners are active participants in all areas of classroom teaching and learning. What questions do you have about actively including these students in classroom lessons? What concerns does this notion raise?

Activities for Further Learning

1. Imagine that you are expecting a new student to enter your class next week. You have no information about the student. You need to find an efficient way to determine as much as you can in a short time. Create a form that can be

used by the front office of the school to help you collect necessary information. Remember to include questions regarding basic information, previous schooling, health information, and cultural information, if possible.

2. Create a floor plan for your ideal classroom of 25 mixed-language students. Indicate where and how students will be seated, the location of the chalkboard and the bulletin boards. Include other areas relative to the age of the students. For younger learners, you may want to include art areas, listening areas, bookshelves, and reading areas. For older learners, you will need to provide storage for reference materials. How does your classroom arrangement provide for flexibility of instruction?

3. Design a bulletin board that provides content-learning information to language learners in a contextualized format.

4. Create some community-building activities that can be used with mixed language populations at both the elementary and middle-school grades. You may want to refer to *Cooperative Structures for Classbuilding* (1995) by M. Kagan, L. Robertson, and S. Kagan. San Juan Capistrano, CA: Kagan Cooperative Learning.

5. Create a list of teaching strategies and techniques that appeal to field sensitive learners. Create a separate list for field independent learners. Compare the lists. Which one best illustrates the classrooms that you attended as a child? Which list describes a classroom that you would like to part of?

6. Choose a reading lesson that you have taught or select a reading lesson from a published program. Adapt the lesson for a group of mixed-language learners using a CALLA format.

7. Read again the teaching behaviors contained in the Sheltered Instruction Observation Protocol (SIOP). Check off the behaviors that are already a part of your teaching repertoire. Now list the ones that you need to learn more about in order to incorporate them into your teaching. Select two of those behaviors and research more about them. If you are currently teaching, start experimenting with these behaviors in your classroom.

8. Create a cooperative-learning content activity that incorporates the four principles of cooperative learning: positive interdependence, individual accountability, equal participation, and simultaneous interaction. Make sure that language skills are a focus of the activity.

PEARSON
myeducationlab)
Where the Classroom Comes to Life   is a collection of online tools for your success in this course, your licensure exams, and your teaching career. Go to www.myeducationlab .com to utilize these extensive resources including videos from real classrooms, Praxis and licensure preparation, a lesson plan builder, and materials to help you in your teaching career.

Suggested Reading

Chamot, A. U. & O'Malley, J. M. (1994). *The CALLA handbook: Implementing the cognitive academic language learning approach.* NY: Addison-Wesley. This is a classic text that should be required reading in every teacher's library.

Cummings, C. (2000). *Winning strategies for classroom management.* Alexandria, VA: Association for Supervision and Curriculum Development. The chapter on bonding and connecting offers many practical activities for creating a cohesive classroom community.

Echevarria, J., Vogt, M., & Short, D. J. (2003). *Making content comprehensible for English language learners: The SIOP model.* Boston, MA: Allyn & Bacon. An excellent description of sheltered instruction with many practical strategies clearly explained with classroom examples.

Meyers, M. (1993). *Teaching to diversity: Teaching and learning in the multi-ethnic classroom.* Reading, MA: Addison-Wesley. This slim volume offers chapters devoted to procedures for welcoming new students into the classroom. Blackline masters and sample information-gathering forms are included.

Scarcella, R. (1990). *Teaching language minority students in the multicultural classroom.* Englewood Cliffs, NJ: Prentice Hall Regents. Scarcella includes chapters on getting to know minority students, promoting interaction, and appealing to a variety of learning styles. This last chapter features teaching strategies for a variety of different learning styles. The Appendix contains descriptions of the major cultural groups in the United States—an excellent resource.

Ventriglia, L. (1982). *Conversations of Miguel and Maria: How children learn a second language.* Reading, MA: Addison-Wesley. This enjoyable and useful text describes the various strategies used by young children when acquiring a new language.

Web Sites for Further Learning

The CALLA Home Page. This site contains an overview of CALLA, references, teacher guides, a video, and other information related to CALLA. Retrieved May 2, 2008.

www.gwu.edu/~calla/

Classroom Strategies for Encouraging Collaborative Discussion. (1998). C. Simich-Dudgeon. This paper includes practical suggestions for promoting collaboration in content classrooms. May 2, 2008.

http://www.ncela.gwu.edu/pubs/directions/12.htm

Kagan Publishing and Professional Development. The main site for Kagan's materials and courses. Look at the Articles section for many discussions relating to cooperative learning. Retrieved May 2, 2008.

http://www.cooperativelearning.com

Language Learning Strategies: An Update by Rebecca Oxford, Oct. 1994. This article points out the importance of learning styles and strategies in affecting language-learning outcomes. Retrieved May 2, 2008.

http://www.cal.org/resources/digest/oxford01.html

Sheltered Instruction Observation Protocol. The SIOP Institute site has informative articles about the SIOP model as well as lesson plans that show how the model can be incorporated into a lesson. Retrieved May 2, 2008.

http://www.siopinstitute.net

References

Brandt, R. (1998). *Powerful learning.* Alexandria, VA: Association for Supervision and Curriculum Development.

California State Department of Education. (1994). *Building bilingual instruction: Putting the pieces together.* Sacramento, CA: Bilingual Education Office.

Carbo, M., Dunn, R., & Dunn, K. (1986). *Teaching students to read through their individual learning styles.* Englewood Cliffs, NJ: Prentice Hall.

Center for Problem-Based Learning. (1993–2008). Home page. Retrieved May 2, 2008. http://www.imsa.edu/programs/pbln

Chamot, A. U. & O'Malley, J. M. (1994). *The CALLA handbook: Implementing the cognitive academic language learning approach.* White Plains, NY: Addison-Wesley.

Cox, B.G. & Ramirez, M. (1981). Cognitive styles: Implications for multiethnic education. In J. Banks (Ed.), *Education in the 80s: Implications for multiethnic education.* Washington, DC: National Education Association.

Cummins, J. (1980). The construct of language proficiency in bilingual education. In J. E. Alatis (Ed.), *Georgetown University roundtable on languages and linguistics* (pp. 76–93). Washington, DC: Georgetown University Press.

Cummins, J. (1984).Language proficiency, bilingualism and academic achievement. In P. A. Richard-Amato, *Making it happen: Interaction in the second language classroom from theory to practice.* (1996). White Plains, NY: Addison-Wesley.

Cummins, J. (1996). *Negotiating identities: Education for empowerment in a diverse society.* Ontario, CA: California Association for Bilingual Education.

Cummins, J. (2000). *Language, power, and pedagogy: Bilingual children in the crossfire.* Clevedon, England; Buffalo, NY: Multilingual Matters.

Delisle, R. (1997). *How to use problem-based learning in the classroom.* Alexandria, VA: Association for Supervision and Curriculum Development.

Douglas, F. (2001). Letter to Harriet Tubman. In A. Applebee (Ed.), *The language of literature.* Evanston, IL: McDougal Littell.

Dunn, R. & Dunn, K. (1993). *Teaching secondary students through their individual learning styles.* Boston, MA: Allyn & Bacon.

Echevarria, J. and Graves, A. (1998). *Sheltered content instruction: Teaching English-language learners with diverse abilities.* Boston, MA: Allyn & Bacon.

Echevarria, J., Vogt, M., & Short, D. J. (2004). *Making content comprehensible for English language learners: The SIOP model* (2nd ed.). Boston, MA: Allyn & Bacon.

Gardner, H. (1983). *Frames of mind: The theory of multiple intelligences.* NY: Basic Books.

Gibbons, P. (2002). *Scaffolding language scaffolding learning: Teaching second language learners in the mainstream classroom.* Portsmouth, NH: Heinemann.

Gifford students learn to grow fish. (July 18, 2003). In *Hometown News.*

Igoa, C. (1995). *The inner world of the immigrant child.* Hillsdale, NJ: Lawrence Erlbaum Associates.

Johnson, D. W., Maruyama, G., Johnson, R., Nelson, D., & Skon, L. (1981). Effects of cooperative, competitive and individualistic goal structures on achievement: A meta-analysis. *Psychological Bulletin, 89*: 47–62.

Kagan, S. (1990). Cooperative learning for students limited in language proficiency. In M. Brubacher, R. Payne, and K. Rickett (Eds.), *Perspectives on small group learning.* Oakville, Ontario, Canada.

Kagan, S. (1994). *Cooperative learning.* San Clemente, CA: Kagan Cooperative Learning.

King-Shaver, B. & Hunter, A. (2003). *Differentiated instruction in the English classroom: Content, process, product, and assessment.* Portsmouth, NH: Heinemann.

Krashen, S. D. & Terrell, T. D. (1983). *The natural approach: Language acquisition in the classroom.* San Francisco, CA: The Alemany Press.

Lawrence, J. (1993). *Harriet and the promised land.* NY: Simon & Schuster.

McCarthy, B. (1987). *The 4MAT system: Teaching to learning styles with right/left mode techniques.* Barrington, IL: Excel.

Nieto, S. & Bode, P. (2007). *Affirming diversity: The sociopolitical context of multicultural education* (5th ed.). Boston, MA: Allyn & Bacon.

Paley, V. G. (1993). *You can't say you can't play.* Cambridge, MA: Harvard University Press.

Peregoy, S. F. & Boyle, O. F. (2004). *Reading, writing, & learning in ESL: A resource book for K–12 teachers* (4th ed.). NY: Longman.

Petry, A. (1996). *Harriet Tubman: Conductor on the underground railroad.* NY: Trophy Press.

Rutherford, P. (1998). *Instruction for all students.* Alexandria, VA: Just ASK Publications.

Scarcella, R. C. & Oxford, R. L. (1992). *The tapestry of language learning: The individual in the communicative classroom.* Boston, MA: Heinle and Heinle.

Seigle, P. & Macklem, G. (1993). *Social competency program.* Wellesley, MA: Stone Center.

Slavin, R. E. (1983). When does cooperative learning increase student achievement? *Psychological Bulletin, 94*: 429–445.

Tomlinson, C. A., (1999). *The differentiated classroom: Responding to the needs of all learners.* Alexandria, VA: Association for Supervision and Curriculum Development.

Torp, L. and Sage, S. (1998). *Problems as possibilities: Problem-based learning for K–12 education.* Alexandria, VA: Association for Supervision and Curriculum Development.

Vygotsky, L. S. (1962). *Thought and language.* Cambridge, MA: MIT Press.

Witkin, H. A., Dyk, R. B., Faterson, H. F., Goodenough, D. R., & Karp, S. A. (1962). *Psychological differentiation.* NY: Wiley.

Wolfe, P. (2001). *Brain matters: Translating research into classroom practice.* Alexandria, VA: Association for Supervision and Curriculum Development.

● ●

CHAPTER 5

Strategies for Oral Language Development

Mike Lawrence, a fifth grade teacher, has been teaching a unit on the properties of liquids to his diverse class of language learners and native English speakers. Mike's students enjoy doing science because he teaches it using a hands-on method that involves all of his students in experiential learning. Yesterday, the class predicted what would happen if Mike put his can of Coke into the freezer. They saw that the bottom and top of the can became convex and were able to report to Mike that this happened because the water froze and increased in volume. Today, Mike has placed his students into small groups to perform experiments on the results of salt on the freezing temperature of water. Each group has a cup of fresh water, an ice cube, a salt shaker, and a piece of thread. They are trying to find ways to pick up the ice cube without using their hands. Marisol's group has figured out that the experiment has something to do with freezing and they are trying to determine how to freeze the thread onto the ice cube. Mike intervenes from time to time to comment and ask thought-provoking questions:

What is the freezing point of water?

That's right, water freezes at 32° F.

How would salt affect the freezing point of water?

Have you seen workers put salt on the streets in winter? Why do they do that? What would happen if you put salt on the ice cube?

If the ice cube melted slightly, how could you get the thread to freeze onto the cube?

As Mike moves around the room, he models the language he wants the students to use ("freezing point," "fresh/salt water," "melt/freeze," "lower/higher," "freeze," "froze," "frozen"). By the end of this lesson, he'll ask each group to report to him on what they have discovered. This will give him further opportunities to help the language learners in the group use the scientific terms and the correct verb tenses. Before groups report their findings to the rest of Mike's class, and write up their summaries, they rehearse by reporting to one another.

What kinds of classroom conditions and activities lead to oral language development in language learners?

• What are the necessary classroom conditions for academic language learning?
• What stages do learners go through before they become proficient in oral language?
• How does the teacher's clarity affect oral language development?
• What structured question and response tools promote oral language development?
• How do teachers scaffold oral language learning and provide for collaborative dialogue opportunities in classrooms?

Conditions for Oral Language Learning

Is learning to speak a new language easy or difficult? It seems the answer to this question, as to so many others, is "it depends." There is general agreement (Goodman, 1986, p. 8; Enright & McCloskey, 1988, pp. 21–29; Hernández, 1997, pp. 162–164; Goldenberg, 2004) that learning is easier when certain conditions are present. Some of these conditions include the following criteria:

• *Language learning is meaningful, purposeful, authentic, and important to the learner.* We have discussed the notion that all language learned must have meaning to the learner. The learning must have a purpose also, and the purpose should be a real purpose, an authentic purpose. Completing a workbook page does not qualify as a real, authentic purpose for learners. But writing a letter to a pen pal, debating a topic, or presenting a science project are examples of authentic and purposeful uses for language. If English language learners (ELLs) see these events as important to their own learning, to their peer group, to their class, to their school, family, or communities, they will be motivated to work diligently.
• *Language learning integrates and explores the development of subject matter, cognition, and language.* Because language is integral to learning anything, and because cognitive development is inextricably linked to language development, these processes cannot be separated. Indeed, the role of school is to integrate and develop learning, cognition, and language because there is no institution outside of school that is dedicated to that goal.
• *Language learning proceeds incrementally, starting from what the learner already knows from prior cultural and linguistic experiences.* English language learners do not come to school as blank slates. Every child has already acquired some knowledge when they enter our classrooms. We need to determine what our new students already know and plan our instruction based upon their cultural experiences, their language experiences, and their school learning experiences.
• *Language learning is social learning.* Students learn language when teachers provide ample, plentiful, and collaborative experiences with peers, teachers, and others in the community. These experiences provide the interest and enjoyment that sparks learners to achieve at higher levels. They also help learners develop the social skills necessary to become bilingual.
• *Language learning proceeds most rapidly when the environment is supportive and accepting, and when there are multiple opportunities for success.* All learning, not

only language learning, is accelerated when these conditions are present. A supportive, accepting classroom can still be a rigorous classroom as long as instruction is scaffolded to ensure learner success.

Academic Language Learning

Unfortunately, these criteria, although worthwhile, do not define many classroom experiences for language learners. Language learning is increasingly difficult even for some of our best students. Fillmore and Snow (2002, p. 30) report that in 1997, 60 percent of the freshmen at the Irvine campus of the University of California who took the English composition competency test failed. One-third of these students eventually enrolled in ESL classes at the university because their level of academic English was not sufficient to support college level instruction. These students were not new arrivals to the country—95 percent of them had lived in the U.S. for eight years or more. Most of them were honor students and 65 percent of them had taken honors and Advanced Placement English courses.

At UCLA, students who had been in mainstream classes throughout elementary and secondary school were shocked to find they were required to take ESL classes. Carlos reported:

> I felt kinda bad, I thought that I knew how to write and stuff, but I guess I didn't. But then I go, well I need the help. My writing is really bad (Brinton & Mano, 1994, p. 14).

Martha, a student in the U.S. since kindergarten, had a more extreme reaction:

> Oh, I remember they told us and I was so—I am going to cry—it's happening again . . . So we get into a group and everybody in my group, I just started talking to them . . . I just wanted to see their reaction—and everybody felt just the same . . . they made a mistake, they just want to fill people in the classes (Brinton & Mano, 1994, p. 14).

What went wrong? Although most of these students had spent more than eight years in elementary, middle school, and high school classrooms, they were not linguistically prepared to succeed in higher education or in the workplace. Although able to speak English well enough to graduate from high school, the English skills they had acquired were not sufficient for a freshman college class. These students needed "well-designed instructional intervention" with "explicit instruction" in academic language (Fillmore & Snow, 2002, p. 31).

What, specifically, is academic language? In Chapter 1, we define Cognitive Academic Language Proficiency (CALP) as Cummins (1996) defined it: language that is cognitively demanding, decontextualized, and relying on a broad knowledge of specific vocabulary, specialized grammar, and academic discourse structures. Textbooks are written in academic language and standardized tests are designed to measure it. The amount of time needed for ELLs to become proficient in this language averages from five to seven years (Thomas & Collier, 2002).

Children become adept at academic language usage through their interactions with their teachers, their course materials, and their peers. Gibbons (2003, p. 3) demonstrates the range of school language **registers** in her description of the following four texts:

> **Text 1** *Look, it's making them move. Those didn't stick.*

> **Text 2** *We found out the pins stuck on the magnet.*

Text 3 *Our experiment showed that magnets attract some metals.*

Text 4 *Magnetic attraction occurs only between ferrous metals.*

It's possible that you won't understand what the child is talking about in text 1 because the language is so restricted to a here-and-now situation. If we tell you that the child is talking in a small group that is experimenting with magnets to determine which objects they will attract, the language becomes clearer. This language is context embedded. The use of the pronouns (e.g., "it, those") is unclear unless you are standing near the speaker. Text 1 is an example of informal speech that is not appropriate for academic talk or written text.

Text 2 is also oral language and indicates what the child reported to her teacher after the experiment was complete. This shift in register shows that the child is able to identify elements of the language that must be specified for the teacher to understand. Thus, the words "pins" and "magnet" help to make the communication more explicit. This text is still highly personal, however, with the use of the pronoun "we," and the general word forms "stuck" and "found out." This text begins to approach the style of academic, written language.

Text 3 represents the child's written report of the experiment. This version reads like an academic and scientific generalization. The verb forms are more specific ("attract") and the results are qualified ("some metals").

Text 4 is taken from a child's encyclopedia and is more generalized than text 3. Rather than talking about "our experiment," the encyclopedia uses the term "magnetic attraction." The verb form "occurs" is far more representative of scientific texts than the child's original statement ("the pins stuck"). "Ferrous metals" replaces "some metals."

The transition from text 1 to text 4 represents the process of linguistic and cognitive development that formal education is all about. The role of the teacher in this process is to provide the support that students need to make this kind of growth. A teacher can assist ELLs in moving from the social language of text 1 to the academic language of texts 3 and 4 by utilizing the following effective teaching strategies:

- Teacher repeats learner's utterances and then recasts them in academic terms.

Teacher: *The magnets stuck to each other. They attracted each other.*

When students attempted to report on what happened in the magnet experiment, they used informal language such as "stuck" and "pushed." The teacher repeated their language, "stuck to each other," and then provided the technical terms necessary, "attract/repel."

- Teacher signals how to reformulate student utterances in ways that are more academically acceptable.

Teacher: *Okay, can I just clarify something? You've got two magnets? They're in line? When you put the two together like that (demonstrating) they attracted each other. Is that right? Okay, can you tell me what you had to do next?*

In this example, the teacher supplied a demonstration of magnetic attraction and modeled the language needed to explain the process. Next, the teacher signaled that the student is to continue with the explanation in a similar fashion.

- Teacher signals a need for reformulating utterances.

Teacher: *Wait just a minute. Can you explain that a little bit more, Julianna?*

Teacher Language Provides the Academic Model Required for Effective Content Learning

Here, the teacher provided opportunities for the student to restate her learning using the models and prompts provided during the dialogue. On some occasions, learners attempted to restate several times, improving each time with the support of the teacher's reformulations and encouragement (Gibbons, 2003).

The result of this kind of learning conversation is that ELLs are exposed to a great deal of redundancy. After working in inquiry groups with other students, they are then asked to report to the teacher or to classmates on their results. During this oral reporting phase, teachers recast the informal language of the students into the formal academic language of the classroom. Teachers also demonstrate their meanings, model the academic language, and urge learners to explain using the academic terminology of school. The oral reporting phase of the lesson, in which ELLs must actually use formal school language while being supported by teacher scaffolding, is critical for building an ELL's ability to learn academic language.

Culturally Diverse Language Patterns

Students from other cultures may come to school with different oral traditions than those that are expected and valued by North American teachers. This can be true even when the children are born in the U.S. The ethnographic research of Heath (1983, 1986) indicates that learners from diverse cultural and economic groups are enculturated to use language in ways that are different from school language. In North America, middle-class parents use conversations with their children to enable them to become competent language users for the purposes of reporting on details, hypothesizing, linear storytelling, drawing inferences, generalizing, and evaluating.

In other cultures, parents use language to socialize, and teach respect for family and/or authority figures. Although storytelling is valued, the form of the oral narrative may vary depending on the culture. Stories in English tend to be linear with the plot directing the progress of the narration. Asian cultures may use a circular structure with the subject approached from a variety of different viewpoints. These stories tend to emphasize character over plot (Gadda, 1994). In the blue-collar African American families studied by Heath (1983), stories were valued if they showed creativity, and were clever or verbally inventive. These stories were closer to performances than oral narratives.

The use of parental questioning varies from culture to culture as well. Middle-class North American parents tend to ask many **display questions.** These are questions where the answer is well known to the questioner. Display questions are valued by schools as a way of assessing children's learning. In other cultures, display questions are rarely asked. Heath (1986, p. 161) reports that the working-class Mexican American parents that she studied "seldom ask questions that require children to repeat facts, rehearse the sequence of events, or foretell what they will do." Their questions focus on information within the family circle, seldom from outside that circle, and rarely use display questions.

Teachers of diverse learners, aware of the range of language patterns that children bring with them to school, need to expand the repertoire of these patterns to include those patterns valued by schools. ELLs can achieve academic success if they are exposed to and taught a range of oral and written language usage. Using language to talk about math problems and solutions, discussing historical events and their effects, talking about characters and events in stories, and questioning processes in science will support our students' mastery of academic language as well as aid their comprehension and retention of content learning.

Oral Language Development

In the progression of developing language skills, listening and then speaking (the aural-oral skills) are usually the first to be acquired. If ELLs are literate in their first language and have studied English as a foreign language, it is possible they will arrive in our classrooms with some reading and writing skills in English, although their comprehension and production may still be limited. Most beginning ELLs in the U.S., however, are young, may have been born in the U.S., and have limited or little literacy in the home language. These students will need to develop their English capabilities by listening, developing understanding, and then beginning to speak.

The four language skills of listening, speaking, reading, and writing are related to each other and complement each other. Though listening and reading are receptive skills, learners must still be cognitively active to engage in them well. The learner acts upon input that is either oral or written, hypothesizes meaning, and interprets the message. For ELLs who are not literate in their home language, listening comprehension generally precedes reading comprehension. The two processes are related in that the ability to interpret oral language is useful in supporting reading comprehension and vice versa. These are internal processes that are difficult to observe and assess. They are not passive processes, however. ELLs use strategies of various kinds to access meaning. While listening, students may use a strategy of watching carefully for gestural cues to meaning, may listen selectively for words that are stressed or repeated, may repeat certain words with a questioning intonation, nod in agreement, ask clarifying questions (e.g., "What is . . . ?" or "Can you repeat . . . ?"), or ask an informant for a translation. While reading, students may use strategies including previewing the pictures and charts in the text, using a dictionary, making an analogy to what is already known, or searching for specific information.

Speaking and writing are productive processes. They require ELLs to create rather than interpret a sentence orally or in writing. Here, young English language learners unconsciously hypothesize the correct language form based upon the rules they have created for the language. This is a process of induction—creating a rule based upon the data analyzed through listening and reading. In this way, the four skills are supportive of each other and promote language development.

Because of the "dynamic interrelationship" (Peregoy & Boyle, 2004) of the four skills, it is helpful to language learning if teachers plan to integrate skill use during instruction. The ability to read target vocabulary on the chalkboard assists listening comprehension. Oral practice in the use of new vocabulary assists reading comprehension. Oral role plays assist in the development of grammatically correct writing. Time spent in written composition helps ELLs to negotiate the rules of grammar that can then be used in oral speech. Efficient teachers know learning accelerates when the four language skills are integrated within their lessons.

In this chapter, we will discuss the growth of oral language within the classroom. We will describe the beginning and intermediate stages of language development, and suggest procedures for supporting language growth in a variety of contexts.

Stages of Oral Language Development

In order to plan lessons appropriately, we need to be aware of the level of English understood and spoken by our students. Krashen and Terrell (1983) defined four stages of language development: pre-production, early production, speech emergence, and intermediate fluency. All ELLs progress through these four stages but not at the same rate.

Teachers of English to Speakers of Other Languages (TESOL) has identified five language levels that overlap somewhat with the Krashen and Terrell levels (TESOL, 2006):

Level 1 Starting: ELLs can communicate basic needs and use high-frequency vocabulary.

Level 2 Emerging: ELLs can communicate about routine experiences; use generalized academic vocabulary, phrases, and short sentences.

Level 3 Developing: ELLs can communicate on familiar matters; use some specialized academic vocabulary and use expanded sentences in writing.

Level 4 Expanding: ELLs can use language in abstract situations and for new experiences; use specialized vocabulary and a variety of sentence lengths with varying complexity.

Level 5 Bridging: ELLs can use a wide range of texts and recognize implicit meaning; use technical academic vocabulary in a variety of sentence lengths and with varying linguistic complexity.

The TESOL levels apply to both oral and written language, whereas the Krashen and Terrell levels apply only to oral language. TESOL does not include a pre-production level but has expanded the Intermediate Fluency level into three separate levels (3, 4, and 5). Level 5, the bridging level, occurs when ELLs are very close to becoming fully English proficient but still require modifications for grade-level material. In the discussions that follow, the TESOL levels will be identified alongside the Krashen and Terrell levels.

Pre-production

The pre-production stage is usually the shortest stage, with most ELLs emerging into beginning speech in a couple of months. However, individual differences occur among learners and we have had students who began to speak in "chunks" of memorized language on their second day of school. We have also had experiences with students who did not speak for an extended period of time. One student, Virgine, was silent for an entire year! At the end of that year, however, she began to speak, not in one word utterances, but in sentences. Although Virgine was silent, she was still learning English.

During the pre-production stage, it is important to engage ELLs in classroom learning experiences even if they are unable or unwilling to speak. We send important expectation messages to learners when we treat them as functioning classroom members. During this time, teachers need to provide comprehensible input and to lower affective filters. Engaging ELLs in social interactions in the classroom will help to fulfill both of these criteria. In our experience, ELLs respond to instruction more quickly if they feel socially secure in our classrooms. Having a friend or a buddy provides that security. English-speaking students who are unused to having a non-English speaker in the classroom may need some help in providing assistance to the ELLs. Offer the partners ways of helping and simplifying language. Help your students to develop empathy for the ELL and monitor their interactions to avoid misunderstandings or conflict.

As seen in Table 5.1, ELLs can usually understand more language than they are able to produce and they are actively learning through listening to our language input. Teachers can support student comprehension at this stage with gestures, scaffolding devices, abundant context clues, lesson outlines projected on the wall, drawings, and simple commands requiring a nonlinguistic response. It's important to model all expected behavior, including simple procedures such as lining up, accessing a locker, or requesting a bathroom pass. Learners at this stage respond well to peer instruction and a buddy's directions. Without forcing students to speak, we can encourage speech emergence at this stage through the use of classroom chants, group songs, raps, and whole group responses. Total Physical Response (TPR), a strategy in which learners show their understanding of new language by responding to teachers' series of commands to perform actions, is highly successful with beginners (Herrell & Jordan, 2007). Predictable books with repeated choral responses are effective in the early elementary grades. Older learners are attracted to rap chants. These activities are even more appealing to many learners when we combine them with rhythmic clapping, finger snapping, or toe tapping.

Though ELLs may not be able to speak English yet, it's important that we continue to speak to them. Smiling, making eye contact, and being aware of body language will carry a great deal of meaning at this stage of language development. It's also helpful to provide modeling of the kinds of language forms learners need during the pre-production stage. The following forms are suggestive:

What's this/that?

Good morning.

Good-bye.

How are you? Fine, thanks.

Table 5.1 Language Development Stages

Stage	Sample Student Behaviors	Sample Teacher Behaviors	Questioning Techniques
Pre-production • Students are totally new to English. • Generally lasts 1–3 months.	• Points to or provides other nonverbal responses. • Actively listens. • Responds to commands. • May be reluctant to speak. • Understands more than one can produce. • Needs survival language.	• Gestures. • Language focuses on conveying meanings and vocabulary development. • Repetition. • Does not force student to speak. • Models all expected behavior. • Encourages students to participate in group songs, chants, and choral responses. • Checks comprehension frequently.	• "Point to . . ." • "Find the . . ." • "Put the ___ next to the ___." • "Do you have the ___?" • "Is this a ___?" • "Who wants the ___?" • "Who has the ___?"
Early Production • Students are "low beginners." • Generally lasts several weeks.	• One- or two-word utterances. • Short phrases. • Initiates conversations by gesturing or using single words. • Can work with rhymes and rhythms. • Continues to rely on buddies.	• Asks questions that can be answered by yes/no and either/or responses. • Models correct responses. • Ensures a supportive, low anxiety environment. • Does not overtly call attention to grammar errors. • Asks short answer WH questions.	• Yes/no: "Is the trouble light on?" • Either/or: "Is this a screwdriver or a hammer?" • One-word response: "What utensil am I holding in my hand?" • General questions that encourage lists of words: "What do you see on the tool board?" • Two-word response: "Where did he go? To work."
Speech Emergence • Students are "beginners." • May last several weeks or months.	• Speaks in short phrases and sentences. • Participates in small group activities.	• Focuses content on key concepts. • Uses expanded vocabulary and responses.	• "Why?" • "How?" • "How is this like that?" • "Tell me about . . ."

Table 5.1 Language Development Stages *(Continued)*

Stage	Sample Student Behaviors	Sample Teacher Behaviors	Questioning Techniques
Speech Emergence *(continued)*	• Demonstrates comprehension in a variety of ways. • Begins to use language more freely but makes many errors in grammar. • Enjoys role playing. • Uses present tense almost exclusively. • Can dictate 3–5 word sentences.	• Models language structures. • Asks open-ended questions that stimulate language production. • Provides frequent comprehension checks. • Uses performance-based assessment.	• "Talk about . . ." • "Describe . . ." • "How would you change this part?"
Intermediate Fluency • Students are "high beginners, intermediate, or advanced." • May require several years to achieve native-like fluency in academic settings.	• Engages in discourse and communicates thoughts more effectively. • Participates in reading and writing activities to acquire new information. • Uses language for concrete problem solving. • Can use present and past tenses. • Can begin to write independently with teacher support. • Can use grammar for substitutions, deletions, and rearrangements of words. • May experience difficulties in abstract, cognitively demanding subjects at school, especially when a high degree of literacy is required.	• Fosters conceptual development and expanded literacy through content. • Continues to make lessons comprehensible and interactive. • Teaches thinking and study skills. • Continues to be alert to individual differences in language and culture. • Uses sheltered instructional strategies.	• "What would you recommend/ suggest?" • "How do you think this story will end?" • "What is the story mainly about?" • "What is your opinion on this matter?" • "Describe/ compare . . ." • "How are these similar/different?" • "What would happen if . . . ?" • "Which do you prefer? Why?" • "Create . . ."

From Grognet, Jameson, Franco, & Derrick-Mescua (2000).

I want . . .

I need . . .

I don't understand.

Can I . . . ?

Modeling two or three language forms, writing the forms on a note card for literate learners, and using context clues to meaning will help ELLs to proceed into the next stage of development, the early production stage.

Early Production (TESOL Level 1)

The early production stage is a continuation of the pre-production stage. At this time, ELLs still require comprehensible input and a low affective filter. They still require social interactions that are supportive and friendly. ELLs are able to attend more to language input at this stage and they are able to respond with one-word answers and then simple phrasal responses.

Reading and writing are not to be delayed until learners can speak English. Reading and writing provide important elements of comprehensible input, and these skills can be included in a school program from the very beginning.

The techniques used in the pre-production stage can be continued at this time. Teachers can also use targeted questioning techniques to include ELLs in the instructional conversation. "Yes/no questions" are the easiest for learners to respond to:

Teacher: *Is this a map?*

Student: *Yes.*

Teacher: *Yes it is. It's a map of the United States.*

In the above example, the teacher asks a simple yes/no question and then expands the student's response in a way that provides more vocabulary and grammatical information to the learner.

"Either-or questions" also require a one-word response but are supportive in that they supply the vocabulary item needed as well as the pronunciation.

Teacher: *Is this a map of the United States or Canada?*

Student: *United States.*

Teacher: *That's right. It's a map of the United States.*

"WH questions" are the next in difficulty. They ask questions such as What? When? Where? These questions require only a one-word response but the response must be supplied by the learner.

Teacher: *What is this?*

Student: *A map.*

Teacher: *That's right. It's a map of the United States.*

In addition, teachers can ask "predictable questions" such as:

How are you?

What's your name?

How old are you?

Do you like ice cream?

These questions are predictable in that ELLs are usually asked about their name and age. Other kinds of predictable questions presuppose the answer. Even so, questions of this sort open up conversations and promote interactions with language that lead to further oral development.

Even when ELLs can only say one word, teachers can use that one word to develop opportunities for comprehensible input. Consider this example from Urzua (1981, p. 9) of a teacher with a five-year-old child:

Child: *Fish.*

Teacher: *Yes it is a fish. A tiny fish. A fish the color of your shirt.*

The teacher in this example is responsive to the child's attempt to interact in the new language and provides additional vocabulary and information in an effort to keep the conversation moving.

In the following example (Urzua, 1981, p. 22), note the repetitions used by the teacher reading a book with a child.

Child: *(Pointing to a picture in the book) Look at that!*

Teacher: *He's sweeping the floor. Oh, he's cross. Show me.* He's cross. Yes, he's cross.

Child: *(Singing a child's song) Na-na-na . . .*

Teacher: *I like that song. It makes me happy.* I like it very much.

Child: *(Pointing to a picture) Cry.*

Teacher: Cry. *The elephant's going* to cry. *Why?* Why did the elephant cry?

Child: *Lion there.*

Teacher: *Oh the* lion *is there. The elephant is afraid of the lion.* He's afraid.

Repetition and vocabulary information are evident in the following example (Urzua, 1981, pp. 40–41) where the child wants to paint a red picture but has chosen the orange paint.

Teacher: *Do you want to paint red?*

Child: *Huh?*

Teacher: *Do you want to paint with* red?

Child: *Yeah.*

Teacher: *All right,* here's red. *There's just a little bit.*

Child: *Okay. This red?*

Teacher: *Uh huh. A little bit of* red . . . *Is it the* red *you want?*

Child: *Ah, this a more?*

Teacher: *I'm gonna put a little water with your* red. *Then you'll have enough* red.

In addition to providing vocabulary, repetition, and information about the structure of the language, teachers also give effective feedback to learners through their conversations. In the following example (Urzua, 1981, p. 30), note the persistence of the teacher as she tries to understand the child. Her final question enables the learner to understand that she needs to elaborate on her message in order to be understood.

Child: *I got a bathing suit . . . A new one.*

Teacher: *You have a what?*

Child: *A bathing suit.*

Teacher: *A baby shoe?*

Child: *A bathing suit.*

Teacher: *Soup?*

Child: *Bathing suit.*

Teacher: *Baby soap?*

Child: *Bathing suit.*

Teacher: *What do you do with it?*

Child: *I put it on and I go swimming.*

Teacher: *A bathing suit. You put it on and you go swimming.*

Speech Emergence (TESOL Level 2)

The speech emergence phase usually lasts longer than either of the preceding two stages. During this time, ELLs experiment with language, though they may make many grammatical errors. As we saw in the preceding examples, however, teachers don't overtly correct errors in oral production. Since the goal is comprehension, it is frequently best to provide the learner with extensions of his or her own language attempts (e.g., "a tiny fish" or "the elephant's going to cry") and continue the conversation. Modeling the correct language serves many purposes. Teacher modeling provides vocabulary, structure, and feedback to learners. But most importantly, it sends the message "I want to talk with you and help you to understand my language."

Teachers can continue to target their questioning to ELL proficiency levels at this stage, asking questions requiring more than a one-word response. If we are aware of the student's ability to use language, we can target our questioning to a level slightly higher than the learner is capable of producing alone. In this way, we challenge ELLs to continue to develop, and we support them while they are learning.

The teacher strategies from the first two stages are still important at the speech emergence stage. In addition, we need to be more aware of checking the comprehension of ELLs. We can check comprehension through a variety of questioning techniques: pair reports and group reports, and nonverbal means such as illustrations, signals, and labeling of diagrams or graphic organizers. At this time, it's also helpful to involve ELLs in performance-based assessments such as role plays, projects, and investigations.

Intermediate Fluency (TESOL Levels 3, 4, and 5)

This is the longest stage of the language development process. Intermediate level ELLs take years to achieve an academic language level that is comparable to their grade-level peers. In Thomas and Collier's final report on their longitudinal study of various models for developing English language in schools (2002, p. 270), they found that when ELLs are "schooled all in second language," in a high-quality program, the process takes, on the average, from five to seven years, but may take much longer for learners with interrupted education, or for those who are in programs that are not well implemented. The implications of this amount of time are staggering. ELLs entering an English language school during the middle-school years may never have enough time to catch up. Indeed, language learning is a process that will last throughout our students' lifetimes. They will continually be confronting new language demands as they progress through school into work or into college, where each new course will overflow with vocabulary challenges.

There are levels within the intermediate fluency stage (see Table 5.1) but the strategies used at each of these levels are similar. Teachers continue to focus on comprehensible input, expanding the input to wider content contexts, readings, and genres. Questioning techniques are also widened, and "open-ended questions" requiring expanded responses become routine at this stage. Grade-appropriate learning objectives will help to ensure ELLs develop conceptually as well as linguistically. It is important to use sheltered learning strategies at this stage as the learning and language demands increase.

Learners at the intermediate fluency level are capable of producing social conversation that is comparable to grade-level peers. This presents a dilemma for teachers who have had little experience with English language learners. It is not unusual for a student to be fluent in language while still lagging far behind in academic skills such as oral debating, persuasion, reading, writing, and test taking. In our experience, teachers who teach these youngsters are often baffled as to why the academic problems persist, often throughout the elementary school years. Because their interpersonal language seems so fluent, teachers tend to view the ELLs as proficient speakers, even though teachers may know that the learners are developing English as a second or third language. It is at this stage that teachers might initiate diagnostic testing to determine why the ELL is not yet proficient and perhaps even if the student has special needs. Tests written in academic language—the same language that requires five to seven (or more) years to learn—may not reveal the language development needs of the ELL.

The most important thing teachers can do for ELLs at this stage of learning is to continue to challenge them cognitively and linguistically while supporting their learning with a variety of sheltering techniques. Consciously focusing on language objectives is crucial at this stage to spur the development of academic language. When learners are able to communicate with social language, their motivation to continue to acquire academic language may falter as the academic language is not necessary to achieve communication. Those ELLs who read widely can also acquire a great deal of language from written materials. Unfortunately, for many ELLs, reading without careful scaffolding and support can be a difficult and frustrating experience because of the challenge of academic language along with the large number of unknown words.

Video Exercise

Communicating with English Language Learners

Go to MyEducationLab, select the topic **Academic Language Development**, and watch the video entitled **"Communicating with English Language Learners"** to observe two teachers explain the strategies they use to communicate with and teach ELLs. Complete the questions that accompany it. You may print your work or have it transmitted to your professor as necessary.

Teacher Tools for Oral Language Development

For oral language to develop in classrooms, students must "interact directly and frequently with people who know the language well enough to reveal how it works and how it can be used" (Fillmore & Snow, 2002, p. 31). The primary person fitting this description is the teacher. In the following section, we describe the kind of language that teachers need to use in classrooms to give clarity to their explanations and directions. Then we describe ways to improve the nature of teachers' question and response interactions with students.

Clarity Tools

Clarity is the process of delivering clear instructions to students—of explaining things well (Saphier & Gower, 1997). It is the primary task of most teachers. We need clarity to introduce new subject matter, to give directions, explain concepts, clear up confusions, and help learners make connections between old and new concepts.

Clear Speech.   The bottom line of clarity is clear speech. The following aspects of effective teacher language are discussed in previous chapters:

- Repetition
- Slower rate of speech with occasional pauses
- Gestures, context, and explanatory devices
- Stress on important vocabulary items
- Modeling correct forms
- Avoidance of unnecessary slang, idioms, and jargon

To this list, we add the following caveats:

- Avoid unknown references
- Avoid sarcasm

Referring to people, places, or things that have no meaning for our ELLs is confusing rather than clarifying. We're always reminded of the second graders who stared blankly as the teacher referred to an object in a story as being "as flat as a phonograph record." It had not occurred to the teacher that these children were too young to have ever seen a phonograph record. The rest of the lesson was spent correcting that error as the teacher pulled her old record player out from the back of the closet and showed the wide-eyed youngsters how the record magically dropped onto the turn table and played.

Unknown, unexplained referents may turn learners' minds away from the focus of the lesson. They can become more of a distraction than a tool for learning. ELLs will not have the same experiences as students growing up in North America. Although they may be familiar with current pop music stars, they might not understand why George Washington is pictured cutting down a cherry tree or what the relationship is between a groundhog and the weather. Teachers can avoid the use of unfamiliar referents, or, when necessary, build the background knowledge necessary for ELLs to understand what they learn. Frequent comprehension checks will alert teachers as to whether referents they are using are familiar or unfamiliar.

Using sarcasm in classrooms is seldom appropriate. Students love humor, and ELLs can appreciate visual and physical humor, as well as some humorous language. But sarcasm is very difficult to understand and is often at someone's expense. What's more, when ELLs see everyone laughing and they don't understand what it's about, they're likely to assume that people are laughing at them. ELLs can be the victim of an inappropriate joke without ever understanding the meaning of the comment.

In addition, effective teachers enunciate classroom language clearly. Teaching talk is different from social conversation. When we misunderstand a friend or cannot quite catch a meaning, we feel free to say "Excuse me?" or "Huh?" Those kinds of cues are not available to children in classrooms. If teachers do not use clear diction, enunciate properly, or pronounce words clearly and appropriately, ELLs have no easy way to retrieve the missing information.

Teachers can also be excellent models for grammar and sentence formation. Long, rambling, or run-on sentences are not as communicative as short, simple sentences. And, since vocabulary is such an important element of subject matter learning, teachers need to use appropriate vocabulary—content-specific vocabulary—rather than substitute more general and vague terminology. ELLs in math classes need to hear the words "numerator" and "denominator" rather than "the number on the top" or "the number on the bottom." They need to learn specific vocabulary items, such as "magnet," "attract," "force," rather than generic ones, such as "thing," "stuff," or "whatcha-ma-call-it."

A teacher's speech assists cognitive academic language learning when it is specific. The following are examples of nonspecific, and confusing utterances to avoid using (Saphier & Gower, 1997):

- Kind of, sort of, mostly, somewhat
- Basically, in a nutshell, so to speak, you know, actually, and so forth
- I guess
- A bunch, a little, some
- Possible, perhaps, maybe
- Generally, ordinarily, sometime
- Somehow, somewhere, someplace, something

Unclear language in the classroom might sound like the following:

This science lesson may *enable you to understand* a bit *about* several aspects *of photosynthesis.* Maybe *you'll remember* something *about photosynthesis from yesterday's lesson?*

The teacher could have improved clarity and comprehension in the following way:

Today we're going to learn the three elements that contribute to photosynthesis. First, who can recall the definition of photosynthesis that we learned yesterday?

Clear, Specific, and Fluent Teacher Language Enables ELLs to Learn Academic Concepts and Vocabulary

The second example is clear as to what the students will learn (three elements). The teacher's question both indicates what they want to know (the definition of photosynthesis) and also gives learners a clue that it was learned yesterday. The use of markers such as "first" provides ELLs with transition points in the teacher's language, again promoting the clarity and comprehensibility of the language.

Finally, teacher language must be as free as possible of false starts and hesitations. These occur when the teacher has not completely thought out what is being said or when the teacher is not really clear about what is being taught. An example might be:

> *Today, we're* uh . . . *going to . . . I'll enable you to understand what* we me . . . , *or what we defined yesterday, as photosynthesis. We're going to review* or present . . . , I'll present the ele . . . *three prerequisite elements that* go wi . . . , *that contribute to photosynthesis.*

Teacher language is the instrument that we use to play our instructional music. In addition to our form and word selections, volume, stress, and intonation enable us to capture the attention of our students.

Explanatory Devices

Explanatory devices contribute to the clarity of our instruction by providing visual clues to the meaning of our oral language. In the preparation phase of instruction, teachers collect the materials they will use to make the input comprehensible to their ELLs. These materials include the following:

- Objects, photos, props, and materials to be used as examples
- Visual organizers such as the Venn diagram, time lines, flowcharts, semantic maps, and tree diagrams. (See Figure 5.1 for examples.)

Figure 5.1 Graphic Organizers Present Visual Pictures That Support Language and Thinking Concepts

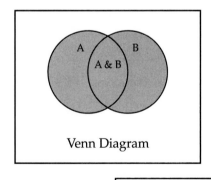

Venn Diagram

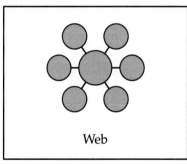

Web

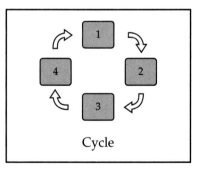

Cycle

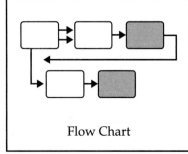

Flow Chart

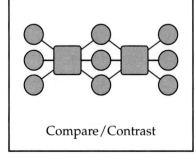

Compare/Contrast

- Demonstrations
- Role plays
- Teacher-created notes or an outline of the lesson to be used by students for later review
- Teacher-created outlines or graphic organizers projected on the wall or monitor—especially useful in upper elementary and middle-school classes where students are expected to write summaries in their notebooks. A visual provides a written clue to the structure of the text and the meaning of the oral language.

Cognitive Empathy

In order to explain things well to ELLs, we must first understand what is inside their heads. Saphier and Gower (1997, p. 190) call this "cognitive empathy"—knowing the information, feelings, and goals learners bring with them into the classroom. When teachers have cognitive empathy with their students, they are able to recognize the moment when misunderstandings occur and then focus on exactly what is not understood in ways that clear up confusion. Cognitive empathy requires teachers to check for understanding of *all* students, *frequently*, throughout the lesson. One moment in particular when checking is critical is when giving directions.

Giving Directions and Stating Reasons for Learning

Clarity requires that teachers clearly think through the steps of their directions. We can do this by imagining our students as they follow our instructions—running a movie in our minds as we watch them proceed. By doing this we can avoid directions such as the following:

Get into small groups and think of an ending for the story we wrote this morning.

In this example, the teacher has not indicated the number of students in the group nor indicated the roles they will play, such as recording and reporting. She has suggested they "think of" an ending but has not told them to write it. These learners will also need some modeling of ways to reach consensus, offer suggestions, and use the language of agreement and disagreement. Without these supports, it is unlikely that the activity will be successful for all learners. Clearer instructions might include these steps:

1. *First, form groups of three. Count off by three.*

   Number 1 is the leader—you get the group started and ask questions.

   Number 2 is the recorder—you take notes.

   Number 3 is the reporter—you tell your group's ideas to the class.

2. *Second, retell the story to one another. You can take turns.*
3. *Third, brainstorm a new ending. Then select the best one and write it down.*
4. *Finally, your reporter will report your answer to the class.*
5. *Now watch as Candace, Araxy, Paul, and I show you how the activity looks.*

Finally, the teacher needs to provide the students with a reason for doing the activity. Students should have a clear understanding of how the activity contributes to the objective of the lesson, the learning from the past, or the learning that will occur in the future. Learners will have greater engagement and effort when they understand the value of their activities.

Question and Response Tools

The teacher-learner dialogue forms the basis of the instructional conversation in classrooms. We have argued for collaborative classrooms where teachers and students negotiate meaning through dialogues that are clear, comprehensible, promote higher order cognitive skills, and are representative of all students in the classroom.

In fact, there is evidence that teacher talk far outweighs student talk in most classrooms. The instructional pattern that predominates in classes from K to Grade 12 is recitation. This is a pattern of:

- Teacher question
- Student response
- Teacher evaluation

Without knowledge, experience, and motivation to teach differently, teachers will teach the way they were taught. Because many teachers have gone to schools where a recitation pattern prevailed, it is difficult to dislodge this pattern from the repertoire of many teachers in classrooms today. Why is a preponderance of recitation problematical for students? Ramirez, Yuen, and Ramey (1991) conducted a study of over 2,000 language-learning students in bilingual and immersion classrooms. They were asked if the classrooms of these learners provided an ideal language learning environment. They responded:

> No. Consistently across grade levels . . . students are limited in their opportunities to produce language and in their opportunities to produce more complex language. Direct observations reveal that teachers do most of the talking in classrooms, making about twice as many utterances as do students. Students produce language only when they are working directly with a teacher, and then only in response to teacher initiations. Of major concern is that in over half of the interactions that teachers have with students, students do not produce any language as they are only listening or responding with nonverbal gestures or actions. Of equal concern is that when students do respond, typically they provide only simple information recall statements. Rather than being provided with the opportunity to generate original statements, students are asked to provide simple discrete close-ended or patterned (i.e., expected) responses. This pattern of teacher/student interaction not only limits a student's opportunity to create and manipulate language freely, but also limits the student's ability to engage in more complex learning (i.e., higher order thinking skills) (Ramirez, Yuen, & Ramey, 1991, p. 8).

Sticking with Your Students.   Environments in which ELLs' use of language is highly restricted will result in less language development. ELLs need opportunities for extended conversations with knowledgeable language users in order to develop the high level of academic language necessary for school success. The recitation classroom limits learners to one-word responses as in the following dialogue (MacLure & French, 1980, as cited in Simich-Dudgeon, 1998, p. 3):

Teacher: *Matthew, what do you think hedges are useful for?*

Matthew: *Corn (quietly).*

Teacher: *Can't hear you, Matthew.*

Matthew: *Corn.*

Teacher: *Hedges are useful for corn? No. Karen?*

Karen: *So the things can't get out.*

Teacher: *So the things can't get out. (Three second pause.) Stop the animals getting into the cornfield to eat all the corn—wouldn't it?*

The teacher in this exchange evaluated Matthew's one-word response (*No*) and went on to the next student. Matthew had no opportunity to explain his response. Although it's very likely that he knew that hedges were related to corn cultivation, he simply couldn't express the relationship without some scaffolding from the teacher. For example, the teacher could say, "Corn? Tell me a little more about that, Matthew."

If Matthew could not tell more about his answer, the teacher had other options. She could ask pinpoint, specific questions to isolate the point of confusion or to provide supportive language structures: "The hedges grow around the corn, don't they? Corn grows behind the hedges." Sticking with a student sends a clear message that we know they can do it and we are there to help them do it successfully. What message does it send when we respond "no" and move on to another student?

Wait Time.   Sometimes we need to slow down the rapid fire question-response recitation pattern to provide enough time for ELLs to think about the question and formulate a response. This time lag is most critical for ELLs who may still be trying to translate the teacher's question while others are answering it. The answer will never be heard and the student slips farther away from becoming a participant in the instructional conversation.

One sixth grader verbalized this in the following way:

[My friend] knows what [the answer is] but he can't actually say it out, and sometimes that happens with people who don't know English, you know. It's just that you can't phrase it right (Simich-Dudgeon, McCreedy, & Scheleppegrell, 1988, as cited in Simich-Dudgeon, 1998, p. 6).

Using sufficient **wait time** helps learners to process questions and to begin to formulate a reasoned response. Wait time requires that we wait for at least three to five seconds before calling on a student to answer a comprehension question. This is sometimes harder than it seems. Most teachers are uncomfortable with silence in the classroom. The average wait time is 0.5 seconds (Saphier & Gower, 1997).

But the results of using wait time make waiting worthwhile. We have noted that more students attempt to respond when we wait a little. We've also noted the quality of the responses improves. Perhaps when students have more time to formulate answers, they process their responses and refine them—not blurting out the first thing that pops into their heads.

Bob Hunter, a middle-school teacher, experimented with wait time in his classroom. He thought that the message he had been sending to his students was a faulty one: *Answering fast shows that you're smart.* In fact, Bob valued thoughtfulness and wanted to curb the impulsiveness of the youngsters in front of him. He also worried about the ELLs in his class who never answered a question, the shy students who never raised their hands, and the learning disabled students who were similarly not included in class discussions.

But Bob's initial experiments with wait time were disastrous. His students became impatient with not being called on promptly. They began to call out, make hooting noises, and in other ways try to get their teacher's attention. Finally, Bob decided to include his students in the experiment. He explained that he was using something called wait time with them and told them the reason why: *We all need to participate and be more thoughtful in our class discussions and comments.* From then on, Bob saw a great improvement in the quantity of responses he received from students who had not participated before.

**Video
Exercise**
**Communication
Skills for
Teaching English
Language Learners**
Go to MyEducationLab,
select the topic
Comprehensible Input,
and watch the video
entitled **"Communication
Skills for Teaching
English Language
Learners"** to observe a
writing lesson and a
writing conference
between the teacher and
an English language
learner. Complete the
questions that accompany
it. You may print your
work or have it
transmitted to your
professor as necessary.

He also noted that responses were more thoughtful. He sent a message to his students through the use of this technique: *What we're talking about is important and I'm going to help you join in this conversation.*

Interactional Structures.   Waiting for students to respond is a good first step. But there are some students who need more than wait time. For ELLs, we have to structure opportunities for oral language development into our lesson presentations. The following structures are suggested as being appropriate for all learners:

- *Use cooperative learning principles as a way of providing more input and negotiated output in small group learning experiences.* Structuring group activities to create positive interdependence and individual accountability ensures that all learners will have simultaneous opportunities to be heard in the classroom.
- *Organize instruction in ways that will create an audience for learning.* Classroom presentations, for example, require learners to acquire both the content and the academic language related to the content in order to report to classmates, schoolmates, parents, teachers, and others in the community. One of the most impressive presentations we have seen at a Board of Education meeting was accomplished by four ELLs, recent arrivals to the U.S., who described their participation in the new high school physics program. Formal presentations are not the only way to promote language growth, however. Informal oral reporting to the teacher is a necessary phase of the lesson that gives ELLs an opportunity to rehearse the content vocabulary and grammar needed for academic learning.
- *Establish long-term dialogues with your students.* We know one teacher, Amy Luray, who met on a scheduled basis, one on one, with each student in her class throughout the year. They talked about progress in learning, set goals for the future, determined ways to provide for support, and prepared for parent-teacher conferences. Other teachers carry on long-term dialogues with their students through dialogue journals in which they converse in writing over the school year.
- *Encourage students to discuss and process new content during the input phase of the lesson.* One technique for doing this in a structured way is called 10-2 (Saphier & Haley, 1993). To use the 10-2 structure, the teacher presents new material for no more than ten minutes at a time. After ten minutes of oral input, the teacher pauses and students share their notes with a buddy, summarizing the concept or discussing a question posed by the teacher. Following the two-minute pause, the teacher may resume ten more minutes of input.

  Ten minutes doesn't seem like a long time, but when listening to complex subject matter in a new language, ten minutes can seem like an hour. We like the fact that 10-2 provides ELLs with a stress-free opportunity to clarify their thinking and understanding with a classmate—and the clarification only takes two minutes. Those two minutes are well spent by the teacher floating around the classroom, assessing the comprehension of learners.

  Opportunities to organize thinking ensure better conceptual development for all learners. The research on 10-2 shows that the English-speaking experimental groups performed better on complex test items, had better retention of the material and more positive attitudes toward the subject matter (Saphier & Haley, 1993). It seems that the 10-2 structure affords all students the time needed to organize new learning into the schema of what they already know and understand—one of the requirements for meaningful learning.

- *Encourage students to discuss and process new content at every phase of the lesson.* Sometimes it is not sufficient to simply encourage students to participate; we must also require their participation. Cindy, a student from Hong Kong, recalled her school silences this way:

> [School] was so difficult. I mean, everybody was in on the conversation. They had class discussions and communicated with each other . . . I felt alone because there weren't that many people that could communicate with me. I was pretty quiet, I think. There was only one student besides myself who was Chinese . . . we didn't talk that much in the beginning . . . she's also kind of shy (Igoa, 1995, pp. 86–87).

Another student, Alice, came to the U.S. from China at the age of eight. She remembers:

> I didn't participate in a lot of stuff. I wanted to. You know, the other kids were doing certain things and I looked at them. I said, "Oh they're having fun. I want to do that." But then, I was reluctant to do that because I felt maybe I couldn't do that, right? Maybe I thought I wasn't good enough to do what they were doing. It was really bad to just sit there and look at what they were doing with the feeling that I wanted to do it but just couldn't (Igoa, 1995, p. 83).

Cindy and Alice longed to participate more fully in classroom discussions. They needed a teacher who structured the class in ways that invited all learners to contribute and scaffolded them to feel secure in their contributions.

Harklau's case study of high-school-level language learners (1994, p. 250) noted that "opportunities to engage in extended interactions with mainstream teachers during classroom instruction were rare." In addition, teachers rarely called on ELL students to speak in class. We have found this to be true in many elementary classrooms as well (Schinke-Llano, 1980).

The benefits to structuring interactional opportunities around content learning are so great for both language and content learning that we recommend using short interactional structures at every phase of the lesson. Examples of these interactional structures are described in Table 5.2.

Scaffolding Oral Language Development

As children progress through school they have opportunities to interact with teachers and with other adults in ways that increase their **linguistic** and **cognitive competency**. Vygotsky (1962) described a collaborative, social context as being the critical component of all learning. He rejected the view that learning occurs by transmitting information from the teacher to the student. He also rejected the view that learning occurs through the individual learner's attempts at discovery and inquiry. Rather, he saw all learning and development as a process of collaboration between the teacher and the learner. Through this collaboration, learners are supported in their language use in order to speak and perform tasks at a level beyond their competency—beyond their **zone of proximal development.**

Scaffolding is a term first used by Bruner (Wood, Bruner, & Ross, 1976) to metaphorically describe the temporary, yet essential, nature of the structures that teachers use to support learning. Oral scaffolding helps maintain the learner's interest, reduce choices, maintain goal orientation, highlight critical aspects of the task, control frustration, and demonstrate a potential activity path (Wood, et al., 1976). Gibbons (2003, p. 10) defines scaffolding as "a special kind of help that assists ELLs to move toward new skills, concepts, or levels of understanding." Scaffolding is thus the temporary assistance by which a teacher helps a learner perform so that the learner will later be able to complete a similar task alone. It is future-oriented—as Vygotsky has said, what a child can do with support today, she or he can do alone tomorrow.

Table 5.2 Interactional Structures

··

1. Learning Buddies	Learning Buddies is a simple structure uniting two learners for a brief period of time to summarize or review learning (Saphier & Haley, 1993). The pairing can be accomplished periodically and can be used to stimulate learning when students appear to be "tuning out" of a presentation. Some teachers like to have students get up and move in order to pair with a buddy. If this is the case, students need to know ahead of time who will be their buddies in order to save time and avoid confusion. Methods of pairing students vary. Saphier and Haley (1993, p. 29) suggest the following ideas:

- Teacher-assigned learning buddies that change from time to time. By assigning buddies strategically, teachers can pair ELLs with language speakers and avoid pairing students who don't work well together. Rotating buddy pairs will ensure that students have opportunities to meet with a variety of partners.

- Randomly selected buddies provide novelty and prevent arguments about buddy assignments. Some teachers use question and answer matching, asking students to match themselves with a student whose answer card matches their question card. For example: "What is the capital of New York state?"

- Another technique for random selection is to create card pairs related to the content learning: word opposites, states and capitals, chemical elements and symbols, dates and historical events.

2. Round the Clock Learning Buddies	Student-selected buddies are problematical in that one student may be left out of a pairing. One technique we like to use to decrease the likelihood of this is Round the Clock Learning Buddies (Saphier & Haley, 1993). Students are given a version of a clock face (shown below) with lines drawn for each number on the clock. Students are instructed as follows: "Put your name on the paper. You will get up (in a minute) and walk around the class making an appointment with twelve other students. Write your name on your one o'clock buddy's clock and ask him to write his name on yours. You won't have a lot of time so you have to work quickly. Complete all twelve appointments on the clock."

Name _____

After about three minutes, call time and ask students to return to their seats. If some have not finished and need an appointment at specified times ask: "Who needs a one o'clock buddy?" Pair the students in this way so that all clocks are complete. Students should be

Table 5.2 Interactional Structures   *(Continued)*

. . . .

	told to keep their clocks with them in class every day. Once completed, the clocks can be used at any time during a lesson when you want to provide language support for learning: "Meet with your five o'clock buddy to share . . . , name . . . , identify . . . , read . . . , or recall three important ideas from today's class." Teachers that we have worked with have modified the Clock Buddies structure in many ways to adapt the technique to their classes. • Our elementary colleagues reduced the clocks in size and laminated them, attaching them to the top of their students' desks. • Our high school colleagues printed the clocks on neon colored paper for easy access. One physics teacher made a wall chart of all clock buddies to eliminate time wasted looking for the clocks. • Other teachers have modified the technique to adapt it to their content learning. The fifth grade teachers in one school created maps of the New England states and used New England Buddies and selected a buddy for each state. They rotated to other regions of the country and were pleased at the amount of map knowledge their students had acquired by the end of the year. • A chemistry teacher created Chemistry Apparatus Buddies at the beginning of the school year to help learners quickly learn the names of the equipment. Others in her department used the structure for Chemical Symbol Buddies. • The French teacher used a map of France and the Spanish teacher quickly followed suit with a map of Spain. • Kindergarten teachers knew that twelve appointments were too many for their young students, but they adapted the technique to Shape Buddies (circle, square, triangle, and rectangle) and then to Primary Color Buddies. There seems to be no end to the variations.
3. Think-Pair-Share (T-P-S)	T-P-S is the simplest structure for brief classroom interactions. At appropriate times (to activate, summarize, or problem solve), teachers ask students to *think* about a question. After a minute or two, learners are asked to *pair* themselves with a nearby buddy and discuss what they have thought about. Finally, learners are asked to *share* with another pair or with the large group. We have found that this structure provides language learners with rehearsal time, practicing or experimenting with the structure of their language. During the sharing time, students may be emboldened to respond, either talking about their own thinking or the thinking of their buddy (Frank Lyman, as cited in Kagan, 1994). Think-Pair-Write is an adaptation that allows for more reflective learners to write their responses before sharing with others.
4. Paired Verbal Fluency (P-V-F)	P-V-F is another structure that provides ELLs with oral language practice. It requires students to listen to a buddy speak and then speak themselves in alternating rounds. The entire structure takes only a few minutes but it can be used for a variety of purposes. It can be used as an activator to help students recall previous learning or to connect to learning that will come in today's lesson. It is also effective as a summarizer when students need to check their understanding of a concept, to process and organize new input, or to clarify misunderstandings.

(Continued)

Table 5.2 Interactional Structures   *(Continued)*

Saphier and Haley (1993, p. 45) describe the basic stages of this structure as follows:

Set Up:	Students pair up and identify who is A and who is B in each pair.
Round I:	A speaks for 45 seconds while B listens.
	B speaks for 45 seconds while A listens.
Round II:	A speaks for 30 seconds while B listens.
	B speaks for 30 seconds while A listens.
Round III:	A speaks for 15 seconds while B listens.
	B speaks for 15 seconds while A listens.

At the end of each round, the teacher signals (with a bell or hand clapping) the time, and students switch speakers. P-V-F provides ELLs with one of those rare moments in a classroom—45 seconds of talking time with no interruptions.

5. Paraphrase Passport

Paraphrase Passport is an excellent technique to encourage ELLs to take part in classroom discussions. In our adaptation of Kagan's (1994) structure, a student contributes a response to a teacher's question. The teacher then asks another student in the class: "What did <u>Tony</u> say?" The student called upon must paraphrase or repeat what the prior student has said.

In our experience, students are surprised when we introduce this gambit into discussions. In most cases, they haven't listened to each other's responses. This is a great loss. We can teach our students to listen if we use Paraphrase Passport from time to time during discussions. The value for ELLs is that it provides a model for language and encourages those students to become a part of the instructional conversation.

6. Talking Chips or Talking Tokens

Talking Chips (Kagan, 1994) is another technique for encouraging oral language use. When students work in small groups to solve a problem or answer a question, we give them a certain number of tokens to use during talking time. Each time a student speaks, they must deposit a token in a container in the middle of the table. At the end of the discussion all tokens must be used. In this way, ELLs who are new to the language are encouraged, even required, to say something to their group members.

Kagan describes a simpler form of Talking Chips. He asks each student to put a chip (such as a pen) in the middle of the table when they talk. That student may not speak again until all other students in the group have deposited their chips also. The dominating members of the group are thus controlled from taking talking time away from others.

7. Stir the Class

Stir the Class (Rutherford, 1998, p. 98) is another structure that involves ELLs in oral language interactions. We have seen this structure used with beginning-level learners with good results even though the learners had very little language. Here's how it works: Each student has a sheet of paper. They are asked to write three names, reasons, examples, causes, etc. about the topic under study. At a signal, the students walk around the class collecting ideas from classmates and sharing their ideas. When the teacher calls time, students return to their groups and share their lists with each other. They could prioritize, categorize, or sort the lists if appropriate.

We saw a teacher use this structure in a fifth grade classroom preparing to study the geography of the U.S. The teacher asked students to write the names of three states on their papers. Basra, a newly arrived student, was able to do this with group help. He then walked around and shared information. He was able to participate because the language demands of the task were not high. One thing that was notable was the big smile on Basra's face as he shared his information with fellow students.

How do teachers scaffold oral language learning opportunities in classrooms? Primarily, teachers provide opportunities for ELLs to use the language purposefully and then support that language use. However, simply listening to a new language is not sufficient to be able to learn and use the new language for academic purposes. ELLs need to be able to talk either to their teachers or to their peers about what they are learning. During teacher-student dialogues, teachers may ask students to report to them on what they have read or learned. Open-ended questions are helpful to begin the conversation. They allow ELLs to select the information they will talk about.

Tell me what you know about . . . ?

What did you discover about . . . ?

What did you find out . . . ?

What can you tell me about . . . ?

As ELLs begin to report, their utterances will be filled with false starts and hesitations. At this point, they need time to express themselves adequately. It is difficult to wait in these situations but we need to wait rather than jump in and solve the language dilemma for the student. We can support ELLs through questioning that focuses on the meaning they are trying to convey. Table 5.3 provides an example of scaffolding of oral language for reporting on a science experiment related to floating and sinking objects. In Table 5.3, the teacher slows down the conversation and waits while the student struggles to report what happened when he placed various items in a bowl of water. The teacher's questions accomplish several purposes. They pinpoint the exact area of confusion in the student's language (e.g., "What goes down?"). They model

Table 5.3 Scaffolding a Science Experiment

Commentary	Teacher	Student
The teacher begins the dialogue with an open-ended question.	"What did you find out?"	"If you put a wood in the water . . . it . . . stay up."
The teacher supplies the target vocabulary item "float," restates the student's sentence, and probes for more information.	"The wood floats? Okay. What else?"	"The thing . . . you put the thing . . . and it . . . it go down."
The teacher's question indicates the specific noun needed for communication to continue.	"What goes down?"	"The screw . . . the screw go down in a water."
The teacher provides the vocabulary item "sink," and asks a cause-and-effect question.	"What causes the screw to sink?"	"The screw sink because it . . . too . . . it too . . . screw too . . . "
The teacher provides two choices for the student to select the appropriate word.	"The screw sinks because it's too light or too heavy?"	"Too heavy . . . The screw sink because it too heavy."
The teacher restates the student's sentence while confirming the meaning.	"Yes, the screw is too heavy and so it sinks in the water. What about the wood?"	"The wood light. The wood float because it light."

grammatically correct sentences (e.g., "The wood floats."). They provide the needed content vocabulary to report on the experiment (e.g., "The screw sinks because it's too light or too heavy?"), and they probe for fuller, complete explanations (e.g., "What else? What goes down? What causes the screw to sink?"). The student leads the conversation and is given the time to develop the language he needs to express his knowledge. Scaffolding in this way enables language learning to occur.

Collaborative Dialogues

Teachers can create opportunities for collaborative dialogues in classroom interactions with ELLs by using a pattern of interaction (Simich-Dudgeon, 1998, p. 3) characterized by

- Teacher question
- Student response
- Teacher-facilitated negotiation of meaning, or feedback

In the following interchanges, teachers paraphrase and recast students' responses in an attempt to help learners comprehend and express the academic concept. Note this pattern in the following exchange between a teacher and several students from a lesson on surface tension recorded in a middle school (Chilver & Gould, 1982, as cited in Simich-Dudgeon, 1998, p. 4):

Teacher: *What do you know about it so far?*

Student: *You can have a skin on top of the water.*

Teacher: *A kind of skin on top of the water, but remember it's not a skin like the skin on boiled milk. You can't scrape it up and take it off and leave it on the side of your plate—you can't do that with it. But it is a kind of skin and various insects can make use of it. Think of one insect that makes use of the skin—Michael?*

Michael: *Mosquito.*

Teacher: *Good, a mosquito. How does a mosquito use this skin? Janet?*

Janet: *It lays its larva underneath it.*

Teacher: *Well, yes, the eggs are laid in water and then what happens to the larva? What does the larva do? Well?*

Student: *Hangs from the surface tension on top of the water.*

Teacher: *Good, it hangs from the surface on the water. Why? Why can't it lie under the water altogether? Why does it need to hang from the surface?*

Student: *It would not be able to breathe.*

Teacher: *Yes, it wouldn't be able to breathe. What it does is put a breathing tube up into the air and breathes that way.*

In the above exchange, the teacher clarifies meaning with students regarding the kind of skin they are talking about by providing a negative but practical example. She then prompts students to think of examples of insects and describe ways in which the insects use the skin. When students respond in ways that are general or vague, the teacher continues to use pinpoint questioning to elicit more specific responses (e.g., "What does the larva do?") Even when students are able to describe the larva as "hanging from the surface tension," the teacher continues to prod to determine why that happens.

The teacher's clarity, pinpoint questioning, repetition, and question focus provide learners with both the language and the content learning they need to achieve. We especially appreciate the fact that this conversation represents ways in which teachers can help students use language to analyze, reflect, and think critically. Although occurring in a classroom, the conversation is closer to being a real discussion than to being a lecture. Talk is used to explore ideas and the teacher is responsive to what the students have to say. In many ways, this conversation exhibits many of the attributes of an instructional conversation.

Instructional Conversations.   These conversations are similar to conversations that take place between adults and children outside of school in that they "appear to support children's advancing linguistic and communicative skills" (Rogoff, 1990, p. 157). The social nature of learning described by Vygotsky (1962) is evident here in that the teacher acts as a facilitator who encourages students to produce many different ideas and fosters a great deal of student involvement. Teacher talk is minimized as students are encouraged to share ideas and then guided to an understanding of the focus of the discussion that the teacher has planned ahead of time. There are rarely correct or incorrect answers in these collaborative discussions, nor is there any evaluation by the teacher. Rather, the teacher guides learners to a consensus or a common foundation of understanding (Goldenberg, 1991, 2004).

Some of the instructional elements (Goldenberg, 1991, 2004, p. 7) found in instructional conversations include:

1. Thematic focus for discussion
2. Activation of prior knowledge
3. Direct teaching when necessary
4. Encouragement of complex language and expression
5. Encouragement of students to determine a basis for statements

The conversational elements (Goldenberg, 1991, 2004, p. 7) are:

1. Few display questions where the answer is known to the teacher
2. Teacher responsiveness to student contributions
3. Connected discussion where one utterance builds upon another
4. Challenging, nonthreatening atmosphere
5. General participation with students self-selecting their turns

Because of their collaborative nature and their ability to involve many students in creating understanding of concepts, instructional conversations are very effective vehicles for teachers of ELLs in content-learning classes.

Assessing Oral Language Development

Oral language proficiency can be accelerated when teachers are aware of the level of proficiency attained by the ELLs in their classes. Through frequent observational assessments, teachers can chart student progress and more closely match instructional targets to developing language forms.

The Student Oral Language Observation Matrix (SOLOM) in Table 5.4 is a useful tool for recording observations of ELLs' progress. The SOLOM gives descriptors of

Table 5.4 Student Oral Language Observation Matrix (SOLOM)

	1	2	3	4	5
A. Comprehension	Cannot understand even simple conversation.	Has great difficulty following everyday social conversation, even when words are spoken slowly and repeated frequently.	Understands most of what is said at slower-than-normal speed with some repetitions.	Understands nearly everything at normal speed, although occasional repetition may be necessary.	Understands everyday conversation and normal classroom discussion without difficulty.
B. Fluency	Speech so halting and fragmentary that conversation is virtually impossible.	Usually hesitant; often forced into silence because of language limitations.	Everyday conversation and classroom discussion frequently disrupted by student's search for correct manner of expression.	Everyday conversation and classroom discussion generally fluent with occasional lapses while student searches for the correct manner of expression.	Everyday conversation and classroom discussion fluent and effortless; approximately those of a native speaker.
C. Vocabulary	Vocabulary limitations so extreme that conversation is virtually impossible.	Difficult to understand because of misuse of words and very limited vocabulary.	Frequent use of wrong words; conversation somewhat limited because of inadequate vocabulary.	Occasional use of inappropriate terms and/or rephrasing of ideas because of limited vocabulary.	Vocabulary and idioms approximately those of a native speaker.
D. Pronunciation	Pronunciation problems so severe that speech is virtually unintelligible.	Difficult to understand because of pronunciation problems; must frequently repeat speech in order to be understood.	Concentration required of listener; occasional misunderstandings caused by pronunciation problems.	Always intelligible, although listener conscious of a definite accent and occasional inappropriate intonation pattern.	Pronunciation and intonation approximately those of a native speaker.

Table 5.4 Student Oral Language Observation Matrix (SOLOM)   *(Continued)*

	1	2	3	4	5
E. Grammar	Errors in grammar and word order so severe that speech is virtually unintelligible.	Difficult to understand because of errors in grammar and word order; must often rephrase or restrict speech to basic patterns.	Frequent errors in grammar and word order; meaning occasionally obscured.	Occasional errors in grammar or word order; meaning not obscured.	Grammar and word order approximately those of a native speaker.

Source: California Department of Education, Sacramento (2007).

language behaviors at five different levels. We might relate level 1 of the SOLOM to the Pre-production stage, level 2 to the Early Production stage, level 3 to the Speech Emergence stage, and levels 4 and 5 to the Intermediate Fluency stage.

The SOLOM is useful in that it provides descriptors for five different elements that comprise language development: comprehension, fluency, vocabulary, pronunciation, and grammar. It is not unusual for an ELL to progress quickly in one area, such as pronunciation, but lag behind in another area, such as grammar. The SOLOM helps us to be aware as teachers that there is no single language developing but a plurality of language elements that develop over time.

The authors have used the SOLOM as an assessment tool to record aural-oral progress. We tape-recorded student oral language responses twice during the school year: once in the fall and once in the spring. In the recordings, our ELLs responded to a series of questions designed to elicit a variety of grammar and vocabulary elements. After taping, we charted the results using the SOLOM as a guide. The descriptors for each of the five levels on the SOLOM enabled us to achieve a numerical score for each language component and finally, a total score. In order to improve the usefulness of the scores, we used two teachers to listen and record results for the same students. In that way, we were able to establish a more reliable score.

The information we gain from planned observations and from unplanned observations in a natural classroom setting provides us with a picture of progress that may be more helpful than a numerical score on a standardized test. This is information that we can share with parents, other teachers, and the students themselves. It is a form of feedback not biased by test validity and shows a clear picture of how language is used within the classroom for a variety of different tasks.

Clipboards can be utilized to record informal observations of student language progress during teacher-student dialogues or during small-group work sessions. We like to keep a list of students on our clipboard to carry it with us as we float around the room, questioning, listening, and interacting with a variety of students. With the clipboard in hand, we can quickly make note of progress or jot down an area for future instruction for each of our students. This clipboard also helps us monitor our attention—keeping track of who's had a chance to speak, and who we've helped individually that day.

Student self-assessment is another assessment tool that helps to promote reflection among ELLs as to their skill development. Simple self-assessment instruments can be used to determine the level of comprehension after a science video, the grammaticality of speech following an oral presentation, or comprehension of a reading passage during social studies. Self-assessment is also useful for helping students to reflect on the social skills needed for classroom cooperative work. Self-assessment can become a routine factor in the content classroom and provide additional information to that gathered by the teacher during formal and informal assessments.

Questions for Reflection

1. In many North American classrooms, children spend much of class time listening while the teacher or a few other students talk. Is it your belief that learning is accomplished through listening? Has this been true in most of the learning experiences you have had in school? What should be the appropriate amount of teacher talk versus student talk in a classroom? Does this vary depending on the age of the students? Why? How should the ratio change for English language learning students?
2. This chapter introduces levels of language proficiency that describe ELLs on their way to full language proficiency. Which of these language levels is most difficult for teachers to assess and instruct? Is grade level a factor? Give reasons for your choice.
3. How is learning oral language in a classroom similar to acquiring a first language? Review the suggestions for oral language development in this chapter and relate how these activities promote learning that is similar to the learning processes that occur when children acquire a first language.

Activities for Further Learning

1. ELLs generally proceed through levels of oral language proficiency. Talk to others in your group to determine: What difficulties do these stages present to the classroom teacher? Which level do you find most difficult to teach? What are the specific problems presented at each of these levels? Does the age of the learner affect the difficulty in teaching learners at each of these levels?
2. Work with your group to determine teaching and communication techniques that are effective for ELLs at each of the oral language development levels. It may be useful to think of techniques for very young learners, for those in the intermediate grades, and for those in middle school.
3. Talk to members of your group about the kinds of oral language activities you have experienced in your elementary and middle-school years. Did your teachers engage you in oral presentations, role plays, puppet shows, songs and poetry, debates, or drama? Did your classroom experiences involve a great deal of individualized work? Was the classroom a silent place or were students involved in collaborative learning? How did your experiences affect your own learning? What kinds of classroom activities are most helpful for language learners? Should activities become more individualized as learners move into middle school? Why or why not?

4. What would Vygotsky say about the amount of teacher talk versus student talk in a classroom? When is teacher talk helpful and when does it become harmful to learning? How can student talk be useful to learning? When is student talk not helpful?

5. Observe a classroom teacher and note the kinds of language used in presentations and input to learners. Is there evidence of modeling of academic language? Record that language and be ready to report to the class about it.

6. Review the list of teacher tools for oral language development included in this chapter. Prioritize the list, putting the most useful tools at the top and the least useful at the bottom. Be able to give reasons for your ordering.

7. Observe a teacher in a classroom engaged in a small group discussion and/or learning. Listen to the teacher's language for examples of Questioning and Response tools or Collaborative Dialogues. Record the language that you hear and be ready to report on it in class.

8. Observe an English language learner in a classroom setting where interaction is taking place—either a small group discussion or project work session. Use the SOLOM assessment chart to determine the quality of the child's oral language development. At which language proficiency level would you place this student? Does the child's teacher concur with your assessment?

PEARSON
myeducationlab
Where the Classroom Comes to Life is a collection of online tools for your success in this course, your licensure exams, and your teaching career. Go to www.myeducationlab .com to utilize these extensive resources including videos from real classrooms, Praxis and licensure preparation, a lesson plan builder, and materials to help you in your teaching career.

Suggested Reading

Anstrom, K. (1998). Preparing secondary education teachers to work with English language learners: English language arts. Washington, DC: NCBE Resource Collection Series #10, Center for the Study of Language and Education, the George Washington University. Ideas for incorporating oral language development into secondary literature instruction are presented in this brief report.

Goldenberg, C. N. (1991). Instructional conversations and their classroom application. (Cooperative Agreement No. R117G10022). Washington, DC: Office of Educational Research and Improvement. This short report provides an excellent overview of instructional conversations with practical ideas for application and a rating scale to assess the use of the technique in the classroom. Other more recent Goldenberg citations expand on teaching and learning in classroom settings for ELLs.

Goldenberg, C. N. (2004). *Successful school change: Creating settings to improve teaching and learning.* New York: Teachers College Press.

Goldenberg, C. N. (2006). Improving achievement for English-learners: What the research tells us. *Education Week,* July 26.

Harper, C. & de Jong, E. (2004). Misconceptions about teaching English-language learners. *Journal of Adolescent & Adult Literacy, 48*(2): 153–162. Authors explore four common misconceptions about teaching English language learners and offer recommendations for effective teaching.

Krashen, S. D. (2003). *Explorations in language acquisition and use: The Taipei lectures.* Portsmouth, N.H.: Heinemann. Krashen continues to explore the nature of language acquisition and learning within the classroom context—an update of his classic 1983 work with Terrell.

Rosenshine, B. & Furst, N. (1973). The use of direct observation to study teaching. In R. M. Travers (Ed.), *Second handbook of research on teaching.* Chicago, IL: Rand McNally. This report includes a classic discussion of Clarity—one of nine variables discussed by the authors that correlate to student growth on standardized tests.

Web Sites for Further Learning

Developing Language Proficiency and Connecting School to Students' Lives: Two Standards for Effective Teaching, Center for Research on Education, Diversity and Excellence, Santa Cruz, CA. This report describes the two standards mentioned in the title and gives classroom examples of how to implement them with language learners. Retrieved May 9, 2008.

http://www.cal.org/resources/digest/daltoneric.html

Fostering Second Language Development in Young Children, National Center for Research on Cultural Diversity and Second Language Learning. This report outlines eight principles to guide educators. It refers to the diverse cultural patterns that language learners bring to the classroom and the process of becoming bilingual. Retrieved May 9, 2008.

http://www.cal.org/resources/digest/ncrcds04.html

Region 15 Graphic Organizers. Graphic organizers found on this site are easy to download and use for structured oral activities. They are available in both PDF and Word format, and in Spanish and English. Retrieved May 9, 2008.

http://www.region15.org/curriculum/graphicorg.html

References

Brinton, D. & Mano, S. (1994). "You have a chance also": Case histories of ESL students at the university. In F. Peitzman and G. Gadda (Eds.). *With different eyes: Insights into teaching language minority students across the disciplines* (pp. 1–21). White Plains, NY: Longman.

Cummins, J. (1996). *Negotiating identities: Education for empowerment in a diverse society.* Ontario, CA: California Association for Bilingual Education.

Enright, S. & McCloskey, M. (1988). *Integrating English: Developing English language and literacy in the multilingual classroom.* Reading, MA: Addison-Wesley.

Fillmore, L. W. & Snow, C. E. (2002). What teachers need to know about language. In C. T. Adger, C. E. Snow, and D. Christian (Eds.), *What teachers need to know about language* (pp. 7–53). McHenry, IL: Delta Systems.

Gadda, G. (1994). Writing and language socialization across cultures: Some implications for the classroom. In F. Peitzman and G. Gadda (Eds.), *With different eyes: Insights into teaching language minority students across the disciplines* (pp. 43–56). White Plains, NY: Longman.

Gibbons, P. (2003). Mediating language learning: Teacher interactions with ESL students in a content-based classroom. *TESOL Quarterly, 37:* 247–273.

Goldenberg, C. N. (1991). Instructional conversations and their classroom application. (Cooperative Agreement No. R117G10022). Washington, DC: Office of Educational Research and Improvement.

Goldenberg, C. N. (2004). *Successful school change: Creating settings to improve teaching and learning.* NY: Teachers College Press.

Goodman, K. (1986). *What's whole in whole language?* Portsmouth, NH: Heinemann.

Grognet, A., Jameson, J., Franco, L., & Derrick-Mescua, M. (2000). *Enhancing English language learning in elementary classrooms.* McHenry, IL: Center of Applied Linguistics and Delta Systems.

Harklau, L. (1994). ESL versus mainstream classes: Contrasting L2 learning environments. *TESOL Quarterly, 28*: 241–272.

Heath, S. B. (1983). *Way with words: Language, life, and work in communities and classrooms.* Cambridge, UK: Cambridge University Press.

Heath, S. B. (1986). Sociocultural contexts of language development. In *Beyond language: Social and cultural factors in schooling language minority students.* Los Angeles, CA: Evaluation, Dissemination and Assessment Center, California State University, Los Angeles.

Hernández, H. (1997). *Teaching in multicultural classrooms: A teacher's guide to context, process, and content.* Upper Saddle River, NJ: Merrill.

Herrell, A. L. & Jordan, M. (2007). *Fifty strategies for teaching English language learners* (3rd ed.). Upper Saddle River, NJ: Pearson Education.

Igoa, C. (1995). *The inner world of the immigrant child.* Mahwah, NJ: Lawrence Erlbaum Associates.

Kagan, S. (1994). *Cooperative learning.* San Clemente, CA: Kagan Cooperative Learning.

Krashen, S. D. & Terrell, T. D. (1983). *The natural approach: Language acquisition in the classroom.* San Francisco, CA: The Alemany Press.

Peregoy, S. F. & Boyle, O. F. (2004). *Reading, writing, and learning in ESL: A resource book for K–12 teachers* (4th ed.). Boston, MA: Allyn & Bacon.

Ramirez, J. D., Yuen, S., & Ramey, D. R. (1991). Final report: Longitudinal study of structured English immersion strategy, early-exit and late-exit transitional bilingual education programs for language minority children. (Contract No. 300-87-0156). Washington, DC: U.S. Department of Education.

Rogoff, B. (1990). *Apprenticeship in thinking: Cognitive development in social context.* Oxford, UK: Oxford University Press.

Rutherford, P. (1998). *Instruction for all students.* Alexandria, VA: Just Ask Publications.

Saphier, J. & Gower, R. (1997). *The skillful teacher: Building your teaching skills.* Carlisle, MA: Research for Better Teaching.

Saphier, J. & Haley, M. A. (1993). *Summarizers: Activity structures to support integration and retention of new learning.* Carlisle, MA: Research for Better Teaching.

Schinke-Llano, L. (1980). Foreigner talk in content classrooms. In H. W. Seliger and M. H. Long (Eds.), *Classroom oriented research in second language acquisition* (pp. 146–165). Rowley, MA: Newbury House.

Simich-Dudgeon, C. (1998). Classroom strategies for encouraging collaborative discussion. *Directions in Language and Education, 12:* 1–19.

Student Oral Language Observation Matrix (SOLOM). San Jose Area Bilingual Consortium. Retrieved May 9, 2008. http://www.cal.org/twi/evaltoolkit/appendix/solom.pdf

Teachers of English to Speakers of Other Languages, Inc. (2006). *PreK–12 English language proficiency standards.* Alexandria, VA: TESOL.

Thomas, W. P. & Collier, V. P. (2002). *A national study of school effectiveness for language minority students' long-term academic achievement.* Retrieved May 9, 2008, from http://repositories.cdlib.org/crede/finalrpts/1_1_final/ or http://crede.berkeley.edu/research/llaa/1.1_final.html

Urzua, C. (1981). Talking purposefully. In C. W. Hayes and C. Kessler (Eds.), *The teacher idea series: A practical resource library for second language teachers,* Volume 1. Silver Spring, MD: Institute of Modern Languages.

Vygotsky, L. S. (1962). *Thought and language.* Cambridge, MA: MIT Press.

Wood, D., Bruner, J., & Ross, G. (1976). The role of tutoring in problem solving. *Journal of Child Psychology and Psychiatry, 17:* 89–100.

• •

CHAPTER 6

Oral Language Development in the Content Classroom

Shelly Sanders is a fifth grade science coordinator and classroom teacher at Pelican Bay Elementary School in Florida. All of her students are native Spanish speakers, the children of migrant workers in the citrus industry. Shelly enjoys teaching hands-on science to her students. Today she is teaching a grade-level lesson concerning the components and functions of plant and animal cells. She has chosen a cookie-decorating activity to help her students practice and learn the concepts and language of the lesson.

Shelly places the students into lab groups and asks each group to choose a materials' handler to help her distribute the materials. As the students begin to work, they talk about the project using both English and Spanish. Dayelle's group includes Gustavo, Janet, Arielli, and Victor, a non-English speaking student. Dayelle confers with Gustavo before translating for Victor.

Gustavo says: "The green one is chloroplasts. It goes close to the nucleus." Gustavo checks his science text and then says: "Your nucleus goes in the middle and ours goes on top." Dayelle and Arielli translate the information for Victor. Since the girls have never studied cell structure in Spanish, they don't know the scientific terms in that language. Instead, they use the English terms they are currently learning.

Shelly circulates around the room while the students work. She observes and listens to the group conversations, occasionally asking questions of each group: "If you have an animal cell, are you going to use chloroplasts? If you have a plant cell, will you need vacuoles? Who needs mitochondria?"

When the cookies are complete, Shelly says, "If you have a plant cell, stand in front of the room with your cell." Eleven students come to the front. "Animal cell people, check their cells. Are they correct?" The students check each other and determine that the plant cells are all correct.

"Animal cell people come on up. Now check these. Some of these look different. Why are they different?" Selene volunteers, "That one (pointing) shouldn't have a . . . (Selene checks her chart) a plant vacuole." "That's right," says Shelly, "this cell shouldn't have a plant vacuole because it's a what? That's right; an animal cell. Animal cells don't contain plant vacuoles." Elissa and Justin quickly remove the plant vacuoles from their cells (Lacina, Levine, & Sowa, 2006, pp. 20–21).

What kinds of classroom conditions and activities lead to oral language development in the content areas of the language arts, social studies, math, and science?

- What language requirements are determined by the content areas of language arts, social studies, math, and science?
- What instructional strategies are effective in each of the content areas?
- How can songs, poetry, chants, and raps be used effectively?
- What are the active listening activities that help to foster the development of oral language?

Content Learning and Oral Language Development

In content classrooms, students are introduced to new concepts and language initially through listening to content presentations and interacting with others concerning the content concepts and vocabulary. English language learners (ELLs) need to be included in these aural-oral activities in order to achieve excellence and to develop academic language skills necessary for success. Each of the following four content areas presents challenges and opportunities for English language learners—opportunities to participate in the oral language of the classroom.

Language Arts

A great deal of the content of the language arts curriculum is learned through reading a text. Written texts are difficult to comprehend because the rich context of conversation is missing, vocabulary often difficult, and sentence length longer and of greater complexity than speech. In addition, literacy skills must be in place to access texts.

A wide variety of literature genres appears in the language arts curriculum K through 8. For example, students are taught poetry, biography, personal narrative, drama, short stories, novels, various nonfiction texts, and speeches. In addition, language arts programs include visual and multimedia literacy, and expect learners to access and understand graphic texts, electronic texts, and film or video. Not all of these genres may be prevalent in the cultures of our ELL students. ELLs may come from cultures in which oral storytelling is more prevalent than written narrative. Youngsters from homes where books are not common and where no one has ever read to them, may have limited knowledge of the typical problem/resolution North American story structure. Yet, ELLs need to learn language arts content in spite of their reading skill proficiency and cultural difference. How can teachers teach this content while accelerating academic oral language development?

Storytelling. Storytelling is a good way to help ELLs learn the linear structure of English expository reading and writing. One effective strategy for assisting new learners is reading aloud. Simple, familiar stories including many pictures are best for beginning-level ELLs. Folk tales from other cultures, including those set in and/or written by authors from your learners' culture, provide a familiar context that will engage student interest.

Picture books are useful in helping ELLs to retell an oral story narrative. Some teachers encourage their ELLs to write their ideas on sticky notes, and use these notes and pictures as **scaffolds** when retelling the story in the picture book.

Teachers can model telling stories for their students using specific strategies to communicate meaning and to move the plot. Story elements can be made more explicit by using graphic organizers. Graphic organizers to support storytelling at the simplest level may include organizers for setting, characters, problem, and outcome (see Figure 6.1).

The cyclical nature of a story or event can be illustrated through a cycle chart. These are particularly useful for children's circle stories. *A Pocketful of Opossums* (Almada, Nichols, & O'Keefe, 2004) is one example of an appealing cyclical story that can be graphically represented on a cycle chart.

To emphasize the linear nature of the plot, use a graphic such as that in Figure 6.2. Include pictures in the graphic to assist meaning and embed context into the story elements.

After reading stories to students and charting them on a graphic, demonstrate an oral retelling and ask students to use the graphic as a scaffold when retelling the story

Figure 6.1 Graphic Organizers Create a Visual Image of the Elements of a Story

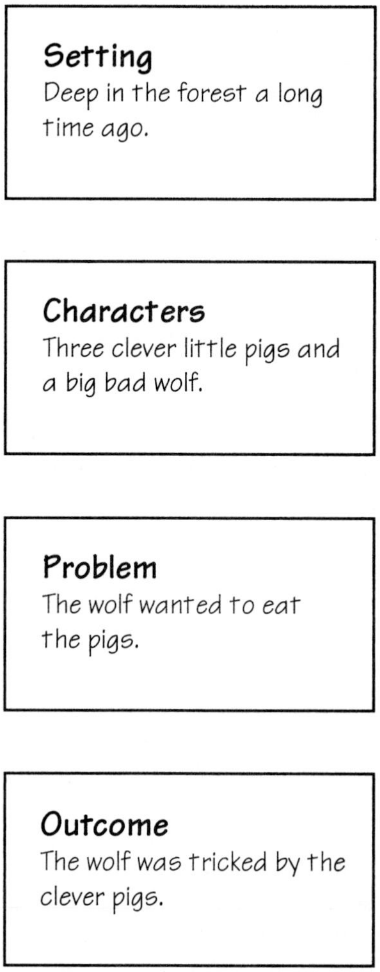

Setting
Deep in the forest a long time ago.

Characters
Three clever little pigs and a big bad wolf.

Problem
The wolf wanted to eat the pigs.

Outcome
The wolf was tricked by the clever pigs.

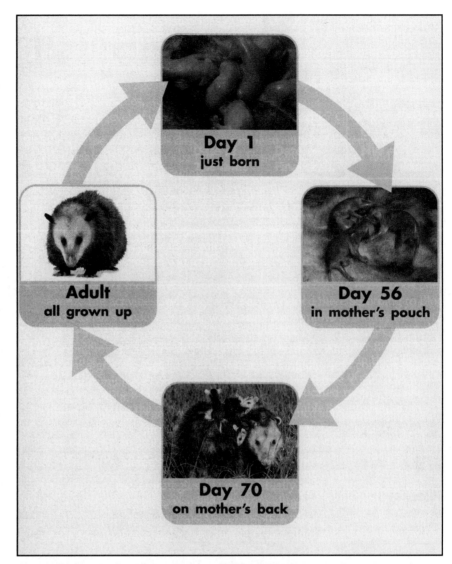

An Example of a Cyclical Story Graphically Represented on a Cycle Chart (from *A Pocketful of Opossums,* Almada, et al., 2004)

to a buddy or to a small group of learners. Inserting signal words of chronology (e.g., *first, next, after a while*) or cause and effect (e.g., *because, so, as a result*) into the graphic will enable students to use these important transition words in their retellings. Later, the same graphics will support a written summary of the story.

Older learners can tell stories about their families, their histories, admired or unusual characters, or immigration stories. Interviewing family members encourages parents to participate in their children's school experiences. Other stories might include tales from the neighborhood or an adventure shared with a friend. You might schedule oral interviews with community members during class time. Before each interview, have the ELLs assist you in developing a list of questions to be asked. Next, ELLs can practice interviewing each other in order to improve their oral questioning skills and to practice note-taking.

The newspaper provides a wealth of material for storytelling. Encourage ELLs to select interesting stories from their city, state, or around the world. Help them to extract critical information from the story and insert it into a graphic organizer (such as the

Figure 6.2 A Graphic Organizer Depicting the Linear Nature of the Story's Plot.

My Story

Setting

Characters

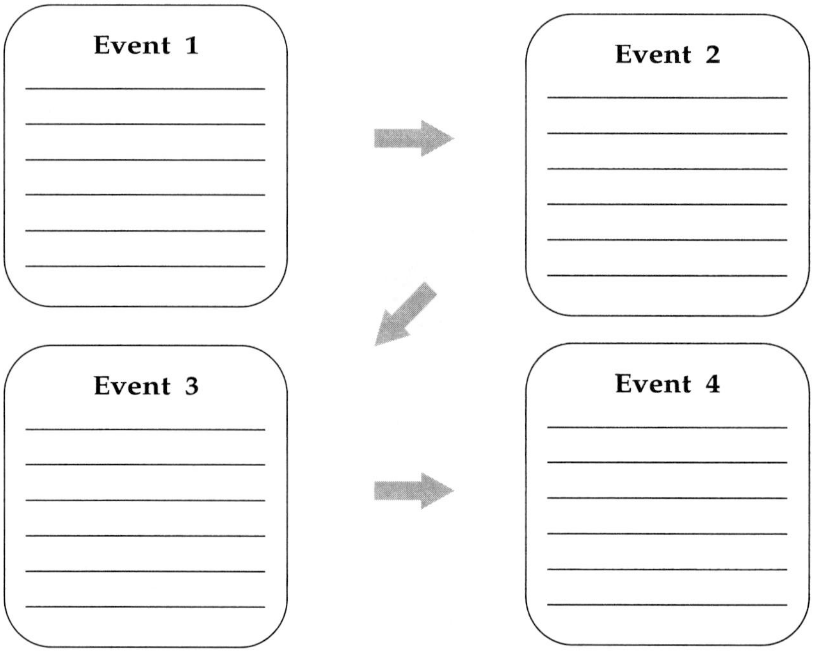

one in Figure 6.1). Important vocabulary can be explained at this time and appropriate signal words chosen for a retelling. The newspaper accounts and the graphics act as scaffolds for the language needed to relate the narratives.

Reader's Theatre. The Reader's Theatre technique (Black & Stave, 2007) offers opportunities to incorporate oral language development into literature study. In this technique, teachers help learners turn a story into a script and then dramatize the action. Even beginning ELLs can learn to comprehend the story and participate in Reader's Theatre in small parts. The teacher supports learners by creating a script (or helping learners to do so), assigning characters, collecting props, and mapping out minimum stage action. Rehearsals provide needed language practice for ELLs with beginning language proficiency. Finally, the production is presented to an audience, perhaps to parents, staff, another class, or the other half of the class.

Literate ELLs can be encouraged to develop a script for the production, the source of the dialogue usually coming from the original story book or folk tale. In this way, all four language skills are integrated into the lesson. New learners are supported in their skill development and benefit from learning about story structure in English.

Social Studies

The social studies present a challenge for English language learners. Textbooks are filled with abstract, multiple-meaning vocabulary and complex, compound sentence forms. Words such as "table," "mean," and "party" take on whole new meanings in a social science context—meanings that are confusing and unfamiliar to ELLs. Passive voice is common while subject referents are often found in the middle (not at the beginning) of sentences. A great deal of the social studies content is intended to be communicated through program materials (textbooks and ancillaries). These texts are usually written at a level that is difficult (sometimes impossible) for ELLs to read.

Historical and geographic referents assumed by the text may be unknown to students. Students educated in other countries will have gaps in their understanding of U.S. government and history. Students with interrupted education will have gaps in their knowledge about social studies of their home countries, as well. Teachers need to carefully probe their students' prior learning—learning that may not have taken place or that is based upon an entirely different curriculum.

Teaching methodology in social studies has sometimes been limited to accessing information in a textbook and answering the questions at the end of the chapter. This style of input and assessment is problematic for ELLs who will not be prepared to comprehend the dense prose of a textbook and unprepared for the principles and concepts contained there. An inability to understand the questions prevents many ELLs from being successful with this teaching style. Fortunately, more contemporary approaches involve student interaction and engagement, and the use of resources, artifacts, and multimedia can make learning relevant and bring it to life.

In addition to these language- and culture-specific problems, teachers must address issues of motivation, and use support and scaffolding strategies to help learners make connections with people of long ago or places they have never seen. How can teachers help ELLs learn the social studies curriculum while acquiring academic oral language skills?

Oral Language and the Textbook. The text is an important learning tool in the social studies classroom, but it is less useful if ELLs are unable to access the information located there. The text can be used, however, for a number of oral language activities that enable ELLs to gradually acquire basic principles, concepts, and academic and technical vocabulary while practicing oral language skills. Activities such as the following take advantage of text graphics:

- Describe what you see in the pictures.
- Describe what you can understand about the charts, maps, and graphs.
- Change the chapter headings into questions. For example, *Volcanoes: What are volcanoes? Where are volcanoes located? Why are volcanoes important?* Try to ask and answer these questions with a buddy.
- Change the chapter subheadings into questions, and ask and answer these with a buddy.
- Ask and try to answer any focus questions found at the beginning of the chapter.
- Tell what you know about the questions at the end of the chapter.
- Find boldfaced or italicized vocabulary, and try to use these words in a sentence or ask a question using the words.

Social studies chapters usually include lists of questions at the end that highlight the important learning in the chapter. These are followed by Application and Expansion activities to help students make connections between the content knowledge and their own prior knowledge and experiences. We suggest that teachers use a strategy called Teach the Text Backward (Center for Applied Linguistics, 1998), beginning with hands-on activities in the application and expansion section and followed by group discussion and perusal of the questions at the end of the chapter. Only then, do students prepare to read the text. Teach the Text Backward progresses from the concrete to the conceptual, from the known to the unknown, and from simple concepts to more difficult ones. The steps for this technique are as follows:

1. Have students complete application and expansion activities at the end of the chapter to help them make connections with the concepts discussed in the chapter.
2. Engage students in discussion of the material, helping them to make explicit their understandings of the major concepts.
3. Enable students to read the questions at the end of the chapter and answer them or make guesses based upon the level of their current understanding.
4. Help students to read and comprehend the text.

Application and expansion activities help students to develop a rudimentary understanding of the underlying concepts in the chapter while making connections to what they already know. For example, in a chapter on immigration, the application activity at the end of the chapter may require students to share some basic facts about their own or their family's immigration history. Students can write the date of their immigration on a large note card and then line up in the classroom in the order of earliest immigration to latest. Students can also tell basic facts of their immigration history such as, *How did you or your ancestors immigrate to the U.S.? Where did you immigrate? Why did you immigrate?* (Students whose ancestors are Native Americans, or students who can't find out when their families arrived might instead tell stories of migration of people of their own ethnic group.) ELLs can be supported in this activity with key sentence frames written on the back of the note card: "My family immigrated from _____." "My family immigrated in _____." "My family came to America by _____." "My family immigrated because _____."

By approaching the text through oral language development, teachers can take advantage of prior knowledge and concrete learning experiences that lead youngsters into new, abstract learning. Their oral language knowledge can be transferred into a written format and the abundant context of the application activities is gradually removed for the more limited context of the printed text.

Oral History.   Because of the reasons above, many teachers are using a teaching approach to social studies that views history as a series of stories. Students link their prior experiences to the curriculum with their backgrounds providing the raw historical data around which the curriculum is structured. Oral history helps students to view themselves and their communities as players on the historical stage (Olmedo, 1993). Because of the oral nature of this learning, ELLs can strengthen their oral language skills while learning content concepts. Oral history relates the students' experiential knowledge, the people and events that have filled their lives, to important social studies concepts and events.

Anstrom (1999, pp. 6–7) provides two examples of relating oral history to students' lives:

1. In preparation for a Civil War unit, ask students about their personal experiences of being different from others in the group. Talk about the fact that these differences can sometimes lead to conflict. Expand the discussion into the political, social, ethnic, and economic differences among people. Relate those

Shared Family Experiences Help Students to See Themselves as Players on the Historical Stage

differences to those existing between the North and the South at the start of the Civil War.
2. For a unit on westward expansion, open with discussion on immigration. Ask language learners to interview their family and/or friends for immigration stories. Relate these in a class discussion to migration patterns to and within the U.S. Ask students to think about how they fit into these patterns as new immigrants to the U.S.

Oral history is best taught within a thematic curriculum structure where topics are studied in depth. Some of the concepts that lend themselves to this approach include: dependence and interdependence, scarcity, migration, acculturation, the impact of change on society, causes and results of war, rights and responsibilities of citizenship, climactic change and the economy, and lifestyles of specific peoples (National Council for the Social Studies Task Force, 1989).

Olmedo (1993, p. 9) has the following suggestions for getting started when teaching oral history:

1. *Identify the concept* you will teach. Make sure that it is grade appropriate and based upon the scope and sequence of the social studies text.
2. *Preview an interview guide* that your students can use to collect the data necessary for the unit. Your students will benefit from constructing the guide with you, suggesting questions, and manipulating question structures.
3. *Translate the guide,* have students translate it, or use the foreign language teachers in your school to help you put the questions into the native languages of the students. Note: Free online translators such as Babelfish (http:// babelfish .altavista.com) are available for many languages. Though these translators are

not yet able to produce clear and accurate text, they can translate many words and help those speaking that language to gain a general understanding of the text. They can also give a head start to a translator. Over-the-phone translations are also available for a fee (e.g., http://www.languageline.com/, which is available for 150 languages).

4. *Practice and record interviews* before sending students into the field. They will need experience in note taking as they interview, using the tape recorder, and being familiar with the questions.

5. *Invite guest speakers* to be interviewed by the class. Record these interviews and help the students to transcribe them afterwards.

6. *Select an interviewee* for students to question. Older relatives are excellent resources. If not available, look for community or church members. Search various institutions, such as hospitals and work sites. Remember that not all ELLs will have family members who are still alive or who are living in this country.

7. *Assign tasks* for students such as interviewing, recording, transcribing, summarizing, or reporting to the class.

8. *Select themes* from the oral interviews that match the concepts in the social studies curriculum and present these to the class.

9. *Compare and contrast experiences* among the interviewees and relate these experiences to readings based upon the experiences of historical figures. Find the similarities and differences among both groups of people.

Our experience with oral history in the upper elementary and middle-school grades was very rewarding. Our ELLs were highly motivated to tell their stories to each other and later to write these stories for a class book. When the local radio station asked for people to submit their immigration stories for a special immigration week, we encouraged our students to send theirs. The children were invited to the radio station to record their stories, which were later aired on the radio.

Dialogues.   The social studies curriculum lends itself to prepared dialogue presentations among and between ELLs of various language proficiencies. Teacher-prepared dialogues conform to the content learning objectives of the lesson but are presented in a familiar context of a conversation. ELLs can practice these dialogue role plays in preparation for presentation to the entire class. The activity aids in oral language development as well as content learning. Audience members may be prompted to ask questions of the presenters in order to engender more attentive listening, or the teacher may ask questions of the audience to recap the material presented in the dialogue.

Dialogues can be differentiated for language levels and can be structured to include important grammatical elements such as past tense verbs and question forms, adverbial clauses, and complex sentences.

Examples of dialogues might include:

*   Antony explaining his conquests to Cleopatra.
*   Lewis and Clark's conversation while planning their expedition.
*   Two citizens of Boston observing the Boston Tea Party.
*   Rosa Parks talking to her husband after her arrest for civil disobedience.

Math

Mathematics has a language of its own. The language is specific (definite), precise (clearly expressed), and logical. Indeed, the National Council of Teachers of Mathematics (NCTM) included math communication as one of its five goals for all students (NCTM 200, 2006). Math assessment is often dependent on knowledge of specific math vocabulary (e.g., *minuend* and *subtrahend*) as well as on the text structures used to communicate mathematically, most obviously in word problems. Consider the following problem:

Number *a* is five less than number *b*. Express the equation for this problem.

Students who have learned that the words "less than" have a specific mathematical meaning and are familiar with the syntax of equations might correctly express the above equation as:

$$a = b - 5$$

An ELL might use the phrase "less" as it appears in a nonmathematical sentence context and express the equation incorrectly as:

$$a = 5 - b$$

Factors Affecting Achievement.   There are a variety of factors influencing the math achievement of ELLs. The level of English language development is an obvious one. An intermediate level of English is necessary for understanding most math word problems. The age of the learner, including developmental level, is a factor. More importantly, however, is the amount of previous learning the ELL has acquired in math.

When Dulce entered our school, she had never been to school before. Although she was placed in the third grade because of her age, she was way behind the other children in language, literacy, and math. Dulce could not participate in the third grade math class until she acquired some basic math skills and language. She needed tutoring in number recognition and naming, counting and grouping. She had to learn basic math symbols such as =, −, +, < and >. She needed to learn the language that clustered around these symbols:

Two plus three equals five.

Five minus two equals three.

Five is greater than three.

Three is less than five.

Dulce was able to learn these concepts fairly quickly because she was eight years old rather than five. Older learners, although they need to learn the basics, will acquire them more quickly than younger learners because they are cognitively more mature. It is important that teachers are aware of students' prior learning so that the gaps in learning can be filled and students can begin to participate in grade-level appropriate instruction.

Another factor affecting achievement is the difficulty of the material. Math is cumulative and, as students advance in school, the amount of math knowledge they are required to know increases while new skills build upon ones previously learned.

Some teachers are surprised to see that ELLs who have been educated in a native language in another country sometimes surpass North American curriculum standards for math. These advanced students are able to compute at a higher level but may not be able to express their thinking and communicate it to others. And so, the ability to convey ideas to others is a factor in their achievement. Some of our ELLs conveyed their thinking in a nonverbal way through computation on the board. It was interesting to us to see that not all math computation is done in the same way. Division, for example, is taught differently in other countries and yet the answers are the same. When ELLs have opportunities to show what they know in math, we empower their learning and prompt them to achieve more.

A final important factor in math achievement is the amount of primary language support children receive for their math learning. In schools with bilingual programs, ELLs are taught in their native languages until they understand the concepts. At that point they transition their knowledge into English. Those ELLs who are taught math in a second language will be at a disadvantage. However, many families are eager to provide support for their children's learning, and math is one area where parents can support school instruction through the use of the native language. We encourage parents to incorporate math concepts into daily life at the elementary level. Telling time, counting, measurement, money, and basic math operations (addition, subtraction, multiplication, and division) are appropriate at this level. Upper elementary and middle-school students can be included in discussions of sales percentages, nutritional components of food, interest payments, and car lease agreements. These math-related topics can be seen to affect the daily life of the family and gain in importance as learners see their families using math to make decisions.

Instructional Techniques for Math Class.   Techniques for teaching math to ELLs are also useful in teaching math to all learners. One of the differences will be found in the emphasis on extensive oral and written language practice needed to communicate mathematical reasoning. Specifically, students will need to learn the following oral skills (Buchanan & Helman, 1993, p. 8):

1. Responding to questions
2. Initiating questions
3. Using English to discuss math
4. Using math vocabulary and grammar
5. Explaining mathematical reasoning

Teachers will need to teach not only the language required by the math objective but also any additional language skills required for communication. For example, when teaching Dulce the symbols < and >, it was also necessary to teach her the comparative use of the term "greater than." To help Dulce remember these, the teacher helped her visualize a hungry alligator that always tried to eat the larger number (shown in Figure 6.3).

When teaching the processes required for a subtraction problem, it will be necessary to teach learners the use of words such as *first, next, then, finally* and other words that signal the steps needed to solve a problem. Word problems often require the use

Figure 6.3 Visuals Help Children Internalize Concepts Such as "Less Than" and "Greater Than"

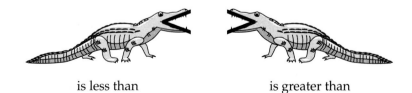

is less than   is greater than

Figure 6.4 Students Can Better Recall the Problem Solving Process If the Steps Are Displayed Prominently

How to Solve a Math Problem in Four Steps
1. Try to understand the problem.
   - Explain it using your own words.
   - Find the important information.
   - Draw a picture.
   - Make an estimate.
2. Determine how to solve the problem.
   - Look for signal words that signal addition, subtraction, multiplication, or division.
   - Look for a pattern between this problem and others you have solved.
   - Break the problem into parts.
   - Write a math sentence.
3. Solve the problem.
   - Record your work carefully and neatly.
4. Check the work.
   - Do the calculations again.
   - Use the proper label (feet, dollars, pounds, etc.).
   - Work the problem backwards.

of the question words *how much* and *how many*. Students choose the appropriate question depending on whether they are working with mass nouns or count nouns.

Presentation techniques in the math class include "think aloud" modeling of the thought processes for problem solving. The overhead projector is a useful tool when teachers need to talk about the steps of problem solving while presenting the steps visually for students. Wall charts with sample problems, solutions, steps needed for problem solving, and math terminology are also helpful for making math reasoning visible to students (as shown in Figure 6.4).

Building on a student's prior experience is especially helpful in math that is cumulative and sequential. Different cultures use different algorithms for solving math problems, and learners may have acquired correct processes and solutions for problem solving that are different from those taught in our schools. We need to look carefully at our learners' work and listen to what they have to say before we assume their work is in error. If, through this process, teachers discover gaps in learning, it may be necessary to modify learning objectives and to differentiate learning in order to help students achieve in the math class.

When Jorge entered our fifth grade math class, we discovered that he didn't know multiplication tables past five. This slowed down his learning as he attempted to count on his fingers whenever a calculator was not available. Tutoring in multiplication, along with opportunities to listen frequently to a recording of multiplication fact songs, soon caught him up to the rest of his peers. Jorge needed a variety of techniques to learn multiplication tables in a new language. Flash cards, multiplication charts, and learning to count by six, seven, and so on, were all helpful as well. The biggest help was a learning buddy who practiced daily with him for short periods.

Effective math teachers relate their learning objectives to the daily lives and interests of their students. Our students always enjoyed learning word problems related to decimal placement by using menus from popular fast food shops. Our older middle school and high school students enjoyed using information related to car purchases, online shopping, and sports statistics.

Though there is occasional controversy regarding math methods, current practice recommended by the NCTM includes frequent use of manipulatives prior to paper and pencil tasks. Even older learners benefit from the use of manipulatives, models, and visuals to help foster comprehension. We saw one teacher use a drink can very effectively to help learners understand the formula for the volume of a cylinder (Figure 6.5). The students had learned a formula for the area of a circle ($\pi \times r^2$). Then the teacher showed a drink can and asked how they could use that formula to determine the volume of the can. The students realized that the shape of the can is similar to a series of disks piled one on top of the other. They said, "If we could measure the area of a series of disks that were 1 cm high, we could combine them to find the answer." The teacher asked the students to measure the height of the can and then told them they had discovered the formula they needed: $\pi \times r^2 \times h$.

Note how the drawing of the can clarifies the process. Drawing pictures to represent a word problem or concept is another helpful tool to assist comprehension of the language of the problem. Effective teachers draw simple, illustrative pictures while reading the problem aloud, emphasizing, clarifying, and scaffolding the acquisition of mathematical terminology and concepts. Practice continues as ELLs create their own drawings and use the drawings to explain the problem orally to a math buddy. Pictures assist learners in forming the mental images that provide context for problem solving in a new language.

The next step in problem solving is to determine which operation is necessary to solve the problem. Isolating the signal words for math operations helps to determine how to proceed with the problem. We like the graphic organizer for math operations shown in Figure 4.3 in Chapter 4. When teachers display this necessary vocabulary on the bulletin boards, ELLs can access it to determine which math operations are appropriate.

Students themselves can be used to demonstrate math problems. To illustrate a number sentence in addition (e.g., $3 + 2 = 5$), the teacher can have three boys stand up, who are then joined by two girls. The reversed algorithm ($2 + 3 = 5$) can be demonstrated by presenting two girls joined by three boys. Children will see that the total is the same in both versions. There are many ways to make math personal. Learners can make graphs of their own hair and eye colors using pictures of themselves, or chart their improvement in typing speed using ratios. Learning new concepts in this way is motivating to students and results in better comprehension and efficient learning.

Figure 6.5 A Drink Can Is Used to Help Students Determine the Formula for the Volume of a Cylinder

Figure 6.6 A Place Value Chart Enables Students to Read Numerals Correctly

Place Value Chart

	thousands	hundreds	tens	ones
45			four	five
873		eight	seven	three
3,279	three	two	seven	nine
8,930	eight	nine	three	zero

Small-group work is essential in math class to help learners generate the negotiation of meaning needed to develop language and to communicate and reason in English. Our fifth grade math students practiced choral recitations of large denominations of money (e.g., "three hundred fifty seven dollars and eighty two cents") before they learned to spell and write the numbers. Middle school students will also need to practice the reading of numbers written in scientific notation:

$8.3 \times 10^3 = 8,300$

Eight point three times ten to the third power equals eight thousand three hundred.

Working together, students can check one another's work, create word problems, explain how to solve problems, report to the teacher, dictate numerals, and practice the vocabulary of math, or keep a log of new math processes and the explanations that they have learned.

Charts, graphic organizers, and visuals or drawings are useful in helping ELLs comprehend mathematical thinking. When teaching place value and the position of digits, use a place value chart such as that shown in Figure 6.6. The chart will help students to read the numbers correctly. When learning the characteristics of triangles, use visuals or geoboards (Figure 6.7) to help ELLs describe each triangle orally using math vocabulary (like words such as "sides" and "congruency").

Figure 6.7 Visuals Support the Oral Descriptions of Three Types of Triangles

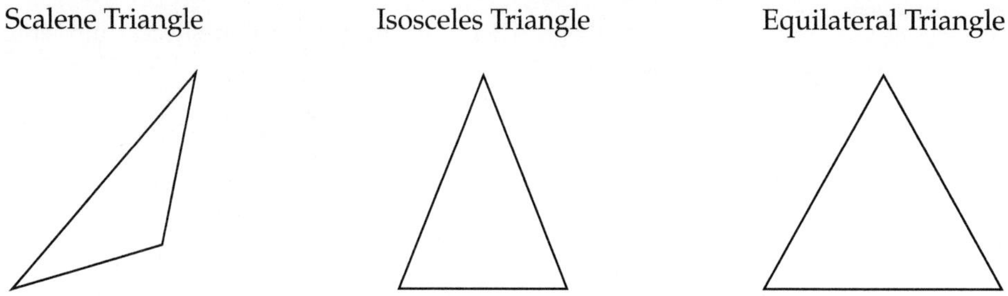

Scalene Triangle   Isosceles Triangle   Equilateral Triangle

Figure 6.8 An Activity for Organizing Fractions by Size (Short, 1991)

$$2\ 1/2 + 13/4 =$$

$$5/2 + 13/4 =$$

$$10/4 + 13/4 =$$

$$2\ 3/4 =$$

$$5\ 3/4 =$$

Video Exercise

Scaffolding for Math Problem Solving

Go to MyEducationLab, select the topic **Academic Language Development,** and watch the video entitled **"Scaffolding for Math Problem Solving"** to observe a teacher working with young learners to develop skills in math problem solving. Complete the questions that accompany it. You may print your work or have it transmitted to your professor as necessary.

The 100s Board helps beginning math students understand basic number concepts such as *even/odd*, and counting by twos, fives, or tens. Cuisenaire rods, dice, and multilink cubes are also helpful in counting. Some numbers are "close confusers" (numbers with similar pronunciation, e.g., 13 and 30, 14 and 40, 15 and 50). ELLs may need a great deal of practice to learn to hear the small differences in pronunciation between the numbers in each pair.

Oral language reporting is an important part of small-group work in math. ELLs can be grouped to work on tasks and then be asked to report orally on the results. For example, when teaching addition of fractions, students can convert to the lowest common denominator, add the numbers together, and organize the math sentence strips into the appropriate order from the largest to the smallest number, as shown in Figure 6.8.

Individual group members, holding the sequenced strips, can read the fractions aloud and ask other class members if they agree with the order they have chosen. Similar tasks include sequencing fractions on a **semantic gradient,** as in Figure 6.9.

Successful achievement in math involves ELLs in:

- Joint problem solving
- Communication of math reasoning (oral and then written form)
- Developing and using the language of mathematics
- Making connections to daily life

When these criteria are met, ELLs can successfully enter the classroom math conversation.

Science

Children are curious about and drawn to scientific investigation. Many of the questions they ask about the world focus on the world of science. The motivation to learn science is an excellent basis for the development of the mental skills and academic language so essential for further achievement. Also, science is best done in the way that children

Figure 6.9 An Activity for Sequencing Fractions on a Semantic Gradient

Sequence the fractions in order from the largest to the smallest.

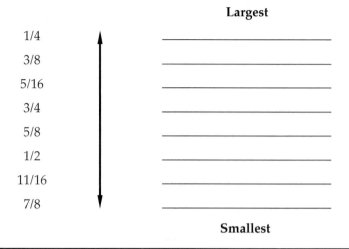

Largest

1/4

3/8

5/16

3/4

5/8

1/2

11/16

7/8

Smallest

most enjoy learning—in a "hands-on" manner. Reading about science is not the same as "doing" science. ELLs need not be prevented from learning by their inability to read dense pages of scientific discourse. Rather, they can engage in processes of questioning, observing, measuring, organizing information, making predictions, and drawing conclusions within a social framework of talk: questions, giving directions, sharing, and comparing information. Such experiential learning provides the context necessary for comprehension of scientific concepts and academic language. The group nature of the inquiry provides scaffolding that supports further achievement.

The National Science Education Standards (NSES), under the auspices of the National Research Council (1996), emphasize the theme of "Science for All." The goal is scientific literacy for all learners. The nature of scientific literacy can be summarized by the NRC definition (NRC, 1996). All students need to be taught to:

- Make observations
- Ask questions
- Investigate solutions
- Communicate results

In the process of engaging in hands-on scientific inquiry, ELLs also learn metacognitive and cognitive skills needed for future learning: questioning, observing, recording information, predicting results, hypothesizing, gathering and organizing data, documenting positions, analyzing, and concluding. These skills are so critical to academic achievement that it would be difficult to imagine a learner being successful in school without their mastery.

Factors Affecting Achievement.   The factors that affect math achievement also affect achievement in science:

- Previous learning
- Age and developmental level
- Level of English

- Difficulty level of the material
- Ability to understand and communicate ideas symbolically
- Native language support

Teachers should be aware that previous science instruction in another country may not be similar to the science taught in North American schools. For this reason alone, it's important to activate ELLs' prior knowledge as much as possible to determine what learners already know, as well as any inconsistencies, knowledge lags, or misunderstandings.

It will be more difficult to instruct those ELLs who have had little or no previous science instruction in grade-level appropriate skills and knowledge. Resources in the home language, including written materials and multimedia, and opportunities to speak and work with speakers of the language are very useful in helping ELLs understand new concepts. Parents with some science background might be helpful in home language discussion of basic science concepts. Teachers can also scaffold the development of science language and concepts through demonstrations, drawings with labeled vocabulary, science lab sheets formatted for easy comprehension, science vocabulary notebooks, word walls, graphic organizers that visually display processes and procedures, and a variety of vocabulary learning activities.

Instructional Techniques for Science Class.   Many of the same general techniques used to teach math are also helpful in teaching inquiry-based science.

- Modeling and/or demonstrating procedures, products, and processes.
- Initiating small-group work that integrates experiential learning and oral reporting which is highly effective for language development.
- Building new learning on the ELLs' prior experience and knowledge.
- Using real objects or models as much as possible

The oral language skills of comprehending, answering and asking questions, communicating scientific information, explaining scientific concepts, and using specialized vocabulary are also comparable to those required for math learning. In the following section, we will describe instructional techniques that are specific to science instruction, and serve the dual function of developing scientific thinking and concepts while encouraging the production of oral language skills related to scientific inquiry.

1. Use visuals—charts, diagrams, and drawings—that contain important information that can be labeled. ELLs who excel in visual representation can offer their drawings as models for the class. Sample tasks include:

   - Draw a group of simple machines and label them.
   - Draw the layers of the Earth and label them.
   - Draw a picture illustrating the process of evaporation. Label the parts and describe the process using the picture as a guide.
   - Use maps and globes for demonstrations and blank maps that students can color code for temperature, rainfall, and so on.
   - Use various graphic organizers to record the stages in the life cycle of various creatures: frogs/toads, butterflies, and so on. Label each stage. Describe how changes occur at each stage.
   - Create tree diagrams of food categories, microbes, and so on. Report to the class giving examples of each category.
   - Complete a flow chart that describes the process of sound transmission. Label each stage in the process and describe the process to the class.

2. Use graphs and charts that contain descriptive information as a resource for language development. Provide key questions on the screen or chalkboard to help students ask and answer questions using the chart. For example:

   - How tall is the ____tree? It's _____ feet tall.
   - How much does a _____ weigh? A _____ weighs _____ pounds.
   - What does the symbol __ stand for? The symbol __ stands for _____.
   - In what state can _____ be found? _____ can be found in _____.
   - Is _____ a metal or a non-metal? _____ is a metal.
   - What is _____ used for? _____ can be used for _____ and _____.
   - What does a/an _____ measure? A/an _____ measures _____.
   - How is _____ measured? _____ is measured in _____.

3. Walk learners through the scientific method. Design simple experiments that require ELLs to work in small groups to observe and record data. Model talking about and proceeding through the steps:

   - State the problem or question.
   - Form an educated guess (hypothesis) of the cause of the problem and make predictions for results based upon the hypothesis.
   - Test your hypothesis by doing an experiment or study (with proper controls).
   - Check and interpret your results.
   - Report your results to the scientific community.

4. Help learners to design and implement experiments and then to report orally to the class on their results. For example:

   - Throw a ball into the air. Count how many seconds it takes to fall to the ground. Record the time. Estimate the height of the throw. Record the height. Report your data to the class. What can you predict about a ball thrown 50 feet into the air? Five feet?
   - Record your buddy's pulse beat in minutes on a chart for three situations: resting, after walking for two minutes, after running for two minutes. Switch places. Report your results to the class.
   - Estimate your buddy's height, foot length, and arm length. Record the estimates on a chart. Measure the lengths using a ruler. Record on a chart. Switch places. Report your results to the class.
   - Line a shoe box with white paper. Line another shoe box with black paper. Place a glass of water into both boxes and put them in direct sunlight. Hypothesize about which box will make the water hotter. After two hours measure the temperature of the water. Record your results and report to the class.

5. **Sort tasks** of various kinds reinforce scientific concepts and help to teach vocabulary. ELLs can sort words by writing them in two columns or by arranging word cards into two groupings. The second method is appropriate for pairs of young learners or any student who enjoys manipulating objects in order to learn. For example:

   - Sort animal names (or pictures of animals) into two groups: warm blooded/cold blooded or vertebrate/invertebrate. Compare with others in your group and give reasons for your choices.
   - Sort igneous/sedimentary/metamorphic rocks into three groups. Compare and give reasons for your choices.

Video Exercise

Scaffolding for Science Concept Learning

Go to MyEducationLab, select the topic **Academic Language Development,** and watch the video entitled **"Scaffolding for Science Concept Learning"** to observe a science lesson with cooperative learning groups. Complete the questions that accompany it. You may print your work or have it transmitted to your professor as necessary.

- Sort all the food eaten by group members in the last two days into seven food groups. Compare with others in your group. What conclusions can you come to about your group's choices?
- Sort pictures of animal feet, paws, hooves, or teeth into categories. How do the feet and the teeth help the animal?

6. Use new learning about science concepts to create rap songs that can be performed for the entire class.

As each of these suggestions indicates, scientific inquiry in the classroom is achieved through the following:

- Asking questions;
- Forming hypotheses;
- Investigating solutions;
- Communicating results.

Science and math are related in their concern for all four elements as well as in the strategies used to teach and promote language competency.

Oral Language Development Every Which Way

The content subject areas provide excellent opportunities for oral language development in classrooms. There are other ways in which ELLs can grow in their language skills, however, and creative teachers use these techniques at all grade levels and within the context of content learning.

Songs and Chants/Poetry and Rap

Music is motivating to many learners. The rhythms of songs and chants entice ELLs to want to participate in group efforts even though their oral language skills are limited. We have observed new learners who memorize rap songs and television jingles because of their infectious rhythms and melodies. These songs are often memorized in "chunks" of language that are unanalyzed by learners on a word-for-word basis. The meaning is understood in a global way but ELLs may be unaware of exactly how many words make up the lyrics or what the individual words mean.

This kind of learning is helpful to ELLs for a few reasons. It gets them into the language immediately, using it for a pleasurable purpose. As such, they often join with others in singing or chanting, and feel a part of the group. In this way, they are eased into the pronunciation, intonation, and rhythms of the new language. Eventually, ELLs will begin to analyze the songs, at a time when they can better comprehend the meaning. At that point, they will often use these chunks of language in their productive speech for communicative purposes.

At the early elementary level, songs are used with hand motions that express the meaning of the song. In this way basic concepts of up/down, over/under, right/left, in/out, and so on, can be taught. We think it's important to incorporate this kind of music into classrooms of diverse learners—even if the teacher is not skilled in singing. The songs bring unity to the class and create a happy feeling among the learners. In addition, real language can be learned in this way. We were always amazed at the amount of language learned by elementary second grade ELLs who participated in our school's chorus. In spite of the complexity of some of this music, the children were able to perform with gusto, acquiring a great deal of academic language along the way.

Many teachers use songs and chants to reinforce classroom learning. We have seen social studies teachers use chants to reinforce lessons of history. Some of these teachers told us that they use commercially produced materials that help ELLs to sing about the American Revolution or the Boston Tea Party. Other teachers have used music, and specifically rap, to help learners memorize information such as the periodic table of the elements. Sue Quinn and Joann Fusare-White from Roth Middle School in Henrietta, New York, use music to help their students memorize mathematical formulas. Some examples of formulas, which are sung to the tune of "Wheels on the Bus," are (as cited in Rutherford, 1998, p. 122):

For *perimeter* of a figure you add the sides,
Add the sides, add the sides.
For *perimeter* of a figure you add the sides
All the way around!

Circumference of a circle is $\pi \times d$, $\pi \times d$, $\pi \times d$.
Circumference of a circle is $\pi \times d$. π is 3.14!

Area of a rectangle is length × width,
Length × width, length × width.
Area of a rectangle is length × width
Only for this shape!

Even without writing musical notation, teachers can take advantage of this technique through the use of rhythmic chants to reinforce learning. A chant is similar to a rap but doesn't necessarily include rhyming. Each statement is said to a rhythmic beat accompanied by toe tapping or finger snapping. Various elements of language can be learned in this way. Imagine the following question and answer format chanted in chorus with one-half of the class asking the questions and the other half answering in a rapid and rhythmic two-beat-per-line cadence:

Group A: *What's the Constitution?*

Group B: *It's the law of the land.*

Group A: *When was it written?*

Group B: *In 1787.*

Group A: *What does it state?*

Group B: *That we are a nation of checks and balances.*

Group A: *Checks and balances.*

Group B: *With three main branches.*

Group A: *Three main branches.*

Group B: *To govern the land.*

Group A: *How many branches?*

Group B: *Three main branches.*

Group A: *What's the first branch?*

Group B: *The legislative branch.*

Group A: *What's the second branch?*

Group B: *The executive branch.*

Group A: *What's the third branch?*

Group B: *The judicial branch.*

Group A: *The legislative branch.*

Group B: *That's the first branch.*

Group A: *The executive branch.*

Group B: *That's the second branch.*

Group A: *The judicial branch.*

Group B: *That's the third branch.*

Group A: *Three main branches.*

Group B: *Three main branches.*

Group A: *Who's in charge of the legislative branch?*

Group B: *The Congress. The Congress.*

Group A: *Who's in charge of the executive branch?*

Group B: *The President. The President.*

Group A: *Who's in charge of the judicial branch?*

Group B: *The Supreme Court. The Supreme Court.*

Teacher and students together can create chants and display them on the wall or board, or provide copies for each student. Performances could be formally presented to other classes or informally practiced in class when a break in routine is needed. Literate learners in small groups could be called upon to write chants as a way of summarizing learning. This is a novel form of assessment that appeals to diverse student learning styles.

The motivations for poetry and rap are similar to songs and chants. Students enjoy these forms of expression. Adolescents, in particular, are drawn to the rap style. The difference between the two techniques is that poetry and rap tend to be more stylized and often use rhyming. These techniques can be explored in much the same way as songs and chants, and can be related directly to content learning.

Presenting a poem, a song, a chant, or a rap is best done within a meaningful context. We like to write the poem or song on a large sheet of chart paper and include rebus pictures or drawings to indicate unknown words. We read the poem to our ELLs with enthusiasm and emotion, and invite them to join us in subsequent readings. We have found it helpful to reproduce these writings for students to include in poetry/song/chant books that they make and illustrate with their own pictures.

One teacher we know selects and creates a poetry month to encourage all of her students to carry a "Poem in Your Pocket." Each student chooses a favorite poem and carries that poem in a pocket. All of the other teachers and students in the school can ask to hear any of these poems throughout the month. They get many repeated readings as others in the school join in the fun of poetry sharing. The ELLs in this classroom benefit from the repetitions of the poetry and the communicative nature of the task.

Role Plays, RAFTs, and Simulations

Role plays are excellent tools for providing oral language practice of subject matter content. There are a variety of ways to include role play into classroom learning but basically, teachers we have observed have used student made role plays or teacher prepared role plays. The advantage of writing a role play for ELLs to perform is that teachers can be sure to include in the role play the language and concepts that are important to the unit. This takes time, however, and when presented to students, can be seen as only a script to follow with little learner investment.

When ELLs write their own role plays, they become more invested in the activity. The role play also works as an assessment of learning. Teachers can see what students have taken from the learning unit as the role play unfolds. Careful planning is needed to be sure that students are successful in their role plays. It is best if the writing is done in small groups and if the teacher presents a **RAFT** (Role Audience Form Time) to guide the writing. A RAFT is a type of role play whereby the teacher creates a scenario about the content being studied (Rutherford, 1998). The teacher assigns a role to the students, determines an audience, a format for the presentation, and a time frame. For example:

- You are a newspaper reporter (role and audience). Your job is to interview (form) Meriwether Lewis, William Clark, and Sacagawea as they reach the Pacific Ocean on November 17, 1806 (time) after exploring the territory between the Mississippi River and the Pacific Ocean. Be sure to determine from each person which aspects of the trip were most momentous for them.
- You are a cloud seeder (role). Your job requires you to fly an airplane, seeding the clouds to promote rainfall for a spring crop (time). Write a presentation (form) that you will give to a group of drought-ridden farmers (audience) explaining the rain cycle and how you will help them to get rain. Answer their questions and convince them to hire you.
- You are a doctor in the local hospital (role and time). Your patient has a heart problem but doesn't understand how the heart is involved in circulation. Role-play an office visit where you explain (form) the system to your patient (audience).

These role plays can be presented within the classroom or to another class of students. They can be copied for each student to read and preserved in a book of role plays created by the class.

Simulations are similar to role plays but in the former, the teacher structures the learning more concretely for learners. For example, students might be asked to set up a store in the classroom and then assume the roles of the clerk and the customer. Some teachers encourage students to write the script for these simulations. This is often done when the simulation is based upon a story read in class, a fairy tale, or a retelling of an event in history.

Potential products for simulations, role plays, and RAFTs are limitless. Students can express their learning in many ways other then through paper and pencil tasks. A quick run through the alphabet can highlight at least 26 products for learning:

1.	Advice column	**7.**	Greeting card
2.	Banner	**8.**	Hand puppet
3.	Comedy act	**9.**	Interview
4.	Documentary	**10.**	Jingle
5.	Eyewitness account	**11.**	Kite
6.	Flannel board	**12.**	Letter to the editor

13.	Mnemonic	**20.**	Tall tale
14.	Nursery rhyme	**21.**	UFO
15.	Owner's manual	**22.**	Venn diagram
16.	Puzzle	**23.**	Web page
17.	Quilt	**24.**	X-ray
18.	Radio commentary	**25.**	Yearbook
19.	Slide show	**26.**	Zodiac chart

WebQuests

A **WebQuest** is an inquiry-oriented lesson format in which most or all the information that learners work with comes from the web. The model was developed by Bernie Dodge at San Diego State University in 1995 with early input from SDSU/Pacific Bell Fellow Tom March, the Educational Technology staff at San Diego Unified School District, and waves of participants each summer at the Teach the Teachers Consortium. Information and a database of WebQuests by other teachers as well as products by learners can be found at www.WebQuest.org. The web site allows teachers to access Web Quests on a wide variety of content topics. Once found, those topics are identified by content area and grade level. Each WebQuest is further divided into an Introduction, Task, Process, Evaluation (with completed rubrics), Conclusion, Credits, and a Teacher's Page with information to help teachers identify the most effective Web Quests for their students.

Increasing the kinds of learning experiences and the products of learning can provide ELLs with a more inclusive classroom experience as well as tap the many diverse learning styles of native English learners.

A Classroom Picture of a RAFT

Cindy Liang, a fifth grade teacher in a mixed classroom of ELLs and native English speakers, uses a Thanksgiving Dinner RAFT to help her students learn about the history of the Pilgrims. Each child in the class is assigned a name of a real Pilgrim to research. As the month continues, students plan a Thanksgiving dinner of authentic foods that they cook themselves and serve to each other and invited guests. Each child, dressed in authentic costume, reacts on that day as the real person in history: speaking of events in their lives and answering questions of those invited to share the feast. More than a simple cooking project, Ms. Liang's class becomes highly engaged with the academic content and learning. In later history units, these students will be able to recall their first person experiences and view historical events in a different way, as events that affected real people and impacted their own lives. This is the kind of transferable skill learning that we aspire to in all of our teaching.

Ms Liang created a RAFT to help structure the Thanksgiving role play:

Role: You are a Pilgrim named _____ living in the New World.

Audience: You are responding to people from another time and telling them about your life.

Form: You are to answer questions addressed to you as completely as possible about your life and your dreams for the future.

Time: The fall of 1621 after the harvest.

Listening In While Not Tuning Out

Comprehending language is very different from simply hearing language. The former is an active mental processing skill, whereas the latter is a function of the ability of our ears to transmit sounds. In Chapter 5, we talked about the importance of listening during the pre-production stage of oral language development. However, it's not only during pre-production that listening is important to learning. Listening is an essential skill for subject matter concept learning as well as for the development of academic language. Students at all grade levels benefit from structured listening activities.

We were visiting a friend with a twelve-month-old grandchild recently. As we watched little Jack play with his toys and interact with his mother and grandmother, it was obvious that he understood a great deal of language. Jack followed his mother's commands and questions to "Come here," "Give me the giraffe," "Do you want your bottle?" "Pick up those papers," and so on. During all this time, Jack rarely uttered a word. Indeed, his mother indicated that Jack only spoke two words: *bot* (bottle) and *no*. In spite of his lack of productive language, Jack is learning language at a normal rate.

Noticing that children learned their first languages by listening and responding to language, James Asher, a psychologist at San Jose State College in California, determined that language could be learned through kinesthetic responses to auditory commands. The many studies conducted to test this hypothesis showed that the **Total Physical Response** (TPR) method resulted in long-term recall of the language (Asher, 1979). TPR reminds us that listening to language should not be a passive activity. We will get better language learning results if students are asked to move their bodies or react in some way as a result of the listening activity.

Sound Discrimination

Beginning-level ELLs will have difficulty perceiving the individual sounds and words of the language. They may be silent for long periods of time as they attempt to discriminate these new sounds that may not exist in their own native languages. Visual learners who are literate will benefit from seeing the words while listening to them. In this way, they can use their literacy skills to promote faster learning. Young, pre-literate children will need a great deal of structured input before they are able to discriminate sounds, comprehend meaning and begin to produce language.

Activities that help learners to discriminate sounds are also helpful to young ELLs who are learning to read. **Phonemic awareness** is thought to be a critical precursor to a child's ability to read. It is defined as the understanding that spoken language is composed of a series of discrete sounds that may be broken down, combined, and manipulated in a variety of ways. The phonemic awareness skills that follow are appropriate for very young learners and for pre-literate English language learners of any age:

- Rhyming: *can, man, fan*
- Segmenting syllables: *im-por-tant*
- Segmenting and blending phonemes: */r-e-d/*
- Manipulating phonemes: *Say cat without the /k/*
- Connecting phonemes to letters: */k/ may be spelled with a c or a k.*

Various full-class activities can be used to promote sound discrimination. A selection follows:

1. Call out a list of known words and ask students to raise their hands when they hear a word that begins or ends with a particular sound or cluster of sounds.
2. Say aloud a pair of words that are either identical or differ in one aspect. The children should stand up if the words are different and stay seated if they are the same. The words may differ in the one area of the particular discrimination skill that you want to practice. For example:

   Fin – thin

   Run – ran

   Fox – fog

   It is particularly helpful for ELLs if you include **minimal pairs** in these activities. These are pairs of words that differ in only one speech sound such as those above. As you can see, this activity can also help you know how learners are progressing at hearing these differences.
3. Play the game "I Am Thinking of . . ." to practice sounds. Say:

   I am thinking of a word that begins with /b/ and is the name of an animal.

   Is it a dog?

   The children answer "yes" or "no" to questions such as these, eventually saying "yes" when asked:

   Is it a bear?

4. Have the children listen as you read aloud a series of words containing a particular sound or inflection. The children should clap when they hear a sound that doesn't belong, for example:

   fat, four, fin, very

   running, eating, kindness, swimming

5. Write two monosyllabic words on the blackboard that contain the same spelling pattern such as:

   cat

   fat

   Ask the students to listen as you pronounce the words and notice that the endings of the words sound the same and rhyme. Ask ELLs to enlarge this list on the blackboard by guessing words that rhyme with "cat" and "fat" and fit the descriptive clues that you give, for example:

   A thing you wipe your dirty shoes on. (mat)

   A thing you use to hit a baseball. (bat)

   After collecting a list of words on the chalkboard, check the children for their understanding of the words by asking:

Which word means an animal that has whiskers?

Which word means a piece of sports equipment?

Your definitions can be adjusted to the ability of the learners and accompanied by drawings. Creating definitions that are a little more difficult than the students' oral language productive ability is one way of enlarging their receptive language abilities.

6. Create Word Bingo by asking students to copy the list of words in activity number 5 onto a bingo grid. As you call out the words, students can place markers on the appropriate words.

Listening for Understanding

The best way to promote listening with understanding is to be sure to talk to ELLs individually every day. Even when students are unable to comprehend much language, they will attempt to understand and use context clues to guess at meanings. Teacher language that is interspersed with various kinds of questions is very helpful to promoting listening skills. Questions, with their rising intonational formats, are quickly identified and they call out for a response. In the beginning, teachers supply the responses for their learners.

Hi Carlos. How are you? What's this? Is this your book bag?

It's a really big book bag. It feels heavy. Is it heavy? No? Not too heavy?

Good.

The repetitions in these conversations, the use of the question words and rising intonation and the obvious reference (book bag) help to put the language learner at ease. These dialogues send the message: *My teacher wants to talk to me!* They also send the message that understanding English might not be too impossible a task.

We have included specific tasks for developing skill in listening with understanding. The tasks range from the easiest to the most difficult. These tasks are adaptable for a variety of subject matter content and the language can be aligned to the proficiency level of the learner. The important element is that teachers focus on the development of listening skills even after ELLs have acquired social language.

1. As we have discussed earlier, hand, facial, and body gestures contribute to the meaning of oral language in the classroom. Routine classroom language that can easily be communicated with gestures includes these expressions: "good morning," "stand up," "sit down," "listen," "look," "give me . . . ," "let's go," "come here," "open your books," "put down your pencil," and "good-bye."

2. Teach classroom routines and directional language by playing Simon Says. You can also ask students to perform an increasingly more difficult series of actions:

   - Walk to the chalkboard.
   - Pick up the chalk.
   - Write the numeral ___ on the chalkboard. (Or write the formula for _____.)
   - Put down the chalk.
   - Walk to your desk and sit down.

Figure 6.10 A Grid Format Activity, "Airport," Teaches Receptive Listening Skills

Flight no.	City	Country	Gate no.	Departure Time
17	Bogotá	Colombia	28	2:45
40	Cali	Guatemala	30	4:32
13	Mexico City	Mexico	17	8:30
70	Cuernavaca	Panama	39	9:15

3. Play Picture Bingo directing students to place a token on a picture of a new vocabulary item. The pictures might be simple, animals of the desert, for example, or more complex such as chemistry apparatus.
4. We like to play Airport to help ELLs listen for specific information related to numbers and time. Draw a grid on the chalkboard such as the one shown in Figure 6.10. The grid should contain columns for flight numbers, cities and countries (in mixed-up order), boarding gate numbers, and times of departure. Call out the information much as a loud speaker at an airport does:

   Flight number 40 for Bogotá, Colombia, leaving Gate 17 at 4:32 PM.

   The student must listen to, remember, and point out the specific times called by tapping with a yardstick on the chalkboard grid. It's important that the student not respond until the announcement is finished. By requiring ELLs to wait before responding, you enable them to develop increasingly longer memory spans. The announcer can control the speed and the quantity of items called according to the ability of the class. The airport activity can also be accomplished in pairs and students can write their responses on paper.

   This activity can be used with any content information that is contained on a chart: the periodic table of elements, the thirteen original colonies with their founders, dates and locations, animal families, and many others.
5. Present students with a group of vocabulary items related to the unit under study. You could write the words on the chalkboard or project them on a screen and accompany them with pictures, if necessary. Then describe one of the items, one sentence at a time. Begin with very general sentences and gradually become more specific. The students must identify the item you are describing. For example:

   It's made of glass.

   It's a measurement instrument.

   It measures heat.

   It contains mercury.

At some point, ELLs will recognize that you are describing a thermometer and indicate the correct word by pointing or naming the item. If the class is very diverse, you may ask learners not to call out but simply raise their hands when they know the answer. In this way you can recognize those who make early guesses but still provide more input for those who are not sure.

The important element of this exercise is the input that ELLs are receiving as you define the objects. Terms such as *measure, made of, contains,* and *heat* are all part of the academic language of the unit. As ELLs listen, they are required to attend to this language and attempt to understand it. The result is that they have more exposure to academic language in a way that requires them to actively process the language.

6. Play the game, "If I Were . . . ." Complete the phrase with a statement related to the unit under study. Students vote on the correctness of the statement, perhaps by showing a signal card labeled True/False or Yes/No.

   If I were a reptile, I would have fur.

   If I were a plant, my leaves would always contain chlorophyll.

   If I were Balboa, I would discover the Pacific Ocean.

7. Describe an event in history or a scientific process based upon a sequence of four or five pictures. Give the pictures to a group of ELLs who have listened to the description and ask them to sequence the pictures correctly. Later, they can retell the event or process.

8. Use dictation to help ELLs extend their memories, develop cognition, listen attentively, and listen with discrimination. Begin with simple sentences containing known grammatical structures and vocabulary. Tell students you will say the sentence only once. They are to listen with their pencils lying on their desks. Hold up your finger, a ruler, or a colorful flag as a signal to begin writing. Say the sentence at a normal conversational speed, then count under your breath to ten before giving the signal. After the dictation, correct the sentence immediately by writing the correct form on the board. If students are not correct, they can use the model to make corrections. ELLs are challenged by this activity and thus motivated to succeed. The ten-second wait will help ensure that they understand and process the oral language before writing. The time wait also helps them develop longer memories for oral language.

9. Even when ELLs are adept at listening and understanding the language of their teachers and friends in conversations, they may have difficulty understanding more formal language presentations such as a lecture, assembly program, or speech. Skills in note-taking are essential to learning from these formal presentation formats. We can help students develop listening and note-taking skills in this way:

   - Distribute copies of a content-related paragraph containing ten to fifteen sentences or refer ELLs to a paragraph in their textbooks. Read the paragraph aloud to the students while they read silently.
   - Next, ask them to close their books and listen to the same paragraph a second time. During this second reading, ask students to take notes on the contents of the paragraph.
   - After the note-taking, go to the board and ask students to tell you the notes they have taken. Write these down. If the students have omitted any important information, include it on the board summary at this time.

- Next, distribute copies of the same paragraph to students with key words or phrases omitted. Read the complete paragraph again and ask students to fill in the blanks as they listen to the reading. After this third reading, you can check the correctness of the students' answers in a variety of ways. Students can read the filled-in sentences aloud, or pair up and compare their answers to a buddy's. Finally, students can refer to the text or the original reading.

As ELLs advance in their cognitive and linguistic skills, you can use this same technique to teach outlining skills by reading a three- or four-paragraph narrative to the class.

Listening and oral language are related skills. Listening is receptive but not passive. Oral language is a productive skill. Development in one skill increases

Table 6.1 Rubric for Oral Language Assessment

	Novice	Developing	Proficient	Expert
Fluency	Speech is halting and fragmentary. There is no continuity in the presentation.	Usually hesitant; description contains long periods of silence.	Description is occasionally disrupted by student's search for correct manner of expression.	Description is generally fluent with rare lapses for correct expression.
Vocabulary	Vocabulary limitations so extreme that no content is communicated.	Difficult to understand because of misuse of words and very limited academic vocabulary.	Occasional use of wrong words; there is evidence of both academic and technical vocabulary and signal words required for description of the content.	Academic and technical vocabulary are used appropriately to describe the content. Signal words are in evidence when required.
Pronunciation	Pronunciation problems so severe that speech is virtually unintelligible.	Difficult to understand because of pronunciation problems; must frequently repeat in order to be understood.	Occasional misunderstandings caused by pronunciation problems.	Description is always intelligible, although listener may be conscious of an accent.
Grammar	Errors in grammar and word order so severe that speech is virtually unintelligible.	Difficult to understand because of errors in grammar and word order; must often rephrase or restrict speech to basic patterns.	Occasional errors in grammar and word order; meaning not usually obscured. There is evidence that the grammar is tailored to the content.	Grammar is correct and tailored to that required by the content.

the development of the other related skill. When we consider the amount of time spent listening in classrooms, we begin to understand the need to make those listening experiences productive ones for all learners.

Assessing Listening and Speaking Skills in the Content Classroom

When assessing listening and speaking skills in the content classroom, teachers need to be clear as to their goals and objectives. Many classroom activities include both language skill goals and content learning goals.

Consider the following directions: "Describe the appearance and composition of two planets in the solar system." This objective includes both an oral language skill (describe) and content knowledge (appearance and composition of two planets in the solar system). In order to assess a student's performance, the teacher needs to separate the content learning goals from the language goals. It is possible that a student has good knowledge of the composition and appearance of the two planets in question, but is unable to fluently and grammatically describe them.

Rubrics are one way to separate the assessment of language skill from content knowledge. Rubrics are scoring scales using numbers or letters that identify the specific criteria used to evaluate a product or presentation. They are most effective when shared with students at the beginning of the learning unit and clearly explained or explicitly modeled. Through a rubric, target performance can be clearly explained, describing several levels of proficiency.

For example, the rubric in Table 6.1 is one that can be used for description in a variety of content subjects. What is important is that the teacher scaffolds the oral reporting task so that all learners can approximate the Proficient level. ELLs might use a graphic organizer or note cards as scaffolds during their descriptions and be given ample opportunity for practice before assessment.

The content knowledge portion of the learning objective can also be assessed through the use of a rubric. This one, however, would be specific to the content and learning requirements. Once, again, students need to see the rubric before the learning unit begins and make reference to it throughout the lesson.

Questions for Reflection

1. What supports do classroom teachers need in order to become academic language teachers in content classrooms in grades K through 8? How can they make considering language development part of their daily thinking and planning about teaching?
2. We have suggested incorporating language objectives for knowledge and skill development into all content classes with ELLs. Which content do you think will be the most difficult for you? Why? Which content class will be the least difficult? Why?
3. Students at all grade levels spend a good deal of class time listening. This is a particularly difficult skill for ELLs to learn. Develop this argument further with reference to various grade levels and then support your thinking with examples of techniques that will ease the load, and promote the language development, of ELLs in content classrooms.

Activities for Further Learning

1. Look back at the instructional techniques recommended for the content areas of language arts, social studies, math, and science. For each content area identify two or three techniques that you consider most helpful to all learners. Share your conclusions with others in your group. Are your choices similar or different? Discuss why each of you has made your choices. Are there other techniques not mentioned that you would include? Share these with your group members.

2. Consider the following lesson plan for an elementary level science lesson on electricity. The plan is designed for students working in small groups. The purpose of the lesson is student investigation of electrical circuits.

   Materials: Cell batteries, insulated wire (with insulation removed at the ends), flashlight bulbs.

   Directions: Experiment to find ways to connect the batteries, bulbs, and wires so that the bulbs will light.

   Vocabulary: Connect, battery, bulb, wire, predict, circuit.

   Predict what the students will report at the conclusion of the experiment. Identify the technical and academic language you want the students to use. Note the kind of grammar needed to report on the experiment in academic language. Talk with your group members about techniques you could use to help students use this formal, academic, and scientific language prior to writing a report.

3. Work with your group to create a rap or a chant that reports on the learning about electrical circuits in academic language.

4. Consult a curriculum guide to devise a lesson plan for a diverse first grade math class. Identify the technical and academic language you want the students to use. Note the kind of grammar needed to communicate about the math learning. Talk with your group members about techniques you could use to help students practice, and use this formal, academic math language in the classroom.

5. Consult a curriculum or standards guide to create a social studies lesson for a mixed language sixth grade classroom. Select the specific objectives (content, language, and learning strategies) and create activities that will promote oral language practice and use within a content learning context.

6. Consult curriculum or standards guides to develop a language arts lesson for an eighth grade classroom of mixed language proficiencies. Develop specific objectives (language, content, and learning strategies), and devise classroom experiences that will require all students to be active participants, practicing and using the target language with appropriate scaffolds.

7. Develop activities that infuse one of the above lessons with music, dance, or artistic expression.

8. Create a RAFT for content learning for each of the above lessons (science, math, social studies, and language arts).

PEARSON
myeducationlab
Where the Classroom Comes to Life   is a collection of online tools for your success in this course, your licensure exams, and your teaching career. Go to www.myeducationlab .com to utilize these extensive resources including videos from real classrooms, Praxis and licensure preparation, a lesson plan builder, and materials to help you in your teaching career.

Suggested Reading

Calderon, M. (2007). *Teaching reading to English language learners, grades 6–12: A framework for improving achievement in the content areas*. Thousand Oaks, CA: Corwin Press. This practical guide is filled with tools for middle-grade teachers with English learners in their classes. It includes lesson templates, rubrics, sample lesson plans in mathematics, science, language arts, and social studies, and descriptions of successful programs.

Fathman, A. K. & Crowther, D. (2006). *Science for English language learners: K–12 classroom strategies*. Arlington, VA: NSTA Press. This book, written by a language specialist and a science teacher, provides a comprehensive guide to teaching language and science together using inquiry-based practices. The text includes an overview of principles that both content areas share, practical strategies and models for lesson and curriculum development, and a review of standards in both areas, along with many resources.

Gomez, S., McKay, H., Tom, A., & White, K. (1995). *Eureka! Science demonstrations for ESL classes.* Reading, MA: Addison-Wesley. This book contains 66 science demonstrations suitable for learners from upper elementary to middle school. There are reproducible pages for student use, excellent and simple line drawings, suggestions for language learning, and detailed instructions for each demonstration. Questions for analysis and application are provided as well as activities promoting student explanations. The demonstrations are grouped into science units including the scientific process, air, force and motion, electricity and magnetism, visual perception, sound, properties of liquids, chemistry, and heat. Teachers with limited knowledge of how to teach either science or second languages will benefit from this material.

Johnston, J. & Johnston, M. (1990). *Content points A, B, C: Science, mathematics, and social studies activities*. Reading, MA: Addison-Wesley. These three slim workbooks present many valuable ideas for teachers who are interested in learning ways to scaffold instruction in the content areas. The materials are aimed at students from upper elementary to middle school. The language requirements and subject matter concepts increase in difficulty from Book A to Book C.

Web Sites for Further Learning

Content-centered Language Learning. This article describes the various models for integrating language learners into classroom and schools. It also discusses methods currently used to teach language learners. Retrieved May 9, 2008.

http://www.cal.org/resources/digest/cranda01.html

"Drama with Poetry: Teaching English as a Second Language Through Dramatization and Improvisation, M. Gasparro and B. Falletta." This article suggests specific poems useful for language learners and offers suggestions on how to teach poetry. Retrieved May 9, 2008.

http://www.ericdigests.org/1994/drama.htm

"Helping English Language Learners Increase Achievement Through Inquiry-Based Science Instruction." Amaral, O., Garrison, L., and Klentschy, M. (2002). A Journal of the Center for Bilingual Education and Research and the National Association of Bilingual Education, vol. 26, no. 2. This report describes an initiative in a large California school district toward the implementation on inquiry-based science at the elementary school level. Standardized report data and components of the program are included. Retrieved May 9, 2008.

http://brj.asu.edu/content/vol26_no2/pdf/ART2.PDF

Integrating Language and Content: Lessons from Immersion, National Center for Research on Cultural Diversity and Second Language Learning. Lessons learned from immersion programs are shared here. The report refers to effective classroom activities and explains how to plan for language learning. Retrieved May 9, 2008.

http://www.ncela.gwu.edu/pubs/ncrcdsll/epr11.htm

Integrating Language and Culture in Middle School American History Classes, National Center for Research on Cultural Diversity. How to plan for an American history unit and examples of specific academic language required are explored in this report. Retrieved May 9, 2008.

http://www.ncela.gwu.edu/pubs/ncrcdsll/epr8.htm

Mathematics for Second-Language Learners (Updated December 2002). The National Council of Teachers of Math outline their position and a rationale for math communication to be taught to second language learners. The short article includes recommendations for teachers and school communities. Retrieved May 9, 2008.

http://www.nctm.org/about/content.aspx?id=6368

Promoting Science Literacy with English Language Learners Through Instructional Materials Development: A Case Study, Fradd, S., Sutman, F., Lee, O., and Saxton, M. Bilingual Resource Journal, Fall, 2001, vol. 25, no. 4, 2001. This article explores science instruction for language learners. The authors collaborated with fourth grade teachers on an instructional design for experiential science. Retrieved May 9, 2008.

http://brj.asu.edu/content/vol25_no4/pdf/ar5.pdf

Reforming Mathematics Instruction for ESL Literacy Students, K. Buchanan and M. Helman. This report discusses teaching math to language learning students who have had interrupted schooling. The authors provide suggestions for clumping objectives, promoting language development and assessment. Retrieved May 9, 2008.

http://www.ncela.gwu.edu/pubs/pigs/pig15.htm

Teaching science to English learners, grades 4–8. Ann K. Fathman; Mary Ellen Quinn; Carolyn Kessler. This information guide contains principles and strategies for integrating language and science education. Retrieved May 9, 2008.

http://www.ncela.gwu.edu/pubs/pigs/pig11.htm

WebQuest. This organization is dedicated to promoting, teaching about, and sharing examples of the use of WebQuests, plans for inquiry learning on the Internet. Thousands of teachers in North America use WebQuests and now many countries are joining where teachers develop WebQuests in many languages. Retrieved May 9, 2008.

http://www.WebQuest.org

References

Almada, P., Nichols, A., & O'Keefe, L. (2004). *A pocketful of opossums.* Barrington, IL: Rigby.

Anstrom, A. (1999). Preparing secondary education teachers to work with English language learners: Social studies. Washington, DC: NCBE Resource Collection Series #13, Center for the Study of Language and Education, Graduate School of Education and Human Development, The George Washington University.

Asher, J. (1979) *Learning another language through actions: The complete teacher's guidebook.* San Jose, CA: Sky Oaks Productions.

Black, A. & Stave, A. M. (2007). *A comprehensive guide to readers' theatre: Enhancing fluency and comprehension in middle school and beyond.* Newark, DE: International Reading Association.

Buchanan, K. & Helman, M. (1993). Reforming mathematics instruction for ESL literacy students, K. Buchanan and M. Helman. Retrieved May 9, 2008. http://www.ncela.gwu.edu/pubs/pigs/pig15.htm

Center for Applied Linguistics (CAL). (1998). *Enriching content classes for secondary ESOL students: Trainer's manual and study guide.* McHenry, IL: Delta Systems.

Lacina, J., Levine, L. N., & Sowa, P. (2006). *Collaborative partnerships between ESL and classroom teachers: Helping English language learners succeed in preK–elementary schools.* Alexandria, VA: TESOL.

National Council for the Social Studies Task Force on Scope and Sequence. (1989, October). In search of a scope and sequence for social studies. *Social Education, 53,* 376–387.

National Council of Teachers of Mathematics (NCTM). (2000). Principles and standards for school mathematics. http://www.nctm.org/standards/

National Council of Teachers of Mathematics (NCTM). (2006). Curriculum Focal Points for Prekindergarten through Grade 8 Mathematics. Retrieved May 9, 2008. http://www.nctm.org/focalpoints.aspx

National Research Council. (1996). *National science education standards.* Washington, DC: National Academy Press.

Olmedo, I. M. (1993). Junior historians: Doing oral history with ESL and bilingual students. *TESOL Journal* (2)*:* 7–10.

Rutherford, P. (1998). *Instruction for all students.* Alexandria, VA: Just ASK Publications.

Short, D. J. (1991). *Integrating language and content instruction: Strategies and techniques.* Washington, DC: National Clearinghouse for Bilingual Education.

CHAPTER 7

Developing Literacy with English Learners: Focus on Reading

Nadia El Naggar works with a multilingual, multicultural second grade class. Eight of her 24 students, who come from five different countries, are being served by the ESOL program, and eight others have been exited from the program, but still need her support in continuing to improve their reading skills. Nadia is the reading teacher of record for all. Let's view a snapshot of one of her full-class, mini-lessons in language arts.

In science, the class has been building an understanding of the growth cycle through the theme, "the circle of life." On this day, Nadia demonstrates the shared reading strategy with a big book called, *A Pocketful of Opossums* (Almada, Nichols, & O'Keefe, 2004), shown in Figure 7.1. She begins the lesson by reviewing a poster the class has studied, which shows four stages in the life of a lion, a chicken, a frog, and a butterfly; and having learners label the pictures. She asks new learners to label the animals; more proficient English speakers to label the stages. Students take turns acting out the four stages for each animal as the class names the animal and the stages. Some children respond with gestures for *yes* and *no* questions; others respond with short answers that Nadia accepts and expands upon.

Next, Nadia asks the children if any of them has ever seen an opossum. Many have not. She shows the children the picture of an opossum on the cover of a big book, and tells the children that this is an opossum. She asks the children to practice saying the word. She then explains that opossums grow from babies to adults, just like people, and this is what the book is about. She introduces the book, models making predictions about what the class will learn with questions (e.g., "How big is an opossum?" or "Where do the baby opossums live?") and encourages the children to make other predictions and ask questions starting with *why, what,* and *where*. They ask:

"What in the pocket?"

"Why no hair?" [on the baby]

"Why is it on its mama's back?"

"Where does possum live?"

After this introduction, Nadia uses the shared reading strategy to support learners as they read and share the text in many ways over several days. With a pointer, she draws the children's

Figure 7.1 Previewing Pictures from a Book, Such As This One, Helps to Set the Stage for Guided Reading

Source: A Pocketful of Opossums, Almada, et al. (2004)

attention to the text as it is read. The first time through, she reads aloud to the children, but on successive readings, more and more children read along. Each reading includes questions and discussions to monitor children's comprehension and maintain their attention. For example, she checks to make sure that all students understand the meaning of "pocket," and has several students show their own pockets.

Following several readings of the story, with children participating more each time (some reading along, some reciting along, some combining reading and reciting, and a few newcomers just watching with keen interest), the teacher uses the text for a variety of literacy-building activities, including letter-sound connections, vocabulary development, summarizing and re-stating, and plotting life cycles on a timeline.

At the end of the week, the teacher sends home a page with the main events in the story pictured and captioned. Children read the story to their parents in English, then retell it in the home language. Parents are proud to listen to and discuss the stories with their children, and sign their children's papers; they're also glad to understand and be involved in what their children are learning.

How do you use reading to develop literacy with English learners?

- What are current approaches to developing literacy?
- What are the unique needs of English language learners (ELLs) who are developing literacy in English?
- What are effective strategies for literacy development of ELLs at different language-learning and literacy stages?
- What are recommendations for schools to ensure that all ELLs are participating in a comprehensive and appropriate literacy program?

What Is Literacy?

Literacy is not just reading. It actually involves all modes of language—listening, speaking, reading, and writing. When learners develop literacy, they learn to construct and convey meaning from their own written texts and the texts of others. They begin to have effective ways to learn about the world, to interact with people in the world, and to be able to influence what happens in the world through the written word. Our goals for English learners are to help them develop beyond merely being *able* to do these things—we want our students to become learners who *choose* to read and write, who *delight* in reading and writing. This chapter focuses on teaching English learners to read, but readers will find many connections to speaking, listening, and writing as well.

Reading is taught in a variety of ways that are often grouped into **top-down approaches** and **bottom-up approaches.** In top-down approaches (Figure 7.2), the focus is on what readers bring into the process, helping them use their world knowledge to bring meaning to the text, then expanding it to develop decoding and comprehension skills in the context of the meaning. In "bottom-up" approaches (Figure 7.3),

Figure 7.2 Top-down Approaches to Reading

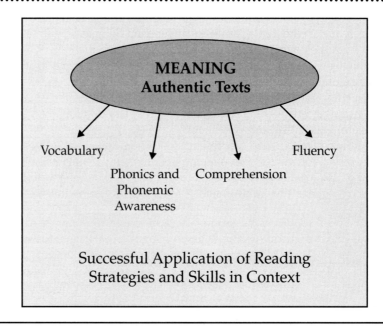

Figure 7.3 Bottom-up Approaches to Reading

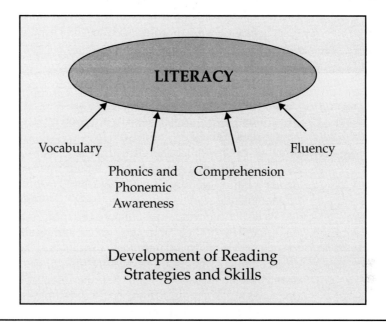

the focus is placed on developing building blocks in sequence—focusing first on developing the ability to hear sounds, then on building decoding skills (associating sounds with letters and letter combinations), and then continuing on to develop word study skills, fluency, and comprehension.

Top-Down Approaches

Top-down approaches to reading include emergent literacy, pioneered by Don Holdaway (1979) and Marie Clay (1997) in Australia and New Zealand, expanded by proponents of the Whole Language philosophy, and of guided reading. This approach views children as beginning to develop written language knowledge from the moment they are first exposed to reading and writing. Literacy development, like oral language development, is a process in which learners act out reading and writing and gradually—with guidance, instruction, and feedback—begin to approximate increasingly conventional reading and writing to get meaning from text. This approach employs literacy development strategies that parallel effective oral language development (Moustafa, 1997). These include providing comprehensible input, scaffolding, and social interaction around literacy that lead students toward mature reading and writing. Emphasis is placed on developing motivation and purposes for reading, helping learners understand the context, gaining meaning from reading, and making meaning with writing. Marie Clay describes reading as "a message-gaining, problem-solving activity that increases in power and flexibility the more it is practiced" (1997, p. 6). Kenneth Goodman (1967) used "a psycholinguistic guessing game" as a metaphor for reading. In this "game," learners develop abilities in using phonemic (letter sounds), semantic (word meaning), and syntactic (word order and grammar) cues to get meaning from a page. The approach does not, as critics have often said, omit the teaching of literacy skills but rather promotes the introduction of literacy skills such as phonics, grammar, and spelling in context as students are ready for them, need them, and in a way that is compatible with their cognitive development. The approach is most effective when the curriculum and well-prepared teachers support the development of the strategies and skills children need, understand the usual sequences of development, and are knowledgeable about effective methods for the introduction and use of the skills and strategies. Top-down elements of curriculum are important for helping ELLs acquire meaning. ELLs need to learn what texts mean either before or as they learn to read them.

Bottom-Up Approaches

By contrast, there has been recent renewed interest in what are called "bottom-up" approaches (Table 7.3), influenced by such publications as that of the Reading First initiative of the No Child Left Behind Act (NCLB) (U.S. Department of Education, 2002). It is important to note that though the research reviewed by the National Reading Panel (National Institute of Child Health and Human Development, 2000) did not include studies focusing on the literacy development and needs of ELLs, the results have been widely disseminated as appropriate recommendations for all readers, regardless of their language background (Stahl, 2002). Likewise, NCLB did not include provisions to accommodate the different language development and content achievement of ELLs, though recently "flexibilities" have been incorporated into the testing requirements for ELLs (U.S. Department of Education, 2002). These "bottom-up" approaches emphasize explicitly developing the component skills of literacy, including developing phonemic awareness, phonics, word study, fluency and comprehension skills, and then putting these together to develop reading proficiency. It is important to note that most explicit literacy approaches in use in grade-level classrooms are dependent on prerequisite oral language proficiency of learners. They assume that learners have acquired the sound system, vocabulary, structures, and patterns of the English language, and use this knowledge to develop the skills of reading. Learners of English do not meet these prerequisites. The National Literacy Panel, convened to "identify, assess, and synthesize research on the education of language-minority children and youth with regard to literacy attainment and to produce a comprehensive report on this literature" (August & Shanahan, 2007), found evidence to show that learners of English benefitted from bottom-up approaches, but primarily for reading at word level—more complex, top-down approaches were important for developing oral language needed for reading and reading fluency, and comprehension ability.

Integrated Approaches

Integrated approaches (Table 7.4) view reading as constructing meaning. Children begin to become readers long before entering school and use invented forms of literacy on their way to conventional reading and writing. In integrated approaches (Figure 7.4), meaning is central, and teachers work to integrate top-down and bottom-up approaches, integrating comprehension and decoding, reader and text, and reader and writer (Birch, 2006). They teach the component skills of reading within the context of authentic, connected texts—texts that are simple and repetitive at first, and then gradually more complex. They sequence skills within thematic units that include relevant, age-appropriate content. They may include the use of leveled readers—texts at levels that very gradually increase in difficulty by carefully and deliberately introducing a few new reading skills and new vocabulary at each level. They may use a guided reading approach (Fountas & Pinnell, 1996, 2001; August & Shanahan, 2007), in which teachers work with small, leveled groups, guiding them to read books at progressively more difficult levels, introducing new features of text and reading strategies along the way, in the context of a variety of rich literacy experiences.

Figure 7.4 Integrated Approaches to Reading

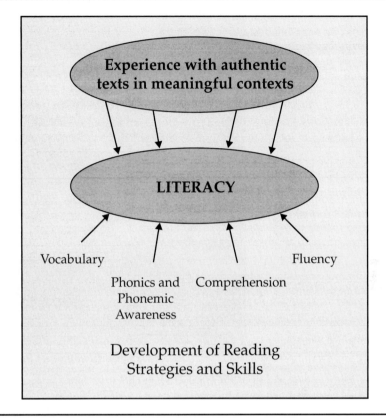

ELLs Developing Literacy Require Special Instruction

With ELLs, teachers of reading cannot assume that learners are able to discriminate the sounds, know the vocabulary, or apply an understanding of the grammar of English, though learners may have parallel skills in another language. New learners of English often cannot tell a word from a nonsense word (e.g., "mat" means no more than "jat"); they often cannot discriminate new sounds of English that are not in their own language (e.g., "sheep" sounds just like "ship"); they cannot discriminate between grammatical and non-grammatical structures (e.g., "he happy" might mean the same, and sound just as correct to the learners as "she is happy"). These elements must be developed before or as learners learn to read the texts that require such discriminations.

What Is Unique About English Language Learners Who Are Developing Literacy?

Most linguists and child development experts are in accord: it is far easier for children to learn to read and write in the language they know best (August & Shanahan, 2007; Hudelson, 1984, 1987; Lanauze & Snow, 1989; Snow, Burns, & Griffin, 1998). So, when possible, it is preferable to give children the opportunity to develop literacy first in their mother tongue. However, given the multilingual classrooms that are the reality in U.S. schools, and the policies chosen by legislators or educators in many areas of the U.S., most young ELLs in U.S. schools are expected to develop initial reading in English.

This Girl, Like Many ELLs, Developed Literacy in Her First Language—Arabic

Likewise, older ELLs are often expected to continue their literacy development in English. This presents unique challenges for school-age ELLs and their teachers. Though the development of ELLs who are acquiring literacy in a new language has many parallels to first language literacy development, there are a number of important distinctions for teachers to keep in mind.

What ELLs Bring

ELLs bring a great deal with them to the literacy table. They already know at least one language, and use it in sophisticated and age-appropriate ways. They have the same cognitive maturity as their native-English-speaking peers. They may have some exposure to literacy in their mother tongue and may have acquired many literacy skills and strategies as applied in another language system. They bring with them rich experiences in one or more cultures. Each day they move between a home culture and a school culture that have wide differences in values and expectations. As teachers, we must respect, use, and celebrate what English learners already know and the unique contributions they bring to our classrooms. Culturally sensitive and responsive programs are important supports for teachers who want to use the strengths their young language learners bring with them.

Transfer of Literacy from Native Language to Second Language.   Though much research is left to be done about the similarities and differences between the native-language reading process and second-language reading processes, researchers have found that processes seem to be more alike than they are different. Heath (1983) refers to transferable generic literacies; Krashen (2003) proposes that second-language reading entails the same basic processes as first-language reading, and

Fitzgerald's (2003) research indicates that the cognitive reading processes of English language learners in the U.S. were similar to those of native-English speakers. Literacy skills from L1 **transfer** to L2. Knowing the level of literacy in L1 can be helpful in determining expectations in L2 reading instruction. Most teachers we have worked with are confident that learners who come with considerable literacy in L1 have a strong advantage in developing reading skills in English. We encourage you to do what you can to find out about your learners' previous schooling. If you are able to locate and use L1 reading and writing assessments for the languages of your learners, these tools will help you in knowing whether you are introducing first-time literacy or helping learners to transfer literacy skills they already have to a new language. If no standardized tools are available, you can still get an idea about your learners' level of literacy development by asking them to read to you from a book written for their age group in the language they know. Does the student know how to handle a book? How fluent is the reading? Likewise, you can ask your ELLs to write something for you in their native language (Figure 7.5 shows one such example). Does the handwriting look as if they have had considerable instruction and practice? Do they write fluently? Is there organization to the way words are arranged on the page? Can the students read to you what they have written? Whatever information you can

Figure 7.5 What Does the 8-Year-Old Who Wrote This Know About Reading and Writing?

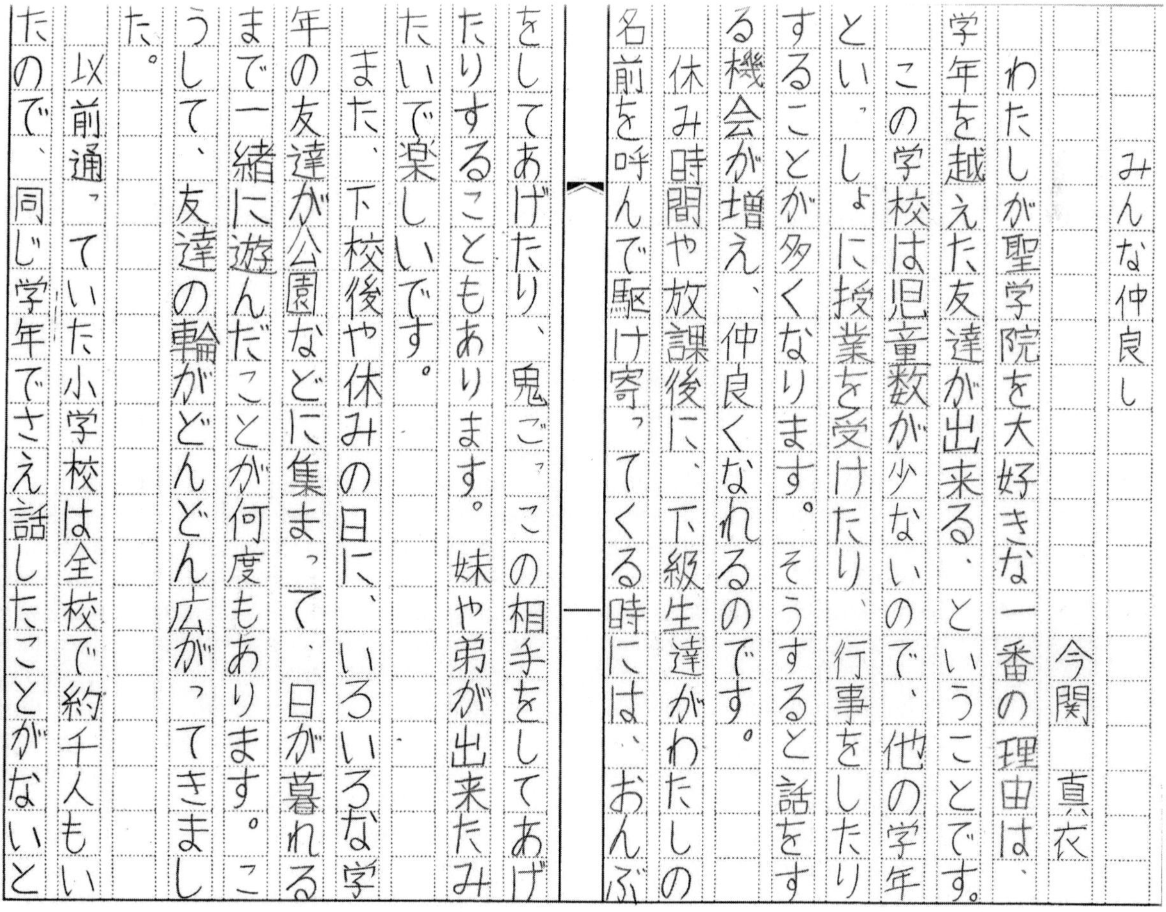

みんな仲良し

今関 真衣

わたしが聖学院を大好きな一番の理由は、学年を越えた友達が出来る、ということです。
この学校は児童数が少ないので、他の学年といっしょに授業を受けたり、行事をしたりすることが多くなります。そうすると話をする機会が増え、仲良くなれるのです。
休み時間や放課後に、下級生達がわたしの名前を呼んで駆け寄ってくる時には、おんぶをしてあげたり、鬼ごっこの相手をしてあげたりすることもあります。妹や弟が出来たみたいで楽しいです。
また、下校後や休みの日に、いろいろな学年の友達が公園などに集まって、日が暮れるまで一緒に遊んだことが何度もあります。こうして、友達の輪がどんどん広がってきました。
以前通っていた小学校は全校で約千人もいたので、同じ学年でさえ話したことがないと

glean on what literacy skills your learners bring to the classroom will help you to teach them better.

What ELLs Need

Language development takes time. Researchers estimate that though children learning a second language can be effective in social language in one to two years, the average time that they take to acquire native-like academic language is about five to seven years (Cummins, 1994; Thomas & Collier, 1997). Native speakers, at age five or six, usually have a vocabulary of more than 5,000 words (Nation, 2001) and have acquired the basic syntax of their first language, which provides a rich basis for learning to encode and decode and comprehend the language they already know orally into written form. We certainly can't wait for ELLs' full acquisition of oral language before we begin literacy instruction as we do with native speakers. In fact, in order to help these students eventually acquire native-like academic language, we need to provide instruction in which oral language development, literacy development, and content learning all support one another. As we provide scaffolded, supportive instruction for students' literacy development, we provide many opportunities for oral language development through rich conversations about the materials learners read and the content they read about. And we remain conscious of the various aspects of language that learners are acquiring—including words and word meanings, sounds and sound systems, language patterns, and cultural and social contexts.

Words and Meanings (Lexical Aspects of Language). Native speakers generally learn to read using language they already use in speech. Learners of English have additional tasks: they must also learn the **lexical aspects of language.** They need to learn what the words mean and how to say them, often using sounds they've never encountered. While we don't delay reading instruction until oral language is well developed, especially for older learners, we must be alert to integrate oral language development with literacy instruction. We carefully assess our students' oral and reading comprehension and employ direct teaching of needed vocabulary. We introduce new words in contexts that make them more easily understood, recycling and re-using new words through thematic instruction to provide the many encounters students will need to learn these terms thoroughly. We also provide background knowledge to make new terms comprehensible to learners who have not had the experiences needed for comprehension.

Sound Patterns and Spelling (Graphophonemic Aspects of Language). As they learn to read and write, native speakers learn to connect sound patterns of words and word parts—ones they already use in listening and speaking—with spelling patterns. These are the **graphophonemic aspects of language.** So when a native-speaking child learns to read "A clock is a circle," the child connects sounds and a spelling pattern to words and concepts they are very familiar with—they know what a clock is and what the word for clock means; likewise with a circle. A new learner of English may know what a clock is and what a circle is (though in this digital age, they may not have seen many clocks with circular faces), and even the concept that "is" can mean "is an example of," but not the English names for these items or concepts. Learners of English have to do more: they don't just learn how to make connections between letters/syllables and sounds they already use to identify words they know. Rather, they hear the sounds (which may not all be present in their home language), know what the words mean, and read those sounds and patterns. Therefore, it is very important to introduce these new sounds in meaningful contexts using words students know or are learning along with pictures and other contextual cues that provide support.

Learners of English should encounter concepts of **phonemic awareness** and **phonics** in the context of meaningful, purposeful, culturally respectful language use, and real words (Enright & McCloskey, 1988). Strategies for developing phonemic awareness for native speakers include shared reading of books that play with sounds, writing with invented spelling, and teaching onsets and rimes (onsets are initial sounds and rimes are the word family endings, e.g., *c -at, r -at, m –at*) using a variety of activities (Cunningham, 1999). With ELLs, additional care must be taken that the language used in these activities is comprehensible to learners or that the learners have the opportunity to acquire the language before or as they are expected to read it. For example, note how the development of phonics skills is complicated when the learners are ELLs by looking at the sample phonics page depicted in Figure 7.6. Native speakers are likely to recognize the objects and associate the appropriate words with a few reminders from a teacher. ELLs, on the other hand, though they may recognize the pictures, may not have the cultural experience of jumping rope, playing a flute, or seeing a mule. Even more likely is that these learners have no idea what the English word for the picture depicts (mug, tube, or June) and may not be able to hear all the phonemes (sounds with differences in meaning in a language) used. Spanish speakers,

Figure 7.6 Sample Pictures from a Phonics Text

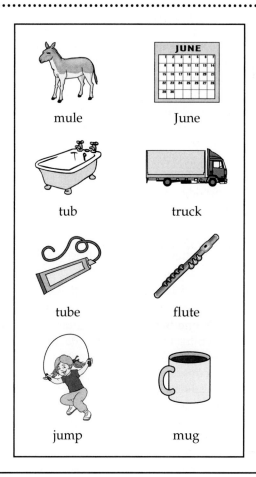

mule   June

tub   truck

tube   flute

jump   mug

for example, would be unfamiliar with the English sound for "j" or the initial consonant blends, or the short "u" sound.

Language Patterns and Grammar (Syntactic Aspects of Language).

Learners of English (as well as speakers of "non-school" dialects) don't just connect print to patterns they recognize, but rather must learn new patterns for constructing grammatical language. They must learn the **syntactic aspects of language.** For these students, it is even more important than for native English speakers that the texts they are learning to read use meaningful language that is both linguistically and culturally accessible. For beginning learners, print should have characteristics that make it easier to remember and learn such as rhyme, rhythm, and repetition; content should be familiar to learners and respectful of their cultural heritage; language patterns should be those frequently encountered in their school and community experiences. Stories such as *Brown Bear, Brown Bear, What Do You See?* (Martin & Carle, 1992) introduce language with universal appeal to new learners of English. Older learners may enjoy age-appropriate, school-appropriate rap songs or jazz chants (Graham, 1978, 2003). Reading selections, songs, and chants with these characteristics all provide rich ways to introduce language patterns. For intermediate and advanced learners, texts should be at children's independent reading or instructional level. If the books are not at this level, teachers should provide adequate scaffolding, or support for learners so that they can make sense of the text and the lesson. (Scaffolding strategies will be discussed in the next section.)

Cultural and Social Contexts (Sociolinguistic Aspects of Language).

First-language learners are often familiar with different ways that language is used with different conversation partners and in different settings. (Linguists call this **register.**) We use different language with family members of different ages, with friends, with teachers and administrators, and in different settings: on the phone at home, in reporting an experiment in a presentation before the class. New learners of English who come from other countries and cultures don't just learn to read the words and language forms that are appropriate in various sociolinguistic contexts; they must learn what language is appropriate when, and then learn the terms and language structures that are used as well. Native speakers intuitively internalize these **sociolinguistic aspects of language.** But ELLs must learn appropriate language and nonverbal behaviors for a very new cultural setting (North American schools) in new cultures (in North America). For example, ELLs from some cultures have learned that making eye contact with adults is rude and disrespectful. Their "polite" behavior may be interpreted by North American teachers as showing lack of interest and disrespect. These differences require teachers to be culturally aware and sensitive, and to use curricula and materials that take into account the wide range of cultures now represented in North American schools.

Home-School Connections.

Research evidence has led to a wide consensus concerning the value of parental participation in students' school achievement, social development, and specifically reading and language development (Heath, 1983; Cummins, 1994). Though parents and teachers may not speak the same language, there are many ways that teachers can support parent participation in their children's literacy development. By integrating oral language development in the context of thematic instruction, phonological awareness, and phonics instruction, contextualized grammatical instruction, and home-school connections with best practices in literacy instruction, we can help children discover the joy of reading as well as the power of access to school and community resources.

Nonverbal Behavior Has Very Different Meanings in Different Cultures, Which Requires Teachers of ELLs to Be Culturally Aware and Sensitive

Differences Between Oral Language Development and Literacy Development. In many ways, oral language and the language of print are the same—we use similar words, our sentences have similar syntax. But there are a number of ways in which literacy development is unlike oral language development. While children learn the oral language of their community, not every culture develops a written language, and not all children learn the written language of their culture. Most children require explicit instruction for successful literacy development. So, effective, balanced literacy instruction requires a print-rich environment in which teachers continue the development of oral language, teach text processing and production strategies, insure cultural background knowledge, and develop decoding and encoding skills (Cloud, Genesee, & Hamayan, 2000). The classroom setting provides input—both oral and print—that is understandable to learners and at the right instructional level. It provides social interaction with and about texts, and explicit instruction in strategies and processes used to make meaning from text. As they introduce language learners to print, teachers demonstrate the pleasure and usefulness that literacy offers us in our lives.

Integrated Literacy Approach. An Integrated Literacy Approach involves integrating meaningful reading and writing, conversations with and about reading, and instruction in reading and writing skills and strategies used in authentic contexts. It meets the needs of a wide range of English language learners for developing literacy. A basic element is providing a print-rich classroom in which students' oral language and literacy development are valued and put to use. The literacy strategies we will recommend gradually move from providing more teacher responsibility to shared responsibility between teacher and learner, to learner-independence in reading.

The Language/Literacy Matrix

Language and literacy skills do not necessarily develop in parallel with ELLs. Some learners may have good first-language (L1) literacy and English language instruction focusing on reading and writing, but still may have had little practice with oral language and be unfamiliar with the sounds of U.S. English. Other learners may have acquired some oral proficiency in English but have not had an opportunity to learn to read in any language. These students may have English oral skills that are more advanced than their reading skills. Teachers who are responsible for the reading development of ELLs should have access to assessments of both types of language learning. Table 7.1, the Language/Literacy Matrix (Freeman, Freeman, McCloskey, Stack, Silva, & Gottlieb, 2004) can help teachers to track both the language and literacy levels of ELLs. Using the results of English language assessment instruments and appropriate reading assessments, place the names of the ELLs in your class in the appropriate boxes. Use these dual assessments in making materials choices and grouping choices, and setting expectations for ongoing assessments.

Levels of oral language development (described in detail in Chapter 5) are listed down the left-hand column. Levels of English literacy development are listed across the top row. Note that your knowledge of childrens' L1 literacy, obtained through formal and/or informal assessment, will also be useful in determining your expectations, your instruction, and your grouping for reading instruction.

Table 7.1 The Language/Literacy Matrix

Stages of Language Acquisition	Levels of English Literacy Development			
	Emergent Literacy	Early Literacy	Early Fluency	Fluency
Stage 1: Pre-production				
Stage 2: Early Production				
Stage 3: Speech Emergence				
Stage 4: Intermediate Fluency				
Stage 5: Advanced Fluency				

Source: Freeman, et al. (2004)

The following are descriptions of the four literacy levels:

Emergent Literacy.   Learners at the **emergent literacy** level understand that print can carry meaningful messages, but are still learning to encode, decode, and understand these messages. They learn basic concepts about books, print, letters, sounds, and writing. They read books that have many kinds of support: they are short; they often have elements of repetition, rhythm, and rhyme with direct match between the words and the pictures. Learners at this level begin to realize that they can get meaning from text and that they can write texts for others to read.

Early Literacy.   Learners at the **early literacy** level understand that books have messages that do not change and that there are certain conventions regarding how print is presented. They begin to read and write simple fiction and nonfiction texts. They know that reading involves finding meaning through using certain problem-solving skills. At this level, learners often read word-by-word, often with a finger pointing at each word.

Early Fluency.   At the **early fluency** level, learners begin to use multiple clues to make meaning from text and are able to understand the main ideas of texts as well as their emotional impact. They rely more on the text, and less on the illustrations to understand the author's message. They use a wider range and variety of problem-solving strategies for reading and determining the meaning of new words.

Fluency.   At the level of **fluency,** learners are becoming mature readers. They make sense of longer and more complex texts approaching or at the level of their native-speaking peers; they use a variety of strategies flexibly to accomplish their reading purposes. They orchestrate all the clues available to them to make meaning: letter-sound relations, the grammar of English, the meanings of words, and the background information and context of the text. When needed, they use self-correction as they read to maintain the meaning of the text. Upper elementary and middle-school readers at this level develop high-level vocabulary and rich comprehension skills to use grade-level academic texts.

What Tools and Strategies Can We Provide to Help ELLs Develop Literacy?

The chart below summarizes strategies that support ELL literacy development. We use the metaphor of **scaffolding,** first introduced by Jerome Bruner (Wood, Bruner, & Ross, 1976) to describe the support that teachers offer to English learners. When workers construct a tall building, they often erect scaffolding—supportive structures around the building to enable them to do their construction work. As the building progresses, scaffolding that is no longer needed is removed. Likewise, teachers provide useful tools and strategies to support learners in developing new language and concepts. And as students become proficient and independent, they begin to use tools and strategies for learning on their own as teachers dismantle unneeded scaffolds and create new, more challenging ones to guide learners toward even higher achievement. This approach is called the gradual release of responsibility model (Brown, Campione, & Day, 1981; Fitzgerald & Graves, 2004) and is shown in Figure 7.7. At early levels in this approach, teachers take most of the responsibility for making the reading task successful; but as learners acquire more skills, they take on more and more of the responsibility for their success.

Figure 7.7 Gradual Release of Responsibility Model

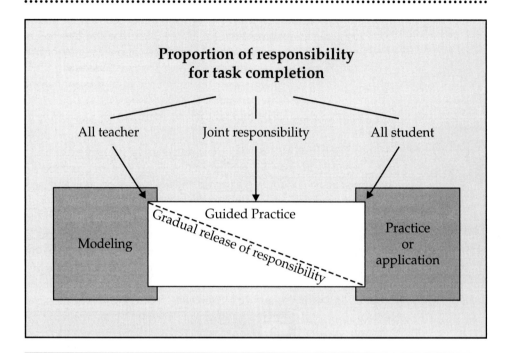

Source: Brown, Campione, & Day (1981); Fitzgerald & Graves, (2004)

We will describe the scaffolding strategies for use throughout literacy lessons (Table 7.2) as well as specific strategies for before, during, and after the reading. We have combined the stages of literacy development into two groups because of the space limits in this chapter, but encourage readers to think of these supports as located along a continuum: from more support to less support; from expectations that the teacher does most of the work in reading to expectations that learners are responsible for making meaning from the text on their own. A number of specific strategies are suggested in parentheses. These are not comprehensive, but are *examples* of the types of strategies to use.

Next, we include brief descriptions of the strategies mentioned for the two reading level groups: Emergent/Early Literacy and Early Fluency/Fluency. We have listed the strategies in alphabetical order to help you find them easily. Then we include a section with additional recommendations for older readers in third grade to eighth grade, both those who are literate in their first language and transferring literacy skills to English, and those who have low-literacy in their first language and are developing initial literacy in English. Table 7.3 lists all the strategy descriptions included in this chapter.

21 Strategies to Support ELL Reading Development

1. Adapting Phonics for ELLs
Levels: Emergent/Early literacy
Grades: All if developing initial literacy

Adapting Phonics for ELLs. Phonics is one of the important components of literacy development at emergent/early literacy levels, but traditional phonics often does not fit the needs of ELLs. If your school provides a phonics program for

Table 7.2 Strategies for Developing Literacy for English Language Learners (ELLs)

	Emergent/Early Literacy	**Early Fluency/Fluency**
Scaffolding Throughout Literacy Lessons	• Provide comprehensible input, checking comprehension frequently. *(Read Aloud)* • Build oral language vocabulary and fluency in meaningful contexts with rich literacy experiences. *(Shared Reading)* • Monitor and develop learners' ability to hear and reproduce English phonemes. *(Choral Reading)* • Develop/reinforce abilities to associate the sounds with spelling patterns of English with letters and word parts. *(Adapting Phonics for ELLs)*	• Provide comprehensible input, checking comprehension frequently. • Continue to build more complex oral language vocabulary and fluency in meaningful contexts. *(Anticipation Guide, Question-Answer-Response or QAR)* • Expand phonics into word study. • Continue to develop listening comprehension, awareness of the differences between L1 and English.
Choosing Texts	• Texts with rhyme, rhythm, repetition. • Illustrations are closely related to text. • Themes are comprehensible across cultures. • Scaffold texts, use selections from texts, or select alternate texts when needed. *(Choosing Texts)*	• Interesting, well-written texts. • Texts have gradually increasing complexity and length. • Texts in which culturally and linguistically diverse learners can see themselves. • Gradually expand to a variety of fiction and nonfiction genres. • Modify texts, use selections from texts, scaffold texts, and select alternate texts when needed. *(Choosing Texts)*
Before the Reading	• Motivate: build concept of reading as a purposeful process of making meaning; develop learners' understanding of purposes for reading. • Review, reread, recite previous texts, chants, and songs. • Teach key vocabulary. *(See Chapter 9)* • Build background knowledge of concepts needed to comprehend text. *(Graphic Organizers, Picture Walk-Through)* • Make connections to learners' own experience and learners' families and communities. *(Language Experience)* • Recommend reading strategies for the text. *(Think Aloud, Guided Reading)*	• Motivate: expand purposes for reading and understanding of a range of genres. • Teach key vocabulary, academic vocabulary, and vocabulary development strategies. • Build background knowledge of concepts needed to comprehend text *(Teaching text structure, i.e., how text is organized). (Also see Chapter 8)* • Make connections to learners' own experience and to learners' families and communities. *(Home-School Connections, Take-Home Reading)* • Focus attention on one or two key reading comprehension strategies. *(Think Aloud, Guided Reading, Teaching Comprehension Skills)*

(Continued)

Table 7.2 Strategies for Developing Literacy for English Language Learners (ELLs) *(Continued)*

	Emergent/Early Literacy	Early Fluency/Fluency

During the Reading	• Use gradual release of responsibility for reading from teacher to learner: Reading to learners, reading with learners, supporting learners' independent reading.
	
	• Teach/reinforce key comprehension skills, literacy skills, and phonics in context through the text. *(Adapting phonics for ELLs)*
	
	• Use read aloud, shared reading, and guided reading techniques.
		• Use a variety of supportive structures to scaffold during the reading:
		  • *Read aloud, audio texts*
		  • *Shared reading*
		  • *Reciprocal teaching*
		  • *Guided reading*
		  • *Jigsaw reading*
		  • *Silent reading*
		  • *Text selection/modification*
		  • *Graphic organizers*
		
		• Teach/reinforce key comprehension skills and literacy skills for identifying words and developing sentence and text-level skills. *(Semantic Feature Analysis)*
		
		• Develop oral skills for talking about text and for fluent and expressive reading. *(Reciprocal Teaching)*

After the Reading	• Develop comprehension through questioning and discussing. *(QAR)* • Teach and apply word-solving tools in meaningful contexts. *(Graphic Organizers)* • Build writing experiences from the reading: e.g., using sentence frames from the text. *(See Chapter 8)* • Support learners as they respond to texts orally, in writing, and expressively. • Make literacy connections with the home. *(Home-School Connections, Take-Home Reading)*	• Continue to develop comprehension and problem-solving through questioning and discussing. *(Anticipation Guide, QAR)* • Continue word, sentence, and text-solving during reading. *(Word Squares)* • Build writing workshops around the genre of the selection. *(See Chapter 8)* • Support learners as they respond to texts orally, in writing, and expressively. • Make literacy and literary connections with the home. *(Home-School Connections, Take-Home Reading)*

learners of English, you may need to make adjustments to the program in order to include these students. First, make sure that your learners are ready for the program. It is difficult to teach phonics with words that students don't know and pictures that are culturally unfamiliar. It doesn't make sense to teach students to read and write sounds they can't yet hear. Before you begin, check that the pictures and language used in the program are comprehensible to the learners. Pre-teach new language you will use in introducing phonics elements or make selections from language that students know. If you have a number of students from the same language background, you may also choose to re-order

Table 7.3 21 Strategies for ELL Literacy Development

Focus on Reading

1. Adapting Phonics for ELLs	12. Jigsaw Reading
2. Anticipation Guide	13. Language Experience
3. Choice Independent Reading	14. Picture Walk
4. Choosing/Adapting Texts for ELLs	15. Point of View
5. Choral Reading	16. Question-Answer-Response (QAR)
6. Feature Analysis	17. Reading Aloud to ELLs
7. Graphic Organizers	18. Reciprocal Teaching
8. Guided Reading	19. Shared Reading
9. Home-School Connections	20. Think-Aloud
10. Instructional Conversations	21. Word Squares
11. Intensive Reading	

the instruction, first teaching the sounds and spelling patterns that will be easier for your learners, then moving on to those sounds of English that are not found in their home languages. Sound-Symbol Transfer Issues for Four Languages Using the Roman Alphabet (Morganthaler, 2004), as shown in Table 7.4, points out which English sounds might prove more difficult for speakers of five common languages of immigrants. Additional information on languages of the ten largest immigrant populations in the U.S. can be found in *Teacher's Resource Guide on Language Transfer Issues for English Language Learners* (Morganthaler, 2004). These include grammar issues (e.g., speakers of Arabic use articles more than speakers of English, and are likely to make errors such as, "I like the sports.") and phonics transfer issues (e.g., Spanish, Vietnamese, Cantonese, and Korean have no short *a* sound as in *hat,* so the word may sound like *hot;* Spanish speakers don't have an initial *s* sound and often add a syllable to words beginning with *s, as in Espanish, or eschool.*). Table 7.4 suggests phonics sequences for beginning students from several cultural groups. The sequences are based on teaching first consonants, then vowels, and by teaching easier sounds—sounds that occur in both the home language and English—first then moving on to sounds that are new to ELLs from each language group.

Understanding and accommodating learners with different language backgrounds. There are many ways that languages differ and it's valuable for teachers to understand a bit about the first languages of the learners in their classrooms. For example, they may have different writing systems. In a **logographic language,** one symbol represents the meaning of a concept, individual word, or part of a word. Arabic numerals and mathematical symbols are examples of logographic symbols. Chinese, Japanese (Kanji), and Korean use logographic systems. In a **syllabic language,** one symbol represents a syllable, or consonant-vowel combination. Japanese and Korean languages both use syllabic writing systems. In **alphabetic systems,** one symbol generally represents one sound. The Roman alphabet is

Table 7.4 Sound-Symbol Transfer

Issues for four languages using the Roman Alphabet. Sounds with transfer issues (from a given language to English) are indicated by bullets.

English Sounds/Symbols	Spanish	Vietnamese	Hmong	Haitian Creole
b as in bat			•	
c as in cat *c* as in cent		• •	• •	•
d as in dog				
f as in fish				
g as in goat *g* as in giant	•		• •	
h as in hen	•			
j as in jacket	•	•	•	
k as in kite			•	
l as in lemon				
m as in moon				
n as in nice				
p as in pig				
qu as in queen	•		•	•
r as in rabbit	•		•	
s as in sun			•	
t as in teen			•	
v as in video	•			
w as in wagon		•	•	
x as in x-ray				
y as in yo-yo				•
z as in zebra	•	•	•	
sh as in shoe	•			
ch as in chair				•
th as in think *th* as in that	•			•

Source: Morganthaler (2004)

used in most European languages as well as Vietnamese and many African languages. Greek has its own alphabet. The Cyrillic alphabet is used in Serbo-Croatian and Russian. In addition to writing systems, languages also have very different vocabularies, grammatical systems, and sounds.

Though it might be very useful, we know it is not likely to be feasible for you to learn to speak all the languages of your English learners. You can, however, learn a little about how their languages work, to help you predict what aspects of language may be easily confused, and what aspects of English may be very new to students from certain groups so that you can prepare to focus lessons on these aspects as appropriate. Another useful source is *The Human Languages Website* by Tyler Chambers, which includes links to rich resources on 209 languages http://www.ilovelanguages.com/).

Video Exercise

Phonics *and* Word Recognition

Go to MyEducationLab, select the topic **Emergent Literacy,** and watch the videos entitled **"Phonics"** and **"Word Recognition"** to observe a teacher conducting a word recognition lesson and a phonics lesson. Complete the questions that accompany it. You may print your work or have it transmitted to your professor as necessary.

Explicit phonics and phonemic awareness. Remember that phonics should be developed in the context of language that is meaningful and purposeful for learners. Though young learners tend to acquire new sound systems easily, sometimes oral development activities are needed to help some learners—especially middle-school and older learners, and learners who seem to have trouble with the sound system—develop the ability to hear new English sounds, and to recognize similar sounds such as rhyming sounds. Phonics sequenced from easy to difficult may be adapted for different language groups. Focus first on hearing differences. Begin sound-letter associations with consonants (in easy-to-difficult order) and then teach vowels through word families. Use known words to teach phonics elements. Teach reading skills through engaging, motivating, texts chosen to be at learners' instructional level. Your school's speech/language assessment process should also include processes for detecting whether ELLs have speech/language issues (e.g., auditory or articulation problems) separate from their language development needs, and for serving those special needs. Keep in mind that learners with special needs will be found with the same frequency among ELLs as among other groups.

2. **Anticipation Guide**
   Level: Early fluency/fluency
   Grades: 3–8

The **anticipation guide** (Herber & Herber, 1993) helps students to develop background information about a topic they will read about as well as to explore their own ideas about the topic and to report on the author's main ideas. The teacher prepares a list of true-false statements about a reading. Before they read the text, learners complete the "you" column on the chart with their own opinions about the statements. They discuss their answers in small groups and explain why they answered as they did. After they read the text, they re-think their responses to the statements according to the information provided in the text and write their answers in the "text" column. Teacher and students discuss their answers, and students are encouraged to support their opinions by returning to the text. See the sample Anticipation Guide in Table 7.5.

3. **Choice Independent Reading**
   Levels: All
   Grades: All

Choice reading is a powerful tool for improving ELL literacy. Teach students to select books for independent reading that interest them and that are at their comfort reading level. (Note that reading levels can vary with learners' interest and motivation.) Provide children with books to choose from and structured, regular time to read alone and to one another. Model by reading yourself during choice reading time. Create opportunities for learners to share and discuss the books they

Table 7.5 Anticipation Guide for "Dealing with Bullying"

Directions:

1. Read the statements below.

2. Before you read the selection, fill out the "you" column. Write "T" if you think the statement is true or "F" if you think it's false.

3. After you read, write your answers in the "text" column. Write "T" if you think the answer is true according to the text. Write "F" if you think the answer is false according to the text.

You (True or False)	Text (True or False)	Statement
		Bullying can be verbal, nonverbal, psychological, or physical.
		Walking away from a bully is a sign of cowardice.
		Only boys can be bullies.
		Bullies are always people who are big, brave, and secure.
		Body language can help you stand up to a bully.
		Never make jokes with a bully.
		If your friends act like bullies, you should join them.
		Talking about bullying—with peers and adults—is often a good thing to do.
		If you see someone being bullied, you should stand up and speak up.

Based on the reading "Dealing with Bullying" at TeensHealth (http://kidshealth.org/teen/your_mind/problems/bullies.html).

read, and to develop their thinking about what they have learned. Beginning readers may choose wordless books, class-made books, picture books, books in their first languages, or audiotapes. With success, support, and guidance, learners will move on to more and more challenging texts and begin to love to read.

4. **Choosing/Adapting Texts for ELLs**
   Levels: All
   Grades: All

Teachers of classes including English learners work with multilevel, multilingual, multicultural classes with wide diversity (Cloud, Genesee, & Hamayan, 2000). They must choose texts carefully to meet the range of students, attending to the following:

- A variety of texts should accommodate students' many purposes for reading; e.g., texts for thematic study, texts for intensive instruction in guided reading, or texts available for students' choice during independent reading.
- Texts should include relevant, needed content that is aligned with mainstream content that learners will need for academic courses.
- Texts should have appropriate cultural aspects—content that the students have the background to understand. They should have positive, accurate, empowering representation of students' cultural groups that avoids

stereotypes or stereotypical settings. (Some groups of American Indians may have lived in Tepees, but historically Indians have lived in many types of homes, and most live in contemporary homes today; members of groups should not be stereotyped by income level, jobs, and so on.)

- Illustrations should show the varieties and contemporary realities of members of ethnic groups.
- Texts should provide contextual support, such as diagrams and illustrations that are interesting, closely complement, and support the text or glossaries that define unfamiliar terms.
- Texts should, as much as possible, meet the proficiency demands of learners in terms of vocabulary, length, grammatical complexity, and background information required. Several leveling systems are in use for determining the demands of a text (e.g., Fountas & Pinnell, 1996, 2001). One system, (Freeman, et al., 2004), has been developed taking into account the needs of English language learners.
- Early texts should offer language authenticity—natural, predictable language based on oral language familiar to students, often with elements of rhyme, rhythm, and repetition that make texts memorable.
- Text content and illustrations should be appropriate for the age level, background, knowledge, and cultures of learners.
- Texts such as powerful stories, memorable language, purposeful content, and fine art should provide intellectual, aesthetic, and emotional satisfaction (Cloud, et al., 2000).

Useful resources for finding appropriate books for Kindergarten to eighth grade learners include the following review journals: *Book Links, Horn Book Guide to Children's and Young Adults' Books,* and *Interracial Books for Children Bulletin.*

Special considerations for choosing texts at the Emergent/Early Literacy Level. In addition to the considerations for all EL students, the following aspects refer specifically to learners at the emergent/early literacy level.

- Select texts that incorporate features that make language memorable, such as rhyme, rhythm, and repetition. This type of text is particularly important for younger learners and learners who have not learned to read in another language. *The Grouchy Ladybug,* by Eric Carle (1996), uses a patterned, repetitive story that introduces values about getting along, as well as concepts of size and telling time.
- Find books in which illustrations closely parallel the text to support comprehension. Elisha Cooper's *Beach* (2006) uses quiet illustrations that carefully parallel the story of a family's day at the beach.
- Ensure that themes of texts are comprehensible across cultures, or provide background to understand them. *Everybody Cooks Rice* (Dooley, 1991), illustrates how cultures are both alike and similar—how one food can be shared among many cultures, but prepared and eaten differently—and allows learners from a number of different cultures to see characters like themselves in a book.
- When grade-level texts are too difficult or too long for English learners, teachers can provide scaffolding in a variety of ways, including: reading the text aloud to learners; providing "walk through" introductions to texts; shared reading, shared reading with audio texts, and guided reading; having learners read along silently as the teacher reads and read the next word aloud when she pauses; and requiring independent reading of selected sections of a text. These scaffolding strategies are described in more detail in the following section.

Choosing Texts at Early Fluency/Fluency Levels

- For learners at the early fluency levels, texts should be well written and of high interest. Whenever feasible, provide learners with opportunities to select texts.
- Texts should generally have gradually increasing complexity and length. Many schools are "leveling" books using designated leveling criteria, such as that developed by Fountas and Pinnell (1996) or Freeman, et al. (2004). Levels enable teachers to select books at students' instructional levels when students know about 90 percent of the words. Students can select books at their independent reading level when they know about 95 percent of the words. Keep in mind that the percentages developed for instructional and independent reading levels have been established for English proficient students, and that English learners would be expected to be challenged by many new words in reading. Also keep in mind that students' high interest and motivation can help them conquer very challenging texts, so children should be encouraged to range beyond their expected levels on occasion.
- Linguistically and culturally diverse learners and their peers should also have opportunities to read books in which they can see people like themselves, people from cultures with which they are familiar, and characters with whom they can identify. *Samir and Yonatan* (Carmi, 2002), for example, with characters from Israel and Pakistan who room together in a hospital, provides middle-school readers with insight on these cultures and on the experience of being an outsider.
- Learners at these levels can be encouraged to expand their reading to a wide range of fiction and nonfiction genres and should be provided with time for choice reading in school.
- To make challenging grade-level texts more comprehensible, teachers can use a variety of strategies, including reading aloud, shared reading, reciprocal reading, guided reading; and reading selections from texts, modified texts, alternate texts, translated summaries, and audio or multimedia support (McCloskey & Thrush, 2006). Scaffolding strategies are described in greater detail in the next section.

Video Exercise

Literature for a Range of Learners

Go to MyEducationLab, select the topic **Content Area Reading and Writing,** and watch the videos entitled **"Literature for a Range of Learners"** (parts 1 and 2) to observe two teachers teaching literature to diverse classes, including English learners. Complete the questions that accompany it. You may print your work or have it transmitted to your professor as necessary.

5. **Choral Reading**
    Levels: All
    Grades: Primary, Intermediate

In **choral reading,** students have their own copies of a text. They all read together. Often the teacher or a student stands in front of the class to lead the oral reading. When reading dialogues, plays, or stories with dialogue, different groups often read different parts of the text. Assessment suggestion: After students are comfortable with a text, have a student lead the choral reading and walk around the room, standing behind individuals as they read. Note their progress on self-stick notes attached to individual folders or on a class checklist.

6. **Feature Analysis**
    Levels: All
    Grades: All

Learners use a grid to explore how terms and concepts are related to one another and to make distinctions between them. They perform a **feature analysis.** The first column lists terms; the first row lists categories. Terms receive a plus sign ("+") if they fit in that category, and a minus sign ("−") if they do not. (See Tables 7.6 and 7.7.)

Table 7.6 Semantic Feature Analysis Category: Types of Books We Read

Early/Emerging to Primary

	Features				
Terms	**Nonfiction: Biography**	**Historical Fiction**	**Fantasy**	**Reader Liked It**	**Takes Place in the U.S.**
Roberto's book: *Tutankhamen's Gift*	−	+	−	+	−
Mikhail's book: *Abiyoyo*	−	−	+	+	−
Niki's book: *Story Painter*	+	−	−	+	+
Raga's Book: *The Librarian of Basra*	+	−	−	+	−

7. Graphic Organizers
Levels: All
Grades: All

Use pictures or designs with graphics to outline text and to illustrate principles within a text. The storyboard, story map, character web, time lines, Venn diagram, ranking ladder, and many other **graphic organizers** can be used effectively (Figure 7.8). After you have demonstrated and taught graphic organizers, encourage students to develop their own to learn from what they have read and to prepare to write.

During reading, use graphic organizers aligned to the structure of the text to assist learners in taking notes and clarifying their comprehension. For example,

Table 7.7 Semantic Feature Analysis Category: Quadralaterals

Early Fluency/Fluency to Intermediate +

	Features				
Terms	**Only Two Parallel Sides**	**Two Sets of Parallel Sides**	**All Sides Are Congruent**	**Two Sets of Congruent Sides**	**All Angles Are Congruent**
Square	−	+	+	−	+
Rectangle	−	+	−	+	+
Parallelogram	−	+	−	+	−
Rhombus	−	+	+	−	−
Trapezoid	+	−	−	*	−

Figure 7.8 Sample Graphic Organizers

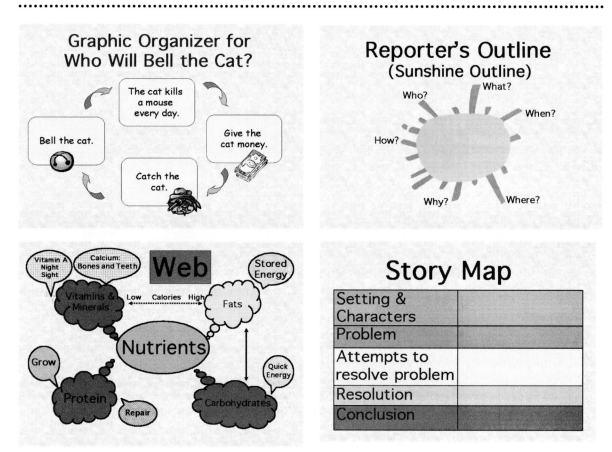

when reading about a central concept or character, use a semantic map as students search the text for identifying attributes. When reading a text organized chronologically, use time lines or flow charts for note-taking important events and/or stages. For cause-and-effect texts, use graphics that clearly identify the cause or causes and the resulting effect(s). Finally, comparison and contrast text organizations can be made more comprehensible with a Venn diagram or double bubble comparison graphic. (See Chapter 5, Figure 5.1, for examples of these graphic organizers.) These graphics can be useful for an oral retelling of the text or as a support for a written summary.

8. **Guided Reading**
    Levels: All
    Grades: Primary and Intermediate; Middle school for early reading.

In **guided reading** (Fountas & Pinnell, 1996), teachers work with small groups with similar reading processes. Books are carefully, progressively leveled to introduce new vocabulary, phonics elements, features of print, and sophistication and length of content. The teacher selects and introduces new books and supports children reading the whole text to themselves, making teaching points during and after the reading. Based on close observation of students' reading, teachers make relevant teaching points during and after the reading.

9. **Home-School Connections**
   Levels: All
   Grades: Primary and Intermediate; Middle school for early reading.

Teachers and schools work to make connections among the school, classroom, and family to help families be engaged in the learning process and to support learners. For ELL families who may have had very different experiences of school, it is important to make efforts toward home-school connections culturally relevant. One example of a culturally and linguistically relevant activity is *At-Home Reading*. After children have mastered texts at school, teachers send the texts home in an envelope with a chart for parents to initial. Students read the books aloud to family members in English, and then summarize the books in the home language. Parents initial the chart and return the book to school. This practice has been shown to have a powerful effect on the development of reading fluency and comprehension, as well as on home-school relations (Tizard, Schofield, & Hewison, 1982).

10. **Instructional Conversations**
    Levels: All
    Grades: All

Through a challenging but nonthreatening process called **instructional conversation,** teachers help students learn to discuss readings at a high level (Tharp & Gallimore, 1988). Teachers provide background knowledge, teach skills or concepts when necessary, and promote students' use of text, pictures, and reasoning to support arguments or positions about text. In the process, teachers ask many open-ended questions, respond to student insights and ideas, and encourage students to take turns with one another, with the teacher as a senior participant in the discussion.

11. **Intensive Reading**
    Levels: Early Fluency/Fluency
    Grades: Middle school

In **intensive reading,** students are directed to read a text several times, each time for a different purpose and using duplicated copies of texts (McCloskey & Stack, 1996). By asking students to underline, annotate, and color-code a text with markers or highlighters, teachers can draw students' attention to literary elements, features of the sound/symbol system, patterns of language, conventions of print, and elements of comprehension.

12. **Jigsaw Reading**
    Levels: Early Fluency/Fluency
    Grades: Intermediate, Middle school

Research evidence shows positive effects of tutoring interactions and small-group cooperative learning tasks (Slavin, 1994; Kagan, 1994; Samway, Whang, & Pippitt, 1995). The **jigsaw** reading technique was first researched by Aaronson (1978). The teacher divides a long reading into sections. One or two individuals in a group read each section and prepare to teach it to the group. When the group meets, each individual teaches the group about the section they have read. The teacher uses a "group quiz" or the "numbered heads together" cooperative learning strategy to assure group responsibility for the content and to assess comprehension.

13. Language Experience
Levels: Emergent/Early literacy
Grades: Primary, Intermediate

Ashton-Warner (2002) first used the **language experience approach** with Maori children in New Zealand, and it has been the subject of considerable subsequent research. After a discussion of a shared or recalled experience, students dictate a narrative as the teacher writes it on a chart, projected computer screen, or transparency. Teacher and students revise and edit the text together. The teacher uses opportunities to teach vocabulary text structures, language structures, and conventions of print. Later, students can use copies of the text as reading texts and as the basis for a series of follow-up activities, including practice with vocabulary, phonics, language structures, comprehension, independent reading, and creative expression.

14. Picture Walk
Levels: Emergent/Early literacy
Grades: Primary, Intermediate

A **picture walk,** a procedure frequently used in guided reading (Fountas & Pinnell, 1996), helps to build learners' interest in a story and set up expectations about what they will enjoy. In addition, a picture walk helps learners focus on using visual cues as they read, a valuable skill for English learners who may find context information in picture cues that will help them comprehend the story. To lead a picture walk, "read" through the pages of the story without reading the words. As you look at the pictures, point out, and have students point out key characters, aspects of the setting, and events, and have them ask questions and make guesses about them. A picture walk will help activate ELLs' prior learning, help learners develop familiarity with the story, enable teachers to introduce and discuss new vocabulary, and make teachers aware of background information that language learners may need to understand the story.

A picture walk might look like this:

- We're going to read *Mrs. Wishy-Washy.* Here's the title, *Mrs. Wishy-Washy,* and here's the author's name. It's Joy Cowley.
- Let's look at the front cover. What do you think this story will be about? Who do you think will be in the story?
- Do you know what this is? (A pig.) What do you know about pigs? What is this pig doing? Why? Who else do you see?
- Let's turn the page. Look, there are the same characters again. Who are they?
- Now what is happening? What do you think will happen next?
- We're almost at the end of *Mrs. Wishy-Washy.* How do you think it will end?
- Now, what do you want to find out when we read the story?
- I wonder what Mrs. Wishy-Washy will say to all the animals?

15. Point of View
Levels: All
Grades: All

For **point of view,** students take on the role of characters in a fiction or nonfiction text, and work to understand the motivation behind the actions of characters from a story (McCloskey & Stack, 2003). Divide the students into groups of three or four. Assign each group a character from the reading. Ask the group to think of at least three questions they could ask that character. Then one member from each group comes to the front of the room and takes on the role of the character. Group members ask the "character" their questions. Other groups may also ask questions of that character. The character answers the questions based on the reading and their background knowledge.

16. Question-Answer-Response (QAR)
Levels: Early Fluency/Fluency
Grades: Intermediate, Middle school

With **question-answer-response (QAR),** learners learn to ask different types of questions and to locate answers in a text. First, model, teach, and practice the four levels of questions of QAR (these questions are based on *Story Painter: The Life of Jacob Lawrence*, by John Duggleby and Jacob Lawrence):

- *Right there questions.* For these questions, the answer is stated in the text— The question asks for facts from the text (e.g., "Where was Jacob Lawrence born?").
- *Think and search questions.* For these questions, students must look for the answer in more than one part of the text. The question asks the reader to bring together information from different parts of the text (e.g., "In what different places did Jacob Lawrence live while he was growing up? How did moving around affect him?").
- *Author and you questions.* For these questions, the answer is a combination of information from what the reader knows and what the author has written. The question asks for information from both the reader and the text (e.g., "What outside influences helped Jacob Lawrence to develop his talent? What did Jacob Lawrence do himself? Which do you think the author sees as most important? Which do you think is most important?").
- *On your own questions.* For these questions, the answer comes from the reader's knowledge and experience. The question asks for an opinion from the reader (e.g., "What talent would you like to develop? How might you do that?").

Prepare a list of questions in the four areas for the students to answer based on a selection from the text. In small groups of 3 to 4, have students read the selection from the text and answer the questions. They indicate the QAR category for each question and justify their decisions. Next, the students read another selection from the text and write their own QAR questions. Groups exchange their questions with other groups, answer them, and categorize them into QAR levels. Eventually, learners develop their own questions in the four categories and use them to discuss the readings.

17. Reading Aloud to ELLs
Levels: All
Grades: All

Reading aloud provides motivation, access, background information, vocabulary development, and builds comprehension skills (Trelease, 2006). After oral discussion to develop the schema (the organizational plan or structure of the text) and explain background information needed to understand a text, introduce the book by reading it aloud to students. If you are reading a picture book or other shorter text, you may choose to read through the text the first time for flow. Then stop to

Reading Aloud Can Provide Learners with Access to a Text That Is Slightly Above Their Instructional Reading Level

ask and answer questions when needed during the second and subsequent repetitions. Ask students which words they don't understand and provide pictures, translations, or definitions as needed. If you are reading a chapter book, you might have learners summarize the previous day's chapter before beginning today's. Reading aloud is a good way to make students familiar with a text to prepare them for other kinds of reading or to provide access to a text that is slightly above their instructional level. It also provides a good model for pronunciation, phrasing, and expression. Audiotapes provide a different, though related, type of reading support for ELLs, and can help them with independent reading. Repeated reading with audio support has been shown to help ELLs in improving their reading.

18. Reciprocal Teaching
Levels: Early Fluency/Fluency
Grades: Intermediate and Middle School

Palinscar (1986) found that when **reciprocal teaching** was used with learners for just 15 to 20 days, students' reading comprehension assessment increased from 30 percent to 80 percent. Follow-up research on the strategy (reported in Oczkus, 2003) has shown it to be effective in many situations. Reciprocal teaching (Palinscar & Brown, 1984) helps students to focus intently on what they are reading by using four key strategies. By consciously asking questions and summarizing content, they learn to understand and remember what is read. English language learners must listen to one another's questions and comments, and teach each other the material. In preparation for reciprocal teaching, students are taught strategies of *summarizing, clarifying, question-generating,* and *predicting.* Teachers model the "teacher role." Then the student "teacher" uses these strategies in questioning and leading the group discussion as readers participate in a dialogue about the text. Each person takes a turn as "teacher," reading a short passage and asking questions about it to the group. Turns may rotate after a paragraph or a longer section.

19. Shared Reading
Levels: Emergent/Early Literacy
Grades: All

For **shared reading,** teachers use engaging, enlarged texts (such as big books, charts, or projected texts), which all learners can easily see, to involve learners in reading together as the teacher uses a pointer to direct students to look at the text being read. A typical shared reading lesson might look like this: a) The teacher and students "warm-up" by re-reading together texts that students have studied previously and are comfortable with; b) The teacher leads pre-reading activities, including building anticipation for the book; discussing the parts of the book, author, and title; reviewing reading skills and strategies, and previewing the pages and making predictions about the text; c) The class participates in multiple readings of the text, with the teacher reading aloud the first time and learners chiming in on more and more of the reading with successive repetitions; teachers stop to discuss needed reading strategies, comprehension skills, elements of phonics, or conventions of print occasionally as the opportunity or need arises; d) The class participates in a variety of activities to follow up on the group reading, such as retelling (with the teacher and then alone) and discussion of the story; mini-lessons on certain reading strategies (e.g., letter-sound relationships, text features, or the writer's craft); e) Students are engaged in a variety of group or individual extension activities, including small-group reading and instruction; listening to the story on audiotape with follow-up activities; creative expression in art, drama, or music; or writing activities using patterns from the text to create new variations.

In **shared-to-guided reading,** designed for ELLs, teachers first "walk" learners through the text, using picture cues to develop vocabulary. Then teachers set the scene, read and reread the text aloud, and help students recall and discuss the content. Students read the book independently or with partners and follow up on reading with recall, skill development, and expressive responses to the literature.

20. Think-Aloud
Levels: All
Grades: All

In the **think-aloud** strategy, the teacher models the internal thinking involved in reading and allows students to observe learning strategies in action. First, determine the learning strategy to be taught and the content you will use; for example, sequencing with a work of fiction, such as *Momotaro: The Peach Boy* (Shute, 1986) at the emergent/early literacy level, or historical fiction, such as *Sacajawea* (Bruchac, 2002). Determine what you want students to know about the strategy; for example, how to place events along a time line. Plan an assessment to determine if students are successful with the strategy, such as a "numbered heads" activity in which learners construct a time line for a chapter of the book. Plan your think-aloud carefully—think about the strategy to be taught, the central concept and key themes of the text, and your own experiences related to the themes. Put notes in the text where you might stop to think aloud.

Introduce the lesson by explaining that a think-aloud is when someone says out loud what they are thinking about how to go about learning. Demonstrate the think-aloud as you read the text. Stop and look at the ceiling or otherwise show when you're stopping to think as you read. For sequencing, use key words such as "Now, what happened first? Second? Third? What was the final event? I am using this sequencing strategy because . . . ." (Note: this may take many repetitions before the students understand it thoroughly.) When students understand the strategy you are using, ask them to practice it using a short section of the reading.

Figure 7.9 Word Square for "Parallel"

Word: Parallel	Symbol or Picture
Translation: *paralelo -a* **My meaning:** *side by side* **Opposite:** *intersecting*	
Dictionary Meaning	**Sentences**
Two lines running side-by-side at an equal distance from one another	*The train tracks are parallel.* *The two stories have parallel plots (math). Two lines that are parallel will never meet.*

21. Word Squares

Levels: Early Literacy/Early Fluency/Fluency
Grades: All

The **word square** graphic organizer (Figure 7.9) is a multidimensional tool for vocabulary development. Students use a variety of ways to explore and remember a new term. To teach the strategy, have students help you create a word square for an unfamiliar word in one of their texts. Show them how to find a translation, how to write the meaning in their own words (they may need to look up the word first), and how to think of an opposite or negative example of the word. Have students look up the word in a picture dictionary, learner dictionary, or translation dictionary (depending on their level), and have them come up with several sentences that illustrate the meaning of the word. Then encourage them to create a pictorial symbol for the word that will help them remember it. After learners have tried word squares with their teacher, they're ready to try with a partner or in a small group, and eventually on their own. Learners can use their word squares to teach one another new, challenging terms.

Issues in Literacy Development with Older English Learners

A recent case study, "Why Mei still cannot read and what can be done" (Li & Zhang, 2004) explores all the factors involved in a Chinese student's failure to develop proficiency in reading and writing in a U.S. public school. Mei, a 14-year-old sixth grader, has failed to learn to read despite spending two years in elementary school with a pull-out ESL program four times a week. The authors reveal much of Mei's problem came from the lack of communication and collaboration among Mei's classroom teachers, her ESL teacher, and her parents. They conclude that teachers—preservice classroom teacher, inservice classroom teachers, and English language development teachers—must learn to work with one another as well as with support staff, administration, and parents, to plan, implement, and supervise an adequate program for each ELD student taking into account all the variables: educational background, native language ability, age of arrival, parents' education and occupations.

Older Learners of English May Have Special Issues in Developing English Reading Skills

Older learners of English have special issues in developing English reading that must be taken into account in all the situations in school in which reading skills are developed and used (de Jong & Harper, 2004). First of all, these learners are not all alike—they have remarkable differences in the background and characteristics they bring to your class. Although each student is unique, we will generalize our descriptions into three groups for clarity (Freeman, Freeman, & Mercuri, 2003). One group includes recent arrivals with adequate formal schooling in their first language. They have academic and literacy skills, and need to transfer these to English, while continuing to develop and maintain their content knowledge. A second group includes recent arrivals who, for various reasons (living in rural areas, poverty, war, membership in language minority, etc.), have had limited or interrupted formal schooling. These students often do not have a strong academic background or reading skills in their home language and, of course, need to develop these in English along with conversational skills. A third group, sometimes referred to as "Generation 1.5" learners, includes long-term English learners, whose schooling has been all or nearly all in the U.S., who have never developed strong literacy in their first language or in English; and who, although they may have good conversational skills in two languages, do not have strong academic skills in either (Roberge, 2002).

So, learners of English may differ on their:

- Level of schooling in any language.
- Level of literacy in their home language or English (or in additional languages—some learners, such as indigenous Guatemalans, may speak different languages at home from those spoken in their schools in Guatemala).
- Level of cultural adaptation—many older students' characteristics, experiences, and educational needs lie somewhere between first-generation adult immigrants and U.S.-born second-generation children of immigrants.

There are several additional issues that present special challenges to developing literacy with older learners. First, there is much more language for them to learn—the content is much more complex for a sixth grader than for a first or second grader: the texts are much longer and the language is more advanced. Second, students also tend to acquire the social language needed to communicate with peers, teachers, and the greater community in a few years (Cummins, 1994; Thomas & Collier, 1997; Hakuta, Butler, & Witt, 2000), but take a much longer time (five to seven years, on average) to perform academically like their English-proficient peers. Teachers often misinterpret learners' oral conversational fluency to imply that students should be performing like grade-level native speaking peers in this time frame, while research shows that the average length of time for learners to perform like native speakers is five to seven years. Third, assessments used at these grade levels are frequently inappropriate because so much of content assessment is integrated with language assessment, and it is therefore difficult for these learners to show what they know about the content on such assessments. Recent development of specific standardized assessments for English learners may prove helpful in this area, but nevertheless have the limitations of standardized tests. Fourth, researchers have found that developing literacy in the first language is often a more efficient route to second-language literacy, but few programs for older learners provide such opportunities, so students must deal with developing initial literacy in a language they don't know very well.

What Are Our Recommendations for Teaching These Older Learners?

While applying the principles and strategies we have outlined in this chapter, pay particular attention to these recommendations:

1. *Find out who your students are.* Recognize their unique needs and differences. Interview students, family members, and other relatives or community members, to find out about students' histories, their ethnic groups, their educational backgrounds, and the languages they know and use. Students often show up with a translator on their first days—take advantage of this opportunity to learn whatever you can. Avoid making assumptions, for example, that a student who arrives from Kenya speaks Kiswahili. There are many indigenous languages in Kenya, and in addition there are many refugee centers where children may have arrived from: Somalia, Ethiopia, or the Sudan. There are parallel situations throughout the world.

2. *Assess your students carefully and continuously.* Expect the unexpected. Students at this age, particularly those with strong educational backgrounds, can progress very quickly and should not be held back by the need to follow a lockstep curriculum. On the other hand, students who are developing initial literacy may take more time and will be likely to need specialized reading instruction from an instructor who understands both reading development and English language development. The ongoing informal assessment techniques in Chapter 10, in addition to the formal English language assessments expected by your school, will help you to know what your learners know and can do, what you should be teaching them, and how quickly they can progress. Be aware, as well, that there will be students with special needs among your English learner population. If a child's progress is clearly not typical, don't wait long to refer the learner. Watch learners carefully and keep track of your observations. Ask parents if children exhibit developmental differences in the home. English learners who are gifted or have certain learning issues may need special education assessment and services. Minimally, specialists can help you develop pre-referral strategies to serve the child appropriately and to continue assessing the child to determine special needs. Be sure to talk to parents or guardians as well about how learners perform in their first language and in interactions at home. These actions can provide very helpful information when determining whether further evaluation is needed.

3. *Provide age-appropriate materials with appropriate challenge.* Although finding appropriate materials for older students has been very difficult in the past, many more materials are available that support older learners who are developing literacy, both through specialized literacy programs, and through fiction and non-fiction library materials. These often correlate to grade-appropriate content-area concepts so that English learners can be focusing on the same standards as their English proficient peers, but with reading materials at an appropriate level. Look for materials that will interest learners, that are related to what their content classes are studying, and that are at an appropriate reading level. Remember that for a book to be at instructional level, learners should know about 90 percent of the words. For a book to be at the independent reading level, learners should know about 95 percent of the words. Because English learners are just developing their English vocabulary, you may find that you will use books that are slightly more difficult for them than ones where they know 90 percent or 95 percent of the words. They may, then, require more scaffolding support in the form of such strategies as graphic organizers, pictures, audio recordings, or book talks.

4. *Provide encouragement and design instruction for success.* This is the age when English learners who are developing literacy may become discouraged with school and either stop trying, or drop out, or both. If you scaffold tasks at which your learners can succeed, and through which they see themselves learning, and offer them encouragement as they attempt more and more challenging learning opportunities, they will see the possibilities for learning, and not be discouraged by their temporary limitations. They will have the hope and support they need to become successful.

5. *Make learning purposeful and meaningful.* Garcia (1999) found that successful teachers focused on topics and concepts that have meaning and relevance for students, and organized their instruction around themes. Through theme study, students build confidence and competence by becoming "experts" in a particular area. Teachers are able to recycle vocabulary, reading skills, and concepts as they focus on answering theme questions that are important to learners.

6. *Make learning culturally relevant.* Learn both with and from your students about their home cultures. Culture is deeply imbedded in our personalities and psyches—it defines who we are. By valuing the cultures of your students, and making these cultures part of what you learn in school, you are affirming your students as people and you are building their senses of self-worth. By providing background information and cultural bridges learners may need to understand the material you teach in class, you help them to learn that they can themselves bridge two cultures successfully, and strive to keep what is valuable in both.

Assessing ELL Literacy Development

Our motto for assessment, is "assess what you teach, the way you teach it." By this, we mean that your teaching and your assessment should be part of the same process, and should work together to promote your students' learning, as well as to inform your teaching, and monitor progress for your parents and your school. To do this, you will use a variety of types of assessment. We address assessment in depth in Chapter 10, but briefly explain here the types of literacy assessment:

1. Standardized reading achievement or **performance-based assessments.**
2. **English language proficiency tests:** standardized assessments designed specifically for ELLs. (These include, for example, the CELDT in California,

ACCESS in a consortium of 16 U.S. states, TELPAS in Texas, and a variety of "off the shelf" assessments determined by individual districts in Florida.)
3. **Holistic measures** of literacy development.
4. Widely-used assessments of specific literacy skills.
5. Assessments from a reading ELD program.
6. Teacher-developed assessments to be used as part of the teaching process.

Standardized Reading Achievement Tests

Many schools are required to use standardized assessments with ELLs. Teachers who work with ELLs should be aware of important issues regarding the use of these tests with ELLs. First, it is very difficult to separate whether these instruments are actually assessing literacy development or whether they are assessing language development because these are often confounded. Second, results may be influenced by issues of cultural background or previous experiences of learners, which may result in instruments not accurately assessing skills. Third, the process of taking an inappropriate assessment may not be harmless—students are often very frustrated and upset when asked to perform beyond their capabilities. Know that many districts and states provide accommodations for ELLs to provide a more level playing ground when students are taking these assessments. And know that the scores students receive on these tests may not tell you much about their learning or your teaching.

English Language Proficiency Tests

As a result of NCLB (2001), states are required to develop or adopt assessments of English language proficiency that can be used to assess learners' and schools' progress toward meeting standards. For example, ELLs in California take the California English Language Development Test (CELDT); in Texas they take the Texas English Language Proficiency Assessment System (TELPAS); in New York, the New York State English as a Second Language Achievement Test; in Florida, districts use a selection of "off-the-shelf" tests, such as the Language Assessment Scales (LAS); and in a consortium of 16 states (the WIDA consortium), districts use the ACCESS test (Assessing Comprehension and Communication in English State-to-State for English Language Learners). Most of these assessments include reading sub-scores to show ELL proficiency. These tests are usually administered upon a learner's initial entrance into a school district for placement, and then administered annually to show progress. Because they are given so infrequently, and because of the time lag in scoring, they are not as useful for informing teaching as they are for measuring school progress over the long term.

Holistic Measures of Literacy Development

Many teachers have found holistic measures of reading, which often provide sub-scores of specific skills, to be very useful in understanding how readers are developing. They can be time-consuming, as they are often individually administered, but provide very rich information about how learners' reading is developing. Remember that the scoring methods for any of these may not be developed with ELLs in mind, and that instructions may state that a pronunciation error, for example, be scored as a reading error. You may have to make accommodations in interpreting results for ELLs. Three types of holistic measures are:

- *Informal reading inventories.* Several **informal reading inventories** are used to get a close look at students' reading. Teachers with training in their use can get a picture of learners' development, and often a grade-level equivalent score that is comparable across schools and programs. These tools, often administered individually, use progressively more difficult passages. Learners read each passage as teachers score their oral reading; then teachers ask a series of questions, or ask for a summary or retelling to assess comprehension.
- *Miscue analysis.* In **miscue analysis,** developed by Kenneth Goodman (Goodman, Watson, & Burke, 2005), learners read set passages and teachers score various aspects of student reading, trying to see how the reader approaches the task. The instrument looks, for example, at self-corrections learners make and at errors that indicate the reader's thinking. Errors might indicate whether learners are attending to syntactic, semantic, or phonemic cues (or some combination) in solving new words.
- *Running record.* The **running record assessment,** developed by Marie Clay (2000), has been used in Reading Recovery and other programs. Teachers can use a variety of texts at appropriate levels for learners and use a coding system to record exactly what learners read, including repetitions, corrections, mispronunciations, and so on. Teachers also ask for a retelling to assess comprehension. The resulting data are then analyzed to determine a number of sub-scores in learners' reading.

Reading Skills Tests

A number of tools have been developed to look at specific skills of reading: for example, phonemic awareness, phonics, vocabulary, fluency, and comprehension. All of these can be useful, but all can also have limitations when working with English learners. The Dynamic Indicators of Basic Early Literacy Skills (DIBELS) (http://dibels.uoregon.edu) for example, is widely used to measure primary learners' development of early skills in phonological awareness, alphabetic principle, and fluency with connected text. The tool does not look at how learners' thinking about reading is developing, and uses items such as nonsense words (Nonsense Word Fluency NWF) that are particularly confusing for ELLs. To add to the confusion on this test, a number of the English words and nonsense words used on the Dibels are *real* words in Spanish, so Spanish-speakers can read these words correctly in their own language but be marked wrong on the Dibels.

Other instruments look at reading fluency, and the speedy recognition of letters and words with accuracy of decoding and expressiveness (prosody). Assessments of fluency include tests such as the Oral Fluency Assessment from Scholastic (1999) (http://content.scholastic.com/browse/article.jsp?id=4445) that measures the number of words read correctly per minute (WCPM) rate. Other fluency assessments are holistic, such as the Multidimensional Fluency Scales (Rasinski, 2003). These four scales provide rubrics at four levels to evaluate a learner's expressiveness, phrasing, smoothness, and pace while reading text. Ratings of fluency do not take English language development into account. The evaluations of expressiveness and phrasing are highly dependent upon comprehension of the reading passage. For example, a lack of expression or improper stress, intonation, and phrasing, are penalized. All of these elements are dependent upon the reader's comprehension of the vocabulary, grammar, and context of the passage.

Vocabulary development assessments include the Peabody Picture Vocabulary Test-4 (Dunn and Dunn, 2007), a test of receptive vocabulary development that the authors claim can be used to evaluate learning in ELLs. We are aware, when using receptive vocabulary tests, however, that the norms of these tests may be affected by cultural differences among learners, their educational gaps, and their language development.

Publisher-made reading assessments. Reading programs (often used with advanced/exited ELLs) and reading components of ELD programs (which can provide comprehensive reading instruction to beginning/intermediate learners) often include assessment packages that can help teachers with appropriate placement of learners in levels of the program as well as with knowing whether the goals of a unit or chapter have been achieved. We encourage you to look at the quality of learner responses as well as at the final score, because, as with other assessments, language development issues may influence results; and also, as with other assessments, learners may have very good, logical, intelligent reasons for giving answers that are scored as "incorrect."

Teacher-made reading assessments. Teachers can develop tests, quizzes, comprehension checks, dipsticking activities, and rubrics and checklists for assessing learner products. They can also use systems for observing student reading and reading habits. These tools all can be used to apply assessment as part of teaching and are highly useful in making sure that your focus is on what learners actually *learn*. Teaching is not, after all, a matter of covering the content, but of working with learners to uncover knowledge, strategies, and skills.

Student self-assessment. Learners, too, can play an important role in the assessment of their reading. They can keep a record of their extensive reading, listing books and authors they've read along with brief summaries. (Some classes include brief book reviews by class members on the class blog or web site.) They can complete a checklist of their reading habits and strategies. They can complete an inventory about what kinds of materials they enjoy reading. All of this information can be used to motivate good reading, and to inform the teaching of reading.

- In Chapter 7, we explored definitions of literacy and selected one for helping us to work with English learners, using all four skills to construct and convey meaning from text. We have looked at top-down and bottom-up approaches to reading and discussed how they might affect ELLs, concluding that using an integrated approach will serve ELLs best.
- We discussed the unique characteristics of English learners who are developing literacy—and how they bring strengths to the literacy table along with specific needs.
- We have considered the multiple dimensions of literacy development, how literacy interacts with language development, and how both must be considered in planning for English learners.
- We then introduced tools and strategies for scaffolding literacy development for English learners at various age and literacy levels—strategies for before reading, during reading, and after reading.
- We raised specific issues regarding literacy development of older learners who are learning to read in English.
- We offered six principles for meeting older learners' unique yet varied needs:

    1. Learn about your students' backgrounds and experiences.
    2. Assess your learners carefully and continuously.
    3. Provide age-appropriate materials that are both accessible and challenging.
    4. Provide encouragement and success.
    5. Make learning purposeful and meaningful.
    6. Make learning culturally relevant.

- Finally, we addressed six types of reading assessments that are used with ELLs in schools.

  - The first, standardized reading achievement (or performance-based) assessments should be used with great care with English learners as results can be invalid for this group—especially beginning and low intermediate learners—and the testing experience traumatic.
  - Other tools, when used appropriately, can provide useful information about English learners. These include English language proficiency tests, holistic measures of literacy development, assessments of specific literacy skills, assessments from reading and ELD programs, and teacher-developed assessments.

Though this one chapter might not offer a comprehensive preparation for teaching reading to your English learners, it can serve as an introduction to the topic and encourage further study of this important area. The following resources are intended to guide deeper exploration. In the next chapter, we continue the literacy discussion with a focus on writing—and look at how writing can be both the cause and the result of English language development.

Questions for Reflection

1. What do you need to know about the ELLs in your classroom in order to effectively teach them reading? How can you get the information you need to know?
2. Reflect on the additional challenges presented by older learners who are developing literacy in English. What suggestions would you make to content-area teachers for scaffolding the reading that students are expected to do in a content class?
3. Review the reading strategies outlined in this chapter. With which ones are you already familiar? With what you know about teaching English learners, how might you change how you use these strategies? Which strategies would you target for further study? Why?

Activities for Further Learning

1. Summarize the differences between native speakers' literacy development and ELLs' literacy development in one of these areas: alphabetics (phonemic awareness and phonics), vocabulary, fluency, and comprehension. Describe some different instructional techniques that might accommodate the learner differences you discuss. Evaluate the materials used in your school to determine adaptations that would improve instruction for ELLs.
2. Observe and take careful notes on a reading lesson with a group that includes English language learners, focusing on the teacher. What strategies does the teacher use? Do you observe differences in the way the teacher works with ELLs? Does the teacher adapt oral language? Does the teacher introduce vocabulary differently? Does the teacher adapt teaching strategies? Does the teacher encourage learners to use certain reading strategies? Is there evidence of cultural relevance?
3. Observe and keep an anecdotal record (noting any interactions with the teacher and the speech and actions of the learner) on a reading lesson with a

group that includes English language learners, focusing on one ELL. Afterwards, analyze your notes. How was the learner successful? What were the learner's challenges? What were the learner's strategies? What would you like to know more about as a result of this activity?

4. Explore the tools available at the Compleat Lexical Tutor web site <http://132 .208.224.131/>. (Retrieved May 9, 2008.) Look at the word lists available. Enter a text that students are expected to read (type the text or cut-and-paste a text file) into the Vocabulary Profiler, the Concordance, and the Hypertext Builder. Describe how these tools might support you in developing your learners' literacy.

5. Select a target age and language level. Visit your school or community library to look for multi-ethnic books on appropriate themes for the learners you have selected. Create an annotated bibliography and give your rationale for including each book on the list.

PEARSON
myeducationlab
Where the Classroom Comes to Life   is a collection of online tools for your success in this course, your licensure exams, and your teaching career. Go to www.myeducationlab .com to utilize these extensive resources including videos from real classrooms, Praxis and licensure preparation, a lesson plan builder, and materials to help you in your teaching career.

Suggested Reading

Campbell, K. (2007). *Less is more: Teaching literature with short texts, grades 6–12*. Portland, ME: Stenhouse. In addition to great questions and strategies for teaching a variety of short-text genres, Campbell also offers excellent suggestions for texts to use with middle-school students, including short stories, memoirs, graphic novels, poetry, children's literature and picture books, and essays.

Cappellini, M. (2005). *Balancing reading and language learning: A resource for teaching English language learners*. Portland, ME: Stenhouse. Cappellini uses the framework of a balanced reading program to outline a complete program for establishing, planning, conducting, managing, and assessing literacy development.

Fay, K. & Whaley, S. (2004). *Becoming one community: Reading and writing with English language learners*. Portland, ME: Stenhouse.

Fitzgerald, J. & Graves, M. F. (2004). *Scaffolding reading experiences for English language learners*. Norwood, MA: Christopher Gordon. Scaffolding is the theme around a comprehensive course in teaching reading to English learners.

Gibbons, P. (1991). *Learning to learn in a second language*. Portsmouth, NH: Heinemann. The practical information in Gibbons's book is related to recent theories in second-language acquisition in a user-friendly way. Included are planning and assessment tools ready to implement in classrooms in which ELLs are not only learning English, but also learning *in* English.

Hadway, N. L., Vardell, S. M., & Young, T. A. (2002). *Literature-based instruction with English language learners*. Boston: Allyn & Bacon. Describes the nature of English language learners in classrooms, language acquisition and literature-based instruction to develop oral language, reading and writing, and to assist learners in responding to culture.

Herrell, A. L. & Jordan, M. (2003*). Fifty strategies for teaching English language learners*, (2nd ed.). Prentice-Hall. Authors provide fifty carefully-selected strategies to help ELL students understand content materials while developing their speaking, reading, writing, and listening skills in English. Strategies include definitions, rationale, and step-by-step implementation instructions and, all are specifically tied to Teachers of English to Speakers of Other Languages (TESOL) standards.

Lu, Mei-Yi. (1998). ERIC Digest: Multicultural Children's Literature in the Elementary Classroom. Bloomington, IN: ERIC Clearinghouse on Reading English and Communication ERIC Identifier: ED423552 http://www.ericdigests.org/1999–2/literature.htm.

Peregoy, S. F. & Boyle, O. F. (2004). *Reading, writing and learning in ESL: A resource book for K–12 teachers* (4th ed.). Boston, MA: Allyn & Bacon. A classic resource for ESL educators, which explores contemporary language acquisition theory while providing suggestions and methods for instruction.

Web Sites for Further Learning

Downloadable take-home books. These books are available for implementing one of the home-school strategies described in the chapter. Retrieved May 9, 2008.

http://www.readinga-z.com/newfiles/preview.html

English Language Development Standards for California Public Schools. This is an example of state standards that provides progressive benchmarks toward meeting district-level standards. Retrieved May 9, 2008.

http://www.cde.ca.gov/re/pn/fd/documents/englangdev-stnd.pdf

I Love Languages (Formerly the Human Languages Web Site). This site includes a comprehensive catalog of language-related Internet resources with more than 2,400 links. Resources include information about languages in 218 language categories, online language lessons, translating dictionaries, native literature, translation services, software, and language schools. Retrieved May 9, 2008.

http://www.ilovelanguages.com/

Lu, Mei-Yu. (1998). International Children's' Literature Bibliography. Bloomington, Indiana: Indiana University School of Education Clearinghouse on Reading, English, and Communication. Retrieved May 9, 2008.

http://www.indiana.edu/~reading/ieo/bibs/intlchlit.html

Slavin, R. E. & Cheung, A. Effective reading programs for English Language Learners: A best-evidence synthesis. Among the findings is evidence of success of programs that teach initial reading in the home language. Retrieved May 9, 2008.

http://www.csos.jhu.edu/crespar/techReports/Report66.pdf

The Vocabulary Profiler (VP) (2006 upgrade). (Original VP by P. Nation, VUW New Zealand & B. Laufer, U Haifa, Israel; Academic Word List (AWL) & sublists by A. Coxhead VUW; WebVP adapted by T. Cobb, UQAM Canada). This site provides a tool for analyzing text. Enter the text and the software will highlight words in different categories in different colors. Categories include words from the first 1000 frequency, words from the second 1000 frequency, words from Averill Coxhead's Academic Word List, and off-list words. The Vocabulary Profiler 2.5 and many more tools are available at the Compleat Lexical Tutor. Retrieved May 9, 2008.

http://132.208.224.131/

"What Elementary Teachers Need to Know About Language." This article, published by the Center for Applied Linguistics, summarizes what teachers should know about language development, and about the English language. Retrieved May 9, 2008.

http://www.cal.org/resources/digest/0006fillmore.html

Word Study for Students with Learning Disabilities and English Language Learners. Outlines the basics of word study with many examples. Retrieved May 9, 2008.

http://www.texasreading.org/utcrla/materials/primary_word_study.asp

World-Class Instructional Design and Assessment (WIDA) Consortium site. The K–12 ESL Standards found at this site are used by a consortium of 16 U.S. states. These standards also form the foundation of the TESOL PreK–12 Proficiency Standards. Retrieved May 9, 2008.

http://www.wida.wceruw.org

References

Aaronson, E. (1978). *The jigsaw classroom*. Beverly Hills, CA: Sage Publications.

Almada, P., Nichols, A., & O'Keefe, L. (2004). *A pocketful of opossums*. Barrington, IL: Rigby.

Ashton-Warner, S. (2002). *Teacher*. NY: Simon and Schuster.

August, D. & Shanahan, T. (Eds.). (2007). *Developing literacy in second-language learners: A report of the national literacy panel on language-minority children and youth*. Mahwah, NJ: Lawrence Erlbaum.

Birch, B. M. (2006). *English L2 reading: Getting to the bottom* (2nd ed.). Mahwah, NJ: Lawrence Erlbaum.

Brown, A. L., Campione, J. C., & Day, J. D. (1981). Learning to learn: On training students to learn from texts. *Educational Researcher, 10*, 14–21.

Bruchac, J. (2002). *Sacajawea*. NY: Scholastic.

Carle, E. (1996, reprint edition). *The grouchy ladybug*. NY: HarperCollins.

Carmi, D. (2002). *Samir & Yonatan*. NY: Scholastic.

Clay, M. (1997). *Becoming literate: The construction of inner control*. Portsmouth, NH: Heinemann.

Clay, M. (2000). *Running records for classroom teachers*. Portsmouth, NH: Heinemann.

Cloud, N., Genesee, F., & Hamayan, E. (2000). *Dual language instruction: A handbook for enriched education*. Boston: Heinle & Heinle.

Cooper, E. (2006). *Beach*. NY: Scholastic.

Cowley, J. (1999). *Mrs. Wishy-Washy*. Aukland, New Zealand: Shorthand Publications.

Cummins, J. (1994). Knowledge, power and identity in teaching English as a second language. In Genesee, F. (Ed.), *Educating second language children*. NY: Cambridge University Press.

Cunningham, J. W. (1999). How we can achieve best practices in literacy instruction. In L. B. Gambrell, L.M. Morrow, S. B. Neuman, & M. Pressley (Eds.). *Best practices in literacy instruction*. 34–45. NY: Guilford.

de Jong, E. & Harper, C. (2004). Misconceptions about teaching English language learners. *Journal of Adolescent & Adult Literacy*, 48: 2.

Dooley, N. (1991). *Everybody cooks rice*. Minneapolis: Carolrhoda Books.

Dowshen, S., Pendley, J. S., & Lyness, D. (2004). *Dealing with bullying*. Kidshealth.org. Available: http://kidshealth.org/teen/your_mind/problems/bullies.html

Duggleby, J., & Lawrence, J. (1998). *Story painter: The life of Jacob Lawrence*. San Francisco: Chronicle Books.

Dunn, L. M. & Dunn, D. M. (2007) *Peabody picture vocabulary test* (4th ed.). Bloomington, MN: NCS Pearson.

Enright, D. S. & McCloskey, M. L. (1988). *Integrating English: Developing English language and literacy in the multilingual classroom*. Reading, MA: Addison-Wesley.

Fitzgerald, J. (2003). New directions in multilingual literacy research: Multilingual reading theory. *Reading Research Quarterly, 38*, 118–122.

Fitzgerald, J. & Graves, M. F. (2004). *Scaffolding reading experiences for English language learners*. Norwood, MA: Christopher Gordon.

Fountas, I. C. & Pinnell, G. S. (1996). *Guided reading: Good first teaching for all children*. Portsmouth, NH: Heinemann.

Fountas, I. C. & Pinnell, G. S. (2001). *Guiding readers and writers (grades 3–6): Teaching comprehension, genre, and content literacy*. Portsmouth, NH: Heinemann.

Freeman, D., Freeman, Y., McCloskey, M. L., Stack, L., Silva, C., Gottlieb, M., et al. (2004). *On our way to English teacher's guide*. Austin, TX: Rigby/HarcourtAchieve.

Freeman, Y., Freeman, D., & Mercuri, S. (2003). Helping middle and high school age English language learners achieve academic success. *NABE Journal of Research and Practice, 1*(1): 110–122.

Garcia, E. (1999). *Student cultural diversity: Understanding and meeting the challenge* (2nd ed.). Portsmouth, NH: Heinemann.

Goodman, K. (1967). Reading: A psycholinguistic guessing game. *Journal of the Reading Specialist, 6*(1).

Goodman, Y., Watson, D., & C. Burke. (2005). *Reading miscue inventory.* Katonah, NY: Richard C. Owen Publishers.

Graham, C. (1978). *Jazz chants.* NY: Oxford University Press.

Graham, C. (2003). *Children's jazz chants old and new.* NY: Oxford University Press.

Hakuta, K., Butler, Y. G., & Witt, D. (2000). *How long does it take English learners to attain proficiency?* (Policy Report). The University of California Linguistic Minority Research Institute.

Heath, S. B. (1983). *Ways with words: Language, life and work in communities and classrooms.* NY: Cambridge University Press.

Herber, H. L. & Herber, J. N. (1993). *Teaching in content areas with reading, writing and reasoning.* Boston: Allyn & Bacon.

Holdaway, D. (1979). *Foundations of literacy.* Portsmouth, NH: Heinemann.

Hudelson, S. (1984). Kan yu ret an rayt en ingles: Children become literate in ESL. *TESOL Quarterly, 18*(2): 221–248.

Hudelson, S. (1987). The role of native language literacy in the education of language minority children. *Language Arts, 65*: 287–302.

Kagan, S. (1994). *Cooperative learning.* Riverside, CA: Kagan.

Krashen, S. D. (2003). *Explorations in language acquisition and use.* Portsmouth, NH: Heinemann.

Krashen, S. D. (2004). *The power of reading: Insights from the research* (2nd ed.). Portsmouth, NH: Heinemann.

Lanauze, M. & Snow, C. (1989). The relation between first and second language writing skills: Evidence from Puerto Rican elementary school children in bilingual programs. *Linguistics and Education, 1*: 323–329.

Li, X. & Zhang, M. (2004). Why Mei still cannot read and what can be done. *Journal of Adolescent & Adult Literacy, 48*(2): 92–101.

McCloskey, M. L. & Stack, L. (1996). *Voices in Literature: An anthology for middle/high school ESOL.* Boston: MA: Heinle & Heinle.

McCloskey, M. L. & Stack, L. (2003). *Visions: Language, literature, content—books A, B, & C.* Boston, MA: Heinle & Heinle.

McCloskey, M.L. & Thrush, E. (2006). Building a reading scaffold with web texts. *Essential Teacher*, pp. 49–52.

Martin, B. J. & Carle, E. (1992). *Brown bear, brown bear, what do you see?* NY: Henry Holt.

Morganthaler, L. (Ed.) (2004). *On our way to English: Teacher's resource guide of language transfer issues for English language learners.* Austin, TX: Rigby/Harcourt Achieve.

Moustafa, M. (1997). *Beyond traditional phonics: Research discoveries and reading instruction.* Portsmouth, NH: Heinemann.

Nation, P. (2001). *Learning vocabulary in another language.* Cambridge, UK: Cambridge University Press.

National Institute of Child Health and Human Development. (2000). Report of the National Reading Panel. Teaching children to read: An evidence-based assessment of the scientific research literature on reading and its implications for reading instruction: Reports of the subgroups (NIH Publication No. 00-4754). Washington, DC: U.S. Government Printing Office. http://www.nationalreadingpanel.org.

Oczkus, L. D. (2003). *Reciprocal teaching at work: Strategies for improving reading comprehension.* Newark, DE: International Reading Association.

Palinscar, A. S. (1986). The role of dialogue in providing scaffolded instruction. *Educational Psychologist, 21*: 73–98.

Palinscar, A. S. & Brown, A. L. (1984). Reciprocal teaching of comprehension-fostering and comprehension-monitoring activities. *Cognition and Instruction, 1*(2), 117–175.

Pearson, P. D. & Gallagher, M. C. (1983). The Instruction of Reading Comprehension. *Contemporary Educational Psychology, 8*(3): pp. 317–344.

Rasinski, T. V. (2003). *The fluent reader.* NY: Scholastic.

Roberge, M. M. (2002). California's generation 1.5 immigrants: What experiences, characteristics, and needs do they bring to our English classes? *The CATESOL Journal, 14*(1): 107–127.

Samway, K. D., Whang, G., & Pippitt, M. (1995). *Buddy reading: Cross-age tutoring in a multicultural school.* Portsmouth, NH: Heinemann.

Scholastic. (1999). *Oral fluency assessment.* NY: Scholastic.

Shute, L. (1986). *Momotaro: The Peach Boy.* NY: Lothrop, Lee & Shepard.

Slavin, R. E. (1994). *Cooperative learning: Theory, research, and practice* (2nd ed.). Boston, MA: Allyn & Bacon.

Snow, C. E. Burns, S. M., & Griffin, P., (Eds.). (1998). *Preventing reading difficulties in young children.* Washington DC: National Academy Press.

Stahl, S. (2002). What the NRP report doesn't say. Keynote address at the Michigan Reading Recovery Conference, Detroit, January. Available at www.ciera.org.

TeensHealth. Dealing with Bullying. Retrieved May 9, 2008. http://kidshealth.org/teen/your_mind/problems/bullies.html.

Tharp, R. G. & Gallimore, R. (1988). *Rousing minds to life: Teaching, learning, and schooling in social context.* Cambridge, UK: Cambridge University Press.

Thomas, W. P. & Collier, V. P. (1997). School Effectiveness for Language Minority Students [Electronic Version]. *NCBE Resource Collection Series.* Retrieved October 11, 2006 from http://www.ncela.gwu.edu/pubs/resource/effectiveness/

Tizard, J., Schofield, W. N., & Hewison, J. (1982). Collaboration between teachers assisting children's reading. *British Journal of Educational Psychology, 52*: 1–15.

Trelease, J. (2006). *The read-aloud handbook.* NY: Penguin.

U.S. Department of Education, (2004). Fact Sheet: NCLB Provisions Ensure Flexibility and Accountability for Limited English Proficient Students. Retrieved May 9, 2008. http://www.ed.gov/nclb/accountability/schools/factsheet-english.html

U.S. Department of Education, Office of Elementary and Secondary Education. (2002). Public Law 107–110. Elementary and Secondary Reauthorization: The No Child Left Behind Act of 2001 (Enacted in 2002). Retrieved May 9, 2008. http://www.ed.gov/policy/elsec/leg/esea02/index.html

Wood, D., Bruner, J., & Ross, G. (1976). The role of tutoring in problem solving. *Journal of Child Psychology and Psychiatry, 17*: 89–100.

CHAPTER 8

Developing Literacy with English Learners: Focus on Writing

Diana Bela has been teaching a science unit on plants to her fourth grade class at an urban school in the Southeast. Her 28 students come from 10 different countries, and have had varied educational experiences and opportunities. Many have had little or no experience with expository writing and most find their fourth grade textbooks difficult to read. Diana has used several of the reading strategies discussed in Chapter 7 to help her learners access the text. Today she wants learners to orally recall what they have learned in science while developing their skills in writing a summary report. She uses the shared writing strategy to encourage a rich academic conversation as she guides learners through the writing process.

The first step in writing is brainstorming. Diana explains that scientists need to write carefully and clearly to explain scientific findings, and that they, too, can write like scientists. The topic today is the theme of the science chapter: the contribution that plants make to our lives. To model this step, Diana asks, "How do plants help us?" Learners are encouraged to skim the science chapter and come up with possible answers. Most of the suggestions are single words or phrases: "wood houses," "cotton clothes," "food," "medicines." Diana offers encouragement as she writes learners' ideas on a graphic organizer on the board (Figure 8.1).

Figure 8.1 How Plants Help Us: A Graphic Organizer

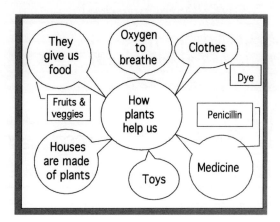

Diana asks learners to categorize, color-code, and group their suggestions. She assigns pairs of students to write a sentence about each idea, encouraging learners to be specific. For example, she says, "It's not very clear to say that plants give us medicine. Let's give an example. What kind of medicine can we get from plants? Right, penicillin is one kind."

Student pairs select ideas from the Web and write drafts of ideas for the essay on sentence strips, which Diana puts in a pocket chart. Students help her to group the ones about similar ideas together to start to build paragraphs. Several students come up with sentences about how plants contribute to our homes (Figure 8.2).

Figure 8.2 How Plants Help Us: Sentences

Houses are made from straw.

Houses are made of wood.

Houses are made of plants.

This gives Diana an opportunity to introduce sentence combining. "This is a little boring to say three times, 'Houses are made of . . . .' How can we combine these sentences into one, more interesting, one? Are straw and wood examples of plants? How can we say that?" Students come up with, "Houses are made of plants, like straw and wood."

As the students read the sentences they have written, they come up with ideas to improve them. Diana gives a little "mini-lesson" on how to "cut and paste" and "insert" words to improve their writing (Figure 8.3).

Figure 8.3 How Plants Help Us: Revised and Combined Sentences

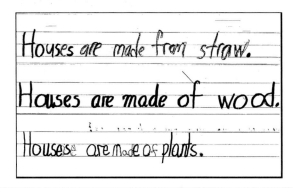

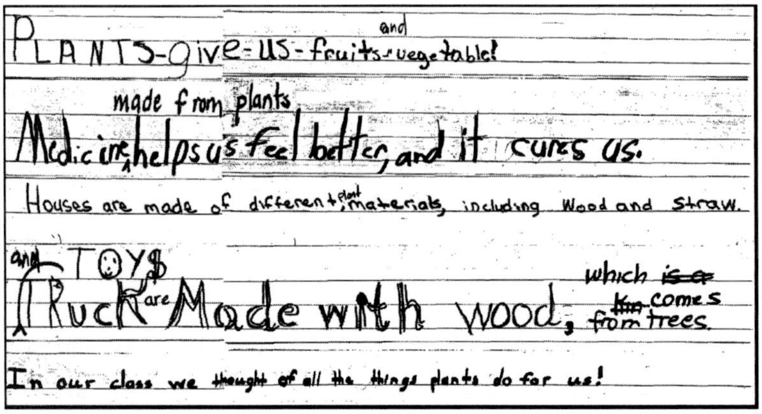

PLANTS give us fruits and vegetables

made from plants

Medicine helps us feel better, and it cures us.

Houses are made of different plant materials, including wood and straw.

and TOYS

Trucks are Made with wood, which comes from trees.

In our class we thought of all the things plants do for us!

After the piece is revised, learners work together to suggest the best sequence for the sentences by physically rearranging the sentence strips. Then they work with the teacher to compose an introductory and concluding sentence. Finally, each individual suggests a title and writes it on a sticky note, and the class votes on the best one (Figure 8.4).

Figure 8.4 How Plants Help Us: Possible Titles

The final piece is carefully written on a chart and posted in the hall outside the classroom. Students are in awe of what they have produced and want to read it over and over again to one another and to anyone who visits. They copy the text to take home to read to their families, adding their own illustrations (Figure 8.5).

Figure 8.5 The Finished Piece: The Plant Team Works for Us

> ### The Plant Team Works for Us
>
> Plants help us in many ways in our everyday lives. Plants give us oxygen and we need oxygen to breathe. We need cotton from plants to make clothes to wear. We use plant dye to make things more colorful.
>
> Plants give us fruits and vegetables. Medicine made from plants makes us feel better and it cures us. Houses are made of different plant materials, including straw and wood. Toy trucks are made with wood, which comes from trees.
>
> In our class, we thought of all the things plants do for us!

How can writing help to develop English learners' literacy?

- Why should we use writing with ELLs?
- How does second language writing develop?
- How can we connect writing to active, interactive learning?
- What are the challenges we face in teaching writing with ELLs?
- How can we establish a rich writing environment?
- What are effective strategies for helping ELLs learn to write?
- How can we use the writing process with ELLs?
- What are ways to assess writing for ELLs?

Why Teach Writing with English Learners?

Recent national emphasis on reading has led to less classroom time, less curriculum emphasis, and less teacher-development of the topic of writing. Sometimes in the past, programs for English learners focused on oral language skills early on, with instruction of writing introduced later with a skills-based emphasis so that English language learners (ELLs) had few opportunities for authentic, purposeful writing in class. Yet, as both Diana's class and research on writing development illustrate (Edelsky, 1993; Hudelson, 1984; Samway, 2006), English learners can clearly benefit from rich and varied opportunities to use writing to construct meaning in their new language.

How Does Writing Develop with ELLs?

Learners pass through similar stages in writing development in both first (L1) and second (L2) languages (Hudelson, 1984). They begin with scribbling, making random marks, and drawing; then begin to use the letter names and initial letters to represent words (e.g., "R EU HP?" [Are you happy?]), move on to phonetic spelling (e.g., "I thot hee waz crazie." [I thought he was crazy.]), and gradually progress to more sophisticated

English Learners Benefit from Opportunities to Use Writing to Construct Meaning in Their New Language

writing with traditional spelling and usage. Older learners who have not learned to write in their first language will pass through similar stages. But there are many unique aspects for English learners beginning to write. One of these is **positive transference**—when learners use aspects of their first language to help them learn to write in their new language (Olivares, 2002). For example, if learners already know how to write in another language, they can make use of many concepts and organizational frames or **schema** they have developed in that language and apply them to the new one. A student who already knows how to write a summary in Russian, for example, can transfer the schema for writing a summary into English (Carrell & Eisterhold, 1988). Learners who have studied a content area can also use cognates they have learned. For example, scientific terms in many languages use Latin or Greek roots and are similar across languages (particularly Romance languages such as Spanish, French, Italian, and Romanian), so words will be very similar and learners, with some instruction and encouragement, can use these similarities to figure out the new terms. Sometimes this application of knowledge from L1 to L2 writing may also lead to **interference** errors in which the rules of one language are applied incorrectly in another, but these are eventually explained and resolved. For example, many Asian and Slavic languages do not use articles, and learners from these groups often have trouble learning how and when to use articles. Teachers will need to learn what their students know about writing in both L1 and L2, and their English proficiency, and set expectations accordingly. Table 8.1 outlines writing expectations of learners across three English language levels according to seven traits of writing (Culham, 2003, 2005). Of course, expectations will also vary according to learners' age and grade level.

Connecting Writing to Active, Communicative Language Teaching and Learning

For ELLs at all levels, writing is an excellent environment for implementing the principles of this book (which are outlined in Chapter 2). Because writing involves productive skills, young writers can be highly active in developing their own creations. They can write about their own knowledge and experiences, providing cultural relevance. They can use collaborative tools in gathering ideas and in responding to one another's writing. Writing builds comprehension because learners better understand how texts are constructed by putting their own texts together. Writing also reveals who the learners are and what they know, to better enable their teachers to connect new knowledge to learners' previous experiences. Writing in content classes can help to develop and cement content learning, enabling learners to work with and apply the content concepts and skills they are developing. Leki (2003) notes that content-based writing, in which learners over time develop knowledge about a topic and make decisions about what to include and how to write about that topic, is useful in preparing English learners for success in the writing they will use in school and beyond. Writing is also adaptable for a multi-level class that includes ELLs. Because learners write at their own levels, writing is an ideal activity for differentiation of instruction for students with different needs, learning styles, backgrounds, and abilities. Through careful use of assessment tools and processes, small group work, and feedback from teachers, teachers can respond to learners where they are, and lead them toward achieving successive levels in their writing development. Writers in a class do not all have to be at the same level, they simply must know where they are in their writing development, and where they are going.

Writing can help language development at early stages (such as when learners know a few words and phrases, and are just beginning to decode and encode the language) by presenting an authentic need to negotiate the letters and sounds and

Table 8.1 Writing Development of English Learners

Writing Aspect	Beginning EL	Intermediate EL	Advanced EL
1. Vocabulary/Word Choice	Vocabulary is limited. Learners translate, avoid words they don't know, use vocabulary sources such as dictionaries and/or ask for help.	Learners know most of the first 2,000 most frequent words, may have trouble with infrequent or "academic" words.	Learners' vocabulary is approaching native proficiency.
2. Sentence Fluency	Writes a few words or sentences.	Writes several sentences.	Writes several paragraphs (depending on age).
3. Sentence Variety	Learners can use one or two sentence patterns.	Learners use several sentence patterns.	Learners vary sentence patterns and have a large repertoire.
4. Organization	Writing does not have evidence of sequencing, or is so short that organization is not apparent.	Writing shows evidence of an organizational plan.	Learners use appropriate organization for the genre chosen.
5. Genre	Learners use the same format for most writing.	Learners know several different writing forms or "schema" and choose among them.	Learners know many different genres and choose appropriately among them to match the purpose of the piece.
6. Grammar	Writer often uses the present tense, and has trouble with word order.	Writer uses more standard word order but makes typical learner errors and interference errors, e.g., -s endings on verbs, articles.	Grammar is similar to that of native speakers with occasional learner errors.
7. Conventions	Attempts at spelling using letter names, L1 sound system. Spaces between letters and words. Punctuation, capitalization, and paragraphs not used consistently.	Writer uses phonetic spelling, with some errors due to differences in sound system between L1 and L2. Generally uses paragraphs, spacing, capitals, and punctuation.	Most high-frequency words are spelled correctly; others are close. Capital letters, punctuation, indentation, and other genre format used accurately and consistently.

apply the phonics skills they are developing. At later stages of language development, writers can develop and polish their productive skills, and better comprehend various genres by trying to compose in them. Well-developed writing lessons and tasks, accomplished at appropriate, increasingly challenging levels, make demands on learners that lead them to build their development of writing ideas as well as all of the writing traits listed above: vocabulary/word choice, sentence fluency, sentence variety, organization, grammar, and conventions.

Challenges of Teaching Writing to English Learners

Writing is a tremendous challenge for learners of English. They have to develop ideas and try to express them in new words, using at once everything they are acquiring in the new language: the words, the sentence patterns, the grammar, the genre, and the conventions of print. In addition, writing involves understanding sociocultural expectations that may be very different and new for the learners. Even if learners understand a genre such as letter writing or essays in one culture, expectations may be very different in another culture. In Spanish, letters are typically more formal and elaborate than in English, and a polite introduction is expected. In Japanese, because everyone in that island culture shares many expectations, it is appropriate to leave cultural understandings unstated—in fact it is demeaning for the reader to state some concepts too explicitly. In English, on the other hand, writers are expected to be so clear that any reader can understand what they mean. Writing is likely to be the last language area for learners of English to master—teachers should not be surprised to see "language learner errors" in students' writing for many years, and to need to spend instructional time addressing them.

Developing a Writing Environment

Samway (1992) describes important characteristics of classrooms that foster rich writing development. Teachers provide learners with opportunities to use writing for real purposes for real audiences, across the curriculum, so that they become enthusiastic and experienced in effectively communicating their ideas. Teachers help learners develop their knowledge of the craft of writing, to understand the relationship between oral language and writing, and to use that knowledge to discuss what they read. Writing is also closely tied to thought processes. Children use writing to help them think and use thinking to improve their writing. Effective teachers of writing develop a "learning community" in which learners see one another as valuable resources and sources of support in the writing process.

Students use their previous experiences with oral and written language to construct new meanings and to further develop their language capacities. For ELLs, using previous experiences manifests itself in two ways (Enright & McCloskey, 1988). First, the "tie back" strategy is when learners use their previous experiences in their home countries' cultures, and language to develop English language and literacy capacities. The second way, the "tie in" strategy is when learners use their experiences in one of the four language processes of listening, speaking, reading, and writing in English to help them develop their capabilities with the other processes. So reading doesn't precede writing and listening doesn't precede speaking: the four modes support one another. Writing key words on the blackboard may help a student listen better; reviewing a concept through paraphrasing it with a partner may cement reading comprehension; writing key words and concepts may prepare a student to talk about them.

To create a writing environment, classrooms both celebrate and connect reading and writing. Teacher and students read together, talk about what they read, write about what they learn and what they think, and the classroom reflects their work—student's written work is prominently displayed along with a celebration of books and authors. The environment is print-rich, with labels and instructions and procedures for readers and writers at various stages. Students are encouraged to read and review books for the class. The classroom provides rich access to words with word walls (Figure 8.6), translation dictionaries, English dictionaries, picture dictionaries, and online sources.

What Is a Word Wall?

An interactive **word wall** is a systematically organized collection of words displayed in large letters on a wall or other large display place in the classroom. It is a tool to use, not just display. Many teachers add a certain number of words each week, depending upon the lesson focus and student needs. Frequently, words in the chart are re-organized according to skills and concepts being developed. On the first day of school in primary grades, the word wall might include only students' names. Later, it might include words with certain vowel or consonant sounds. Teacher and students might pull out rhyming words, or word families or certain parts of speech, or words that are pronunciation challenges, or words that are Spanish cognates, or words that are useful in writing about the topic they are studying: estuary. All students, but particularly English learners, will find the word wall a tremendous resource when they're writing. In addition, the teacher can save time when asked about writing words by simply pointing to the word wall. For example, "Lake is in the 'take' word family. Look under T for Take. Write 'take' but start it with an 'l'."

Getting Started: Interactive Writing

Support your learners' early efforts through interactive writing. Interactive writing works well to introduce concepts of writing to beginners. Writing begins as a dialogue, a conversation between writers that can provide a bridge between the informal and interactive nature of conversation and the more formal and solitary nature of writing. Learners can have a natural means to negotiate meaning through real, purposeful written exchanges. Four examples of interactive writing are message boards/mailboxes, interactive journals, content learning logs, and literary logs.

Message Boards/Mailboxes. Set up a bulletin board where learners can stick messages, or stack and label milk-carton mailboxes where folded notes can be tacked or placed with the name of the intended recipient on the outside. If you have the resources, use e-mail or classroom software for message exchange. Begin writing short notes to students asking questions, commenting on their successes, relating interesting events, or perhaps just drawing and labeling a little picture. (If your class is large, you may choose to write some of your messages on the board to the group in general, or to send an e-mail message to the class and have learners write individual responses.) Encourage learners to use the message board/mailboxes/e-mail to communicate with one another as well as with you. Monitor the bulletin board and set up clear expectations for good etiquette in its use.

Interactive Journals. Dialogue journals and letters help to engage learners in the personal process of negotiating meaning (Hadaway & Young, 2006). Encourage learners to write frequently in a bound journal, notebook, or folder about topics of their own choice. (You may choose to provide on a chart or the board a few suggestions or prompts for when learners feel "stuck.") Exchange questions, report personal experiences, make promises, evaluate classroom activities, offer contributions to the class, apologize, give directions, complain, or state opinions. In your responses to student writing, remember these basics:

- Use a direct conversational style, matching the length and level of reasoning to the student's proficiency and cognitive ability.

Figure 8.6 Detail of a Word Wall

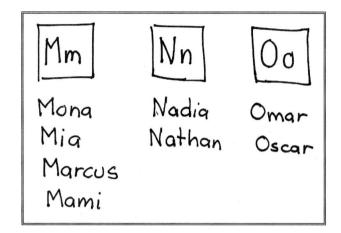

- Offer new and interesting information in your responses and model writing slightly more complex than your student's.
- Ask real questions that seek student opinion and information that you don't know.
- Direct corrections may not be appropriate in writing intended to be a conversation. You may choose to correct indirectly by using the same language of your learners with errors "fixed" in your responses. Note common types of errors that occur and provide the class with "mini-lessons" on these topics.
- Some older learners, on the other hand, may be eager to have you point out their errors. Discuss this with the writers to determine some aspect of writing they want your feedback on, and, if the writer requests it, make a few corrections in that area when you respond.

In the interactive journal excerpt in Figure 8.7, which shows the correspondence between Thuy, a fifth grader from Vietnam, and her homeroom teacher, Ms. O'Brien,

Exchanging Messages Is Motivating and Effective for Beginning Writers

Figure 8.7 Excerpt from Interactive Journal

I have friends. I have two peoples frend. One people is Leon. I don't know one people's name. I like Scial Studys. It class very funny. I make with my map. It map is elevation map. I like school.

9/17

Dear Thuy,

I'm happy that you like school and that you have two new friends. I hope you will show me the elevation map you made with crayons in your social studies class. You should be good at maps because you traveled halfway around the world to come here! Where did you stop on the way to the U.S.?

Ms. O'Brien

note how Ms. O'Brien provides indirect feedback for spelling, grammar, conventions, and format. Notice, too, how she raises the level of language just a little, challenging Thuy to raise her reading and writing to a slightly higher level.

Content Learning Log.   Have learners keep a log of what they are learning in their math, science, or social studies class. At the end of each class, learners write in their logs a statement summarizing something important they want to remember from the day's lesson. Figure 8.8 and Figure 8.9 show learning log entries from units on fractions at different grade levels.

The statement might be in the form of pictures about what certain fractions look like. Or learners might document processes they used to do computations with fractions. For example, in a math lesson on fractions, learners might illustrate fractions in various formats; they might document the processes they use to compute fractions; they might summarize lessons, write main ideas or main points, or write directions to teach someone else a process.

Literary Journals.   As part of your independent choice reading program (see Chapter 7), you can have your students keep literary journals. For these, learners write down in a section of their notebook or in a separate bound composition book the title and author of each book they read along with a brief review. Provide sharing times for students to read their reviews and make recommendations to one another for future

Figure 8.8 Excerpt from Grade 2 Math Journal: Fractions

reading. Read to learners brief reviews of books for their age and level. Keep a literary journal yourself and model giving "book talks" from your written reviews. In order to provide comprehensible input to different levels of learners in your class, your model book talk might include, for example, showing the class your favorite picture spread from a picture book, giving a very short summary, stating a thought about the theme or themes of the book, and offering a curious question that readers might like to find the answer to by reading the book. Hadaway and Young (2006) suggest that more advanced learners make a new journal (five to ten pages folded in half and stapled) for each book they read and make an entry after they finish every three to four chapters. Teachers provide open-ended prompts such as, "I predict . . .," "My favorite part . . .," I connect . . .," or "I would change . . .," (p. 203). Before class discussions, students circle or highlight particular parts of their journals they want to share with the group.

Figure 8.9 Excerpt from Grade 4 Math Journal: A Rule for Adding Fractions

Remember this!   February 23

When you add things, they have to have the same name.

  3 kids + 2 kids = 5 kids

The name is kids. The total is five kids.

When you add fractions, they have to have the same name, too.

  2/8 + 5/8 = 7/8.

2 eighths plus five eights is seven eights.

The name is eighths. The total is seven eighths.

Video Exercise

Learning about Journals in the Primary Grades

Go to MyEducationLab, select the topic **Writing**, and watch the video entitled "**Learning about Journals in the Primary Grades**" to observe a teacher conducting a lesson about "My Friend's Journal." Complete the questions that accompany it. You may print your work or have it transmitted to your professor as necessary.

Scaffolding Learners Through the Writing Process

An integrated, process approach to writing has many advantages for students' language learning. For beginning readers, reading their own writing or that of their peers gives learners the opportunity to practice reading texts written with words that are part of students' speaking vocabularies. In this way they are challenged by reading words they know, not by trying to learn the meanings of words at the same time as learning to read them. Students learn reading and writing skills, such as encoding and decoding the sounds of the language, in a purposeful, meaningful context and so are more prepared to comprehend what they read. Writing also helps learners to become more independent language learners—they must use many resources—peers, teachers, books, dictionaries, word walls, word analysis skills, and understanding of genre. Writing gives teachers the opportunity to show how these skills serve real purposes for written communication. ELLs who write frequently learn spelling and grammar skills better, and gain a better understanding of the types of writing as they use them in their composition, beyond what they can learn with only focused lessons.

Writing educators (e.g., Hudelson, 1984; Calkins & Mermelstein, 2003; Graves, 2003; Samway, 2006) used observations of the way professional writers work to describe the **writing process** as the various steps a writer goes through in the process of developing a final piece. This process is not always the same for each writer or each piece, however, and does not always proceed in a linear pattern through all the steps. Nevertheless, guiding learners through these stages can help them understand the processes involved in careful writing. The steps can serve as a guideline for teachers in helping ELLs discover effective writing processes to use to achieve their own goals for writing as they meet their school's *and* state's writing standards (e.g., WIDA writing standards, used by a consortium of states, for grades 3 to 5 Standards: http://www.wida.us/Resources/standards/html/classroom/domain/3-5/writing.html). The steps can also be adapted to different genres, including various types of writing that students use in different content areas: For example, writing in time sequence or cause and effect in social studies (e.g., the fishbone graphic organizer in Figure 8.10); or writing about a scientific cycle (e.g., the graphic organizer for a cycle in Figure 8.11).

Steps in the Writing Process

1. *Pre-writing:* This is the stage in which the learner has experiences, reads, listens, conducts experiments, interviews people, comes up with ideas, and then reviews and collects his or her thoughts about the piece to come. Preparation for writing might include rich conversation, jotting down lists, selecting and using graphic organizers for the writing genre chosen, studying features of a certain genre, and/or outlining. For ELLs, preparation will also include developing vocabulary and practicing certain language forms that will be used in a piece.

2. *Drafting:* In this stage, writers try to get ideas down on paper, attending more to content than form, and working fairly quickly so as to keep the train of thought going. They might use content journals or "quickwrites," for this process. Young, beginning learners may only take their writing to this stage. The initial draft might be the final draft. The feedback may come in the form of general "mini-lessons" the teacher creates after reading and assessing the children's work and determining which standards and skills need to be addressed. Incorporating new learning may happen with the next draft. For older, more proficient learners, some writing pieces might be left at the draft stage; others may be selected for reviewing and revising.

3. *Sharing and reviewing drafts:* During this stage, writers read their writing to themselves and to others and think about and discuss how they might improve

Figure 8.10 Fishbone Graphic Organizer Showing Cause and Effect

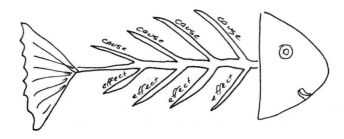

the writing. For example, they might review how to make it more complete, to sequence it better, to organize it well, to use words well, to include the right amount of detail, and/or to make the piece interesting. Learners may refer to standards, criteria, or checklists to assess their works in progress. Teachers of English learners help students develop the language needed for students to talk about their writing and may also introduce peer learning strategies such as Encourage, Question, Suggest (EQS) (see explanation in Table 8.2) to help learners respond effectively to each other's writing.

4. *Revising:* In this stage, learners try to include the ideas for improvement that came up in sharing and reviewing their drafts. Some teachers use individual or small-group writing conferences to help learners plan their revisions and to give learners feedback and encouragement in this stage. ELLs may need extra support in this stage as their writing usually reveals areas in which their language is still developing. Teachers cannot focus on all the errors learners make, but must choose important and developmentally appropriate concepts to teach.

5. *Editing:* When the content of the piece is determined, writers go back once more to edit and polish the piece, checking their capitals, usage, punctuation, and spelling. Rog (2007) includes an editing mini-lesson for young learners to

Figure 8.11 Cycle Graphic Organizer

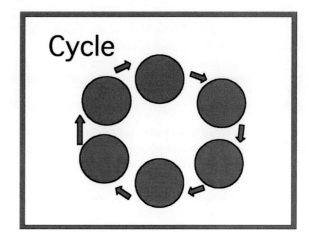

help them edit their own writing, referring to these four elements as "CUPS." We have included several editing checklists that can be adapted for your learners and used for this stage of the process. (See Tables 8.4, 8.5, and 8.6.)

6. *Publishing:* The final stage in the writing process is a celebration of the accomplishments of writers. Writing can be published in many ways: it might include having the student, the teacher, or others read it aloud; it might be posting in the classroom or on the class web site; writing might be collected into classroom books; learners might send it home and read it aloud to family members and retell it in the home language; or it might be sent in to a children's publication or writing contest.

The Shared Writing Process

Before we ask ELLs to write, we need to provide them with some of the tools they'll need. They will need good sources for ideas, lots of words and phrases about their topic, and appropriate language structures and patterns to express their ideas. But it's not enough to tell them how to access and use these tools; we need to *show* them by modeling the tools in use. In the opening vignette to this chapter, Diana used **shared writing** to model and guide learners through the process. Let's take a careful look at the strategies she used in this way of modeling writing.

Shared writing is a collaborative process through which learners provide content for a text and the teacher provides scaffolding for the text's construction. The teacher takes the lead in showing learners that when they have an experience or learn something or think about something, they can talk about it, write it down, refine their writing, and share it with others. Shared writing shows learners how writing is done, and helps them understand how it's possible for them to be writers. It can help to:

- Develop interest in and enjoyment of writing.
- Demonstrate purposes of writing.
- Provide participation in all stages of the writing process.
- Enable learners to understand the planning and organization involved in constructing various kinds of texts.
- Provide opportunities to teach language—vocabulary, grammar, usage, and conventions of spelling and punctuation.
- Provide models for students' independent writing.

Build Background.   Begin with a shared experience, a memory, a read-aloud text, a content concept you're studying. You might, for example, share and discuss a story or nonfiction text, take a walking field trip, or interview a visitor. Have learners dictate as you take notes. Generate words and ideas for the writing as you construct. One class had a visitor from the United Kingdom. They asked about elementary schools there and compared the visitor's answers with their own school using a Venn Diagram (Figure 8.12).

Read the Draft and Discuss Revisions.   As you discuss revisions, incorporate teaching/review of appropriate strategies and skills of the reader/writer. Introduce features of the text structure you are using. Use your assessment of students' independent writing to determine skills to be addressed in shared writing. For the compare/contrast lesson, the class reviewed **signal words** and frames for comparing and contrasting (Figure 8.13).

Demonstrate organizational features and elements of the writer's craft. The teacher at Indian Creek explained that there were two ways to write a compare/contrast essay.

Figure 8.12 Venn Diagram Comparing Indian Creek and Edmund Campion Schools

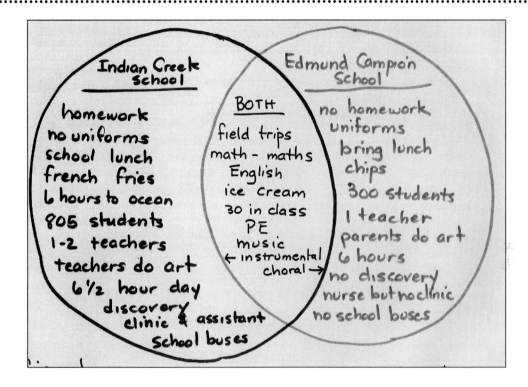

One way is to write about one thing, then write about the other. The other way is to compare the two in each category. The teacher also helped learners to see that using a variety of different signal words helped. (See Figure 8.14 for Indian Creek's finished essay.)

Revise the writing in front of everyone, referring to editing and revision tools. You may want to physically cut and paste the piece so the writers can see how it's done. Work to have everyone involved in the writing. You will need to vary your questioning and

Figure 8.13 Signal Words

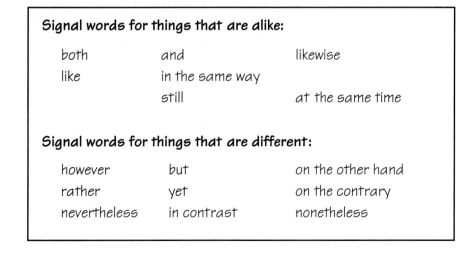

Signal words for things that are alike:

both	and	likewise
like	in the same way	
	still	at the same time

Signal words for things that are different:

however	but	on the other hand
rather	yet	on the contrary
nevertheless	in contrast	nonetheless

Figure 8.14 Comparing Indian Creek and Edmund Campion Schools

------

Comparing Our School with
Edmund Campion School in England

We had visitors from England. They helped us compare
Indian Creek School in the United States to Edmund
Campion School in England.

We learned that both schools have field trips. Children at
both schools study math (they call it "maths" in England),
English, music, and PE.

There are some ways both schools are different. At
Indian Creek, students do not wear uniforms but at
Edmund Campion they do. Children have homework at
Indian Creek, but they don't at Edmund Campion.

Students in England bring their lunch. At Indian Creek,
most students eat in the cafeteria. Our school has a
clinic with a nursing assistant. They have no clinic, but
they do have a nurse.

Our school is much larger. We have 805 students and
Edmund Campion has 300. At Edmund Campion parents
help with art, but teachers do art at Indian Creek. We
study only English. They study English and French. Most
students walk to school but we have one bus at Indian
Creek. There are no busses at Edmund Campion School.

We like going to school at Indian Creek, but we'd love to
visit Edmund Campion!

------

your task expectations for ELLs at various levels—some might use the lesson to learn a few new key words and one pattern for comparing (e.g., "At Indian Creek students don't wear uniforms, but at Campion, students do wear uniforms."). Others will be able to take advantage of the genre discussion and be ready to write their own pieces.

Put the Piece to Work.   Post the writing (with illustrations) in the classroom and find ways to use it to reinforce what students have learned: use it for reading activities; encourage learners to copy the writing in their notebooks; have a student read it to anyone who comes in the room; send home copies for students to read to their families. Additional strategies for scaffolding writing are included in Table 8.2.

Table 8.2 More Strategies for Scaffolding Writing

Strategy	Writing Stage	Procedure
Reading Aloud Examples of the Genre/Skill	Pre-writing	Provide good examples of the genre you ask learners to use. For example, when they are writing a narrative, you will want to teach them to use a strong lead—one that invites readers into the story and "grabs" them with questions they want answered. Collect

Table 8.2 More Strategies for Scaffolding Writing   *(Continued)*

Strategy	Writing Stage	Procedure
		strong leads from professional writers and from student works (to use anonymously). Offer learners some good examples of strong leads and discuss why they work. E. B. White starts *Charlotte's Web* with, "Where's Papa going with that ax?" (White, 2004). A newspaper article begins, "Let's talk about tattoos" (Gartner, 1993).
Semantic Mapping/ Graphic Organizers	Pre-writing/ drafting	Use graphic organizers to make the structure and organization of a piece of writing visible and clear to all learners. For example, learners might use the "Fishbone" Graphic organizer to outline a piece that describes cause and effect. (See Web resources for more examples of graphic organizers.)
Quickwrite	Drafting	A Quickwrite is an activity to help learners generate ideas and develop fluency. Ask learners to write about their topics for a limited time (3–5 minutes), without stopping. Assure students that spelling and grammar are not important in a Quickwrite. What's important is to get as many ideas down on paper as possible. If someone doesn't have anything to write, she can just write her name over and over until she gets a new idea.
EQS	Sharing and reviewing drafts	EQS (Encourage, Question, Suggest) helps learners develop skill in responding to others' writing. Over time (several days to several weeks, depending upon age and language level), help learners develop the three skills of *encouraging, questioning,* and *suggesting.* With each skill, first model the skill yourself, then model with a student partner, and directly teach the language that learners will need to use the technique. Below are descriptions of the skills and the language that learners will need to use them.

E: *Encourage:* Offer the writer interest and encouragement by telling them specific things you like and why.

Language samples for encouraging:

- "The giant is a funny character."
- "I could tell that you read a lot about penguins."
- "I liked the surprise at the end."
- "The first sentence made me want to read more."

Words for encouraging:

Good, great, interesting, funny, detail, read, happy, silly, laugh, sad, curious, surprise, suspense, mystery, choose

Q: *Question:* Ask questions to help the writer to be clear and to include important details.

Language samples for questioning:

- "What does the giant look like?"
- "What happens to the penguins in the winter?"

(Continued)

Table 8.2 More Strategies for Scaffolding Writing   *(Continued)*

Strategy	Writing Stage	Procedure
		• "Did you give any hints of (or foreshadow) the surprise?"
		• "Why did the story end that way?"
		Words for questioning:
		• Who went . . . ?
		• Why did . . . ?
		• Did you . . . ?
		• Where did . . . ?
		• How will you . . . ?
		• When will . . . ?
		S: *Suggest:* Gently suggest different choices and possible improvements.
		Language samples for suggesting:
		• "Could you tell me more about what the giant looked like and what clothes she wore?"
		• "What about adding a picture of the penguins?"
		• "Maybe you could put something in earlier about how she was afraid to fly. What do you think?"
		• "What verb could you use instead of 'is'?"
Sentence Combining	Revising	Sentence combining helps students make their writing clearer and more sophisticated. It provides teachers a chance to show how to create more complex sentences by taking out repetition, creating adjectives, and using "signal words" to create phrases and clauses within sentences.
		Before sentence combining: I have a brother. He is four. He likes to play soccer with me. When he can't score he gets mad. He won't go home. Sometimes I let him score.
		After Sentence combining: My four-year-old brother loves to play soccer with me, but he gets so mad when he doesn't win that sometimes I let him score just so we can go home.
Computer Reformulation	Revising/ editing	This is a variation of *reformulation* (Allwright, Woodley, & Allwright, 1988; Tocalli-Beller & Swain, 2005), a strategy in which native speakers reformulate language learners' texts and then the two discuss the process and the results. Use an online translator such as Babel Fish, which translates between many European languages, as well as Chinese, Japanese, and Korean. http://babelfish.altavista.com.
		Have learners write in L1 on the computer (or have someone enter their writing) and translate by computer into English. (The results will be inaccurate, but helpful in getting you started.) Then collaborate with the class and the writer to revise the piece into a translation of what the writer intended to say.

Table 8.2 More Strategies for Scaffolding Writing *(Continued)*

Strategy	Writing Stage	Procedure
Writing Conferences	Revising/ editing	Set aside time while students are writing to meet with individuals to talk about their writing. Spend most of your time listening, encouraging learners to share their writing and share how they want to improve it. Focus your comments on a few writing traits and skills you have covered or are working on in class. Work toward improvement, not perfection.
Spellchecker/ Writing Software	Editing	Online spell-check and grammar-check programs and thesauruses can be very helpful to EL writers if the writers learn that these tools only provide guidance, not authoritative answers. Take time to teach learners how to use the tools to help them re-think and question their writing choices. After electronic checking, they may need to go on to use other resources, such as a dictionary.
Author's Chair	Publishing	Every writing day, provide an opportunity for a young writer to sit in the "author's chair" to read aloud from his or her work. Lead the class in providing feedback in the form of encouragement and questions about the work.
Classroom Library/ Web Site	Publishing	Set up a library in your class, or in the school library for student publications. Make this library available during choice reading times and encourage parents to come to school to read and listen to their children's works. Alternately, put your learners' writing (with scanned artwork) on a secure class web site, where students and parents can read and enjoy the works.

Assessing Writing

Video Exercise

Assessing Writing in Middle School

Go to MyEducationLab, select the topic **Writing**, and watch the video entitled "**Assessing Writing in Middle School**" to observe a teacher helping middle school learners develop and assess narrative writing. Complete the questions that accompany it. You may print your work or have it transmitted to your professor as necessary.

Today's teachers and learners are feeling the pressure of high-stakes writing exams, often with cut-off scores required for secondary school graduation. The learning curve required for English learners is very sharp, but we can't focus on everything at once: we must pace our day-to-day writing expectations on what learners can do now and what they can learn to do next, keeping the final proficiency goal in mind. Ongoing assessment tools can help teachers and learners to observe and document writing progress, to determine short-term goals for the next challenge to tackle, and to provide feedback to learners and parents.

Mini-Lessons and Checklists

When Diana first started teaching writing, she felt that she wasn't a good writing teacher if she didn't find and mark every mistake in a student's paper. The result of this level of correction for an ELL is a paper with so many red marks that it "bleeds," discouraging the student and preventing them from wanting to try again. Meanwhile, the teacher hesitates to assign writing tasks and face still more piles of papers to correct. A guide who was helping a group of climbers attempt the overwhelming task of climbing Mount Everest asked his group, "How do you eat an elephant?" The answer was, of course, "one bite at a time." A mountain climber, after very careful planning, must take one step at a time up Everest. To an English learner, learning to write and climbing Mount Everest may both seem like unachievable goals, but the solution is to take one bite at a time—to conquer small goals in writing development (and retain them) and to celebrate one's progress along the way. When we learned to target certain criteria for a piece of writing—criteria that learners understand, want to, and are able to meet—the process becomes achievable and pleasurable.

When new learners of English come into your classroom, try to get samples of the students' writing in their first languages. You will know a lot just from looking at that text. Does the handwriting indicate that the child has written a lot? Is there a clear sense of organization and order to the page? Is the child confident or hesitant? Is the writing fluent? This information, though just an introduction, can help you begin to learn to know about your students, their history, and educational background.

Determining Goals: Standards for ELL Writing

TESOL, an international professional organization for teachers of English to speakers of other languages, recently updated the TESOL K–12 ESL standards to become the TESOL PreK–12 Proficiency Standards, incorporating the use of language to achieve content goals and meet content standards (TESOL, 2006). These standards are an extension of standards developed by the World-class Instructional Design and Assessment (WIDA) Consortium for a group of 16 of the U.S.

The standards documents are organized to include five grade clusters (PreK–K, 1–3, 4–5, 6–8, and 9–12), five ESL levels (Starting Up, Beginning, Developing, Expanding, and Bridging Over), and four core content areas (language arts, math, science, and social studies). They can also be selected by classroom framework, large-scale framework, or they can be combined.

Standards, sample descriptors, and ways to use the standards can be accessed through the TESOL text (TESOL, 2006), or downloaded from the WIDA web site: [http://www.wida.us/Resources/standards/elp_files]. You can generate specific standards for your class's grade-level, language level, and purpose (classroom or large-scale framework) using the online WIDA ELP Standards Wizard: [http://www.wida.us/Resources/standards/wizard]. For example, the new social studies standard 5 is: "English language learners *communicate* information, ideas, and concepts necessary for academic success in the area of *social studies.*"

The sample descriptors shown in Table 8.3 were generated from the Wizard by selecting classroom framework, grade levels 3 to 5, writing, and social studies. The

Table 8.3 WIDA English Language Proficiency Standards: The Language of Social Studies

Writing Domain: Engage in written communication in a variety of forms for a variety of purposes and audiences.

Standards	Level 1 Entering	Level 2 Beginning	Level 3 Developing	Level 4 Expanding	Level 5 Bridging
Social Studies	Reproduce historical highlights from time lines or visually supported newspaper headlines.	Produce entries for historical journals from time lines or visually supported newspaper headlines.	Maintain historical journals in chronological order based on time lines or newspaper headlines.	Produce reports from historical journals (using technology).	Produce historical documentaries from multiple sources (using technology).

Source: WIDA ELP Standards © 2004, 2007 Board of Regents of the University of Wisconsin System

Table 8.4 Writing Self-Assessment

How I Write

What I think	☹	😐	☺
Details			
Beginning, middle, end			
Makes sense			
Punctuation: (.), (!), (?)			
Capital letters			
Spelling			
I like my story			

descriptors give an idea of how the standards can be aligned to both content goals for writing and levels of proficiency of your English learners.

Once the focus standards and descriptors for a unit have been determined, it's time to develop "mini-lessons" for the "elephant bites" that will become your writing lessons. Lucy Calkins (Calkins, 1994; Calkins & Mermelstein, 2003) first used the concept of "mini-lessons" to model and teach aspects of writing. A mini-lesson is a short, five- to ten-minute lesson at the beginning of writing time that provides explicit instruction on a specific writing technique or skill. Assessment is an ongoing part of every lesson; you can teach learners how to use various assessment tools as they write, conference, revise, and edit. Diana, in the vignette at the beginning of this chapter, conducted several mini-lessons to build the skills learners needed, including one on inserting and cutting and pasting text, one on sentence combining, and another on writing a title.

Checklists are useful for helping learners understand the expectations for writing, for encouraging learner self-assessment, and for giving teacher feedback. For beginning

Table 8.5 Editing Checklist: Spelling and Word Choice

1. I checked the spelling of the following words in the textbook, in a dictionary, or with a friend: ☐

2. I asked (name and relationship, e.g., my sister Marta) _____ to check my spelling. ☐

3. I used a computer spellchecker. I had misspelled the following words: ☐

4. I chose appropriate and specific words. Three specific words I used are: ☐

5. I looked up the following words in the dictionary: ☐

6. I used the following strong verbs instead of "to be": ☐

7. Other: ☐

Table 8.6 Persuasive Essay Rubric

	Quality			
Criteria	**1**	**2**	**3**	**4**
My Position	I do not say what my position is.	I define my position but it is confused or unclear.	I define my position clearly.	I clearly define my position and explain why it is controversial.
Reasons Supporting Position	I do not give reasons that support my position.	I give one or two reasons that support my position somewhat but provide little evidence for it.	I give three reasons that support my position and provide evidence, examples, or statistics for all three.	I give clear and compelling reasons (at least three) that support my position and provide many examples, statistics, or other evidence.
Reasons Against the Position	I do not give arguments against my position.	I admit that there are arguments against the position but don't explain them.	I discuss arguments against my position, and provide some evidence to support the arguments.	I thoroughly discuss arguments against my position and provide examples or statistics as evidence.
Organization	My writing is disorganized.	My writing shows evidence of organization but sometimes gets off topic. There are few transitions between paragraphs.	My writing has a clear beginning, middle, and end. I generally use appropriate transitions between paragraphs to support the logic of the argument.	My writing is well organized, has a strong opening, strong supporting evidence, and a satisfying conclusion. There are logical transitions between paragraphs.
Closing	I forgot to write a closing.	My closing does not remind my audience of my argument.	My closing reminds the audience of my argument and restates the most compelling piece of evidence for it.	My closing restates my argument and cites the most compelling evidence for it.
Sentences	Too many confusing sentences make my essay hard to read.	My sentences are often awkward. Some run-ons and fragments.	I wrote well-constructed sentences that show evidence of variety.	My sentences are clear, well-constructed and varied with compound and complex construction evident.
Conventions	Multiple errors in spelling, punctuation, and grammar make my paper hard to read.	Too many errors are distracting to the reader but do not impede communication.	My spelling is correct. I make few errors in grammar and punctuation.	I use first-person form, with grammatical sentences, correct punctuation, and spelling.

Table 8.7 Running Record of Writing Pieces

Name

Topics	Date of 1st draft	Date of Questions	Date of 2nd draft	Date of Final draft	Rating: E = Excellent VG = Very Good G = Good NW = Needs work
1.					
2.					
3.					
4.					

learners, the purpose is to focus attention on aspects of writing. For example, the checklist in Table 8.4 is designed for beginning learners in primary grades to assess their own writing. As learners develop, they can use more details in their assessment tools. The checklist in Table 8.5 helps them to consider issues of spelling and word choice. As learners progress, they can use more sophisticated rubrics to assess their writing. Rubrics, such as the persuasive essay rubric in Table 8.6, can be designed to fit the genre that learners are using.

Writers can also keep track of their own process, noting what pieces they are working on, what ones they complete, and what their self-assessment is. Stack (2001) has her students keep notes on a form called a "running record of writing pieces," shown in Table 8.7.

Writing is clearly one of the best activities for teaching ELLs. Writing helps us "start where students are," because all learners write at their own levels. Learners at all levels can write right away—at beginning levels, this writing may include drawing, writing in another language, or pointing to pictures or telling the teacher words to write down. With lots of practice and exposure, feedback from teacher and peers, careful ongoing assessment, and rich responses to their writing, each child can steadily grow as a writer. Writing provides powerful ways for learners to construct and remember the language they are learning, and to apply what they know in their first language to a new one. Writing works best when understood as a developmental process; we can communicate to learners that they don't have to get everything right the first time; they just need to work to do something a little better each time. And we can celebrate each small step of the way as our learners become powerful, fluent, resourceful, and imaginative writers.

Questions for Reflection

1. What aspects of writing were addressed in Diana's lesson? What elements of "the writer's craft" did she teach?
2. Why is writing an activity that is particularly suited for helping ELLs acquire English? How does it connect to the principles outlined in Chapter 2?

3. What are differences between the writing process in various content areas, e.g., language arts, social studies, science, math, the arts?

4. Given the limitations of time and the large number of students in classrooms, how might you organize your writing time to use your time and your students' time well?

5. What are some ways you can use student writing to enhance school-home connections?

Activities for Further Learning

1. Develop a writing "mini-lesson" to scaffold one of the aspects or traits of writing in Table 8.1. How will you include modeling, explaining, scaffolding practice, and independent practice? How will you design your lesson to include learners at various language levels?

2. A new ELL enters your class. This student is from a language background that no one in the classroom speaks. How might you begin to assess this learner's knowledge of writing in L1 and English? What assessment tools might you develop/use? What other resources might you need? What rubric might you use or create?

3. Create an annotated list of Internet resources for students to use in their writing and/or for teachers to use in teaching writing. You might search for dictionaries/translation sites in various languages, including English; useful graphic organizers; and rubrics for assessing writing at your chosen grade levels.

4. Plan and conduct a shared writing lesson about a particular genre (e.g., thank-you letter, personal narrative, persuasive essay, compare/contrast essay, report of experiment, analysis of data, or explanation of a process). Assess and evaluate your lesson. Did learners progress toward achievement of the goals? Were you able to include learners at a variety of levels in the class? Did you make adaptations of the task to meet the levels/needs of ELLs?

5. Create a collection of good examples of a trait or genre you plan to teach: For example, a collection of strong first sentences, a collection of good endings, examples of conversation, examples of transitions, advertisements, letters, reports, essays, and so on. You may use published work, student work, or your own examples. Develop a rubric and use it to analyze each piece, evaluating elements such as appropriateness for the grade/level of your learners, qualities of the writing, and so on.

6. Plan a word wall to assist a specific class that includes English learners. What will you include on the first day of school? How will the word wall change through the school year? What activities will you incorporate into your class to make use of the word wall? What are some lists of words that you plan to add over the year? (Note: There are many word wall lists available on the Web that you might consult.) How might you adapt/enhance your word wall for the ELLs in your class?

7. Design a writing center for a classroom that includes specific resources to meet the needs of the ELLs in that class. You might consider picture dictionaries and other vocabulary sources, translation tools, computer and software, a variety of writing and drawing materials, models and examples of writing, rubrics, various writing prompts/task cards, and journals. Explain the purpose of the materials and resources you include and the procedures you will establish for using the writing center.

myeducationlab Where the Classroom Comes to Life   is a collection of online tools for your success in this course, your licensure exams, and your teaching career. Go to www.myeducationlab .com to utilize these extensive resources including videos from real classrooms, Praxis and licensure preparation, a lesson plan builder, and materials to help you in your teaching career.

Suggested Reading

Barrett-Dragan, P. (2005). *A how-to guide for teaching English language learners in the primary classroom.* Portsmouth, NH: Heinemann. This book, written by a classroom teacher, takes the reader through the first twenty days of school, showing how to get ELLs started in their language acquisition, as well as how to build an inclusive classroom community that supports their learning.

Chen, L. & Mora-Flores, E. (2006). *Balanced literacy for English language learners, K–2.* Portsmouth, NH: Heinemann. The authors focus on seven aspects of balanced instruction to help ELLs develop and expand literacy skills: interactive read-aloud, emergent story book read-aloud, shared reading, reading workshop, writing workshop, guided reading, and word work.

Franklin, E. (Ed.). (1999). *Reading and writing in more than one language: Lessons for teachers.* Alexandria, VA: TESOL.This book discusses issues in K through 12 literacy with bilingual learners. Ten chapters from various contributors offer different viewpoints speaking from real classroom experiences, offering evidence and examples from teachers and students.

Hadway, N. L., Vardell, S. M., & Young, T. A. (2002). *Literature-based instruction with English language learners.* Boston: Allyn & Bacon. Hadway and Young's chapter, "Negotiating Meaning Through Writing" provides a clear explanation of the issues in ELL writing development, and provides principles and examples for helping beginning learners start to write, particularly using interactive writing.

Hudelson, S. (1984). Kan yu ret an rayt en ingles: Children become literate in ESL. *TESOL Quarterly, 18*(2), 221–248. The author shares and carefully analyzes the writing of young bilingual students who are developing English language skills, offering recommendations for effective practice.

Samway, K. D. (2006). *When English language learners write: Connecting research to practice, K–8.* Portsmouth, NH: Heinemann. Samway connects the latest research on ELLs and language acquisition to effective classroom practices incorporating research on how ELLs' writing develops and steps to take in providing instruction responsive to ELLs' needs.

Web Sites for Further Learning

Babel Fish Translation. This online tool from AltaVista translates words and phrases from Chinese, Dutch, French, German, Greek, Italian, Japanese, Korean, Portuguese, Russian, and Spanish into English and vice versa. These translations are frequently inaccurate, but may help in getting started. Revising the translations together is also a very useful classroom activity with rich learning opportunities. Retrieved May 16, 2008.

http://www.babelfish.com

Celebrating Cultural Diversity Through Children's Literature. Robert Smith provides links to annotated bibliographies of multicultural children's books from a variety of cultural groups, categorizing them by genre, and providing approximate grade levels. Evaluations of the books are not implied, nor are they included. Retrieved May 16, 2008.

http://www.multiculturalchildrenslit.com/

English Language Learners, Classroom Drama, by Dana Loy. From *The Quarterly* from the National Writing Project, 2004. Dana Loy of the National Writing Project writes about how her eighth graders collected, wrote, and performed stories from their culture and how deeply everyone (especially the teacher) learned from the process. Retrieved May 16, 2008.

http://www.writingproject.org/cs/nwpp/print/nwpr/1286

Graphic Organizers. This site offers a large collection of easy-to-download graphic organizers to use in writing. They're available in both PDF and Word formats. Retrieved May 16, 2008.

http://www.region15.org/curriculum/graphicorg.html

I Love Languages. This site is a comprehensive catalog of language-related Internet resources with more than 2,400 links. Though the links have been hand-reviewed, they are of uneven quality. Nevertheless, the access to lesser-known languages, online language lessons, translating dictionaries, native literature, translation services, software, language schools, and so on, is highly useful. Retrieved May 16, 2008.

http://www.ilovelanguages.com/

International Children's Digital Library. The International Children's Digital Library has nearly 200 titles selected by national libraries, authors, and publishers representing 45 different cultures, and is aiming for 10,000 titles. All of the books open online, fully illustrated, and in their original languages. This site may be useful in finding a text in your students' languages for them to read as well as in helping you learn a little about some of those languages. Retrieved May 16, 2008.

http://www.icdlbooks.org/

Lucy Calkins's Mini-Lessons and Rubrics, Samples. This site offers sample rubrics, mini-lessons, and conferences, along with a brief video of Lucy conducting a writing conference. Retrieved May 16, 2008.

http://www.unitsofstudy.com/samples.asp

Smithsonian Photography Initiative. Smithsonian provides an online repository from Smithsonian museums for teachers and learners to sequence, tag, and save for use in inspiring and illustrating writing. Retrieved May 16, 2008.

http://www.photography.si.edu/

Topics: An Online Magazine for Learners of English. This online magazine includes lots of cultural information for students learning about other countries. It also invites and includes writings by English learners about where they're from. It includes a language center for writing development and polishing, and a teachers' corner with Web projects and teaching techniques. Retrieved May 16, 2008.

http://www.topics-mag.com/

Writing Checklists. This site has five examples of checklists for student self-assessment of writing. Retrieved May 16, 2008.

http://www.mlmcc.com/File/PUBLICATIONS/2007FiveEditingChecklists.pdf

Writing Fix. Sponsored by the Northern Nevada Writing Project, and organized around the six traits of writing, the Writing Fix offers interactive writing activities and activities for all types of learners, including tools, games, lessons, and areas for publishing. Retrieved May 16, 2008.

http://www.writingfix.com

References

Allwright, R. L., Woodley, M. P., & Allwright, J. M. (1988). Investigating reformulation as a practical strategy for the teaching of academic writing. *Applied Linguistics, 9:* 236–256.

Calkins, L. M. (1994). *The art of teaching writing* (New ed.). Portsmouth, NH: Heinemann.

Calkins, L. M. & Mermelstein, L. (2003). *Launching the writing workshop.* Portsmouth, NH: FirstHand.

Carrell, P. L. & Eisterhold, J. C. (1988), Schema theory and ESL reading pedagogy. In P. L. Carrell, J. Devine, & D. E. Eskey (Eds.), pp. 73–92. *Interactive approaches to second language reading,* Cambridge, UK: Cambridge University Press.

Culham, R. (2003). *6 + 1 traits of writing: The complete guide for grades 3 and up.* NY: Scholastic Professional Books.

Culham, R. (2005). *6 + 1 traits of writing. The complete guide for the primary grades.* NY: Scholastic.

Edelsky, C. (1993). *Writing in a bilingual program: Había una vez.* Norwood, NJ: Ablex.

Enright, D. S., & McCloskey, M. L. (1988). *Integrating English: Developing English language and literacy in the multilingual classroom.* Reading, MA: Addison-Wesley.

Gartner, M. (1993). Tattoos and freedom. *The (Ames, Iowa) Daily Tribune.*

Graves, D. H. (2003). *Writing: Teachers and children at work* (20th anniversary ed.). Portsmouth, NH: Heinemann.

Hadaway, N. L. & Young, T. A. (2006). Negotiating meaning through writing. In T. A. Young & N. L. Hadaway (Eds.), *Supporting the development of English learners.* Newark, DE: International Reading Association.

Hudelson, S. (1984). Kan yu ret an rayt en ingles: Children become literate in ESL. *TESOL Quarterly, 18*(2), 221–248.

Leki, I. (2003). Research insights on second language writing instruction [Electronic Version]. *CAL Digest.* Retrieved May 16, 2008 from http://www.cal.org/resources/digest/0306leki.html.

Olivares, R. A. (2002). Communication, constructivism and transfer of knowledge in the education of bilingual learners [Electronic Version]. *International Journal of Bilingual Education and Bilingualism,* 5(1). Retrieved May 16, 2008 from http://www.multilingual-matters.net/beb/005/0004/beb0050004.pdf.

Rog, L. J. (2007). *Marvelous minilessons for teaching beginning writing, K–3.* Newark, DE: International Reading Association.

Samway, K. D. (1992, Spring). Writers' workshop and children acquiring English as a non-native language [Electronic Version]. *NCBE Program Information Guide Series.* Retrieved May 16, 2008 from http://www.ncela.gwu.edu/pubs/pigs/pig10.htm.

Samway, K. D. (2006). *When English language learners write: Connecting research to practice, K–8.* Portsmouth, NH: Heinemann.

Stack, L. (2001). *An introduction to writers' workshop for English language learners.* Unpublished manuscript, San Francisco.

TESOL. (2006). *PreK–12 English language proficiency standards.* Alexandria, VA: TESOL.

Tocalli-Beller, A. & Swain, M. (2005). Reformulation: The cognitive conflict and L2 learning it generates. *International Journal of Applied Linguistics, 15*(1): 5–28.

White, E. B. (2004). *Charlotte's web.* NY: HarperTrophy.

Young, T. A. & Hadaway, N. L. (Eds.), (2006). *Supporting the development of English learners.* Newark, DE: International Reading Association.

CHAPTER 9

Structuring and Planning Content-Language Integrated Lessons

Kathy Gill is teaching her fourth grade class a unit on fables. Her students have read many of Aesop's fables and Kathy has asked students to interview family members for examples of fables from their native cultures. Kathy's students have brought these stories to class and shared them with the group. Kathy has gathered the stories together and produced copies for the class.

Today, Kathy is distributing two stories to each of her six classroom groups. The stories are brief. The first one is one of Aesop's fables and the other a fable brought by one of the children from home. Kathy wants the students to find commonalities in each of the stories, eventually defining the characteristics of a fable.

Kathy has assigned jobs for each of the four children in each group. One child is the reader and has the job today of reading the stories to the others. One student is a reporter and will report the results of the group work to the class as a whole. One student is the writer who will write the results and the fourth student is the manager and timekeeper. This student's job is to keep the work moving along, and make sure everyone understands their tasks and finishes the work on time. Kathy has assigned her English language learners (ELLs) to groups where she knows they will be supported by their classmates. She has assigned tasks to these students based upon their language abilities. For example, her beginning-level ELL is assigned to be a timekeeper in a group where one other student can speak her language.

Kathy has provided job tents for each student. The folded oak tag "tent" states the job name and pictures it as well. There are descriptions of what the job entails on each card, along with "frames" suggesting language these learners might use. The class has used these cards before—Kathy is sure many of the students understand their jobs—but she wants to check to be sure.

Kathy: *Mario, you are the reader today. What will you do?*

Mario: *I will read the stories to my group.*

Kathy: *Okay, and what will you do, Marta?*

Marta: *I listen to the stories and find the thing in common.*

Kathy: *(nodding) What does Marta mean by "in common"?*

> Several children raise their hands and Kathy waits for five seconds for all to think about her question. Then she says,
>
> **Kathy:** *Turn to your buddy and tell your buddy what Marta means by "finding the things in common" in the two stories.*

How do teachers structure lessons for content-language integrated classes?

- What are the six characteristics of lessons that support learning?
- What are the three kinds of objectives for integrated lesson planning?
- Why do we activate prior knowledge?
- How can we teach vocabulary so that it will be retained by learners?
- What is the nature of language and content input?
- How do we proceed through guided practice?
- What activities are appropriate for independent practice?
- How can students summarize what they have learned?
- How can we conduct assessment throughout the learning experience?

Lesson Characteristics That Support Learning

Lesson planning for a grade-level classroom of diverse English language learners requires careful thought and structure in order to integrate the content and language learning needs of all students in the classroom. Effective teachers make adjustments to their lessons that lead to achievement gains for ELLs. These teachers carefully structure their language use, teach grade appropriate content, integrate all learners heterogeneously in instructional groups that support practice, and provide corrective feedback. The element that sets apart these classrooms more than any other may be the conscious planning for language development occurring in mixed language content classrooms. Whether our subject matter is science, math, or social studies, the language of the content is an important part of the learning of the content.

In our discussion of lesson planning, we will keep in mind the elements of good lessons that have been found to relate to achievement gains for English language learners. The following six factors are critical features (Wong Fillmore, Ammon, McLaughlin, & Ammon, 1985, pp. 125–143).

Teacher-Directed Instruction

The language of the teacher during instruction can provide valuable input to ELLs and better access to the curriculum. High-quality student-teacher exchanges have been found to exist in exemplary math and science programs in California where teachers were trained in second language techniques (Minicucci, 1996). But these high quality exchanges are not the norm in mainstream classrooms. Teachers in one study (StoopsVerplaetse, 1998) commonly used imperative directives ("Open your books to page 45") asked few questions, and rarely asked high-level cognitive or open-ended questions of ELLs. Lindholm-Leary (2001) found a high number of directives in math classrooms. Harklau (1994) found that by secondary school, teachers rarely adjusted their lectures to increase comprehensibility for ELLs. Students tuned out of the lessons for the most part and busied themselves by working on homework assignments or reading the text. The result of this impoverished language environment over a period of time was to diminish comprehensible input and decrease access to the curriculum. Teachers who have limited or poor language interactions with students have very little notion of their students' language levels. Since they rarely hold extended conversations with them, they can be widely off the mark when asked to rate their language abilities. A reciprocal interaction model of instruction in which teachers engage in genuine dialogue with their students is more beneficial in the development of higher-order cognitive skills and provides better access to the curriculum than a traditional transmission teaching model (Berman, Minicucci, McLaughlin, Nelson, & Woodworth, 1995; Doherty, Hilberg, Pinal, & Tharp, 2003; Tikunoff, 1985).

Content teachers can accelerate content comprehension and language growth by adjusting their language patterns in order to model the language forms related to the specific content area studied. These forms change from one area of content to another. Science lessons may stress present tense verbs, measurement terms, and specific vocabulary: "Cut thin slices of a beet so that they can be placed on a microscope depression slide and viewed with the lowest power (4X)." Social studies texts contain many present perfect and past tense forms, use adverbials of time, and are language dense: "The March on Washington for Jobs and Freedom on August 28, 1963, riveted the nation's attention. Rather than the anticipated one hundred thousand marchers, more than twice that number appeared, astonishing even its organizers." Math word problems use specific language closely related to the processes required for problem solution: "Measure the following objects using the metric scale. Convert the measurements to the English scale by multiplying or dividing." Effective teachers isolate this language, model it, and provide opportunities for their students to use it appropriately.

Heterogeneous Grouping

When grouped with English-speaking peers, ELLs are able to hear more correctly-formed language than when isolated in ELL-only classes. In integrated classrooms, the language input of both the teacher directions and the students' responses create a range of English proficiency that, if comprehended, provides a source of content-related grammatical structures and vocabulary. Students are expected to participate more in mixed than in ELL-only groupings and if the teacher has planned effectively, they will have reason and opportunity to output language. This output potential is essential to language acquisition (Swain, 1985; Izumi & Bigelow, 2000). As learners use what they know in the new language, their fellow learners help them to determine whether their communication is effective or not. In studies of small-group interactions among ELL-only groups (Pica, Lincoln-Porter, Paninos, & Linnelli, 1996), researchers found that the group interactions assisted language learning even when the source of the interaction is another ELL. Help from other students, whether native speakers or ELLs, apparently provides the language practice that can assist learners to develop new grammar forms and learn academic vocabulary (Wong Fillmore, 1989; Pica, et al., 1996).

The integration of technology into the content curriculum provides other opportunities for ELLs to work in heterogeneous groupings with English-only classmates. Cummins, Brown, and Sayers (2007) report on implementing approaches to promote literacy and engagement among minority learners using technology as a means to develop higher-order learning. Dixon (1995) reports effective learning for middle school students on spatial visualization tasks and concepts of reflection and rotation when compared to a traditional textbook approach. It appears that well-managed cooperative learning, on the whole, promotes higher achievement levels in ELLs (Calderón, Tinajero, & Hertz-Lazarowitz, 1992; Calderón & Carreon, 1994; Calderón, Hertz-Lazarowitz, & Slavin, 1998). Negotiation of meaning and adjustment of output relates to language gains. But perhaps the most important element of heterogeneous grouping is the assurance that English language learners will work on grade level and with cognitively appropriate content.

Appropriate Content

Wong Fillmore, et al. (1985) found a relationship between the level of instruction, the level of language, and the academic outcomes of classroom programs (p. 129). ELLs excelled when the level of instruction provided was high and when the teachers were demanding. This outcome was especially notable in the Hispanic students in the study. In certain classrooms, teachers were skilled at organizing and presenting grade appropriate materials in ways which engaged English language learners and aided their comprehension. Content-free, simplified materials could not hold learner interest as keenly as appropriate grade-level content. Many studies have agreed that a meaningful and academically challenging curriculum is a core component of effective programs for ELLs (Tikunoff, 1985; Ramirez, 1992; Berman, et al., 1995; Montecel & Cortez, 2002; Doherty, et al., 2003). An emphasis on learning basics such as the alphabet, numbers, and colors does not provide appropriate content learning for older learners. By engaging learners in age-appropriate content material they will learn the basics as well as a great deal more.

Attention to Language

Effective teachers place an emphasis on communication and comprehension and plan ways to help ELLs enter the instructional conversation of the classroom. Using consistent language patterns for regular routines, teachers help their students quickly learn the transitions that occur in any lesson or school day. We saw this clearly in one kindergarten class where we observed a newly arrived Chinese student. Although he did not yet speak or understand English, he participated loudly by sing-songing his teacher's announcement: "It's clean-up time. It's clean-up time." at the end of the play period.

The location of the instruction in the classroom and the materials used help to mark transitions between lessons. Formulaic expressions and routine beginnings and endings of lessons are further aids to English language learners' comprehension. Clearly labeled daily agendas and lesson outlines provide the patterned routine so necessary for older learners. Consistent lesson formats for instruction help learners to anticipate what will come next and be prepared to participate. Merchant and Young (2000) create a weekly syllabus called the *Sci Fire News* at the beginning of each week for their mixed language science classes. The syllabus alerts students to activities, announcements, and assignments for the coming week.

Attention to language occurs when teachers plan for the content language necessary to learn the content. In Dana Richmond's middle-school algebra class, many of the students were not able to explain how they solved problems using appropriate math vocabulary. Dana knew the vocabulary was crucial to understanding the algebraic concepts and that it would be tested at the end of each unit. And so she provided opportunities for groups of learners to work together in creating their explanations and then presenting them to the class along with the correct problem solutions. Learning these terms in isolation, Dana discovered, was not effective. The language and content learning needed to be integrated and Dana needed to plan for that integration.

The integration of language and content objectives has been explored (Berman, et al., 1995; Minicucci, 1996; Echevarria, Short, & Powers, 2003) as a way of providing better access to the curriculum and higher achievement for ELLs. Indeed we advocate the addition of a language development component in every content classroom containing ELLs.

Supported Practice

Teachers support language learning when they support students' opportunities to practice the language within a content context. Language output is as important as language input (Swain, 1985). The form of support can be visual, verbal, graphic, or interactional. When students work in groups or enter into discussions with their teachers, the interactional support enables them to use newly acquired language in a variety of ways. They are able to determine what works and are supported by more experienced listeners to negotiate what they want to say. Wong Fillmore (1989) says teachers need to plan their elicitation questions carefully in order to engage learners at each level of proficiency. This "response tailoring" might mean the teacher plans to ask simple *yes-no* or *either-or* questions of beginning English learners while presenting intermediate learners with open-ended questions.

Planning for supported practice also means teachers plan in advance not only the kind of language they will use for various levels of learners but also plan the language output that will result. They plan how to support the output through a visual, graphic, or interactional context. And so, intermediate ELLs may describe the process of metamorphosis using a graphic organizer to structure their language and vocabulary. Beginning learners will also describe the same process with the same organizer but may answer only by pointing to pictures in response to the teacher's questions: "Where is the butterfly? Show me the caterpillar. What happens after the caterpillar makes the cocoon?"

Video Exercise

Lesson Characteristics That Support Learning for ELLs

Go to MyEducationLab, select the topic **Sheltered Content Instruction**, and watch the video entitled **"Lesson Characteristics That Support Learning for ELLs"** to observe a first grade class involved in making body graphs. Complete the questions that accompany it. You may print your work or have it transmitted to your professor as necessary.

Corrective Feedback

Learners can receive feedback on their language use in ways that encourage learning, and don't lead to embarrassment. These include modeling correct answers in responses that address the meaning learners were trying to convey; providing elaboration with this modeling to expand and improve language used; asking questions to help learners clarify what they mean; noting common errors and using them to develop mini-lessons for individuals, small groups, or the whole class; providing rubrics to help learners detect their own errors; and pointing to models or rules on the wall to help learners correct errors and promote learner self-evaluation. Sometimes it might be important to simply ignore the language error and attend solely to the meaning a learner is trying to convey. Olivier (2003) reports that the ways in which teachers use language affect how learners modify their language. If teachers give constructive feedback, learners tend to use the feedback to rephrase. Feedback and open-ended questions from fellow students in small-group settings also provide the data for modification of output and development of grammar (Pica, et al., 1996).

A Lesson Format for Integrated Learning

Keeping in mind the six characteristics of lessons that work, we propose a lesson format for integrated content and language instruction that is based upon a three-part structure: *Into, Through, and Beyond* (some teachers call this structure *Before, During, and After*). The organization of our lesson is based upon work in cognitive psychology, particularly on the view that knowledge is constructed and that the focus of instruction should be helping students to develop learning and thinking strategies rather than to help them memorize and acquire facts. In Mayer's cognitive model of knowledge construction (1992), he describes three learning processes necessary to meaningful learning:

1. Selection of information to be learned and added to the "working memory"
2. Organization of information in the "working memory" into a coherent whole
3. Integration of the organized information into the other knowledge structures already existing in the "working memory"

For meaningful learning to occur, learners must proceed through all three processes (see Table 9.1). They first select information that is necessary to the learning experience, focusing on this information and not attending to other information in the environment, the textbook, or lecture. In order to select appropriately, learners must comprehend the information and make their selections based upon their understanding of the new information. In reading a textbook passage, for example, learners must understand the information in the text before they are able to select the information that is most important for the learning experience.

After the selection process, learners organize the selected information into a coherent whole. Organizing the totality of a story might mean learners are able to answer specific questions about the story and retell the story according to an organizing principle.

The final step is integration of the whole topic into the schema of what learners already know about the topic. This presupposes learners are aware of what they already know and their current information has been activated through classroom experiences, such as discussions with the teacher. Integration of the information requires learners to arrange the new information in some way, perhaps hierarchically, temporally, or spatially. For example, in learning about Juan Ponce de Leon, learners might place the name of the individual within the category of known explorers. The timeline of de Leon's life and the location of his explorations also can be meshed with known histories of other explorers and areas of exploration in the New World. Without this integration of the new information, long-term learning does not take place.

The three part lesson format described here corresponds to Mayer's description of the cognitive processes leading to meaningful learning.

Into the Lesson: Defining Objectives, Activating, and Preparing for Learning

In the Intro phase of the lesson, teachers prepare for the new learning. Preparation involves determining and clearly communicating objectives, activating what learners already know about the topic, motivating them to learn more, providing a perspective for the learning, and stimulating learners to begin processing the new information.

Defining Content Objectives

This is the first step in planning a lesson. When teaching English language learners, we want to think about three different kinds of objectives:

1. Content objectives that are grade appropriate and cognitively challenging
2. Language objectives that identify the language needed for the content to be processed, learned, and communicated

Table 9.1 A Three-Part Lesson Format for Comprehensive Lesson Planning

Theme: What "big idea" or topic will connect this lesson to others I will teach this week or month?

Lesson Phase	Lesson Components	Questions for Lesson Planning
Into the Lesson	Content Objectives	What *specifically* do I want my students to know or be able to do at the end of the lesson? How can I *communicate* the objective to my students? Is my objective *measurable?* What contextual *supports* can I provide for learning?
	Language Objectives	What specifically do I want my students to be able to understand, say, read, or write by the end of my lesson? How can I communicate the objective to my students? Will I be able to measure this objective? What contextual *supports* can I provide for learning?
	Learning Strategy Objectives	What learning strategy will I teach or *demonstrate* to help my students learn better? How can I *communicate* the objective to my students? Is my objective *measurable?* What contextual *supports* can I provide for learning?
	Activating Prior Knowledge	How will I help students to focus their attention on what they *already know* about the information or the skill in today's lesson?
Through the Lesson	Vocabulary	What vocabulary will the students be using? How will they *use the vocabulary?* Does the vocabulary reflect the *content* I am teaching?
	Language and Content Input	How will the new information be conveyed to my students? Will they listen to it, read it, or engage in research to discover it? How can I support the input with *context* and *scaffolding?*
	Guided Practice	How will I help my students *practice* the new information or skill in a way that will help them to be successful? Can I incorporate a *collaborative activity* into this practice? How will I *check their understanding* of the new information?
Beyond the Lesson	Independent Practice	What assignments or homework shall I have my students complete to facilitate long-term *retention?* Does the assignment reflect the *variety* in my students' learning styles?
	Summarizing	How can I help my students to *demonstrate, tell, or write* what they have learned today?
	Assessment	How will I know what *each* of my students has *learned* in this lesson?

3. Learning strategy objectives that promote thinking about learning, analysis, and reflection

As shown in Table 9.1, the questions we ask ourselves when planning for instruction concern the specificity of the objectives, our ability to communicate them and measure their effectiveness, and the degree to which we can support the learning.

- What specifically do I want my students to know or be able to do at the end of the lesson? Is my objective measurable? How can I communicate the objective to my students? How can I support their learning?
- What specifically do I want my students to be able to understand, say, read, or write by the end of my lesson? How will I communicate the objective to my students? Will I be able to measure this objective? How can I support their learning?
- What learning strategy will I teach or demonstrate to help my students learn better? How can I communicate the objective to my students? Is my objective measurable? How can I support their learning?

Specificity in defining objectives helps us to focus more clearly on what it is we want students to learn during our lessons. This kind of thinking is more effective than thinking about the activities we are going to use or how to get the students involved in the learning. We have to think about those aspects of the lesson, too, but they do not determine learning outcomes in the same way as specific content objectives, clearly communicated. Objective writing is best done in terms of what the students will do and not what the teacher will do. Thus, we like to think in terms of language where the student is the subject of the objective, for example: "The learners will be able to identify three causes for the fall of the Roman Empire," or "Learners will illustrate the four stages in the life cycle of a frog."

We advocate the use of Bloom's Taxonomy of Thinking Skills (Bloom, Englehart, Furst, Hill, & Krathworl, 1956) to bring more specificity to our thinking about objectives. Table 9.2 lists the Taxonomy or six levels of cognitive thinking defined by Bloom, et al.; the next columns indicate cue words that are highly specific to that level of thinking. These cue words, when used to write content or language objectives, bring clarity to our thinking and to the thinking of our students concerning what they are going to learn or be able to do.

The six levels of cognition on the Taxonomy begin at the Knowledge level, the level of naming and labeling, equivalent to the level of the two-year-old who asks Mom "What's dat?" This is the level of vocabulary learning and it's a good place to start content lessons. As we proceed through our lessons, we move through the hierarchy, giving students opportunities to comprehend and apply knowledge. It would be a mistake to end learning at this point, however. Students will not achieve meaningful learning unless they also analyze the information, synthesize the learning to form a new whole, and evaluate the material for a given purpose. Although it may not be possible to achieve each level of the hierarchy for every lesson, it is essential to teach to the higher levels for a substantial part of each learning unit. Standardized testing requires students to compare-contrast, compose, persuade and argue—all higher-order skills. And it is through teaching at these higher levels that ELLs are able to develop the language and cognitive skills they need to communicate about complex content.

Defining Language Objectives

Language objectives are essential for English language learners to become language users. We cannot assume that learners will develop language through classroom immersion. Academic language is used primarily in schools and textbooks; in order for

Table 9.2 Bloom's Taxonomy of Thinking Levels

Level	Cue Words		
Knowledge Recall Remembering previously learned material.	• Observe • Repeat • Label/Name • Cluster	• List • Record • Match • Memorize	• Recall • Recount • Sort • Outline (Format Stated) • Define
Comprehension Translate Grasping the meaning of material.	• Recognize • Locate • Identify • Restate • Paraphrase	• Describe • Tell • Report • Express • Explain	• Cite • Document/Support • Summarize • Precise/Abstract
Application Generalize Using learned material in new and concrete situations.	• Select • Manipulate • Sequence • Organize • Imitate	• Use • Frame • Apply • How to • Show • Demonstrate	• Dramatize • Illustrate • Test/Solve • Imagine (Information Known)
Analysis Break down/ Discover Breaking down material into its component parts so that it may be more easily understood.	• Examine • Classify • Distinguish • Differentiate • Outline (No format given)	• Map • Relate to • Characterize • Analyze • Conclude • Question	• Compare and Contrast • Research • Debate and Defend • Refute • Infer
Synthesis Compose Putting material together to form a new whole.	• Propose • Plan • Compose • Formulate	• Create • Invent • Design	• Construct • Imitate • Imagine • Speculate
Evaluation Judge Judging the value of material for a given purpose.	• Compare (Pro/Con) • Prioritize/Rank • Judge • Decide	• Rate • Evaluate • Criticize • Argue • Justify	• Convince • Persuade • Assess • Value • Predict

Source: Adapted from Zainuddin, Yahya, Morales-Jones, & Ariza (2002, pp. 257–258).

learners to acquire it, teachers create language objectives and provide opportunities for structured practice of the language.

The kinds of language objectives we focus on are determined by the nature of the content learning. If, for example, the lesson is devoted to the Gold Rush, we will expect learners to use past tense verbs to describe historical events. The language of maps entails place names and passive voice constructions (e.g., "The center of gold panning was located in the Yukon. The Yukon is situated in . . ."). Susan Sillivan (2000) teaches a unit on Marketing and the Media to her eighth grade students. She includes objectives relating to the language of persuasion such as: "Identify persuasive language in TV commercials," "Take a position and support it," and "Create a commercial using persuasive language."

We like to determine language objectives by thinking backwards. After determining content objectives and the activities required to achieve those objectives, we think about what students need to do with language to complete those activities successfully. For example, students may read a passage in a text, report on information either orally or in writing, listen to and understand others in small-group work, or take notes from an oral presentation. Each of these activities involves a language skill such as listening, speaking, reading, or writing. Language content is also involved, such as using punctuation, writing a chronological essay, completing a graphic organizer, or using content-specific vocabulary or specific grammatical constructions. We like to run the lesson through our minds as if viewing a movie. We imagine our students working on the activities we have chosen and try to identify the language they will need to be successful. Often, we will find the language we want to teach in the textbook or in other materials used to inform the class. This language will be required by all students, whether they are English language learners or not.

The next step is to communicate the content and language objectives to our students both orally and in writing. Communication of learning goals is critical to achieving those goals. We have been told by principals and supervisors that the most effective teachers are very clear about the goals of their lessons. After spending five minutes in their rooms, you are sure to know exactly what the learners are being taught to know or do. In addition to orally informing students, it is important to write the objectives on the board where they can be referred to easily. ELLs who cannot clearly understand that oral language will have a second chance to understand the written communication. Once learners know what they need to learn to be successful, they are able to set about learning. Communicating this information gives all students the opportunity to be a part of the instructional conversation.

Determining how we are going to assess our objectives is another part of the preparation phase of the lesson. We may want learners to end the lesson by writing a short summary in their learning logs, sharing their summary with a partner, creating an illustration, answering a quick question on a sticky note, responding to our summary questions through symbols (such as "thumbs up" and "thumbs down" symbols), or writing a "Dear Teacher" letter. We need to remember that we may be assessing both content and language knowledge, and the nature of the lesson determines the nature of our assessment. If we have a reading-skill goal in mind, we may want learners to demonstrate comprehension by completing a graphic organizer summarizing the text passage. Assessing oral skills will require an oral response either in large- or small-group format. Listening skills can be the most difficult language mode to assess because we can't see inside our students' heads. We can, however, ask students to produce language orally or in writing that demonstrates comprehension.

Defining Learning Strategy Objectives

Learning strategies are an important part of lesson preparation for all of our students. These strategies form the core of the CALLA approach, which is discussed in Chapter 4. For English language learners, learning strategies are particularly important.

ELLs use these strategies to help them compensate for their lack of classroom language proficiency. They learn strategies that help them become better learners, such as:

- Organizing main ideas
- Planning how to complete a learning task
- Listening to information selectively
- Checking their own comprehension, and
- Planning when, where, what, and how to study

Learners also need to know how to

- Use reference materials
- Take notes
- Summarize
- Relate new learning to prior learning
- Predict and infer meanings

During class, they must be able to

- Ask questions of the teacher and their peers
- Work with others in a group

Once again, we cannot assume our students have learned these essential strategies. If we want learners to use learning strategies to achieve, we have to plan for their use.

Rona Wilson begins each year with her seventh grade students by concentrating on social learning strategies of questioning, praising, participating, and cooperating. She plans lessons where she defines the social skill, models the skill, and then sets up situations that require her students to practice each of the skills. Rona supports the English language learners in her class by writing the language necessary to the skill on large charts that she keeps hanging on the wall. For praising, she writes items such as "That's a good idea," "Well done," and "Good job." Question starters might include phrases such as "What do you call . . . ?" "How can I . . . ?" and "Do you have . . . ?" After a while, students no longer need the wall words as they incorporate the language into their growing language systems.

Performance Indicators

These are observable, measurable language behaviors that teachers can assess as students engage in classroom tasks. Performance Indicators are similar to language or content objectives, but they contain three elements of classroom progress critical to the success of ELLs:

1. *Content information* derived from the content curriculum, state, and national standards. Examples include: math operations, human body systems, or initial consonant clusters.
2. *Language functions* that indicate how the language is used in communicating. Examples include: persuade, defend, and interpret.
3. *Support or strategy* that scaffolds the communication act enabling ELLs to be successful with developing language skills. Examples include: using

manipulatives, visuals, graphic organizers, or working in small groups (TESOL, 2006, p. 43).

Performance indicators provide the three essential elements needed for successful instruction of ELLs in content classrooms. Both content and language objectives are clearly specified. In addition, an element of support is indicated to ensure that the learning experience is structured in a way to help ELLs be successful. Examples of supports and strategies for content and language learning include social (interactional) supports, material supports, and learning supports.

Social supports

- Small group learning
- Interactive structures that encourage discussion and active participation (Buddy Talk, Think-Pair-Share, and so on)
- Cooperative learning structures (numbered heads together, group work with designated roles, roundtable/round robin, Jigsaw, and so on)
- Study buddies
- Study groups

Material Supports

- Graphic organizers
- Pictures, props, and gestures
- Advance organizers, outlines, structured notes, T-lists
- Picture dictionaries, learner dictionaries, translation dictionaries, word source software
- Alternative and modified texts

Learning Supports

- Learning strategies (note-taking, selective listening and reading, summarizing, organizational planning, effective memorization, prediction, and so on)
- Vocabulary learning tools (personal dictionaries, Word Squares, visualization, and so on)

When supports and scaffolds are combined with language and content objectives, teachers can modify instruction for differing proficiency levels. For example, a performance indicator targeting the content of plants (grade level 1 to 3) might require beginning level learners to:

Draw and label local plant or animal species from real life observations, experiences, or pictures (TESOL, 2006, p. 65).

The same content for an intermediate level learner might require a different language function and a different support structure such as:

Compare physical attributes of local plant or animal species from real-life observations, experiences, or pictures, using graphic support (TESOL, 2006, p. 65).

In this last example, the language function (compare) requires a comparison graphic organizer as a support structure. As teachers respond to multiple levels of language proficiency in classrooms, they modify the language functions and support structures while teaching the required content to all learners.

Activating Prior or Current Knowledge

Activation takes place while proceeding Into the Lesson, immediately after the communication of objectives. It is one of the most important ways teachers help learning to occur. The educational psychologist, David Ausubel (1968), has said it is the "single most important factor influencing learning." Why is this so? Once learners are aware they already know something about a topic, it is no longer viewed as totally new. Learners won't give up on themselves before they start but will be willing to continue the learning dialogue, especially once they have made an initial contribution to the conversation. Learners feel empowered at the outset of instruction.

They also feel cognitively engaged and focused on the new learning. We like to think of it as attaching Velcro to the brain. The new learning "sticks" because our students have become participants in the exploration of knowledge in our classrooms.

Activation also serves the teacher's purpose of finding out what learners already know about the topic and clearing up any misconceptions they may have about it. This information helps teachers to adjust instruction to learner's previous knowledge as well as to their interests and cultures. The teacher may discover her students mistakenly believe all rivers flow from the north to the south or seasons occur because of the distance of the Earth from the Sun. This misinformation will need to be clarified before further learning can take place.

The question we need to ask during this phase of the lesson is: "How will I help students to focus their attention on what they *already know* about the information or the skill in today's lesson?" There are many techniques used by teachers to activate learning. All of them have in common the effect of getting learners cognitively engaged and ready to accept the new learning. Let's look at a few we have found to be useful at a variety of grade levels.

Semantic Mapping. This is sometimes called Spider Mapping. We like to use large pieces of chart paper to create our semantic maps (Figure 9.1). We draw a circle with the content topic printed in the center and then lead students in a brainstorming session to tell what they know about the topic. With ELLs, you'll notice few of them will raise their hands to contribute to these brainstorming sessions. In order to overcome this problem, we like to ask students to brainstorm in buddy pairs first, setting a goal of two or ten ideas per pair depending on the age of the students. This rehearsal time gives our students more opportunity to prepare their language and then contribute to the group. Once the semantic maps are complete, we can begin the process of grouping ideas. In the Our Community map, the various vocabulary words relating to the community have been grouped under headings such as "Stores," "People," "Transportation," and "Community Buildings." The grouping process teaches an important learning strategy to young learners; the language used to process the grouping leads to vocabulary and grammatical structures, such as: "Trains go under transportation," and "The policeman belongs in the People group."

The K-W-L Chart. This chart (Figure 9.2) is a fixture in many classrooms. It works as a useful activator asking students about the lesson content: What do I *know*? What do I *want* to know? What did I *learn*? We like to use it with students at every grade level. The first question, What do I know?, is similar to the question we ask when brainstorming semantic maps. In this situation, however, we may need more than a one-word answer. We used the K-W-L chart when preparing students for a lesson on Christopher Columbus. We asked students to tell us all they knew about the famous explorer and then wrote the answers on the chart. In some cases, we modeled the fact that we weren't sure of some ideas of our own. We placed these ideas on the chart with a question mark. We wanted students to know it's all right

Figure 9.1 The Semantic Map Is a Visual Picture of How the Vocabulary in the Unit Is Related

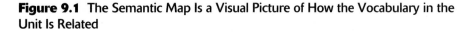

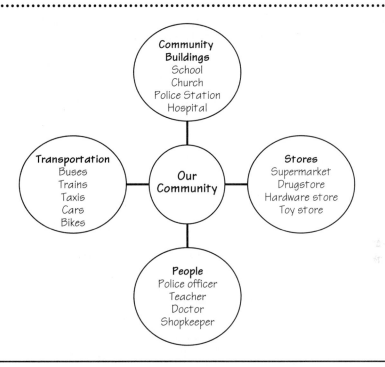

not to be sure of all their answers and the question marks led us into the next question What do I want to know? This question usually produces a long list of questions, a perfect road map for structuring the rest of our lessons in the unit. Asking and answering these questions empowers students to take charge of their own learning. They feel as if they are learning the things that are important to them, not imposed upon them. The K-W-L Chart also reveals many different misconceptions—some of our students told us they thought Columbus was Chinese and lived around 1957! The last question, "What did I learn?" provides the summarizer we need for the learning experience and allows us to assess each student's learning as well. These charts hang on the classroom walls throughout the learning unit provoking, guiding, and summarizing learning.

Wordsplash.   This is a collection of vocabulary words and phrases taken from a text that the students will read for content information and "splashed" across a large chart (Saphier & Haley, 1993). We carefully tailor the construction of these Wordsplashes to both the content we wish to focus on and the language necessary to express that content. In the example in Figure 9.3, students are about to read about chemical reactions. We have included the verb phrases needed to make cause-and-effect statements about chemical reactions shown on the chart, for example: "Chemical reactions are caused by interactions of molecules. Rust is caused by iron molecules combining with oxygen. Chemical reactions occur when molecules interact." We instruct students to work in buddy pairs to write sentences using the vocabulary on the chart.

Students must predict the relationships between the words and the concepts in order to write their sentences. Many learners make guesses because they have limited

Figure 9.2 The K-W-L Chart Provides a Framework for All Phases of the Lesson

What I Think I Know	What I Want to Know	What I Learned
Christopher Columbus was an explorer. He was Chinese? He lived in 1957? He sailed on a ship.	Where did he live? When did he live? Where did he explore? Why is he famous?	

understanding of the vocabulary on the chart. Nevertheless, all learners can be mentally involved in the activity of trying to use these words and become familiar as a preparation for later learning. After writing the sentences, we read the textbook and determine whether our guesses are correct or not. At this point, we like to ask our students to change their sentences to make them correct. For young learners, we write student sentences on the board and correct them in small groups.

Corners.   Merchant and Young (2000) use this cooperative strategy to assess their students' prior knowledge in their unit on scientific measurement. Students are divided into four groups and proceed to the four corners of the room, where they are given a task. In the measurement unit, they are asked to take their science journals with them and record their answers to the questions written on the chart in each corner. Students work together to create answers and then move on to the next corner

Figure 9.3 The Words and Phrases on the Wordsplash Can Be Combined to State Important Concepts from the Unit

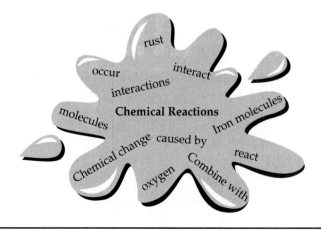

at a signal. In other versions of corners (Kagan, 1994), students are asked to take a stand in response to a question, such as "What causes air pollution?" The four corners of the room are each labeled with a different response: "Car exhaust fumes," "Cigarette smoke," "Factory emissions," and "Wildfires." Students choose one of the four answers, and then go to a corner to share their reasons for making that choice. Some teachers then ask students to visit other corners and listen to the reasons behind the other choices. Another option is to appoint a spokesperson for each group who shares the reasons with the class.

Carousel Brainstorming. (Saphier & Haley, 1993). This is a good activator to use at the beginning of a unit of study. For this activity, we place charts around the walls of the room. Each chart has a heading or questions related to a sub-unit of the major topic. For example, when fifth graders are about to study the regions of the U.S., we might ask questions such as:

- What are the major crops of the Pacific Northwest region?
- What important historical events happened in the Pacific Northwest region?
- What do you know about the geography of the Pacific Northwest region?
- What states are located in the Pacific Northwest region?
- What natural resources are located in the Pacific Northwest region?
- What manufactured products are produced in the Pacific Northwest region?

Students move in small groups around the room attempting to write what they know on each chart. We like to give each group a different color marker to distinguish itself. At the end of the activity, each group returns to the original chart and proceeds to read what others have written there. If you can't hang charts on the wall, pass the charts around to table groups.

Through the Lesson: Input for Active Understanding, Vocabulary Development, and Practical Purpose

The Through phase of the lesson is where a great deal of learning occurs. This is the lesson delivery phase. It is also the phase where the teacher continues to connect new learning to previous knowledge and to the learner's interests and culture. Practice and application of learning takes place during this phase of the lesson with emphasis on interaction among the learners, comprehensible input, and scaffolding of the learning.

Vocabulary Learning

We like to ask the following questions when planning for the Through phase of the lesson in regard to vocabulary:

- What vocabulary will the students be using?
- How will they use the vocabulary?
- Does the vocabulary reflect the content I am teaching?

Vocabulary selection occurs as we think about the nature of the content and the language we want to teach. There is an important distinction to be made in the kinds of vocabulary we select for our lessons. Content-specific, technical vocabulary represents terms necessary to learning the content (Snow, Met, & Genesee, 1989; Beck, McKeown, & Kucan, 2002; Genesee, 2006). For example, in a unit on the Civil Rights movement, we need to teach segregation, desegregation, boycott, and integrate. These words must be taught to the entire class as they will, most likely, be new to most learners, even those who speak English.

In order to talk about civil rights, however, there are other vocabulary items, academic, or textbook language, which are not specific to the civil rights content, but are part of an educated speaker's vocabulary. For the civil rights example, we might want to use adverbial phrases such as:

- In 1957 . . .
- After the arrest of Rosa Parks . . .
- When the Supreme Court ruled . . .

Certain verbs are also necessary such as:

- Ensure basic freedoms
- Abolish slavery
- Amend the Constitution
- Enact laws

When choosing the vocabulary we are going to teach, we need to be aware of both the technical and the academic vocabulary needs of our students. Different content subjects require different academic language. By reading the science, math, and social studies texts used in schools, we can familiarize ourselves with the language necessary to talk about each of these subjects.

Content vocabulary is not immediately acquired, even by students who speak English. In a study of 646 eighth grade students in Australia (reported in Miller, 1993), researchers asked the English-speaking students to define 20 math terms that they had used in their math course throughout the year. The terms were:

sum	digit	quotient	remainder
equal	angle	diameter	subtract
fraction	meter	factor	divide
denominator	perimeter	average	difference
measure	circle	product	whole

On average, the students were able to define four of the terms correctly. When allowed to use symbols, diagrams, or examples to assist their definitions, the students averaged eleven correct definitions. It would seem that vocabulary, even those terms that are essential to content learning, is difficult to learn unless teachers place emphasis upon vocabulary instruction.

Frequent, brief, and active interactions with new vocabulary yield the best learning. For this reason, it is probably not helpful to give English language learners a long list of new vocabulary items and ask them to find the definitions in the dictionary or to use the new vocabulary in a sentence. Most learners will not understand the vocabulary definitions because they are written in unfamiliar academic language. Writing a sentence using a new vocabulary item is more of a testing than a teaching technique. Learners need to know the grammatical function of the word and the context of use before they can create sentences with the term.

Effective teachers choose a few critical vocabulary items and work with these to help students make connections meaningful and relevant to their own lives. In some cases, the vocabulary will be similar to a native language. For example, Spanish has many cognates to English—words that are closely associated in meaning and form. The following techniques are ones that have been effective with our students.

Sentence Context.   It is helpful to place the new vocabulary within a context of a sentence. Learners can be encouraged to make predictions about the meaning. For example in the sentence, "Sally the pig uses her snout to roll a basketball across the floor," learners can guess that a "snout" is a part of the animal's body.

Sentence frames are helpful in supporting word use for academic language structures. For example, the frame, "The _____ ensures that _____," can be used in a variety of contexts:

- The Constitution ensures that _____
- The Civil Rights Act ensures that _____
- Title IX ensures that _____

By providing the frame and encouraging student use of the structure, we can enable students to better use and maintain the academic language in their vocabularies.

Semantic Mapping.   This is another tool for providing meaning to new vocabulary. We like to write the new word in the center of the map and ask students to tell us:

- What is another word that has a similar meaning?
- What is an example of this word?
- What is the opposite of this word?
- What is a definition of the new term in your own words?

Word Square.   Learners can use the same questions to create a word square. We included a word square in Table 2.1 in Chapter 2. word squares are note cards divided into four quadrants. Students write the new vocabulary item in the top left hand corner and then work with a buddy or a small group to fill in all four quadrants by answering questions such as those used in semantic mapping. We change the questions depending on the age and language levels of our students.

Student Self-Assessment and Drawings.   One of the most effective techniques we have used with our students is one that we came upon by accident. One day we had been asking our students to evaluate their own learning of vocabulary, a useful learning strategy. The students were asked to work with a buddy to determine how well they knew each of the new words. If they could define the word, they checked "I Know It" on the practice sheet. If they were unsure of the meaning, they checked "I Kind of Know It," and if they could not guess at all, they checked "I Don't Have a Clue." We used these self-evaluation charts to help learners focus on the words they needed to learn. After talking about the meanings and sharing the meanings with their classmates, we asked the students to draw pictures of the words they didn't know to help them remember them for the next day. An example from one student (Table 9.3) shows the scribbled word balloon for muttering, the little twins for resembles, and the angry face for frown. At the end of the unit, students indicated that the self-drawn pictures helped them the most in retaining meaning of the new vocabulary.

The important element in all of these activities is that learners are actively participating in the experience, an important principle of learning. Active participation does not

Table 9.3 After Self-Assessing Their Vocabulary Knowledge, Students Can Draw Pictures to Help Remember Unknown Words

	I Know It	I Kind of Know It	I Don't Have a Clue
muttering			√
electricity	√		
frown			√
earned	√		
resemble			√

always mean moving around the classroom. But it doesn't mean sitting passively either. For students to learn most efficiently, we believe they must be actively engaged in the learning experience. Sometimes, this means writing or talking about the new vocabulary as in the examples in Table 9.3, where students were asked to create word squares with a buddy. Sometimes it means drawing pictures or completing a graphic organizer with new terminology. Sometimes it means asking students to respond with Thumbs Up/Thumbs Down as we define a new word or place markers on a Bingo card covered with new vocabulary in response to a definition.

Vocabulary development is essential to success in reading and writing in content classrooms. Learners cannot read effectively if they cannot understand the meanings of the words in the text. For this reason, it's important to teach vocabulary in every lesson.

Language and Content Input

The questions we need to ask in regard to the content and language input phase of the lesson are:

- How will the new information be conveyed to my students?
- Will they listen to it, read it, or engage in research to discover it?
- How can I support the input with context?

Input that is comprehensible and conveyed to the learner as clearly and as concretely as possible is the goal for this phase of the lesson. Additionally, if we can connect the new learning to what our students already know or to their cultural backgrounds, we can increase their understanding in ways leading to long-term retention.

How can we make new learning comprehensible? For oral instructional input, it's important to be aware of the **clarity** of our language input to students. We try to avoid idiomatic expressions, jargon, and slang as much as possible. We speak clearly, not too rapidly, and underlie all that we say with repetition of the important phrases and ideas. We accompany our oral language with gestures that lead to meaning: pointing to words, pictures, or objects, demonstrating with body gestures (with a smile, a shrug, a frown, or with fatigue), and using word stress and pauses to highlight important language.

We incorporate as many **explanatory devices** as possible into our input. These devices include visual aids, writing on the chalkboard, charts, drawings, graphs, maps, real objects, graphic organizers, and models. We bring objects from home and use objects in the classroom to help students comprehend our oral language.

Teacher **modeling** is an important part of how we help students understand new input. Effective teachers provide models of the processes and products they want their students to engage in and create. One teacher we know used classroom objects, such as a ruler and a small block, to help her students understand the concept of a lever. She placed the block on the windowsill and inserted the ruler under the sill using the block as a fulcrum to lift the window. The simple machine was then diagrammed on the chalkboard as students recalled what they had seen her do. The parts of the machine were labeled ("load," "effort," "fulcrum," "lever") and students made their own drawings with labels. Next, students used rulers and blocks to work in small groups and determine other jobs this simple machine could accomplish in the classroom. The modeling by the teacher and the later hands-on learning opportunity, ensured that all learners in the class understood the nature of the lever as an example of a simple machine.

If we have begun teaching with an **activator** that causes students to ask questions, such as those on the K-W-L chart, we can begin the Input phase of the lesson using those questions as a guide. Working in small groups, learners can use picture books, texts, maps, and other resources to find answers to their questions.

Barbara Agor (2000), in a sixth grade unit on the Middle Ages, used a picture walk and brainstorming as activators for her lessons. She began by having students ask questions based upon their exploration of the many picture books she had provided. Barbara wrote these questions down and used them to help guide her instruction. She introduced activities to aid her students' comprehension of the period. The class created time lines, stretching from the Middle Ages to the present. They added important events to the time line throughout the unit as learners became aware of the major changes occurring during this period of history. Students also made lists comparing and contrasting "Things we have today" and "Things they had then." They used these lists to write personal letters to a time traveler from the Middle Ages, alerting him to the changes he would encounter in this century.

Interaction between learners provides a further help to comprehension of new learning. We try to use buddy pairs and small groups frequently. We determine ways to help the students interact positively with one another (positive interdependence) and to assess each learner's individual growth (individual accountability). In a unit on Guatemala, Betty Wein, with the help of her third graders, first gathered many books and artifacts from the country. She then divided her class into groups of four and used the Jigsaw strategy to divide up the learning. Each student was responsible for determining one of the following:

Video Exercise

Activating Knowledge and Vocabulary for ELLs

Go to MyEducationLab, select the topic **Sheltered Content Instruction**, and watch the video entitled **"Activating Knowledge and Vocabulary for ELLs"** to observe a fourth grade teacher and her class involved in preparing to read about coral reefs. Complete the questions that accompany it. You may print your work or have it transmitted to your professor as necessary.

- Food products
- Clothing and housing
- Geography
- Weather

Betty asked all of the students in the Food product group to work together using books, pictures, and home interviews to learn about the major food products of Guatemala. She did the same with the other three groups. By the end of their research, students were able to return to their "home" groups and report on what they had learned. Students took notes on a chart that were later used to create essays about Guatemala. The essays helped Betty determine what each student had learned as a result of her unit.

Content and language input that is characterized by student comprehension and interaction is effective input. We can be assured our students understand the concepts and language of the topic. Comprehension alone is not sufficient to ensure long-term learning, however. Next, we need to guide students in practice and application of the new knowledge and skills.

Guided Practice

In regard to the guided practice phase of the lesson we ask:

- How will I help my students practice the new information or skill in a way that will help them to be successful?
- Can I incorporate a collaborative activity into this practice?
- How will I check their understanding of the new information?

The Jigsaw Strategy

Jigsaw is a technique that aids language and content input by fostering interaction among learners. Content is broken up into related parts, like interlocking pieces in a jigsaw puzzle, in order to stimulate interaction among learners and improve student comprehension. Learners become experts on one portion or piece of a topic and share their expertise with others. Learners are also able to study a portion of a large amount of information and hear summaries of the rest from peers. Everyone shares responsibility for learning.

Procedure:

- Divide participants into "home groups" of about four students.
- Assign each person in a home group an "expert number."
- Assign each expert number a section of the reading.
- Students reassemble into "expert groups," based on their numbers.
- They read their assigned section of the text and determine how best to teach the material to their home groups.
- Experts return to their home groups and take turns teaching the content learned in their expert groups to their home groups.

During guided practice, we need to provide scaffolding to help our students be successful in their first practical use of the new skills. This kind of guidance, at the beginning of the practice session, greatly increases the rate and degree of learning. Scaffolds also help to support the learner's first attempts to express or write about the new learning.

It is at this stage of the lesson where we guide students step-by-step through the processes of the task. If we want learners to write about what they have learned about the history of the Navajo, for example, we need to show ways to talk about Navajo characteristics. Using a semantic map listing Navajo characteristics, we can model sentences that describe the Navajo lifestyle then invite our students to orally describe the Navajo, using the same **key sentence frames,** while being supported by the semantic map.

The Navajo _____ for _____.

used bows and arrows	hunting
rode and tamed horses	work
wore woven headbands	decoration
raised cattle and sheep	food

Further practice occurs as we invite our students to interact with each other using the new language. Instructing students to "tell your buddy all about the Navajo" is an opportunity to provide English language learners with supported practice in using the new language and structures.

Nancy Wong provided guided practice for her third grade students in their science unit based on the life cycle of the salamander. After students had opportunities to observe the animals, listen to stories about them, and leaf through many picture books, Nancy wanted her students to become responsible for the care and feeding of the animals. Each day, she gave a mini-lesson on one aspect of care such as feeding, cleaning the aquarium, handling, and so on. She supported the major points by writing them on a chart. She then gave her students opportunities to tell each other what they had learned about the care of their classroom pets. Eventually, Nancy wanted the students to create their Salamander Care and Feeding manual to be used in the third grades in the school. The daily oral practice helped her students not only to learn the information but to be able to talk about it and write about it.

We can clearly communicate the need for classroom activities if we create a *practical purpose* for learning. Betty Wein accomplished this goal by helping her students to present the results of the Guatemala unit at an open school night. Barbara Agor (2002) invited interested groups from the school to see and hear her students talk about the Middle Ages. Nancy Wong created a practical purpose for her third graders when she suggested her students use their Salamander Care and Feeding manual to teach the classroom next door how to care for the salamanders they would have in their own classroom for the following month.

Teachers such as Betty Wein, Barbara Agor, and Nancy Wong are able to guide their students' learning step-by-step because they are always aware of what their students understand and what they do not. They *check for understanding* throughout the lesson. This is an important element in teaching sometimes forgotten because of the lack of time and the large number of students in our classrooms. But checking for understanding is essential to knowing which students are with us and which ones are not.

Keep in mind the need to check if *everyone* is understanding. If you ask a question and one learner answers well, it doesn't mean that the rest understand. Many ELLs might not choose to raise their hands in class or might not volunteer quickly enough after attempting to comprehend the teacher's question. So we need strategies to include them in our comprehension checks.

We need to find ways to determine the understanding of

- All of our students
- Frequently
- On the same topic or concept
- During instruction

This kind of checking is what Madelyn Hunter has called **dipsticking** (Saphier & Gower, 1997). In the same way that mechanics use a dipstick to check for oil in a car's engine, teachers use techniques to check for comprehension in the minds of our students.

Dipsticking can be accomplished using recall or comprehension questions. If we use only recall questions, however, we may not be sure students have a good understanding of the concept. ELLs may be able to recall a one-word answer for the teacher but not really understand how that word relates to the whole topic. Comprehension questions are better at assessing complete understanding. To answer a comprehension question, students must understand the concept or guiding principle that is being assessed. For example, in order to answer this question, "What have we read about Geronimo that tells us he was not a Navajo?" students must understand the characteristics of the historic Navajo people. The question, "Does refrigeration represent a physical or a chemical change?" also requires an understanding of an underlying principle of chemistry. Thus, we may need to ask a number of questions at several different levels, both recall and comprehension, so that each student can communicate the extent of his or her current understanding and also achieve success with the realization of that learning.

Checking every student in the class, frequently, may seem an impossible task. But there are techniques that can help us to accomplish this goal. The **one-question-quiz** is used when the teacher wants to check comprehension of all students. She asks a summarizing question and students write the answer while the teacher circulates through the room noting which students can respond correctly.

Asking questions to the entire class and telling them to answer with a *buddy*, is another way to check understanding. We've seen teachers who float around the room listening to answers and then say, "Tell me what your buddy told you," to assess students they haven't yet heard from.

Thumbs up/thumbs down is a signal response that gives us a quick check of which students are confident in their answers and which ones are hesitating. The teacher says, "Paul Revere was a silversmith who made a midnight ride to warn the British," and students respond with thumbs up. If she says, "John Paul Jones once said 'Give me liberty or give me death,'" students respond with thumbs down.

Other signal responses involve the use of *note cards*. One third grade teacher we know gives her students cards with a multiplication sign on one side and a division sign on the other. She reads word problems and asks her students to show the appropriate sign for solving the problem. In English class, her students use cards to identify correct punctuation, parts of speech, or run-on sentences (RO). We like to use hand signals, too. Sometimes we teach a letter from sign language such as *r* to signify "reptile" and *m* to signify "mammal." Students enjoy using these signals to identify animals or animal characteristics. Checking vocabulary can be done quickly using signals, also. Write two words on the chalkboard labeled number 1 and number 2. Define one word and ask students to show the correct number by raising one or two fingers.

Thumbs Up Is a Quick Assessment Tool That Encourages Students to Be Actively Involved in the Learning Experience

One of our favorite comprehension checking devices is using the **slate.** We have used slates with students of all ages and found them to be one of the most effective techniques for gauging comprehension of simple recall information; assessing math computation; and practicing phonics skills, language mechanics, or spelling. We model the process by holding our own slates, asking a question, quickly writing the answer, and then asking students to "show your slates." We take a quick scan of the room and show our slate with the correct answer. Students can quickly self-correct with this immediate feedback. Our students are strongly motivated to participate in this task. It is low-stress and fun, and even beginning English language learners will feel comfortable participating.

Individual slates resembling miniature chalk boards are sold in educational supply stores. These can be expensive and require the use of chalk and an eraser that may be messy. We have also used dry erase board cut into about 9-inch by 12-inch rectangles as a cheaper alternative. These require the use of special dry erase markers. The cheapest and easiest slate we have used is a piece of white paper slipped into a see-through page protector. Most of these can be written on and erased with a tissue (we suggest you check before buying, though, as they can be made of many different materials). If the page protector has been three-hole punched, students can keep these in their ring binders for easy access.

While listening to these definitions, sentences, or characteristics, all of our students are involved in learning and all of them are listening to our language. This is an important time in the classroom. These moments create excellent opportunities for language input. The students are attentive, they are listening, and they are primed to respond to our language. Even though the time spent in checking is registered in minutes, the gains for learners are enormous. We, too, learn a great deal about our students at these moments. This learning helps us to know if students need additional guided practice or if they are ready to move into the next phase of learning—independent practice.

Beyond the Lesson: Providing Reasons for Further Communication

Independent Practice

Independent practice is the phase of the lesson when we want our students to internalize the new learning by integrating it into the other knowledge structures or **schema** that already exists in their brains. During this phase we ask ourselves:

- What assignments or homework shall I have my students complete to facilitate long-term retention?
- Does the assignment reflect the variety in my students' learning styles, interest, knowledge levels, and proficiency levels?

The arena of the classroom is a "here and now" situation. We have advocated for the use of situational activities with scaffolding supports, such as visuals and realia. We have also advocated for a great deal of interaction within the classroom to provide opportunities for real language use. At some point, our learners need to move beyond this "here and now" context in order to expand language use and promote learning retention.

Billows has described the learner's situation as "four concentric spheres with the learner at the center" (1961, pp. 9–12):

- Sphere no. 1: This is "what the learner can see, hear, and touch directly." This is the arena of the classroom.
- Sphere no. 2: This is "what the learner knows from his own experience, his daily life, what he has seen and heard directly but cannot see or hear at the moment." This might describe the student's neighborhood, home, or native country.
- Sphere no. 3: This sphere represents what the learner "has not yet experienced directly, but what he can call to mind with an effort of the imagination, with the help of pictures, dramatization, charts and plans."
- Sphere no. 4: The fourth sphere is "what is brought into . . . mind through the spoken, written or printed word alone, without help through audio-visual aids."

The role of the teacher is to support learners as they move outward through these four spheres to achieve the last sphere, where learners can read printed text with no visuals or contextual supports and achieve comprehension through the language alone. It's interesting to note the progress of this movement is in line with what we know about good teaching. We suggest effective teachers begin instruction with the "here and now" and attempt to help learners activate what they already know about the topic from prior learning or experience. As learners progress in their understanding, teachers use techniques and materials to promote learning beyond the realm of the classroom. The final outcome results when learners can read a text or take a standardized examination and comprehend the material well.

The movement from Sphere number 1 to Sphere number 4 requires careful planning, as we have suggested. In addition, it is helpful to think about the movement of the language growth occurring as learners move through these four spheres. Mohan (1986, p. 110) describes this progress as an increase in the distance between the speaker and hearer of the language. He arranges the discourse in order of increasing distance:

1. Reflection
2. Conversation
3. Correspondence
4. Publication

Reflection occurs within the learner himself. There is no distance because the speaker and hearer are one. Conversation occurs between a speaker and hearer who are face to face. Correspondence is writing for a known audience, for example, a letter to a pen pal or an essay for the teacher. Publication is "impersonal communication" for an unknown audience where feedback does not exist, as in a newspaper article. As the distance between the speaker and hearer grows, the level of difficulty of the language grows. The lack of feedback at level four requires the highest level of language skill because there is no context other than that created by the language itself. As our learners progress in their language skills and cognitive growth, their goal is the level of publication.

In another kind of distance, Mohan (1986, p. 110) describes the distance from the speaker to the topic of the language. The levels reflect the "increasing abstraction" created between the experience and the description or verbalization of the experience.

1. Drama   2. Narrative
3. Exposition   4. Argumentation

Drama, for example, in the form of a role play, is closely related to telling a story about content experience. Narrative is more abstract as students attempt to report back on a learning experience. Exposition relates to generalizing about learning, perhaps in the form of an essay. Finally, argumentation is the most abstract, at the theory level. Here students might engage in a debate.

These two kinds of distances reflect growing cognitive and language abilities in our students. Mohan (1986) describes the "Show and Tell" experience of kindergarten or first grade students as a face-to-face, conversational exchange "somewhere between drama and narrative." This experience also reflects Spheres 1 and 2 in Billows's (1961) scheme. The child makes a transition between home experience and school experience.

Older English language learners still require concrete classroom experiences characteristic of "Show and Tell," such as science experiments, but these experiences need to be reflective of appropriate grade-level content learning. Older learners also need to move beyond the level of face-to-face conversation and role play into the world of interviews, reporting, research, generalization, and theory.

During the Beyond phase of the lesson, we attempt to move our students beyond the "here and now" aspect of practice and application, and into a more abstract realm of using language to communicate beyond the classroom. We have discussed a few examples of teachers who took their learners beyond the classroom experience and created culminating activities at the end of a unit to communicate to a wider audience and in a more abstract form of discourse. Agor's (2000) students reported on the Middle Ages to members of the school community. Nancy Wong's students taught other third graders how to care for salamanders and wrote a Care and Feeding manual to support their instruction. Fifth grade teachers we have worked with created opportunities for Beyond classroom experiences when they culminated their experiential science unit with a science fair. The fair was attended by parents, school board members, and members of the community. Each student was responsible for presenting a science experiment visually in the form of a display and also reporting to others about the experiment, answering questions, and clearing up misunderstandings.

Another interesting and challenging form of Beyond the classroom experience is called service learning. Service learning gives learners the chance to apply the content of their studies to real problems in their communities (Allen, 2003). Service learning is more than volunteerism because of the academic goals that are integral to the program. In the most rigorous forms of service learning, students analyze real problems in their communities, such as traffic congestion or pollution, and then plan ways to create social change. Planning bus routes to save fuel, doing research on plants that will reduce pollution, and convincing local authorities to plant drought resistant plants in states with water shortages are some of the projects students might tackle. The language requirements of these projects help students to communicate beyond the level of the classroom and connect them with the real world in which they live.

The Beyond phase of the lesson allows learners to participate in lesson formats that are varied and that provide novelty. For many of our students, paper and pencil tasks do not relate to their learning styles and may not reflect their intelligence and creativity. The notion of variety in learning is an important one when there are diverse language learners in the classroom. The variety of languages and cultures will surely reflect a variety in learning style as well. If we can appeal to our students to use language to communicate, tease, entertain, and inform, we are enlarging their levels of discourse. Using language to create songs, poetry, plays, radio shows, and debates for an audience of others ensures our students will retain their learning over time.

Summarizing

The summary phase of the lesson relates back to our content, language, and learning strategy objectives. In this phase of the lesson, we ask:

- How can I help my students to tell or write what they have learned today?

Summarizing learning can be done by students at the end of each lesson. We want our students to expect to be challenged on their learning each day. Summarizing sends a strong message to students that they are responsible for the learning of the objectives that were communicated at the start of the lesson.

Too often, teachers skip this stage of the lesson because of time constraints. But summarizing need not take up a lot of class time. Some of the techniques we enjoy using take no more than five minutes but they help all learners to integrate their new learning with what they already know about the topic. Summarizing also helps learners to self-assess their own learning—an important learning strategy.

- **3-2-1** is an easy but effective summarizer activity (Saphier & Haley, 1993). The teacher writes the three requirements for the summary on the board: recall information from the lesson, show understanding of the topic, and analyze the concept. Then, students respond in writing that is collected. Notice how the 3-2-1 elements increase in cognitive complexity. For example, in the following example, the "3" requests students to simply recall. The "2" asks for a comprehension level of understanding. The "1" is at the level of analysis in Bloom's (1956) Taxonomy of Thinking Skills.

   3 characteristics of the historic Navajo people
   2 major differences between the Navajo and the Apache people
   1 reason why you would have preferred to be either a Navajo or an Apache in the past.

- The **ticket to leave** (Saphier & Haley, 1993) is an excellent summarizer when little time remains at the end of the class. Students are asked to respond to the teacher either in writing or orally. Teachers can collect the "tickets" as students leave the class or stand at the door listening to student responses. Examples of questions might be:

   - Answer the question on the board (written as the day's objective).
   - Write one thing about today's content that leaves you puzzled.
   - Name the most important thing you learned in today's class.
   - Be able to give three reasons why . . .

- **Learning logs** are student notebooks that record short summaries of a lesson. Some teachers like to use them at the end of every lesson, collecting them from time to time to check on their students' comprehension. Learning logs can be freely written as a summary or can be structured; it depends on the age and ability of the students. It is best to use open-ended questions to structure a learning log question. Recall questions tend to be answered in short phrases that limit the development of language skills and fall short in helping students to structure their own comprehension of the lesson.

Some open-ended questions useful in promoting a lesson summary are:

- Tell what you learned today about . . .
- What do you know now about . . . that you didn't know before?
- What did you understand about today's lesson? What don't you understand yet?
- What were the most important points from today's discussion?
- Explain your understanding of . . .

- **Draw a picture/diagram** (Saphier & Haley, 1993) is most effective with topics that can be represented visually. You can give students a blank piece of paper and ask them to draw or diagram a topic, or you can provide a diagram, outline, or graphic organizer for students to complete. Some examples of this technique are the following:

- Complete the flow chart to include all of the steps in the process.
- Draw a picture of the main character as described in today's reading.
- Draw a diagram of the process of *photosynthesis*.
- Indicate where each of the three battles occurred on the map.
- How does an apple grow? Draw the main stages.

Assessment

The assessment phase, although written here as the last phase of the lesson, really takes place throughout the learning experience. The question we ask about assessment is:

- How will I know what each of my students have learned in this lesson?

We have previously discussed comprehension checking or dipsticking, which takes place with all students throughout the lesson. Dipsticking is an important source of **formative assessment** information for teachers—ongoing knowledge of student performance to guide instruction. It may be too late to assess at the end of a lesson or at the end of the unit. At that point, we have no time to reformulate our lesson, change our techniques, or provide for additional guided practice. Assessment needs to be ongoing and classroom based.

Another kind of assessment—**summative assessment**—is used at the end of the learning experience—at the end of a unit of study, or often at the end of the school year, to provide information to report to parents as well as to evaluate programs, schools, districts, and states. Summative assessment is sometimes done in the form of district-level testing, departmental testing, or standardized testing.

The type of assessment we are primarily addressing here is formative assessment. This kind of assessment is the ongoing collection of information gathered both during and after instruction in order to determine how well a student is progressing. The more frequent and varied our assessment is, the better it will be able to determine achievement. If we only rely on weekly quizzes to assess students, we will have a limited picture of achievement. If, however, we use weekly quizzes, learning logs, dipsticking, student reporting, group quizzes, role plays, and group presentations, we will have a variety of ways to inform our instruction and to create a clear picture of the learner's achievement.

Questions for Reflection

1. Reflect on the six lesson characteristics supporting and promoting achievement for language learning youngsters. Arrange these in a hierarchy of priority from most important to least important. Defend your choices with examples from life experience.
2. The lesson format described here (Into, Through, Beyond) is based upon a cognitive model of knowledge construction. Does this model imply that knowledge is constructed rather than memorized or learned? What are the differences in these viewpoints?
3. Essential to this chapter's view of learning is the integration of language activities in every part of the lesson. Can this be done with learners who are newcomers and beginners in English? How?

Activities for Further Learning

1. Two teaching characteristics that support learning for language learners are heterogeneous grouping and appropriate grade-level content. Teachers who are not familiar with techniques for teaching diverse classes have difficulty teaching challenging and grade-level content to students of mixed achievement levels. What problems can you foresee in these situations? What problems might teachers have? Students? Parents? What strategies and suggestions can you offer to teachers to support achievement gains for all learners in heterogeneous learning situations?
2. Teacher language has been mentioned as an important characteristic of effective instruction for English language learners. Teacher language that is unclear leaves students confused as to what is expected of them. Too often, this leads to inattention and discipline problems. Think about the language you use with students in the arena of giving instructions. Create a series of instructions for students that incorporate the aspects of clarity mentioned in this chapter: body gestures, simple language, repetition, explanatory devices, oral and written support.
3. We have said lessons for English language learning students need to have specific, measurable objectives for content, language, and learning strategies. Use the Bloom Taxonomy in this chapter to create content, language, and learning strategy objectives for two different lessons: elementary science and middle-school social studies.
4. Checking for understanding becomes more important when English language learning students are in our classrooms. Teachers cannot assume all learners will understand the directions for an activity or the new content information. Talk in your group about the suggestions given here for dipsticking activities. Which ones are you already familiar with? Which ones can you imagine using in a class of mixed-language users? What other methods can you suggest for checking the understanding of your students?

5. Vocabulary learning is crucial for academic success. Students need to learn both technical vocabulary and academic vocabulary. In order to have some hands-on experience with both kinds of vocabulary, review typical teacher language in the area of

   - Classroom routines
   - Directions

   You might find examples of this language in teacher manuals, textbooks, or prior to standardized testing. What aspects of this language are typical of academic language? Which words are used routinely but may need clarification? How could you help students understand this language?

6. Select a textbook passage used by students. Analyze the language of the text and isolate the technical vocabulary and the academic vocabulary (or grammar). How could you help students understand and learn this language?

7. Imagine you are teaching a third grade class in multiplication. You are entering the Guided Practice phase of the lesson. What scaffolds could you use with students to help them be successful in their first experiences with multiplication?

   Now think about a sixth grade social studies lesson on the topic of latitude, longitude, the equator, and the Tropics of Cancer and Capricorn. How could you support students in their guided practice of these concepts?

8. Describe examples of "Beyond the Classroom" communication that could be incorporated into each of the lessons described in question number 7.

PEARSON
myeducationlab)
Where the Classroom Comes to Life is a collection of online tools for your success in this course, your licensure exams, and your teaching career. Go to www.myeducationlab .com to utilize these extensive resources including videos from real classrooms, Praxis and licensure preparation, a lesson plan builder, and materials to help you in your teaching career.

Suggested Reading

Echevarria, J., Vogt, M., & Short, D. J. (2003). *Making content comprehensible for English language learners: The SIOP model* (2nd ed.). Boston, MA: Allyn & Bacon. An excellent description of sheltered instruction with many practical strategies clearly explained with classroom examples.

Hill, J. D. & Flynn, K. M. (2006). *Classroom instruction that works with English language learners.* Alexandria, VA: ASCD. Authors review research on effective teaching, and particularly effective teaching of ELLs, and show how these strategies can be implemented in multicultural, multilingual classrooms. Strategies include cooperative learning, summarizing and note-taking, reinforcing effort and providing recognition, use of nonlinguistic representations, and involving parents and the community.

Mohan, B. A. (1986). *Language and content.* Reading, MA: Addison-Wesley. One of the classic books relating to the integration of language and content in classrooms. We appreciate the knowledge framework described here, which advances students in the growth of language and in cognition as they explore content.

Piper, T. (2002). *Language and learning: The home and school years* (3rd ed.). Upper Saddle River, NJ: Merrill. This book has much to delight those who are interested in the subject of language and children. Chapter 9 is relevant in its discussion of the relationship between language and cognitive growth. Chapter 10 discusses school language in both its positive and negative aspects. The discussion of teacher language is especially relevant here. Chapter 12 details ten principles for language learning.

Web Sites for Further Learning

Center for Research on Education, Diversity & Excellence (CREDE). This site has developed materials related to its five standards for effective pedagogy:

1. Joint productive activity
2. Language and literacy development
3. Contextualization/meaning making
4. Challenging activities
5. Instructional conversation

The site provides a self-assessment rubric for teachers, descriptions of classroom practice with specific indicators of good practice, multimedia tools, and related links to content organizations and information. Retrieved April 7, 2008.

http://www.crede.ucsc.edu/

ColorinColorado is a very useful site for lesson plan development. One section shows how to adapt a lesson plan for ELLs. In addition, the site provides podcasts of famous ESL authors and webcasts from experts in the field discussing issues of second language teaching and learning. Retrieved April 8, 2008.

www.colorincolorado.org/educators/content/lessonplan

ERIC has on file a collection of over 2,000 lesson plans from U. S. teachers. They are divided into subject areas such as the arts, health, math, physical education, science, social studies, language arts, vocational education, and literacy, among others. Retrieved April 7, 2008.

http://ericir.syr.edu/Virtual/Lessons/

EverythingESL is Judie Haynes's web site. Judie is an ESL teacher from New Jersey. Her site contains content-based ESL lesson plans and links to other sites. The "Ask Judie" section contains viewer's questions with responses from the teachers in the ESL field. Retrieved April 8, 2008.

http://www.everythingesl.net

References

Agor, B. (2000). Understanding our past: The middle ages. In S. Irujo (Ed.), *Integrating the ESL standards into classroom practice grades 6–8.* Alexandria, VA: TESOL.

Allen, R. (2003). The democratic aims of service learning. *Educational Leadership, (60)*6: 51–54.

Ausubel, D. P. (1968). *Educational psychology: A cognitive view.* NY: Holt, Rinehart and Winston.

Beck, I. L., McKeown, M. G., & Kucan, L. (2002). *Bringing words to life: Robust vocabulary instruction.* NY: The Guilford Press.

Berman, P., Minicucci, C., McLaughlin, B., Nelson, B., & Woodworth, K. (1995). *School reform and student diversity: Case studies of exemplary practices for English language learner students.* Santa Cruz, CA: National Center for Research on Cultural Diversity and Second Language Learning, and B. W. Associates.

Billows, F. (1961). *The techniques of language teaching.* London: Longman.

Bloom, B., Englehart, M., Furst, E., Hill, W., & Krathworl, D. (Eds.). (1956). *Taxonomy of educational objectives: The classification of educational goals. Handbook I: Cognitive domain.* NY: David McKay.

Calderón, M. & Carreon, A. (1994). Educators and students use cooperative learning to become biliterate and bicultural. *Cooperative Learning Magazine, 4:* 6–9.

Calderón, M., Hertz-Lazarowitz, R., & Slavin, R. (1998). Effects of bilingual cooperative integrated reading and composition on students making the transition from Spanish to English. *The Elementary School Journal, 99:* 153–165.

Calderón, M., Tinajero, J., & Hertz-Lazarowitz, R. (1992). Adapting cooperative integrated reading and composition to meet the needs of bilingual students. *Journal of Educational Issues of Language Minority Students, 10:* 79–106.

Cummins, J., Brown, K., & Sayers, D. (2007). *Literacy, technology, and diversity: Teaching for success in changing times.* Boston, MA: Pearson.

Dixon, J. K. (1995). Limited English proficiency and spatial visualization in middle schhol students' construction of the concepts of reflection and rotation. *Bilingual Research Journal, 19*(2): 221–247.

Doherty, R.W., Hilberg, R.S., Pinal, A., & Tharp, R.G. (2003). Five standards and student achievement. *NABE Journal of Research and Practice, 1*(1): 1–24.

Echevarria, J., Short, D., & Powers, K. (2003). School reform and standards-based education: How do teachers help English language learners? Technical report. Santa Cruz, CAS: Center for Research on Education, Diversity & Excellence.

Genesee, F. (2006). *Educating English language learners: A synthesis of research evidence.* NY: Cambridge University Press.

Harklau, L. (1994). ESL versus mainstream classes: Contrasting L2 learning environments. *TESOL Quarterly, 28:* 241–272.

Izumi, D. S. & Bigelow, M. (2000) Does output promote noticing and second language acquisition? *TESOL Quarterly, 34*(2): 239–278.

Kagan, S. (1994). *Cooperative learning.* San Clemente, CA: Kagan Cooperative Learning

Lindholm-Leary, K. J. (2001). *Dual language education.* Avon, UK: Multilingual Matters.

Mayer, R. E. (1992).Cognition and instruction: Their historic meeting within educational psychology. *Journal of Educational Psychology, 84:* 405–412.

Merchant, P. & Young, L. (2000). Investigating how much: Linear, volume, and mass measurement. In S. Irujo (Ed.), *Integrating the ESL standards into classroom practice grades 6–8,* (pp. 55–84). Alexandria, VA: TESOL.

Miller, L. D. (1993). Making the connection with language. *Arithmetic Teacher, 40*(6): 311–316.

Minicucci, C. (1996). Learning science and English: How school reform advances scientific learning for limited English proficient middle school students (Educational Practice Report No. 17). Santa Cruz, CA: National Center for Research on Cultural Diversity and Second Language Learning.

Mohan, B. A. (1986). *Language and content.* Reading, MA: Addison-Wesley.

Montecel, M. R. & Cortez, J. D. (2002). Successful bilingual education programs: Development and the dissemination of criteria to identify promising and exemplary practices in bilingual education at the national level. *Bilingual Research Journal, 26:* 1–22.

Olivier, R. (2003). Interactional context and feedback in child ESL classrooms. *Modern Language Journal, 87*(87): 519–533.

Pica, T., Lincoln-Porter, F., Paninos, D., & Linnell, J. (1996). Language learners interaction: How does it address the input, output, and feedback needs of L2 learners? *TESOL Quarterly, 30,* 59–84.

Ramirez, J. D. (1992). Longitudinal study of structured English immersion strategy, early-exit and late-exit transitional bilingual education program for language-minority children (Executive Summary). *Bilingual Research Journal, 16*(1–2): 1–62.

Saphier, J. & Haley, M. A. (1993). *Activators: Activity structures to engage students' thinking before instruction.* Carlisle, MA: Research for Better Teaching.

Saphier, J. & Haley, M. A. (1993). *Summarizers: Activity structures to support integration and retention of new learning.* Carlisle, MA: Research for Better Teaching.

Saphier, J. & Gower, R. (1997). *The skillful teacher: Building your teaching skills.* Carlisle, MA: Research for Better Teaching.

Sillivan, S. (2000). Mastering the art of persuasion: Marketing and the media. In S. Irujo (Ed.), *Integrating the ESL standards into classroom practice grades 6–8,* (pp. 85–112). Alexandria, VA: TESOL.

Snow, M. A., Met, M., & Genesee, F. (1989). A conceptual framework for the integration of language and content in second/foreign language instruction. *TESOL Quarterly, 23(2):* 210–217.

Stoops Verplaetse, L. (1998). How content teachers interact with English language learners. *TESOL Journal, 7(5):* 24–28.

Swain, M. (1985). Communicative competence: Some roles of comprehensible input and comprehensible output in its development. In S. M. Gass and C. G. Madden (Eds.), *Input in second language acquisition,* (pp. 257–271). Rowley, MA: Newbury House.

Teachers of English to Speakers of Other Languages, Inc. (TESOL). (2006). *PreK–12 English language proficiency standards.* Alexandria, VA: TESOL.

Tikunoff, W. (1985). Applying significant bilingual instructional features in the classroom. Rosslyn, VA: National Clearinghouse for Bilingual Education (ERIC Document Reproduction Service No. ED 338 106).

Wong Fillmore, L. (1989). Teaching English through content: Instructional reform in programs for language minority students. In J. Esling (Ed.), *Multicultural education and policy: ESL in the 1990s* (pp. 125–143). Toronto, Canada: OISE Press.

Wong Fillmore, L., Ammon, P., McLaughlin, B., & Ammon, M. S. (1985). Learning English through bilingual instruction: Executive summary and conclusions. (Final report to National Institute of Education). Washington, DC: U.S. Department of Education.

Zainuddin, H., Yahya, N., Morales-Jones, C., & Ariza, E. (2002). *Fundamentals of teaching English to speakers of other languages in K–12 mainstream classrooms.* Dubuque, Iowa: Kendall/Hunt.

CHAPTER 10

Assessment Tools for the Integrated Classroom

Annie Watt's second grade class takes a district-developed reading test twice a year to evaluate the effectiveness of reading instruction in the grade. Annie had been hopeful that Julio, an English language learner (ELL) in her class, would do well on the test. She watched him as he attempted to read the text passages and answer the questions, and cringed as he became outwardly upset.

Waving his hand wildly to get her attention, he called out, "Ms. Watts, Ms. Watts, what's this word mean?"

Annie knew she couldn't help Julio with word meanings and suggested that he "take his best guess."

The test seemed to take forever. Julio gave up after an hour and put his head on his desk until others in the class were finished. Annie breathed a sigh of relief when she could send the children out to the playground at the end of the session.

When test results arrived weeks later, Annie was dismayed to see that even simple reading passages and questions were too difficult for Julio. For example, Julio responded incorrectly to the following questions:

1. Joe and Jim are playing football. Joe picks up the ball and runs to the goalpost. Who do you think is the winner of this game?
2. Select a breakfast food from this list:
   a) pancakes   b) a sandwich   c) rice
3. Sandy and Tim want to play baseball after school. Sandy is bringing his bat and ball. What do you think Tim will bring to the game?
   a) a net   b) a glove   c) a racket
4. Jane knew that spring had arrived when she saw her first
   a) tulip   b) icicle   c) pumpkin

Annie began to rethink her earlier evaluations of Julio. Perhaps he wasn't making as much progress as she had thought. Why were these questions so difficult for Julio?

How do teachers assess the progress of English language learners in their classrooms?

• What is assessment?
• What are the critical factors affecting assessment of ELLs?
• What are the fundamental principles of assessment for ELLs?
• What are examples of authentic, performance-based classroom assessment?
• How do standards affect classroom assessment?

What Is Assessment?

In our discussion on assessment, we focus on teachers and practitioners who instruct English language learners in content and language learning in classrooms of many different types: ESL **pull-out,** ESL **push-in, bilingual, dual language,** and multilingual, multi-level content classrooms in elementary and middle schools.

The measurement issues in these classrooms are complex because a variety of different kinds of measurement of learning takes place in public schools. In this chapter, we will refer to three types of assessment of learners:

• Standardized testing
• Classroom-based ongoing assessment (that can include teacher-made tests or tests from a published program)
• Program evaluation

Standardized Testing.   The narrowest in focus of the three types of assessment, standardized tests are designed by test developers to measure discrete skills at one moment in time. Tests are developed for **reliability**—that students will score the same on different administrations of the test, and **validity**—that tests really measure what they are designed to measure. Standardized tests have been developed by states and national companies for many content areas. Specific tests have also been developed for ELLs to show their levels of English-language development.

Classroom-Based Assessment.   This type of assessment refers to the gathering of information on a wider basis over a period of time. Formats for classroom-based assessment are varied and may include teacher observations, tests developed by teachers or publishers to be used as learners progress, rubrics to be applied by teachers to student products, such as writing, presentations, and multimedia products; checklists, surveys/questionnaires, and anecdotal records. Classroom-based assessment is ongoing and can occur at every stage of instruction. The purposes of classroom assessment include:

• monitoring student achievement
• planning and improving instruction
• providing communication to parents and school personnel
• providing students with information and feedback about their own progress

Program Evaluation.   With the broadest scope of the three, program evaluation seeks information about schools, teachers, and large groups of students for the purposes of:

- monitoring the effectiveness of an educational program
- determining the effectiveness of teaching and learning in a school district
- attaining accountability for state standards and reporting summary information
- ensuring equitable educational opportunities on the national level

Standardized testing, which often takes place in the spring in public schools, is frequently used in program evaluation. Other kinds of school data (e.g., attendance, drop-out rates, etc.) are often included as well. It is possible to use many other kinds of information in program evaluation, such as that described under classroom evaluation, but in today's schools, standardized tests dominate. Under the No Child Left Behind Act (NCLB) of 2001, standardized tests are used to determine school effectiveness. Schools must demonstrate levels of achievement and improvement, or be subject to escalating levels of consequences, one of which might be the "restructuring" of the school (which could lead to a new administration and the requirement that teachers re-apply for their jobs). This legislation has put tremendous pressure on schools and teachers to assure that students perform well on standardized tests. At present, a number of states are beginning to use a promising new growth model of using data from standardized tests that evaluates learners on their yearly growth rather than their achievement of grade-level equivalent scores.

Different Types of Assessment.   Assessment for ELLs can be categorized further by type and purpose of assessment. Table 10.1 compares criterion-referenced to norm-referenced, language proficiency to content proficiency, and direct performance to indirect performance assessments (TESOL, 2001, p. 12).

Table 10.1 Comparing Assessment Test Types, Purposes, and Formats

Criterion-Referenced	Norm-Referenced
Student performance is compared and rated against a set of predetermined criteria. The criteria might be determined by a state or content standard, a teaching objective, a performance indicator, or a teacher-created rubric.	Student performance is compared and ranked relative to similar populations in the state or the country.
Language Proficiency	Academic Proficiency
Student language performance is assessed globally in regard to listening, speaking, reading, and writing skills.	Student performance of curricular content and skill is assessed.
Direct Performance	Indirect Performance
Student performance for specific knowledge is assessed through a demonstration of ability. An example is an oral report or a written essay.	Student performance gains are assumed through assessment of one aspect of a skill. For example, answering comprehension questions or taking a vocabulary quiz assesses aspects of reading. Often, listening comprehension is assessed indirectly.

Adapted from *Scenarios for ESL standards-based assessment,* TESOL (2001, p. 12)

What Are the Fundamental Principles of Classroom-Based Assessment for ELLs?

We propose four fundamental principles for ELL classroom assessment. Assessments should:

- Provide fair, reliable, and valid information.
- Inform teaching and improve learning.
- Use multiple sources of information for assessment.
- Use familiar instructional techniques.

Conduct a Fair, Reliable, and Valid Assessment

Fairness is an essential attribute of the teacher/student relationship. Most children ask for and respond well to a teacher who is fair. Fairness in assessment occurs when all students have an equal chance to show what they know and can do. Fairness does not mean that all students must be treated exactly the same. In fact, treating all students the same may be very unfair. For example, requiring beginning ELLs to take standardized tests that do not provide any meaningful information and give the learners an experience of failure and frustration is very unfair.

To achieve this goal of fairness in assessment for ELLs, teachers often need to provide accommodations. For example, when working with math word problems, teachers can scaffold the tasks by providing models of appropriate problem solving that students can then apply in other situations. Teachers can ask students to work in buddy pairs so learners have a chance to negotiate the meaning of questions. Teachers can provide oral language practice in describing problem solutions before moving to the writing phase of the lesson. If we ask ourselves the following questions, we may be better able to adjust our assessments to pass the "fairness test":

- Did the student understand the question sufficiently to answer it?
- Did the student, in fact, answer the question that was asked?
- Am I evaluating the student's content understanding or the student's language?
- Did I provide the student with the support needed to respond to my assessment (support in terms of a peer, an outline, a cloze passage, a list of terms, a graphic organizer, pictures or realia, native language translation, etc.)?
- Have I told students what I am evaluating and modeled a desired product?
- Have I clearly specified the criteria on which evaluation is based?
- Am I evaluating the process or the product or both?

By answering and responding to the above questions, teachers will be assured that all students in the class will have the opportunity to show what they know or are able to do.

Reliability.   Reliable assessment occurs when there is consistency and dependability in results that occur over a period of time, when scored by different raters. Holistic assessment of writing, for example, is reliable when the raters are trained in the same holistic scoring technique and achieve consistency among themselves when scoring the same writing passages. Reliability in assessment of oral language occurs when trained raters use taped oral language samples with a criterion-referenced rating scale, such as the Student Oral Language Observation Matrix or SOLOM (see Table 5.4 in Chapter 5) to mutually assess vocabulary, fluency, syntax, and other aspects of oral language.

Validity.   When assessment instruments measure what is intended, they are said to be valid. The interpretations made from valid tests or assessments are deemed adequate and appropriate, and curriculum and instructional decisions can be adjusted based on the results. When learners don't understand the language of a test, using that test to determine their knowledge of content is not valid. It is difficult to achieve valid results with one-shot testing. Rather, we should use multiple, appropriate measures to get a rich picture of what learners know and can do. Classroom-based, informal assessment that is varied and reflects the classroom teaching style can best achieve a broad and valid picture of the learner's skills and knowledge.

The issue of validity is probably the most compelling issue in assessing ELLs. Poor language proficiency may prevent ELLs from displaying their content knowledge gains adequately. Cultural differences may confuse ELLs who may not come from cultures with experiences similar to those of test developers. Therefore, when assessing content, teachers should assure that they are measuring content learning and not assessing ELLs' cultural understanding or language proficiency. The following questions help to pinpoint the problem:

- Am I assessing language knowledge or knowledge of the world?
- Am I assessing knowledge of the world available to all cultures or only to particular cultural groups?
- Am I assessing the content objectives or the language skills of the student?

Valid assessment occurs when teachers assess the content objectives they intend to assess regardless of the language used to express that content. Creating specific objectives and rubrics for assessment is helpful in ensuring valid assessment.

Consider the issue of validity in the assessment example in Figure 10.1. A seventh grade student has written a response to the teacher's request for a paragraph summarizing what has been learned about the pyramids of Egypt. Reading this paragraph, you cannot help but note the many grammatical errors, and the influence of the student's native Spanish in the word choice and word order of the language. In order to evaluate the work, however, the teacher needed to refer to the directions given for the task and the rubric distributed to students for assessment. The teacher's directions were the following:

- Use the information on your graphic organizer to write at least one paragraph summarizing what you have learned about the pyramids of Egypt.
- Include a topic sentence, supporting details, and a conclusion.

Miguel's teacher used the rubric in Table 10.2 to assess his pyramid paragraph. When evaluated according to the task directions and the rubric, we can see that a valid assessment concerning the content, organization, and neatness of the paragraph gives this student a passing grade. He has comprehended the information about the building of the pyramids, their location, and their time frame, and provided an example of the greatest pyramid, in Giza. In addition, the student has learned and used the vocabulary necessary for the concept of pyramid building: "Pharaoh," "pyramid," "Egypt," "sled," "slaves," "barge," "tomb," and "stone." The assessment of the paragraph according to the rubric is a **product grade.**

The additional assessment of the language of the paragraph is a **process grade.** The grammatical errors in the paragraph, such as the lack of past tense verbs, must be noted by the teacher and lessons planned for helping the student to use verbs correctly in discussions of history. These types of ELL writing errors (e.g., verb tenses, word choice, word order, and articles) are persistent for many years, even after ELLs have

Figure 10.1 Summary of What a Seventh Grade Student Had Learned About the Pyramids of Egypt

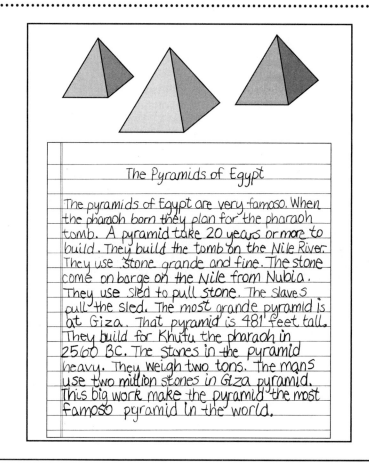

The Pyramids of Egypt

The pyramids of Egypt are very famoso. When the pharaoh born they plan for the pharaoh tomb. A pyramid take 20 years or more to build. They build the tomb on the Nile River. They use stone grande and fine. The stone come on barge on the Nile from Nubia. They use sled to pull stone. The slaves pull the sled. The most grande pyramid is at Giza. That pyramid is 481 feet tall. They build for Khufu the pharaoh in 2560 BC. The stones in the pyramid heavy. They weigh two tons. The mans use two million stones in Giza pyramid. This big work make the pyramid the most famoso pyramid in the world.

exited from English Language Development (ELD) programs, and it is important that classroom teachers be comfortable addressing them. In this situation, lessons addressing common issues can be integrated into the instructional plan as part of future learning about Egypt. An assessment can be made on this learning objective separate from the content that the language conveys. Assessment of content knowledge is thus accomplished separate from language ability.

Separating product grades from process grades in the content classroom promotes valid assessment. To assess both at once puts a heavy burden on the ELL student. Process and product are both important but without separating the two, teachers may never get a clear picture of what a student is learning in the content classroom. The picture will only show what the student has not yet learned.

Inform Teaching and Improve Learning

Assessment that informs teaching begins with a scrutiny of the teacher's mastery objectives. What is it that the students are to know or be able to do at the end of the instructional period? By aligning assessment closely to the content, language, and thinking-skill objectives in the unit, teachers will have a clear direction for instruction. In many cases, these assessment techniques do not take time away from teaching, but

Table 10.2 Rubric for Evaluating a Student's Content Learning in a Unit on Egypt

Name: _Miguel Morales_

Topic: _Pyramids of Egypt_

Criteria

	1	2	3	4	Points
Organization	No topic sentence, few supporting details and no conclusion.	Missing either a topic sentence or conclusion. Details are scanty.	Topic sentence is present with a conclusion. More than three details present.	Topic sentence and conclusion are clearly stated. Many details support the topic.	4
Content Knowledge	Student does not have grasp of information; student cannot answer questions about the subject.	Student displays general content knowledge and demonstrates basic concepts.	Student displays specific content knowledge and basic concepts.	Student demonstrates full knowledge (more than required) of content.	3
Neatness	Work is illegible.	Work has three or four areas that are difficult to read because of illegible handwriting.	Work has comprehensible handwriting.	Work is neatly done. Handwriting is legible and clear.	4
				Total points:	11/12

enhance it, and can be integrated into various stages of the lesson plan: activating prior knowledge, checking for understanding, observations, questioning, interactional learning strategies, slates, sort tasks, and signals.

Effective classroom-based assessment improves student learning. An example of an improved learning opportunity is the pyramid rubric used in Table 10.2. By creating a rubric and sharing it with learners, the teacher has provided a snapshot of what a good performance looks like. With this snapshot in hand, a student has a greater chance of achieving at a high level.

Other learning opportunities are presented to students when teachers:

- Support learners' practice sessions before oral presentations.
- Provide multiple opportunities for learners to achieve desired outcomes (re-teach and re-test).
- Teach learners how to support one another in reviewing, revising, and editing writing.
- Teach the use of graphic organizers as organizing tools for research and writing.
- Provide scaffolding for all forms of assessment.

Scaffolding is one way of reducing the language demands of the content classroom by providing contextual supports for meaning. But scaffolding can also be used to provide language support for content assessments. Manipulatives, graphic organizers, and visuals are examples of support structures. Examples of scaffolded assessment include the following (O'Malley & Valdez Pierce, 1996):

- *Exhibits or projects* that involve students in comprehending, organizing, and presenting content information
- *Visual displays* that enable students in comprehending vocabulary and content in order to complete graphic organizers, diagrams, or semantic maps
- *Organized lists* through which students present concepts or terms they have organized, sorted, or sequenced in some way
- *Tables or graphs* that demonstrate student organization, interpretation, and comprehension of data
- *Short answers* that ask students to focus on specific content area concepts

All of these examples control the language load on ELLs while allowing them to report on the extent of their content learning. The examples in Table 10.3 show common classroom tasks and the ways that teachers can scaffold those tasks depending on the proficiency levels of the learner.

Use Multiple Sources of Information

The best strategy for assessing ELLs is to use a varied approach to collecting information from multiple sources during classroom instruction. Though tests (even multiple-choice tests) can provide useful information, this information is necessarily narrow. One-shot testing cannot inform teachers as to the breadth and complexity of student understanding. Rich assessment uses multiple measures of learner success.

Writing portfolio assessment is an example of assessment that is informed through multiple sources of information. It provides opportunities for teachers and students to evaluate multiple writing pieces over a period of time. Students create writing in various genres and revisit selected pieces at later dates, self-assessing, rewriting, and perfecting with the help of teacher conferencing. Portfolios enable students to develop needed learning skills as well as increase their writing competencies. Table 10.4 lists and describes some of the categories of assessment techniques that are available to classroom teachers.

Use Familiar Instructional Techniques

One of the reasons why many ELLs may have difficulty with discrete skills tests, standardized tests, and summative evaluation in general is that the format of the assessment instrument is alien to their experiences in the classroom. Lack of experience with testing can lead to "test errors" or errors that result from the testing situation, rather than lack of knowledge of the content being tested. For example, students taking standardized tests make incorrect responses by writing too lightly on the bubble answer sheet or by skipping a row of answer bubbles. Classroom teachers often prepare students for standardized tests by providing learners with practice test experiences on marking answers, using time well, checking answers, and guessing that is appropriate for the test.

Since ELLs have limited experience in North American classrooms, their experience with test formats may also be limited. For these students, assessment that arises

Table 10.3 Scaffolding for Classroom Assessment

Assessment Task	Without Scaffolding	With Scaffolding
Make an oral presentation with note cards.	• Work individually to organize content. • Summarize on note cards. • Present to the class.	• Team two students. • Provide a graphic organizer to structure the presentation. • Divide the presentation in half. • Provide opportunity for oral practice with coaching before the final presentation.
Summarize a text reading.	• Read the chapter. • Write a summary.	• Provide hands-on activation experiences to uncover the concepts in the text. • Preview the pictures and graphics in the text. • Create questions from the bold print headers. • Make predictions about possible answers. • Provide a chapter outline. • Read the questions at the end of the chapter. • Team to read the chapter together. • Take notes on a T-list or semantic map.
Write a word problem.	• Create a word problem using your own numbers. • Provide a numerical equation. • Write the word problem story and question	• Provide a cloze form of a word problem or a model problem. • Provide key sentence frames for the problem questions. • Provide a context for the problem. • Work with a buddy to create a problem. • Act out a word problem.
Write an essay describing the characters, plot summary, and setting of a narrative text.	• Provide an outline of the essay organization.	• After modeling, fill in the descriptions of plot, setting, and characters on a graphic organizer. • Complete the missing information on a cloze essay.
Define a concept.	• Write a paragraph describing the concept.	• Create a list of descriptors. • Label a picture that is provided.

Adapted from O'Malley & Valdez Pierce (1996)

from familiar instructional techniques produces the most reliable, valid, and fair information about student achievement. In brief, we recommend that teachers assess what has been taught in the ways that it was taught.

Assessment techniques can be incorporated into every phase of the lesson. Indeed, checking comprehension throughout instruction assures teachers that all students are engaged in the instructional conversation. Madelyn Hunter's description of

Table 10.4 Assessment Techniques for ELLs

Areas of Assessment	Student Tasks
Oral Language Assessment	• Point to the answer, picture, or object. • Draw a picture. • Use a signal to respond. • Write an answer on a slate. • Respond to one word, yes/no, either/or questions. • Engage in buddy or group talk. • Paraphrase concepts. • Explain orally. • Present an oral report. • Respond with Numbered Heads Together, Think-Pair-Share, or other active learning strategies.
Reading Assessment	• Record concepts on a graphic organizer. • Record concepts on a T-list. • Listen and respond to a recorded book. • Engage in buddy reading. • Engage in reciprocal reading. • Read to the teacher. • Retell the story. • Engage in a directed group discussion. • Answer comprehension questions. • Complete a cloze passage.
Writing Assessment	• Record new learning in a journal. • Write to the teacher. • Engage in writing as a process. • Meet with the teacher for a writing conference. • Write from a graphic organizer. • Write in various genres: letter, poem, report, book review, slide presentation, compare/contrast essay, expository "how-to" essay, persuasive essay, literary analysis, etc. • Contribute regularly to a portfolio of writing that is evaluated by the student and the teacher.

(Continued)

Table 10.4 Assessment Techniques for ELLs *(Continued)*

Areas of Assessment	Student Tasks
Content Assessment	• Create a poster or mural. • Label a graphic organizer. • Role play to show understanding. • Use pair or group reports. • Complete a cloze passage. • Complete a project. • Conduct research with oral interviews, the computer, or the library.
Other	• Self assessment. • Portfolio assessment. • Skills and strategies checklists.

Video Exercise

Portfolio Assessment for ELLs

Go to MyEducationLab, select the topic **Assessment,** and watch the video entitled "Portfolio Assessment for ELLs" to observe an elementary level ELL in a portfolio conference with her teacher. Complete the questions that accompany it. You may print your work or have it transmitted to your professor as necessary.

dipsticking (first discussed in Chapter 9) fits our criteria (Saphier & Gower, 1997). The metaphor of dipsticking comes from the act of checking the oil in your car. In dipsticking, teachers make a quick check of student comprehension. The attributes of dipsticking require that teachers check the comprehension of

- All of their students
- Frequently
- On the same topic or concept
- Throughout the lesson

Dipsticking can be accomplished in every phase of the lesson—from activation of prior knowledge to the summary at the end. Traditional classroom assessment involves teachers asking individual learners questions about what has been covered. This can be useful, but is very time-consuming, and can lead the teacher to think that everyone understands when in truth only the few who volunteered to answer the questions "got it." To check the comprehension of all students, it is most efficient to use a variety of strategies and techniques in which many learners can respond at once. Some of the active learning strategies we have recommended in this book (shown in Table 10.5) can also be used to check student comprehension during instruction.

What Are the Critical Factors Affecting Assessment of ELLs?

Formative versus Summative Assessment

Summative assessment is evaluation at the end of learning to determine whether or not learners have achieved goals. Standardized tests are an example of summative evaluation and are typically administered at the same time of year annually to compare

Table 10.5 Active Learning Strategies for Every Phase of the Lesson

Lesson Stage	Assessment Technique
Into the Lesson: Activate Prior Knowledge/Assess Pre-knowledge	• K-W-L chart • Wordsplash • Semantic map • Corners • Carousel brainstorming • Picture previews • Open-ended questions • Buddy talk • Line ups • Stir the class
Through the Lesson: Input for Active Understanding	• Signals • Think-pair-share • Buddy talk • Teacher questioning • Jigsaw the information • Anticipation guides • Word splash
Through the Lesson: Guided Practice	• Reciprocal reading • One question quiz • Thumbs up • Slates • Signal cards • Sort tasks • Line-ups • Cooperative learning groups • Numbered heads together
Beyond the Lesson: Independent Practice	• Cooperative learning groups • Biopoems • Sort tasks • Project learning • Inside-outside circle • Journal entries

(Continued)

Table 10.5 Active Learning Strategies for Every Phase of the Lesson *(Continued)*

Lesson Stage	Assessment Technique
Beyond the Lesson: Summarizing	• Ticket to leave
	• Homework
	• Journal entries
	• ABC summary
	• 3-2-1 summary
	• Slates

learners with others in the same grade as well as to compare the performance of schools, districts, and states. High-stakes standardized tests are used to determine, for example, whether learners may move on to the next grade or graduate from high school.

The No Child Left Behind Act (NCLB) of 2001 was enacted to improve the educational achievement of economically disadvantaged and minority children, including ELLs. It declared that schools would be held accountable for assisting all children to meet state standards and pressured states to include ELLs in large-scale assessment programs. States have responded by administering standardized tests to learners throughout the grade levels in math, language arts, and science.

The recent emphasis on large-scale assessment has had both positive and negative consequences for ELLs. Benefits from NCLB arise from the emphasis on raising standards for all students; schools are invested in the success of ELLs, who are challenged more than ever before to meet higher levels of academic achievement. On the other hand, major decisions regarding school funding, grade-level promotion, and graduation are often made on the basis of the standardized testing program. ELLs are at a disadvantage to show true achievement gains on these assessments because of problems with validity, fairness, and language load (Coltrane, 2002).

ELLs can be stigmatized by standardized summative testing. Their limited language skills bring the reliability and validity of the test into question. Some states, schools, and districts do not test ELLs until they have been in an instructional program for one to three years. Others require that ELLs be tested with everyone else, on the same instruments. In an urban district in California, the district sued the state over requirements of early testing of ELLs on standardized tests, which, the city argued, did not provide useful information on learners and could negatively affect them. At one point in the arguments, a district administrator challenged those involved with a math test in Chinese, and asked if the English-speakers in the room felt that this test would show what they knew about math. This simple but dramatic demonstration made it clear to many that early use of such tests is not useful or advisable.

Even if testing is delayed, standardized tests present problems for EL learners. For this reason, accommodations in the testing process are allowed in many states. An accommodation is a change either to a test or to a testing situation that increases an ELL's access to the content of the test while still preserving test validity (Rivera, 2006). Accommodations may include (but are not limited to):

- Extended time periods for testing.
- Use of a dictionary (bilingual, English to English, or customized for the particular test).

- Separate setting with an ESOL teacher.
- Translated or extended explanation of test directions.

Accommodations to the language load of the test can benefit ELLs taking standardized tests. The elimination of passive voice constructions, extraneous vocabulary, and lengthy compound/complex structures increases learner comprehension of the content question, affecting student response and improving test validity. When linguistically loaded questions are simplified, ELLs have been shown to increase their test scores (Abedi, 2002).

Other accommodations are being explored to increase the validity of standardized testing for ELLs. Charlene Rivera, the Executive Director of George Washington University's Center for Equity and Excellence in Education (CEEE), has researched state education department policies and practices to accommodate ELLs and found that, for the most part, state departments are inconsistent within and across states in regard to exemptions from testing, modifications of testing, and the use of alternative tests (Rivera, Vincent, Hafner, & Lacelle-Peterson, 1997). The Center for Research on Evaluation, Standards, and Student Testing (CRESST) recommends that policy makers and educators develop nationwide consistency with the following (Abedi, 2002):

- Modifying test questions to reduce unnecessary language complexity and thus narrow the performance gap between ELLs and native English students.
- Providing customized dictionaries (customized to the language of the test questions only) to provide an alternative to standard dictionaries.
- Monitoring and evaluating intended and unintended accommodations to determine effects on ELL achievement as well as native English student achievement.

A number of assessments have been used to determine the language proficiency of ELLs, including the Language Assessment Scales (LAS), the Woodcock-Muñoz, the Language Assessment Battery (LAB), and the CELDT. Recently, as a response to NCLB, new standardized tests (e.g., the ACCESS Test for ELLs at http://www.wida.us/assessment/ACCESS.aspx) have been developed specifically to assist in appropriate placement of ELLs and to show ELL growth in language proficiency. Though designed to show levels of proficiency, they cannot take the place of ongoing assessment in the classroom.

Formative Assessment

Formative assessment is assessment that takes place as learning is developing. It includes the multiple ways that teachers gather information about their students' learning throughout the instructional process and use this information to evaluate their own teaching and their students' learning. Formative assessment is ongoing, occurs during instruction, and guides the teaching process. Much formative assessment is informal and occurs on-the-spot as the teacher observes students, converses, asks questions, conducts quick-writes, or engages in any number of classroom tasks that are not specifically graded according to a set of criteria (Echevarria, Vogt, & Short, 2004). Other forms of formative assessment are conducted as part of the instructional process, guided by standards and classroom objectives, graded and/or documented through the use of a checklist, anecdotal record, classroom quiz, or other data-collection technique. As such, formative, classroom-based assessment expands on the single test approach; assessment becomes part of teaching, and assessment tools closely resemble the instructional tools of the classroom.

Informal classroom-based assessment provides teachers with the information they need to determine if students comprehend the content and are achieving the objectives of the lesson. It is essential in helping teachers to adjust instruction, re-teach, provide tutoring in special skills, or move on. Assessment, then, is not relegated only to the end of the lesson but is used during every phase of the lesson to determine prior knowledge, to clear up misconceptions, and to determine the level of understanding of the new concepts.

Cultural Issues in Testing

Annie Watts, the teacher we described in the chapter introduction, instinctively felt that her student Julio was making progress in reading in her classroom. But when she administered the district test, the test indicated that Julio did not comprehend the meaning of the reading passages well. Annie never considered that the questions that Julio was asked to respond to were based on content that he had never been taught and that were not a part of his culture. Baseball and breakfast food are culturally associated with the specific North American culture. Julio enjoys and plays what he calls football, but that game is referred to as "soccer" in the U.S. Finally, flowers that grow in the spring are not common in Julio's neighborhood or in the town in Central America where he was born.

Few diagnostic tools have been designed specifically for children who are exposed daily to two languages—one at school and the other at home (Valdes & Figueroa, 1994). In fact, "standardized" assessments presume a high degree of homogeneity of experiences among students. English language learners for the most part are not represented adequately by any existing norm samples (Ortiz, 2001). When differences exist between the experiences of the norm-referenced group and the children taking the test, bias can exist that renders the assessment less valid (Figueroa & Garcia, 1994; Ortiz, 2001).

Examples of test items requiring specific cultural knowledge have been illustrated by Mohan (1985, pp. 124–125) from widely used tests such as the following:

An example from the Stanford Diagnostic Reading Test, Form X, Level 1, number 3:

1. Our flag contains one _____ for every state.
(a) stripe   (b) star

From the Gates McGinitie Reading Test, Form 3M, number 1:
2. Sam won at marbles because he could ___ straighter than Bill.
(a) show   (b) shoot   (c) draw   (d) run

From the Comprehensive Test of Basic Skills, Form 4, Level 9, number 1:
3. Bill ran out on his front porch to watch the fire truck. He lives in _____
(a) a big apartment.   (b) a city house.   (c) a trailer.

Major testing corporations employ panels of experts to eliminate cultural bias from their standardized assessments, but state testing agencies are not always capable of this level of review. It would be preferred if the norm-referenced populations used for testing purposes included adequate numbers of language minority students. Assessment in two languages would also produce a more adequate picture of an individual's global ability.

Certainly, Congress has spoken on this issue in the Improving America's Schools Act of 1994 that calls for assessing Limited English Proficient (LEP) students relative to state content standards, and "to the extent practicable in the language and form most likely to yield accurate and reliable information on what students know and can do, to determine mastery of skills in subjects other than English" (sec. 1111) (b) (3) (F) (i–iii) at http://www.ed.gov/legislation/ESEA/toc.html.

Cultural bias in testing is difficult for classroom teachers to recognize because culture is intrinsic to people who are raised in it. Like the air around us, we don't notice it until it's changed or taken away. And yet the results of bias in testing can have permanent effects on children. Tests such as the ones mentioned previously are used in schools to make important decisions about children's

- Classroom placement
- Reading group placement
- Need for special education placement
- Placement in classes for the gifted
- Selection of remedial programs
- Selection of remedial learning materials

Unless children have been specifically instructed in the rules of marbles or the symbolism of the stars and stripes on the American flag, it is inappropriate to test them on those cultural items in the name of testing reading comprehension. Awareness of cultural bias and alertness to its presence in instruments used in our schools will help classroom teachers prevent some inappropriate placements of children.

Formative assessment can also be culturally biased. Teacher-made tests tend to reflect the cultures teachers live in and are familiar with. Those who write tests for textbooks also tend to make use of their own life experiences. We need to consider what our learners have experienced and work to create assessments that are geared toward the content and language objectives taught in the classroom.

Language versus Content

Language issues can easily color assessment of content learning in the classroom. When assessing learning of social studies concepts, for example, teachers may ask students to write summary paragraphs or essays. The grammatical errors in the writing, however, may have an effect on the teacher's reading of the concepts expressed in the essay. When creating math word problems, ELLs will have difficulty expressing their intent in the language of mathematics. Although learners may show that they understand the concepts of the problem, their language may give teachers the impression that students understand less than they actually do. The same type of problem may ensue in an oral discussion of literature. Learners' receptive skills may be much more advanced than their productive skills. Teachers' questions may be answered slowly, haltingly, and with inappropriate vocabulary and grammar, making it appear that students understand little about what they have read. Once again, poor language skills give the impression that the student does not understand the content concepts. Teachers have difficulty knowing whether the student lacks content knowledge or lacks language skills to express that knowledge.

What Are Examples of Authentic, Performance-Based Classroom Assessment?

As we have seen, classroom-based assessment often involves some kind of "performance" in which a learner constructs a response: for example, responses to questions, story retelling, oral presentations, role plays, writing pieces, captioned artwork, media products, and so on. Constructed-response assessments can improve educational achievement for ELLs by helping learners to demonstrate learning and transfer learning from one application to another while developing mental habits, skills, and abilities that will aid the student in lifelong learning (Valdez Pierce, 2002). We must also work to make this type of assessment valid by using rubrics, checklists, and other means to specify to learners what a good performance looks like and exactly how their performances will be evaluated.

Performance-based assessment is authentic when it is consistent with the kind of instruction used in the classroom involving knowledge and skills closely resembling those needed in the real world (Valdez Pierce, 2002). Authenticity in assessment involves "multiple forms of assessment that reflect student learning, achievement, motivation and attitudes on instructionally-relevant classroom activities" (O'Malley & Valdez Pierce, 1996, p. 4).

As previously noted, standardized testing frequently does not reflect classroom instructional techniques or the learning that has actually taken place within the classroom. Certainly, standardized tests do not give teachers information regarding student motivation or attitudes. We need day-to-day assessments to amass a more complete picture of learners to help guide teachers' future instructional planning.

Performance-Based Assessment (PBA)

PBA generally falls into three types: *products, performances,* and *process-oriented* assessments (McTighe & Ferrara, 1998; Valdez Pierce, 2002). All three types can be used in the classroom with ELLs for different learning goals and for students at differing levels of language proficiency.

Table 10.6 provides examples of three types of performance-based assessments for use with ELLs. The types of assessments, their benefits, and the language levels at which these assessments are appropriate are included. Also included are two different leveling systems: the four level system (Pre-production, Early production, Speech emergence, and Intermediate fluency) introduced by Krashen & Terrell (1983) and the 2006 TESOL proficiency levels (Level 1 Starting, Level 2 Emerging, Level 3 Developing, Level 4 Expanding, and Level 5 Bridging).

In our view of classroom assessment, (which includes performance-based, authentic, ongoing, constructive-response information gathering) the goal is not merely rote learning of content facts (though, of course, it includes some of this), but the development of the mental habits, skills, and knowledge that learners will need for lifelong learning of both language and content, and their subsequent success in life. These include the ability to collect, comprehend, and analyze information, work collaboratively with others, solve problems, and perform complex, real-world tasks (Darling-Hammond, Ancess, & Falk, 1995). Three additional features of performance-based assessment help learners to achieve this goal: self-assessment, visible criteria, and rubrics.

Self-Assessment

Self-assessment that routinely accompanies instruction helps learners to process their own skill development and to take responsibility for their own learning, and guides them in the acquisition of the kinds of study skills, attitudes, and practices that will lead to greater learning achievement. For example, the checklist in Table 10.7 encourages students to assess their use of academic oral language. The assessment clearly conveys the kinds of oral language tasks that students will be able to accomplish at the end of the learning unit (in this case, a unit on the pyramids of Egypt).

Table 10.6 Performance-Based Assessments at Varying Language Proficiency Levels

Product Assessments	Benefits	Language Proficiency Levels: TESOL 2006	Language Proficiency Levels: Krashen & Terrell, 1983
Illustrations	• Limited language load required for expression of content learning.	• Level 1 Starting • Level 2 Emerging	• Pre-production
Projects	• Opportunity to display content learning outcomes in a team environment and with limited language requirements.	Levels 1–5 • Starting • Emerging • Developing • Expanding • Bridging	• Pre-production through intermediate fluency
Poster Board Presentations	• Posters act as a scaffold for the oral language of the content presentation.	Levels 2–5 • Emerging • Developing • Expanding • Bridging	• Early Production • Speech Emergence • Intermediate
Dioramas	• Content learning display with a limited language load.	Levels 1–5 • Starting • Emerging • Developing • Expanding • Bridging	• Early Production • Speech Emergence • Intermediate Fluency
Lab Reports	• The format of the report acts as a scaffold for the description of a scientific process, opportunity to evaluate specific vocabulary learning.	Levels 3–5 • Developing • Expanding • Bridging	• Intermediate Fluency
Portfolios	• Offer an opportunity to display long term progress in content and language in multiple formats.	Levels 1–5 • Starting • Emerging • Developing • Expanding • Bridging	• Pre-production through intermediate fluency

Table 10.6 Performance-Based Assessments at Varying Language Proficiency Levels   *(Continued)*

Product Assessments	Benefits	Language Proficiency Levels: TESOL 2006	Language Proficiency Levels: Krashen & Terrell, 1983
Graphic Organizers	• Limited language required for the content learning display.	Levels 1–5 • Starting • Emerging • Developing • Expanding • Bridging	• Early Production • Speech Emergence • Intermediate Fluency
Bio Poems	• Summarizing tool for social studies and/or language arts that is scaffolded through the use of a modeled format.	Levels 3–5 • Developing • Expanding • Bridging	• Intermediate Fluency
Journals and Learning Logs	• An enduring sample of student language achievement, vocabulary acquisition, and a record of content learning.	Levels 1–5 • Starting • Emerging • Developing • Expanding • Bridging	• Early Production • Speech Emergence • Intermediate Fluency
Performance Assessments			
Role Plays	• Opportunity to assess oral language usage and content learning in a scaffolded role play framework.	Levels 2–5 • Emerging • Developing • Expanding • Bridging	• Speech Emergence • Intermediate Fluency
Oral Presentations	• Opportunity for oral language and content assessment supported with practice and notes.	Levels 3–5 • Developing • Expanding • Bridging	• Speech Emergence • Intermediate Fluency
Interviews	• Opportunity to use practiced oral language structures (such as questions) multiple times while requiring comprehension of an unknown response.	Levels 2–5 • Emerging • Developing • Expanding • Bridging	• Early Production • Speech Emergence • Intermediate Fluency

(Continued)

Table 10.6 Performance-Based Assessments at Varying Language Proficiency Levels   *(Continued)*

Performance Assessments	Benefits	Language Proficiency Levels: TESOL 2006	Language Proficiency Levels: Krashen & Terrell, 1983
Debates	• Opportunity for oral language and content assessment that is scaffolded with team support, notes, and pre-written questions.	Levels 4–5 • Expanding • Bridging	• Intermediate Fluency
Group Discussions	• An informal oral language observation opportunity providing data on content learning	Levels 2–5 • Emerging • Developing • Expanding • Bridging	• Speech Emergence • Intermediate Fluency
Demonstra-tions	• Oral language and content assessment with realia, practice and notes as scaffolds.	Levels 3–5 • Developing • Expanding • Bridging	• Speech Emergence • Intermediate Fluency
Process-Oriented Assessments			
Self-assessments	• Opportunity to self-assess language, reading and writing skills, learning goals and study skills.	Levels 1–5 • Starting • Emerging • Developing • Expanding • Bridging	• Pre-production through Intermediate Fluency
Learning Logs	• Opportunity to self-assess logical thinking, writing, content learning and vocabulary usage.	Levels 2–5 • Emerging • Developing • Expanding • Bridging	• Speech Emergence • Intermediate Fluency
Think-Alouds	• Opportunity to self-assess in an aural-oral modality.	Levels 3–5 • Developing • Expanding • Bridging	• Intermediate Fluency

Table 10.7 Self-Assessment: Content Unit on Egypt
• •

Check (√) the box that describes your language.

Task	Not well	Okay	Well	Very well
1. I can describe a pyramid.				
2. I can describe how pyramids were built in the past.				
3. I can understand my teacher talking about the pyramids of Egypt.				
4. I can understand a television program about pyramid building.				
5. I can give an oral report on pyramid building.				

The self-assessment in Table 10.8 is a generic self-assessment for listening and speaking behaviors. Here, the teacher has indicated ways in which students can communicate better in the classroom.

Reading self-assessments can help learners know what good reading habits are and if they're using them. Even in primary grades, learners can rate themselves using a rubric like the one in Table 10.9. Study skills and learning goals can also be incorporated into self-assessment instruments, as shown in Table 10.10.

Visible Criteria

Performance-based assessment is enhanced when teachers share the criteria they will use to evaluate learning with students and parents. Visible criteria that are specific, communicated, and comprehensible to the learners improve the performance of ELLs (Valdez Pierce, 2002). Methods of sharing criteria range from sharing examples of possible products with students (e.g., essays, lab reports, book reviews, poems, and essays) to the modeling of processes (e.g., lab skills, math computation, writing as a process, and oral reporting) to the use of rubrics that will eventually be used in evaluating learners' products and processes. Teacher modeling and sharing with good student models provide students with clear targets for their own products and performances. Models make visible the achievement levels that we expect our students to attain.

Table 10.8 Self-Assessment: Listening and Speaking in the Classroom
• •

Circle the word that tells how well you talk and listen in class:

When talking in class, I:

1. Ask my classmates for help;	Never	Sometimes	Often
2. Use my hands and face to add meaning and show feeling;	Never	Sometimes	Often
3. Draw a picture to help explain something;	Never	Sometimes	Often
4. Use a different way of saying something if I am not understood;	Never	Sometimes	Often
5. Use a synonym when I can't think of a word.	Never	Sometimes	Often

Table 10.9 Self-Assessment: Good Reading Behaviors

Circle the face that shows how often you do these things.

What I do	Not Often	Sometimes	Usually
1. I read every day.	☹	😐	☺
2. I listen to my teacher read.	☹	😐	☺
3. I like to read.	☹	😐	☺
4. I read at home.	☹	😐	☺
5. I borrow books from the library every week.	☹	😐	☺

Rubrics

As we have seen, **rubrics** are useful tools for both learners and teachers to evaluate products. Rubrics list the specific criteria used to evaluate a product or presentation and then indicate performance levels on a scoring scale that uses numbers, letters, or other descriptive labels. Teachers share rubrics with students prior to the learning experience and provide clear explanations and examples so that all learners will understand the criteria. Often, rubrics are accompanied by models of acceptable or outstanding products.

Table 10.10 Self-Assessment Checklist: Active Learning Behavior

Put a check (√) next to the active learning strategies you use.

	Not Often	Sometimes	Usually
1. I listen carefully to directions.			
2. I take notes from the blackboard.			
3. I study new vocabulary with my buddy.			
4. I ask for help if I don't understand something.			
5. I have a special place and time to study at home.			
6. I do my homework every night.			
7. I read every day.			
8. I check my written work for errors.			

Rubrics can be designed for both teachers' and students' use. For learners, the rubric may be rewritten in language that students can easily understand and that will guide them during the learning process. Often, learner rubrics are developed for specific projects such as the Pyramid Unit Rubric in Table 10.2. It is also very useful to develop learner rubrics for tasks and genres used frequently, such as process writing.

Rubrics designed for teacher use are often more complex and complete than those learners will use. Sometimes teachers on a grade-level team develop common rubrics for their use; other times rubrics are devised by grade levels, schools, or districts to evaluate specific student learning goals such as oral language, writing, or math problem-solving. The Student Oral Language Observation Matrix (SOLOM) scale (Table 5.4, Chapter 5) is one example of a district-made rubric for teacher assessment of oral language.

Whether rubrics are developed for student or for teacher use, it is important that the criteria are precisely defined according to what a student should know or be able to do at the end of the learning experience. Qualities of the student's product or performance are made specific so that students can assess their own learning and work to raise their achievement levels. Rubrics provide richer and more useful feedback to learners than a single letter or number grade, because they make it clear why learners scored as they did. Finally, rubrics ensure that assessment is fair and equitable because learners are made aware of what is being assessed and what performance is expected if they are to achieve at a high level.

Research supports the notion that rubrics lead to higher achievement gains in learners. Marzano (2000) reports on a study (Wilburn & Felps, 1983) that compared math achievement in middle school students using two assessment approaches: criterion-based rubrics and a norm referenced, point-based approach. Average achievement gains were 14 percent higher for students using rubrics than for those who did not. Particularly high gains were achieved by low-achieving students using rubrics as compared to higher-achieving students. The average improvement was 24 percent higher than the average improvement of students assessed on the point-based approach. In addition, the rubric group showed more positive attitudes toward math, the content-area focus of this study.

Fuchs and Fuchs (1986) analyzed 21 different studies examining the use of rubrics. They found that when teachers used rubrics to make decisions about students, student achievement increased by 32 percent as compared with students whose teachers did not use rubrics. "Apparently, asking teachers to conceptualize the classroom progress of students by using rubrics encouraged teachers to clearly define the knowledge and skill strengths and weaknesses of their students and to act on them to promote student growth. Presumably, this perspective was passed on to students, who, in turn, improved their achievement" (Marzano, 2000, p. 63).

Following is an example of a writing rubric devised for third grade ELLs who are learning to write essays. Note that the criteria are clear; they include what the teacher has taught the students and how they are expected to perform.

Compare the elementary-level writing rubric in Table 10.11 to the one in Table 10.12, which is designed for the middle-school level. Note that the teacher uses four levels of performance and provides more detail in describing the performances in Table 10.12. The four-column rubric in Table 10.12 displays a range of proficiencies wider than the three-part rubric in Table 10.11. Generally four-column rubrics are preferable to three-column rubrics in that they allow for descriptions of outstanding performances in all categories, providing goals to challenge even the most advanced learners in your class. In a four-column rubric, the third column, the proficient category, is the target for all students. This column describes the skills and knowledge that will be accomplished by learners who have mastered the lesson content.

The goal of the Likert-scale rubric in Table 10.13 is to assess student achievement on a range of study skills taught in conjunction with an elementary unit on the amphibian

Video Exercise
Authentic Assessment for ELLs

Go to MyEducationLab, select the topic **Assessment**, and watch the video entitled "Authentic Assessment for ELLs" to observe an upper elementary level math class involved in performance-based assessment. Complete the questions that accompany it. You may print your work or have it transmitted to your professor as necessary.

Table 10.11 Generic Essay Writing Rubric: Third Grade Level

Your Writing Includes:	1	2	3
Parts of an Essay	No clear introduction, body, or conclusion. Theme is unclear.	Introduction, body, and conclusion are not easily identified.	Introduction, body, and conclusion are easily identified.
Paragraphs	You do not use paragraphs.	Your paragraphs are missing a topic sentence or only contain one or two details.	You include at least three paragraphs. Each paragraph has a topic sentence and about 3 details.
Ideas	You have no clearly developed ideas.	You have only one or two developed ideas.	You have at least three ideas that clearly develop your theme.
Words	Your vocabulary is limited and general.	You use mostly basic vocabulary but only a few descriptive words.	You use at least 5 interesting, descriptive words.
Sentences	You use little or no punctuation or capitalization, and unclear sentences.	Your sentences can be understood, but contain missing capitals, missing or incorrect punctuation, and some misspelled words.	Your sentences are neatly written and include capitalization, punctuation, and correct spelling.
Handwriting	Your handwriting is sometimes difficult to read because it is not neat or legible.	Your handwriting is legible.	Your handwriting is clear, neat, and legible.

life cycle. Teachers give students copies of the rubric at the start of the unit to clarify the learning goals they need to attain to achieve at a high level. They explain the terms carefully so that ELLs will be able to use the rubric appropriately. Learners then assess their own ability to use the desired study skills with a Likert scale. At the same time, the teacher can assess the students using a similar rubric.

The Amphibian Observation Rubric in Table 10.14 identifies the same goals as the rubric in Table 10.13, but from the point of view of the teacher. This rubric contains specific criteria for each of the goals. Middle-school math content is assessed in the four-column rubric for a geometry lesson on quadrilaterals in Table 10.15.

The combination of self-assessment checklists, scales, and rubrics provides students with a clear picture of how to achieve at progressively higher levels. These tools also provide clarity for teachers, parents, and others in the school community about what is taught and assessed in the classroom.

How Do Standards Affect Classroom Assessment?

Standards have been developed in the U.S. in many content areas (math, science, social studies, etc.) and at national and state levels for each of the grades PreK–12. In addition, Teachers of English to Speakers of Other Languages (TESOL) has developed

Table 10.12 Generic Essay Writing Rubric: Middle School Level

	Novice	**Apprentice**	**Practitioner**	**Expert**
Purpose	• Writing lacks purpose. • Shows little understanding of concepts and assignment. • Does not state a main idea.	• Purpose is unclear. • Shows a minimal understanding of concepts and assignment. • Does not state the main idea. • Unrelated ideas are included.	• Purpose is evident. • Demonstrates a proficient understanding of concepts and assignment. • States the main idea. • Unrelated ideas may be included.	• Purpose is clear. • Establishes a thorough understanding of concepts and assignment. • States the main idea. • Remains on topic throughout.
Content Focus	• Topic is undeveloped. • Few to no details to support the topic.	• Topic is minimally developed. • Few details or examples support the topic.	• Topic is developed. • Details and examples are sufficient to support the topic.	• Topic is clearly and fully developed. • Contains extensive, relevant detail and examples to support the topic.
Organization	• Progression of ideas is difficult to impossible to follow. • Transitions are lacking. • An element of format (introduction, body, conclusion, beginning and ending sentences) is missing.	• Some organization is evident but progression of ideas has major inconsistencies. • Transitions are lacking or used incorrectly. • An element of format is missing or weak.	• Ideas are organized and progression of ideas evident. • Transition words are used. • Complete format is evident.	• Ideas are ordered logically and are easy to follow. • Transitions are used throughout to aid coherence and unity. • All format elements are included.
Grammar, Usage, Mechanics	• Writing is filled with errors that impede communication.	• Writing has errors that at times begin to impede communication.	• Errors are evident but writing is fundamentally grammatical and communicative.	• Few, if any, errors occur.

Table 10.13 Self-Assessment Checklist: Learning Strategies for a Unit on Amphibians

- The aquarium contains a clump of frog eggs. Soon the eggs will grow into tadpoles and eventually grow into frogs.

- Observe the eggs every day and notice how the eggs change.

- Write or draw what you observe in your notebook.

- Think about how well you are doing this task.

	Never	Rarely	Sometimes	Usually	Always
1. I look carefully at the aquarium animals every day.					
2. I work with a friend to talk about what we see in the aquarium.					
3. I plan how I'm going to record my observations.					
4. I record my observations every day.					
5. I ask my teacher or a friend if I don't know the correct words to use in my notebook.					
6. I check my science notebook before I give it to my teacher.					

two standards documents specifically for English language learners (1997, 2006). There is no shortage of standards' documents available for students and teachers.

Teachers find standards very helpful in identifying the specific content to be taught at a grade level within a school year. However, some districts and states have developed standards that are more helpful than others. Consider the following characteristics of good standards in evaluating your district/state standards (Lacina, Levine, & Sowa, 2006, pp. 37–39):

1. *Standards must be clear* for teachers, parents, and students to understand what they will teach and what they will learn. This means that content standards should be detailed and precise enough to guide a teacher's instructional program.
2. *Standards must be specific.* When written in a general and vague manner, they leave teachers wondering about their interpretation and provide a barrier to student learning. Asking ourselves if a standard can be measured is one test of standard specificity. Note: Many standards that are written broadly also use subcategories of performance indicators and/or rubrics to specify performances expected within each standard.
3. *Standards must be comprehensive* with adequate breadth and depth to enable students to understand the content area at every grade level.
4. *Standards must be manageable,* that is, not overwhelming for the teacher or impossible to implement within the course of a school year.

Table 10.14 Rubric for Assessing Students' Learning Strategies in a Unit on Amphibians

Task	Poor	Fair	Proficient	Outstanding
1. Observe aquarium animals.	Observe once or twice.	Observe twice a week.	Observe almost every day.	Observe daily.
2. Talk with a friend about your observations.	Talk once or twice.	Talk twice a week.	Talk almost every day.	Talk daily.
3. Plan a record of your observations.	Write a few words about the animals in your learning log.	Write descriptive observations in your learning log.	Create an observation plan with sentence length descriptions.	Create an observation plan such as a daily diary with sentence length descriptions plus a chart or table.
4. Record your observations.	Record once or twice.	Record twice a week.	Record almost every day.	Record daily.
5. Use a dictionary, ask a buddy, or ask the teacher for the meaning of unknown words.	Avoid using new words.	Take a guess at the meaning of new words.	Ask a buddy for the meaning of new words.	Ask the teacher or a buddy for the meaning of new words.
6. Edit your science notebook for neatness, spelling, complete sentences, clear meaning, and daily observations before giving it to the teacher.	Avoid editing the notebook.	Edit the notebook for neatness.	Edit the notebook for spelling and neatness.	Edit the notebook for spelling, neatness, and complete sentences.

5. *Standards must be rigorous* for all students and set high expectations for them.
6. *Standards must be public* so that teachers, parents, and students are aware of what the target is and all can have a part in hitting it squarely.
7. *Standards must include a balance between skills and knowledge.*
8. *Standards must be cumulative* in that the skills and knowledge learned at one grade level are used to build increasingly more complex and abstract levels of skills and knowledge in the next grade level.
9. *Standards must be measurable* in order to be easily assessed.

Table 10.15 Polygon Rubric for Middle School Students to Self-Assess Math Learning

··

Polygons: Identification, Classification, and Computation of Quadrilaterals

	Awful	**Awkward**	**Average**	**Awesome**
Identify Geometric Quadrilaterals	• Identifies quadrilaterals by name with less than 60% accuracy.	• Identifies quadrilaterals by name with 60% accuracy.	• Identifies quadrilaterals by name with 80% accuracy.	• Identifies (or matches) 7 quadrilaterals by name with 100% accuracy.
Draw the Quadrilaterals	• Draws 7 quadrilaterals correctly. • They are not measured or marked. • Proportion is not correct in all drawings.	• Draws 7 quadrilaterals correctly. • Angles are measured incorrectly or marked incorrectly on some drawings. • Proportions are not correct in all quadrilaterals.	• Draws 7 quadrilaterals correctly. • Angles are measured and marked with few errors. • Proportions are correct.	• Draws 7 quadrilaterals correctly. • Angles are correctly measured and marked. • Proportions are correct.
Classify Quadrilaterals	• Can classify fewer than 7 quadrilaterals but cannot cite side and angle characteristics.	• Can classify fewer than 7 quadrilaterals by referencing either side or angle characteristics.	• Can classify 7 quadrilaterals by referencing side and angle characteristics.	• Can classify 7 quadrilaterals by referencing side and angle characteristics.
Compute the Perimeter of Quadrilaterals	• Computes perimeter with less than 60% accuracy with the help of a calculator.	• Can compute perimeter with 60% accuracy but may need a calculator.	• Can apply formulas to compute perimeter with 80% accuracy.	• Can independently and correctly compute perimeter with 100% accuracy.

When all of these characteristics are in place, teachers can use standards documents to guide instruction and create meaningful assessment. Table 10.16 is an example of a standard from the Sunshine State Standards of Florida (State of Florida, 1996) fourth grade to fifth grade science content area and addresses the topic, "Processes of Life."

The general learning arenas in Figure 10.16 are made more specific in the Grade Level Expectations, where benchmarks are provided for each standard (see Table 10.17). The benchmarks are specific to number 5 in Standard 1: "Knows that similar cells form different kinds of structures" (SC.F.1.2.5).

From this progression of general standards to benchmarks to grade level expectations, Shelly Marx, a fifth grade science teacher in Florida, is able to construct a

Table 10.16 Florida Science Standard 1 for Grades 4 and 5.

··

Processes of Life

Standard: The student:

1. describes patterns of structure and functions in living things. (SC.F.1.2)

2. knows that the human body is made of systems with structures and functions that are related.

3. knows how all animals depend on plants.

4. knows that living things are different but share similar structures.

5. knows that similar cells form different kinds of structures.

---

grade-level unit for her class, which includes both ELLs and proficient English-speaking students. The standards and benchmarks provide her with a level of specificity, clarity, and comprehensiveness, yet are manageable within the time frame available to teach the unit. The progression of knowledge from the fourth to the fifth grade reminded Shelly of what students had learned in previous years. However, Shelly could not take this learning for granted, particularly because many of her students were children of migrant farm workers who rotated in and out of the school according to the requirements of the citrus season.

Shelly developed a unit based upon her state's guidelines that she used when she assessed her students' learning. For example, when teaching the parts of plant and animal cells, Shelly determined which aspects of plant and animal cells she wanted students to know and understand. The science text provided her with some of this information and Shelly adapted the material, prioritizing the most important elements of cells and their functions, and creating science, language, and study skill objectives based upon this information.

Shelly determined that she would need multiple assessments for her cellular unit to accommodate the diversity of her classroom. Four of the students were beginning language learners from Mexico and Central America; other students were functioning bilinguals; a few were monolingual English speakers; and several were designated special education students. Several of these groups required differential assessments. Shelly planned that her assessments would include:

Table 10.17 Grade Level Expectations for Florida Science Standard 1

···

Grade Level	Expectations
Fourth grade student	1. knows that living things are composed of cells.
	2. knows that processes needed for life are carried out by cells.
Fifth grade student	1. uses magnifying tools to identify similar cells and different kinds of structures.
	2. knows the parts of plant and animal cells.
	3. understands how similar cells are organized to form structures (e.g., tissue, organs) in plants and animals.

- Frequent comprehension-checking throughout instruction
- Peer review and evaluation of final cell products
- Summary paragraph of a nonfiction reading on cellular structure
- Short quiz
- Venn diagram comparing plant and animal cells, and their structures
- "Cellular cookie" showing the structures created using candy and decorative frosting

In order to ensure that all students in the class would accomplish the assessments successfully, Shelly provided multiple scaffolds throughout the lesson:

- Sticky-note summaries in the text books
- Class and individual Venn diagrams
- Summaries in the science notebooks
- Small supportive groupings with mixed L1 and L2 speakers
- Use of the native language for clarification among groups
- Individual vocabulary cards listing cellular structures and their functions
- Classroom charts and handouts on which to take notes

After determining her assessments based upon state standards, Shelly fleshed out her objectives for the lesson (see Table 10.18).

As we have seen, standards and assessments were the starting point in Shelly's planning for her fifth grade science class. Starting with standards and the assessment of those standards assured Shelly that all of her students would be working at rigorous, grade-level content learning. Her instructional practices were part of her assessment plan and included techniques that were familiar to the students. Her scaffolding and variety of instruction and assessment ensured her that all students would have access to the learning and be assessed in a fair, reliable, and valid manner. Finally, Shelly used multiple sources of information for her assessment throughout the learning process rather than relying on a quiz or test at the end of the unit. Shelly's planning for teaching and assessment is itemized in Table 10.19.

ELLs assessed according to the principles described here and illustrated in Shelly's classroom will have the opportunity to display their content-learning strengths while acquiring the language they need to become fully functional in an English language classroom. Equitable, varied, and scaffolded assessment is the foundation of good instruction.

Table 10.18 Shelly's Science Lesson Objectives

Type of Objective	Specific Objective
Content Objective	Students will describe the components and their functions for both plant and animal cells using a completed vocabulary card of cellular structures and functions.
Thinking/Study Skill Objective	Students will match the cell components with their functions on a chart.
Language Objective	Students will use the target vocabulary to describe the differences between plant and animal cells; and tell the functions of parts of the cell using a vocabulary card and a class chart.

Source: Lacina et al. (TESOL, 2006, p. 19)

Table 10.19 Shelly's Assessment and Instruction Plans

1. Identify state content standards for the topic. Locate the appropriate benchmarks. Identify grade-level expectations for the prior grades leading up to the current grade level.

2. Determine content, language, and learning skill objectives for the grade-level expectations.

3. Determine a variety of assessment procedures that will adequately assess learning for all language proficiency levels in the class.

4. Identify appropriate scaffolding for assessments: interactional grouping and structures, pictorial and graphic supports.

5. Determine a variety of activities that will enable all students to reach the proficient level for each objective.

6. Determine methods of scaffolding instruction.

7. Clearly communicate objectives to all learners.

8. Communicate and demonstrate success to all learners in the form of rubrics, self-assessments, models, demonstrations, and/or completed products.

Questions for Reflection

1. We have advocated for differentiated assessment techniques that are adjusted to the needs of the learner. By adapting assessments, we have argued that language learners can receive more equitable treatment in evaluating their content learning. What might the arguments be against this thinking? How would you explain your method of assessment to parents of monolingual students?

2. Many teachers have difficulty differentiating between the language of the student and the content learning expressed in that language. Others in the school community may not understand how a student can receive a grade of B on an assignment that contains ungrammatical elements. Can these assignments be proudly displayed on bulletin boards in school hallways? What responses would you give to critics of this grading system?

3. Assessment should be grounded in state, national, and content standards. Others would argue that assessments should be grounded in the strengths and needs of the students in the classroom. Prepare arguments for both of these positions.

Activities for Further Learning

1. Summative assessments can sometimes contain elements of cultural bias. Conduct an analysis of a summative assessment used in your state or school district. Determine the percentage of cultural bias in that assessment.

2. Using the listings of classroom instructional practices in this chapter, create an assessment that rates content learning separately from language learning.

3. Choose/create a lesson plan for content learning. Write a student rubric that can be used to assess student learning of that lesson.

4. Devise an observation checklist that teachers can use to evaluate the aural-oral skills of students while engaged in group work and discussion.

5. Choose one of the lessons in the thematic units at the end of this text and create a student rubric for that lesson.

6. Devise two self-assessment instruments that students at two different grade levels can use to self-assess one of these language areas (e.g., reading, writing, listening, or speaking).

7. Create an assessment plan using at least five different forms of assessment for a lesson or unit you have created or taught in the past.

8. Standards are often the starting point for good assessment. Look at the standards in your state for math, science, social studies, and language arts. Are the standards and benchmarks sufficiently specific to determine learning objectives and assessments? Choose a content area, select standards for that content at a specific grade level, and determine assessments and objectives for a diverse class of learners based upon those standards. Argue for or against the usefulness of your state standards.

PEARSON
myeducationlab
Where the Classroom Comes to Life is a collection of online tools for your success in this course, your licensure exams, and your teaching career. Go to www.myeducationlab .com to utilize these extensive resources including videos from real classrooms, Praxis and licensure preparation, a lesson plan builder, and materials to help you in your teaching career.

Suggested Reading

August, D. & Hakuta, K. (1998). *Educating language-minority children.* Washington, DC: National Academy Press. This short volume summarizes a report entitled *Improving schooling for language-minority children: A research agenda* (1997). The chapter on student assessment itemizes the key findings of the research in that report.

Brown, J. & Hudson, T. (1998). The alternatives in language assessment. *TESOL Quarterly, 32*(4): 653–676. The authors examine three types of assessment useful for classroom purposes. They then describe how teachers can best select appropriate assessments for various objectives.

Carr, J. & Harris, D. (2001). *Succeeding with standards: Linking curriculum, assessment, and action planning.* Alexandria, VA: Association for Supervision and Curriculum Development. This book describes a comprehensive plan for aligning local curriculum to local, state, and national standards. Although not aimed specifically at ELLs, the authors are concerned with improving academic performance for all students.

Leung, C. & Lewkowicz, J. (2006). Expanding horizons and unresolved conundrums: Language testing and assessment. *TESOL Quarterly, 40*(1): 211–234. In an article scrutinizing the state of assessment in the TESOL profession, the authors discuss current concerns in standardized testing as well as key issues in classroom-based teacher assessment of second-language learners.

Short, D. (1993). Assessing integrated language and content instruction. *TESOL Quarterly, 27*(4), 627–656. This is a practical article that explores content instruction for ELLs and the various ways to assess their learning in classrooms PreK–12.

Teachers of English to Speakers of Other Language, Inc. (2006). *PreK–12 English language proficiency standards.* Alexandria, VA: TESOL. A resource for teachers seeking to align content standards with language learning standards. The volume includes standards for language arts, social studies, math, and science as well as the TESOL standards for social, intercultural, and instructional purposes within a PreK–12 school setting. Varying language proficiencies are included with appropriate performance indicators.

Web Sites for Further Learning

Assessment and Evaluation on the Internet. ERIC/AE Digest. In this digest, Internet resources of particular interest to the assessment community are identified. Retrieved April 8, 2008.

http://www.ericdigests.org/1996-1/evaluation.htm

Center for Research on Evaluation, Standards and Student Testing (CRESST). This site contains a wealth of material on assessment. The Teachers Page contains materials related to assessments and rubrics. The rubrics are explicit in defining clear criteria for assessment. Student samples of writing are rated here by various criteria. In addition, the Teachers Page contains links to articles on standards and measurements, and accountability. Retrieved April 8, 2008.

http://www.cse.ucla.edu/products/teachers.html

Language Accommodations for English Language Learners in Large-Scale Assessments: Bilingual Dictionaries and Linguistic Modifications (December, 2005). This study from the National Center for Research on Evaluation, Standards, and Student Testing (CRESST) at the University of California, Los Angeles, focuses on the validity, effectiveness, differential impact, and feasibility of accommodation strategies for ELL students. The study found that some of the strategies were effective in increasing the performance of ELL students and reducing the performance gap between ELL and non-ELL students although the effectiveness of accommodation may vary across grade levels. Retrieved April 8, 2008.

http://www.cse.ucla.edu/reports/r666.pdf

Kathy Schrock's Guide for Educators. This web site includes many teacher-friendly examples of rubrics, graphic organizers, and assessment information especially appealing to teachers of learners in grades K–6. Retrieved April 8, 2008.

http://school.discovery.com/schrockguide/assess.html

Middle School Assessment and Evaluation. This site is dedicated to multiple issues affecting middle-school teachers in the assessment of learners. Retrieved April 8, 2008.

http://www.middleweb.com/ContntAssess.html

References

Abedi, J. (2002). Assessment and accommodations of English language: Issues, concerns, and recommendations. *Journal of School Improvement, 3*(1). Retrieved May 18, 2008 from http://www.icsac.org/jsi/

Coltrane, B. (2002). English language learners and high-stakes tests: An overview of the issues. *CAL Digest* EDO-FL-02-07. Retrieved May 18, 2008 from http://www.cal.org/resources/digest/ 0207coltrane.html.

Darling-Hammond, L., Ancess, J., & Falk, B. (1995). *Authentic assessment in action: Studies of schools and students at work.* NY: Teachers College Press.

Echevarria, J. Vogt, M., & Short, D. J. (2004). *Making content comprehensive for English learners: The SIOP model* (2nd ed.). NY: Pearson.

Figueroa, R. A. & Garcia. E. (1994). Issues in testing students from culturally and linguistically diverse backgrounds. *Multicultural Education,* Fall: 10–19.

Fuchs, L. & Fuchs, D. (1986). Effects of systematic formative evaluation: A meta-analysis. *Exceptional Children, 53*(3): 199–206.

Krashen, S. D. & Terrell, T. D. (1983). *The natural approach: Language acquisition in the classroom.* San Francisco, CA: The Alemany Press.

Lacina, J., Levine, L. N., & Sowa, P. (2006). *Collaborative partnerships between ESL and classroom teachers: Helping English language learners succeed in preK–elementary schools.* Alexandria, VA: TESOL.

Marzano, R. (2000). *Transforming classroom grading.* Alexandria, VA: Association for Supervision and Curriculum Development.

McTighe, J. & Ferrara, S. (1998). *Assessing learning in the classroom.* Washington, DC: National Education Association.

Mohan, B. A. (1985). *Language and content.* Reading, MA: Addison-Wesley.

No Child Left Behind Act of 2001. 107th Congress of the United States of America. Retrieved from http://www.ed.gov/legislation/ESEA02/107-110.pdf

O'Malley, J. M. & Valdez Pierce, L. (1996). *Authentic assessment for English language learners: Practical approaches for teachers.* Reading, MA: Addison-Wesley.

Ortiz, S. O. (2001). Assessment of cognitive abilities in Hispanic children. *Seminars in Speech and Language, 22*(1): 17–37.

Rivera, C. (2006). Using test accommodations to level the playing field for ELLs. Presentation at the LEP Partnership Meeting, Washington, DC, August 28–29, 2006. Retrieved May 18, 2008 from http://www.ncela.gwu.edu/spotlight/LEP/Presentations/Charlene_Rivera.pdf

Rivera, C., Vincent, C., Hafner, A., & Lacelle-Peterson, M. (1997). Statewide assessment programs: Policies and practices for the inclusion of limited English proficient students. *Practical Assessment, Research & Evaluation, 5*(13). Retrieved May 18, 2008 from http://pareonline.net/getvn.asp?v=5&n=13

Saphier, J. & Gower, R. (1997). *The skillful teacher: Building your teaching skills.* Carlisle, MA: Research for Better Teaching.

State of Florida, Department of State (1996). *Science: Pre K–12 sunshine state standards and instructional practices.* Tallahassee, FL: Author.

Student Oral Language Observation Matrix (SOLOM). San Jose Area Bilingual Consortium. Last retrieved May 18, 2008. http://www.cal.org/twi/evaltoolkit/appendix/solom.pdf

Teachers of English to Speakers of Other Languages, Inc. (1997). *ESL standards for PreK–12 students.* Alexandria, VA: TESOL.

Teachers of English to Speakers of Other Languages, Inc. (2001). *Scenarios for ESL standards-based assessment.* Alexandria, VA: TESOL.

Teachers of English to Speakers of Other Languages, Inc. (2006). *TESOL PreK–12 English language proficiency standards in the core content areas.* Alexandria, VA: TESOL.

Valdes, G. & Figueroa, R. A. (1994). *Bilingualism and testing: A special case of bias.* Norwood, NJ: Ablex.

Valdez Pierce, L. (2002). *Performance-based assessment: Promoting achievement for English language learners.* ERIC/CLL News Bulletin. Retrieved April 8, 2008 from http://www.cal.org/resources/archive/news/2002fall/performance.html

Wilburn, K. & Felps, B. (1983). *Do pupil grading methods affect middle school students' achievement: A comparison of criterion-referenced versus norm-referenced evaluations.* Unpublished document. Jacksonville, FL: Wolfson, H. S. (ERIC Document Reproduction Service No. ED 229 451).

CHAPTER 11

Putting It All Together Thematically: Developing Content-Based Thematic Units

Donna Norman's fourth grade district curriculum includes the study of various regions of the U.S. For the next three weeks, her class will explore the Southwest region. Donna teaches a mixed class of learners that includes six children who are learning English as a second language. Five of these students are boys. Donna has met with her grade-level colleagues, Sally and Bob, to talk about ways to integrate the teaching of the history, geography, and peoples of the Southwest with the language arts skills that she emphasizes for all of her students. After looking at the district curriculum and assessing the needs and interests of the students, Donna, Sally, and Bob decide to teach a three-week integrated unit called "War and Peace in the Old Southwest."

Donna knows that this theme will appeal to her students—especially the boys. Donna also thinks that the theme is broad enough to include content objectives related to struggles between Native Americans and cattle ranchers; warfare over scarce resources; conflicts between warring Native American groups, hunting, and gathering populations; and challenges from the harsh environment.

In the past, Donna has motivated her students by engaging them in concrete experiences that help them to understand the big picture of the learning unit. But this unit has her stumped. Living in the Northeast, she has little access to Native American artifacts. Donna confers again with Sally and Bob, and they brainstorm ideas. Finally, they agree on a combination of simulation and story-reading to introduce the unit. The teachers arbitrarily divide each class into two groups, Navajos and Apaches and provide cloth headbands labeled with the name of each tribe. Once the headbands are in place and the tribes identified, Donna explains to her class what will happen next:

"For the next three weeks we will learn about your people who lived in the American Southwest long ago. We will learn how your families functioned, how you found food, the crafts you produced, your religions, where you lived, who your enemies were, and some of the major struggles you had in your lives. Your job is to learn about your own tribe so that you will be able to explain it to others from outside the Southwest region. We will start today reading a story about one young boy who lived in the Southwest years ago and his relationship to a wild white horse."

How do you develop content-based thematic units?

- What is thematic instruction?
- Why teach thematically?
- How are thematic units structured?
- What about standards in a thematic unit?
- How is content curriculum organized in a thematic unit?
- How is language curriculum organized in a thematic unit?
- How can learning strategies be incorporated into thematic instruction?

What Is Thematic Instruction?

Thematic instruction for English language learners (ELLs) refers to an approach to teaching where an organizing principle, point of view, or theme is used as the "conceptual glue" integrating content area knowledge with language learning. The content/language learning is organized and sequenced around developmentally appropriate broad-based themes that may take several weeks to complete. Students have opportunities to learn concepts in depth, participate in a wide variety of activities that foster learning, and develop the academic language skills necessary to read and write about the new learning.

Thematic instruction comes from an educational tradition that structures curricula around activities reflecting the interests and experiences of the learners. Dewey (1916) expressed this philosophy, which focused on active participation of learners in activities related to life experiences; and Mohan (1986, p. 40) reiterated that "Doing is not an alternative for knowing: it is a way of knowing. And activity is not an alternative to talk: it is a context for talk." Activity-based language learning grows out of Dewey's basic principles.

Although thematic instruction is not the only way to organize learning for ELLs, it is the most effective and efficient organization scheme that we have encountered. Because we know that our students have a limited time in the classroom, and yet are required to learn to the same high level as their classmates, it is necessary to organize instruction in such a way that vocabulary, concepts, grammar, and language skills are constantly reused and recycled. Thematic instruction makes this possible.

Thematic instruction can be structured in a variety of ways depending on the age of the learners and the preferences of the teacher and the school. Theme units are traditionally determined by district curriculum and teacher choice but may also be generated by student inquiry and interest. Integrated learning units and interdisciplinary instruction are examples of thematic instruction from the primary to the secondary school level. The term **thematic instruction** represents the continuum of instructional options from units to courses—all of them characterized by the integration of learning within the classroom.

Marina Sanchez has developed thematic units for her primary class that include several low to intermediate ELLs. One that she usually teaches in October centers on the characteristics of animals, but Marina calls it her "Monster" unit. She uses the children's excitement about Halloween and their natural curiosity about monsters to motivate them to learn the scientific characteristics and academic language used to describe the various aspects of animals: their physical descriptions, habitat, diet, methods of obtaining food, sleep cycles, and other interesting information. Although the children begin the unit learning about mythical and strange monsters, they eventually begin to focus on the real animals that are interesting to them. The month-long unit takes the children through many different areas of learning. They begin with comics and mythological stories, and proceed to singing and marching in monster parades, reading library books, exploring information on the computer, organizing information on graphic organizers, reporting on various animals, and finally, creating their own monster animals with pictures and oral reports describing their life habits.

Criteria for Thematic Instruction

Marina's unit incorporates the nine principles of Activity-Based Communicative teaching and learning. These principles overlap with instructional criteria that are thought to produce effective thematic instruction (Enright & McCloskey, 1988; Peregoy & Boyle, 2001).

1. *Active, Varied Engagement:* Thematic instruction offers variety in many ways, in class groupings, in skill use, in topics and choices, in methods of learning, in task difficulty, in roles and responsibilities, and in presentations. There are many ways for children to learn about the themes and each student can become expert in at least one of them. Marina's students read comics and myths, sang and marched, explored the computer, completed graphic organizers, and reported on and drew pictures of their monsters. The goal is total engagement of all learners.

2. *Cultural Relevance and Student Interest:* Thematic instruction is successful when teachers are able to match the instructional goals of the state or district curriculum to their own students' interests, lives, and cultures. As the unit progresses, students often take the lead in the direction of the inquiry as they suggest new questions to explore and use their own experiences to guide them. Those students who like to sing were delighted with Marina's monster parade. But others in her class were far more interested in exploring learning on the computer and in the library. All of her students related well to the mythological creatures described in their home cultures. For some of her students, creating drawings of their own imaginary monsters was the high point of the month.

3. *Collaboration:* Collaboration enables ELLs to practice language in an academic context, develop a broad range of language functions, and increase academic vocabulary. Students work together with buddies, small groups, various teachers, and their families to negotiate their understanding of content and determine the meaning of the new language and concepts. For this unit, Marina expanded the instructional conversation of the classroom by using

A Monster Unit Is Powerfully Motivating to Young Elementary Students

student pairs and small group work projects. Marina's student groupings changed as activities evolved. Other adults in the school were consulted when questions needed to be answered. For example, the school librarian was used to help with the research; and the fifth grade teacher, Ms. Leary, was questioned about her extensive knowledge of birds.

4. *Learning Strategies:* Learning strategies expand student learning beyond the classroom and maximize learning potential. Marina used the computer frequently during this unit. Skills that the students had learned in the computer lab could be practiced in her classroom. Marina focused on search strategies for specific information for this unit. In addition, she used graphic organizers once again, a learning strategy that her students were becoming accustomed to throughout all of their learning.

5. *Comprehensible Input with Scaffolding:* The teacher determines that forms of sheltering and scaffolding need to be used for each of the activities in the unit to ensure that all students are participating as fully as possible. The monster unit utilized many pictures of both real and imaginary animals. These spiked the students' interest and helped them understand the new terminology. Graphic organizers supported the writing assignments, and group work ensured that each student had multiple opportunities to speak and be spoken to.

6. *Activating Prior Knowledge and Building on Prior Experience:* Students need to reflect upon what they already know about the topic in order to be ready to learn more. Marina Sanchez reminded her students of the unit they had studied the year before on toads and frogs. She also encouraged them to think about monster stories they knew from their own cultures. Some students recalled hearing the story of Bigfoot and described that mysterious creature. Others told about Nessie, the Loch Ness monster. Many of the children knew a great deal about dinosaurs. Far from blank slates, her students had their own experiences to bring to the topic.

7. *Integration of Content Learning with Language:* As students proceed through the unit, their language skills develop, particularly in connection with the vocabulary and methodology required by the topic. Marina's students were learning the language and methodology of zoologists. The vocabulary of the topic became increasingly accessible to them as they used it in a variety of activities and learning formats. Their final reports and presentations reflected this language growth in addition to the information they had learned about animals.

8. *Differentiation:* Thematic units can accommodate differences in language, literacy, cognitive levels, dimensions of learning, learning styles, and interests because units extend over a period of time when content learning can be explored in a variety of different ways and on a range of language proficiency levels.

9. *Clear Goals, Feedback, and Purpose:* Students are involved in purposeful activities for which there is an audience and a goal. Marina's students knew they had to learn about animal characteristics to be able to design their own monsters, report on them to the class, and display them during the Halloween season. Marina was also clear in her feedback to students by providing abundant modeling, both of processes and products, and using rubrics for oral presentations.

Video Exercise

Culminating Event of a Thematic Unit

Go to MyEducationLab, select the topic **Sheltered Content Instruction,** and watch the video entitled **"Culminating Event of a Thematic Unit"** to observe a third grade class during the culminating event of a thematic unit on the desert. Complete the questions that accompany it. You may print your work or have it transmitted to your professor as necessary.

Marge Gianelli (1991) is a big fan of thematic instruction. As director of bilingual and ESL programs at Canutillo Independent School District near El Paso, Texas, she worked for over five years to develop content-based thematic units for grades K through 6. The school district was concerned about the fragmented nature of children's learning in their traditional classrooms. Students were confused about what they were learning and reading scores were low. After the introduction of thematic instruction, the results have been "dramatic." Teachers enjoy teaching this way, learners are interested and involved, and reading has increased and improved. Gianelli attributes the success to, among other things, the in-depth involvement of students in a great deal of meaningful language within a supportive learning environment.

The teachers at the Canutillo School District proceeded to organize for thematic instruction in much the same way that Marina Sanchez did. They began by scouring their state and district curricula to determine possible themes. It is important that the themes have broad relationships to those topics typically required in the content curriculum of a grade level. Marina Sanchez knew that her third graders would be spending the year in science and social studies learning about plant and animal habitats from four regions of the world. She chose her monster theme to provide some of the language, skills, and knowledge her students would need for that content.

The next step in the process is to determine the specific content area topics to be studied. Most teachers don't have a district curriculum committee to do this for them. Instead, they use their students to help plan the unit. Barbara Agor (2000), a middle-school teacher in Rochester, NY, enlisted her students to help her plan a unit on the Middle Ages. Barbara began by overwhelming her students in the first days of the unit with what she calls the "book circle"—a circle of books all around the room, differentiated for reading proficiency and all dedicated to the Middle Ages. Barbara gave her students time to look through as many books as possible, about three minutes per book on the first day. Later, they went through these books a second time with colored sticky notes, marking important pages and pictures, writing questions, and focusing on topics. The sticky notes were used when Barbara helped the class create a graphic organizer of all the topics they wanted to study. The graphic helped them to group topics and create subtopics under major headings. Barbara also had a question wall where she wrote student questions as they popped up. The graphic organizer and the question wall acted as a road map for the rest of the unit.

From here, Barbara sequenced the activities, collected and adapted materials for differing language proficiencies, and created content and language objectives. For the next five weeks, her students learned about the Middle Ages (dates, places, lifestyles, problems) and they also learned how to ask questions, report, imagine, research, and present information about the Middle Ages, a combination of content and process, and skills and knowledge.

Why Teach Thematically?

"Everything is connected to everything else" (Sylvester, 1995, p. 140). Whether we study ecology or the neural networks of the human brain, we will find that connections are vital to the health and growth of the intellect and the planet. Brain research has shown us that what we call learning results from the connections between neurons in our brains. As our neural networks grow and develop, we get smarter and are able to transfer our learning from one sphere of knowledge to the other. Thematic instruction enables students to see the connections between aspects of the curriculum and to make those connections in their brains.

Connections between neurons are supported by the growth of dendrites—spiny tree-like projections that help electrochemical impulses leap from one neuron to another. It is through active learning experiences that dendrites are produced. Wolfe (2001, p. 187) reminds us that "The person doing the work is the one growing the dendrites." In thematic instruction, the student is the one doing the work while the teacher facilitates learning. Thematic instruction emphasizes dynamic, experiential, inquiry-based learning over passive-listening classrooms. The idea of action here refers to mental action primarily, those activities involving choices, research, and problem-solving. Students are involved in processes of constructing meaning and discovery. They seek to find answers rather than being told answers. This kind of learning is optimal for all learners. "When combined with opportunities for collaboration, thematic instruction creates optimal content, language, and literacy learning opportunities for both native and non-native English speakers" (Peregoy & Boyle, 2001, p. 79).

Thematic instruction assists the brain in an innate effort to create patterns and thus give meaning to new information that would otherwise be dismissed and forgotten. New information is organized and associated with previously relevant information, connecting neural networks in the brain into connected patterns, and thus increasingly developing the ability to comprehend wider and more complex contexts. In the early grades, teachers are better able to see the connections, themes, and underlying principles than are the children because adults have a wider array of accumulated knowledge with which to make connections. But older learners can make these connections for themselves as they have had more time to accumulate sufficient data and to see patterns emerge. Interdisciplinary and cross-disciplinary models in middle and high schools create more relevance for learners, helping students to see how economics relates to geography, math to music, and the linkages between ecology and politics (Jenkins, 1998).

The unique nature of thematic instruction also encourages memory enhancement. Consolidation of new information into long-term memory requires deep processing and/or multiple opportunities for recollection and use with the brain's executive functions. These repetitions reinforce the neuronal connections of the brain's axons, dendrites, and synapses. When neuronal connections are stimulated, dendrites are strengthened, and memory becomes more enduring (Willis, 2006). In thematic instruction, the brain perceives information repeated in multiple ways and in a variety of contexts. This process makes encoding of that information more efficient and more enduring. The result is consolidation of information:

> Consolidation of information involves using the most effective strategies to first acquire information and then practice and rehearse it. The best-remembered information is learned through multiple and varied exposures followed by authentic use of the knowledge .by processing it through the executive function centers (Willis, 2006, p. 30).

Thematic units provide a learning experience that facilitates consolidation of information and long-term memory storage. Thematic learning also enhances the brain's ability to create patterns from new content information and to make connections between related content areas, such as the connections between science and math or the relationship between literature and history.

Many school districts have chosen to sequence curricula thematically because of the belief that learning is most likely to occur and be transferred from one situation to another when concepts and activities are interrelated in the classroom as they are outside the classroom (Richard-Amato, 2003). In addition, thematic instruction provides the context and concrete experiences necessary for many students, including ELLs, to learn abstract concepts. The collaborative nature of these experiences motivates and involves students while providing them with a purpose for learning. Indeed, Ritter (1999) reports a study that suggests that the engagement rates of students were higher for thematic instruction than for single-subject lessons. Teacher observations and student self-perceptions confirmed that third and fourth graders in the study were more involved in learning when social studies, reading, and math were integrated than when they learned those subjects individually.

Language skills are placed at center stage throughout thematic instruction. Collaborative problem solving, project work, inquiry-based research, and sharing of information enable learners to use and hear both social and academic language. The social language skills for communicating and functioning within a small group are facilitated as the groups assign roles, make suggestions, praise, edit, and create together. The sharing of information between and within groupings requires the use of the academic language related to the content subject. Reading and writing skills develop as students are exposed to source material within and outside the textbook. Writing skills also develop as students are required to present information that they have learned with others. Finally, the integration of these skills makes more effective use of classroom time than if they were taught individually in separate lessons. Thematic instruction is time efficient.

How Are Thematic Units Structured?

It is clear that . . . we need to develop an organizing framework of language and thinking skills that apply across the curriculum. We need to go beyond techniques that help a student understand a particular lesson; we need to help the student to acquire the ability to develop this understanding independently. This calls for general language and thinking skills that can be transferred. The organizing framework must help the students to connect work in the language class and the content class.

Bernard Mohan, 1986, pp.18–19

All thematic units require structure—a skeleton upon which teachers can develop the content, language, and thinking objectives they wish their students to learn. The nature of that skeleton will differ from teacher to teacher, but there are some general principles that apply to the structuring of all thematic instruction. We will consider three:

- Concrete to abstract learning
- Low to high cognitive levels
- Simple to complex content structures

Concrete to Abstract

Thematic instruction is a process of organizing learning experiences along a continuum of increasing abstraction. Recent brain research emphasizes this approach, and our own experiences reinforce that thinking. There are at least three kinds of learning that help neural networks to form:

- Concrete experience
- Representational or symbolic learning
- Abstract learning

This continuum of abstraction (shown in Figure 11.1) begins with practical, "hands-on" concrete experience. Experiential learning is most effective in producing long-lasting learning. In fact, the strongest links in the brain's neural networks develop as a result of concrete experience (Wolfe, 2001). When we think about our own learning, we realize that we didn't develop our computer skills by reading books about the computer but by actually using it. Even though we have studied foreign languages in classrooms, our language skills began to grow and develop when we traveled to countries where those languages were spoken. We finally understood the

Figure 11.1 Learning Progresses from Concrete Experience and/or Visual Representation to Abstract Learning
....

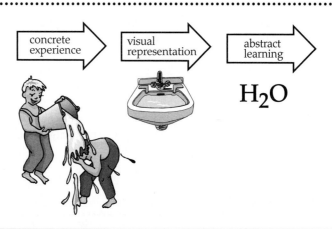

usefulness of algebra when we had to comparison shop for mortgage rates, determine the rate of earnings or loss from our stock portfolios, or predict how long a car trip might take us.

Teachers of young children are aware of the importance of concrete experiences. Play is an important part of the kindergarten curriculum and "hands-on" learning is crucial to primary education. Older learners also need concrete experiences to begin to develop an understanding of difficult abstract concepts.

Representational or symbolic learning is the next level of abstraction. Using pictures and graphics, teachers can help learners to understand new concepts. However, these tools are only as useful as the degree to which learners have had concrete experience with the concept. Showing a picture of a computer to a child who has never seen or used one may not lead to retention of that image or the word identifying it. Understanding a visual diagram of the water cycle is easier when children have had experiences seeing condensation on the side of a cold glass and monitoring rain clouds.

Abstract learning involves acquiring concepts through words and numbers. Reading about concepts and learning through reading is possible when "students have a strong neural network formed by concrete experiences and representations" (Wolfe, 2001, p. 138). Indeed, there are many concepts that require abstract learning. Abstract ideas such as "democracy," "culture," and "justice" can be understood by learners depending on their age, level of language development, number of examples provided by the teacher, prior knowledge, and amount of student involvement in related experiences (Wolfe, 2001).

The continuum from concrete to abstract reflects the kinds of language needed to process learning experiences. Concrete experiences require language for here-and-now, face-to-face dialogue. This language is simpler than the academic language required for abstract learning. The thinking skills required also increase in complexity as students move along the continuum from simple to complex, concrete to abstract. The interconnections between content, language, and thinking skills (Figure 11.2) provide a model for teachers of language learning students. Thematic instruction allows us to sequence learning events in such a way as to introduce academic terminology within a meaningful context of a concrete experience and gradually increase the abstraction of the learning activities, the complexity of the language, and the difficulty of thinking skills required.

Figure 11.2 Thematic Units Integrate Three Kinds of Skill Development Within Carefully Planned Lessons

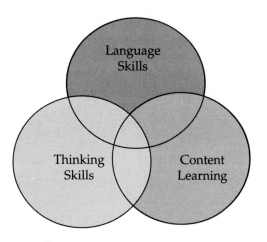

Low to High Cognitive Levels

Bloom's Taxonomy (Bloom, Englehart, Furst, Hill, & Krathwohl, 1956) is a framework that can be used to structure thematic learning experiences from a low cognitive level to a high cognitive level. We introduced using the taxonomy in Chapter 9 as a resource for developing content and language objectives. Here, we suggest that the hierarchy can also be used as a framework for structuring learning experiences for thematic instruction.

Bloom designed the hierarchy to describe six levels of thinking, from the concrete and practical knowledge level to the abstract levels of analysis, synthesis, and evaluation. The cue words appended to the chart in Chapter 9 (in Table 9.2) provide suggestions for the learning activities that could occur at each level. Table 11.1 shows the taxonomy of thinking levels and includes examples of those activities.

From the few suggested activities, we can see that language demands increase as the teacher moves from the knowledge level, where students are asked to identify vocabulary and recall information, to the synthesis and evaluation levels, where they are asked to persuade others of their point of view, debate, and use language to propose solutions to problems. In order to challenge ELLs cognitively and advance them linguistically, we need to involve them in tasks beyond the application level of cognition. This is one of the greatest challenges of working with ELLs—providing cognitively challenging material without overwhelming learners linguistically.

Simple to Complex Content Structures

Bloom's Taxonomy gives teachers a framework for sequencing language and thinking skills, but is not explicit about the nature of the content-learning concepts that must be integrated unto the unit of instruction. Mohan (1986) provides helpful suggestions regarding content integration (Table 11.2). Mohan advises previewing the content unit to get a general, overall sense of the knowledge structures within the content learning. By knowledge structures, we mean the informational structures used to convey the content information. If the content is dedicated to describing the attributes of a concept or an individual, we can say that the knowledge structure is *description.* If the

Table 11.1 Learning Activities on This Hierarchy Proceed from a Low Cognitive Level to Higher Cognitive Levels

Thinking Levels	Activities
Knowledge Remembering previously learned material.	• Name the state. • Define photosynthesis. • Label the parts of a flower. • List characteristics of Greek drama.
Comprehension Grasping the meaning.	• Explain the life cycle of a butterfly. • Summarize the story of . . . • Identify the hero-heroine. • Explain how the digestive system works.
Application Generalize; use the material in new and concrete situations.	• Illustrate the setting of the story. • Act out the fairy tale. • Sequence the life cycle of a frog. • Demonstrate the solution of a math problem on the chalkboard.
Analysis Break down material so that it is more easily understood.	• Compare the two characters in . . . • Map the best route for your vacation trip. • Research the products of . . . • Infer the reason why the solution turned color.
Synthesis Compose; put material together to form a new whole.	• Construct a dinosaur that could swim and eat meat. • Design a playground for our school. • Propose a campaign platform. • Design a contour map for an alien landing field.
Evaluation Judge the value of material for a given purpose.	• Convince the class of the value of your product. • Persuade the group to end the story your way. • Decide which character is the most heroic. • Evaluate the benefits of immigration.

Source: Levine (1995)

topic lends itself to a recount of historical events, we may focus on *sequence*. Learning about the conflicts, decisions, or dilemmas of a situation is a *choice* structure. In most learning situations, these three structures can be based within a concrete situation or can be represented visually through pictures or graphics.

In the thematic unit that Donna Norman and her colleagues developed, she began by searching the school library and the book room for fiction stories about the Southwest. She found a copy of a book entitled *White Horse* (Robinett, Bell, Rojas, & Goldstein, 1970), which told a poignant story of a Native American boy and a proud

Table 11.2 Mohan Suggests Using These General Procedures for Organizing Information in Thematic Units
••

1. Preview the content to get an "overall sense" and determine specific, practical cases or examples that will illustrate the more abstract theoretical knowledge.

2. Choose a specific example that you can present as a picture story, demonstration, drama, experience, film, process, or narrative.

3. Present the general, theoretical knowledge in charts, tables, or other suitable forms such as reading passages. At times, enable students to gather and express this information themselves.

4. Use the particular case to illustrate general principles, and use general principles to help the students interpret the particular case.

5. Use the knowledge structures of the particular case (description, sequence, choice) to develop corresponding thinking skills and language skills. Do the same for the knowledge structures of the general information (classification, principles, evaluation). Using graphic organizers, charts, or other visuals will help you to do this easily with ELLs.

Adapted from Mohan (1986, p. 34)

white horse. This text provided her with a concrete situation that would be appealing to her students and arouse their interest. The knowledge structures of *White Horse* can be viewed in terms of Mohan's framework (see Figure 11.3). Donna wanted to help her students *describe* the characters and setting of the story, specifically the little boy, the horse, and the southwestern region in which they lived. Donna helped students find this information through a series of before, during, and after activities that are part of her routine for reading-skill instruction.

Next, Donna helped the students to focus on the *sequence* of events in the story and the *choices* that the boy and the horse made as a result of those events. In this way, Donna helps her students to focus on a specific situation, understand the situation, and use their language skills to interpret meaning from that situation. From here, Donna began to focus on the more abstract content information that she wanted her students to learn: notions regarding the lifestyles of historic Native American groups, agrarian versus hunting economies, relationships between geography, food supply, and culture, and others. For this aspect of the unit, Donna used the general, theoretical knowledge structures of *concepts* and *classification, principles,* and *evaluation.*

Classification refers to how concepts and ideas are related to each other. In Donna's unit, she focused on the agriculture of the regional tribes, the differences in family structure of Navajo and Apache, and their settlement and nomadic patterns, religion, and warfare. By comparing two tribes in this way, her students came to understand some of the *principles* that govern all cultures. These principles include the cause-and-effect factors relating to agrarian and nomadic economies, the methods by which we study cultures, and the norms by which we evaluate their successes and failures. Finally, Donna helped her students to *evaluate* the lifestyles of the Native American tribes and determine why they made the choices they did.

Donna knew that her students would learn a great deal of language as they proceeded through this unit because she planned to choose language arts activities that reflected the structure of the content that she was teaching. She used Bloom's taxonomy to suggest activities that related to each of these knowledge structures. For

Figure 11.3 A Unit on the Southwest Begins with a Concrete Situation Related to a Story and Proceeds to Include Theoretical Concepts Related to Geography, History, and Economics

Specific, Practical Action Situation		General, Theoretical Background Knowledge	
Description	•a large white stallion	•Navajo food gathering •Apache hunting practices	**Concepts and Classification**
Sequence	•rode across the plains •hunted by horse thieves	•Navajo are agrarian •Apache are nomadic	**Principles**
Choice	•live in captivity or die	•compare Navajo and Apache lifestyles	**Evaluation**

example, for *description,* Donna used cue words from the knowledge and comprehension levels. *Sequence* lent itself to the level of application. Analysis dealt with the *concepts* she presented and the *principles* she wanted her learners to determine for themselves. The last level of both the hierarchy and the knowledge framework is *evaluation.* This was the culmination of the unit as students evaluated their own learning as well as the cultures they had studied.

Once Donna had structured the content she wanted to teach along these general lines, she slotted activities into the unit in their proper sequence. Donna planned several activities before she began to teach but usually selected others as she proceeded based upon the learning needs and interests of her students. It was also at this time that she differentiated each of the activities to accommodate the various language and literacy proficiencies in her classroom. For example, Donna used reciprocal reading often to help learners read for specific information in texts. She used graphic organizers to help organize the information in preparation for writing. And she appealed to the families of a few students who had familiarity with the Southwest to share their knowledge with the class through structured student interviews and slide shows.

What About Standards in a Thematic Unit?

Recent reform movements in education brought about a move toward the development of rigorous standards aimed to help all learners achieve at the highest levels. These **content standards** have provided teachers and curriculum writers with explicit information on what children at each grade level should know or be able to do. The standards are now being aligned with testing programs, curriculum frameworks, instructional materials, professional development efforts, and pre-service education. They have become the foundation of much educational effort in the U.S.

ELLs have not been eliminated from the standards movement. The English Language Arts (ELA) standards are intended for all learners—both first- and second-language learners and many teachers use these standards to guide their instruction. ELA standards are necessary but not sufficient for the many children learning English in public schools. Those learners have needs that extend beyond the scope of the Language Arts standards. As a result, Teachers of English for Speakers of Other Languages (TESOL) developed and published *ESL Standards for PreK–12 Students* (1997, p. 2). These original standards serve to:

- Articulate the English development needs of ESOL learners.
- Provide directions to educators on how to meet the needs of ESOL learners.
- Emphasize the central role of language in the attainment of other standards.

The ESL standards are organized around three main goals:

- Goal 1: To use English to communicate in social settings.
- Goal 2: To use English to achieve academically in all content areas.
- Goal 3: To use English in socially and culturally appropriate ways.

The second goal is the one that most teachers feel is in their domain of experience. Goal 2 includes the kinds of standards that teachers are familiar with, such as helping students to use language to process subject area information. Goals 1 and 3, however, are crucial to the success of Goal 2. If students are unable to use language in the social setting of the classroom, or use it in appropriate ways, learning of content will not occur. For this reason, we believe that teachers need to become aware of these standards and use them in planning for instruction. Table 11.3 specifies the three goals with nine standards and indicates some **progress indicators** for each. Progress indicators are those observable behaviors that indicate students are showing progress in meeting the standard.

The ESL standards can be incorporated into thematic instruction at the point where the teacher identifies the content-area standards and objectives for the unit. These standards will provide guidance in selecting appropriate language objectives for the unit. For example, when Donna Norman planned her unit on the American Southwest, she wanted students to work together in cooperative groups researching historical and cultural aspects of either the Navajo or Apache Indians. Donna realized that the language learners in the class needed help in working linguistically in small groups. She consulted Goal 2, Standard 1 for specific progress indicators that addressed the needs of her students. Donna selected the following:

- Use polite forms to negotiate and reach consensus.
- Negotiate cooperative roles and task assignments.
- Take turns when speaking in a group.

Once Donna had specified the behaviors she wanted her students to learn, she devised activities to help them practice these behaviors. For the first objective, Donna created a list of polite negotiating forms and listed them on a large chart that she kept hanging in the classroom for easy reference. She modeled the forms with a small group of students, then gave all the groups an easy task to complete while practicing the polite forms. Donna observed and recorded the results, praising those groups that used the polite forms most consistently. In later group sessions, Donna reminded her students to continue their practice and encouraged them from time to time.

Table 11.3 ESL Standards for PreK–12 Students (Abridged)

Goal 1: To Use English to Communicate in Social Settings	**Standard 1:** Students will use English to participate in social interaction.	**Sample Progress Indicators** • Volunteer personal information. • Describe feelings, interests and opinions. • Ask for permission. • Offer and respond to greetings, compliments, invitations, introductions, and farewells.
	Standard 2: Students will interact in, through, and with spoken and written English for personal expression and enjoyment.	**Sample Progress Indicators** • Describe storybook characters. • Listen to, read, watch, and respond to stories, songs, poems, plays, films, computer programs, and magazines. • Express enjoyment. • Talk about favorites. • Express humor.
	Standard 3: Students will use learning strategies to extend their communicative competence.	• Test appropriate use of new vocabulary, phrases, and structures. • Recite poems or songs aloud. • Associate realia or diagrams with written labels to learn vocabulary or construct meaning. • Practice recently learned language.
Goal 2: To Use English to Achieve Academically in all Content Areas	**Standard 1:** Students will use English to interact in the classroom.	**Sample Progress Indicators** • Share materials and work successfully with a partner. • Ask a teacher to restate directions. • Use polite forms to negotiate and reach consensus. • Negotiate cooperative roles and task assignments. • Take turns in groups.
	Standard 2: Students will use English to obtain, process, construct, and provide subject matter information in spoken and written form.	**Sample Progress Indicators** • Define, compare, classify objects. • Construct a graphic. • Edit/revise written assignments. • Use contextual clues. • Take notes. • Synthesize, analyze, evaluate information. • Locate information in text or reference materials.

Table 11.3 ESL Standards for PreK–12 Students (Abridged)   *(Continued)*

	Standard 3: Students will use appropriate learning strategies to construct and apply academic knowledge.	**Sample Progress Indicators** • Use cues to know when to pay attention. • Scan/skim a book to locate information. • Rehearse and visualize information. • Take risks with language. • Rephrase, explain, revise, expand information to check comprehension.
Goal 3: To Use English in Socially and Culturally Appropriate Ways	**Standard 1:** Students will use the appropriate language variety, register, and genre according to audience, purpose, and setting.	**Sample Progress Indicators** • Express humor. • Interact with an adult appropriately. • Make polite requests. • Write a letter to an adult. • Prepare and deliver a persuasive presentation to different audiences.
	Standard 2: Students will use nonverbal communication appropriate to audience, purpose, and setting.	**Sample Progress Indicators** • Respond appropriately to a teacher's gesture. • Obtain a teacher's attention appropriately. • Use appropriate volume of voice. • Determine the appropriate distance to maintain while conversing. • Maintain appropriate level of eye contact with audience.
	Standard 3: Students will use appropriate learning strategies to extend their communicative competence.	**Sample Progress Indicators** • Observe language use and behaviors of peers in different settings. • Rehearse different ways of speaking according to the formality of the setting. • Test appropriate use of newly acquired gestures and language. • Rephrase utterances.

Source: TESOL (1997)

For the second objective, Donna held a class discussion asking students to brainstorm ways to negotiate roles and assignments in their small groups. She posed "What if . . ?" questions that represented some of the problems she thought might occur in her class:

- What if one person doesn't want to accept the assignment?
- What if the same person always takes the same role?
- What if some students are not capable of handling assignments as well as others?

The students were able to generate many solutions to these questions that Donna collected on a Group Work chart that remained hanging in the classroom.

For the third objective, Donna used a cooperative learning structure called Talking Chips (Kagan, 1994). She asked each person in the group to place a "chip" such as a pen in a cup in the center of the table when they wanted to talk. The chip stayed in the cup and could not be used again until all students in the group had spoken. Donna felt this activity would encourage her language learning students to speak during the group work while preventing other students from monopolizing the conversations.

More recently, TESOL issued a second volume of standards, *PreK–12 English Language Proficiency Standards* (2006). This second volume expands on the first by addressing the content learning needs of ELLs in four areas: language arts, mathematics, science, and social studies. These instructional arenas are further differentiated into five levels of language proficiency over twelve grade levels and into the four language skills of listening, speaking, reading, and writing. Table 11.4 shows a sample from the grade 6 to 8 science standard in the domain of listening exemplifying how suggested performance indicators are differentiated and scaffolded as students increase their language proficiency from Level 1 through Level 5. Another sample from the speaking domain (in Table 11.5) illustrates social studies content in grades 6 to 8.

The PreK through 12 English Language Proficiency Standards provide an excellent model for teachers as to how to differentiate and scaffold for language learners in their classrooms. As many classrooms now have ELLs at varying language proficiencies in classrooms, ranging from very limited speakers to those at the transitional level, the examples in Tables 11.4 and 11.5 illustrate how a teacher can provide for multiple learning opportunities in the same classroom on the same topic.

Organizing Content Curriculum in a Thematic Unit

Most teachers of content subjects take guidance from their state and/or district curricula and standards when planning instruction. This has become increasingly important due to federal- and state-mandated standardized testing required at certain grade levels, especially in the language arts, math, and science. We encourage teachers to attend to required content curricula and work to use it in ways that meet the needs of all learners, including ELLs. Content curricula provide another way to structure thematic learning.

Table 11.4 The Performance Indicators Differentiate Listening Skill Levels for Language Proficiency While Maintaining Similar Science Content

Domain	Topic	Level 1	Level 2	Level 3	Level 4	Level 5
Listening	Atoms Cells Molecules	Identify elements within models or diagrams according to oral directions.	Match oral descriptions of functions of various elements with models or diagrams.	Arrange models or diagrams based on sequential oral directions (e.g., stages of mitosis or fission).	Reproduce models or diagrams based on visually supported tapes, CDs, videos, or lectures.	Design or construct models or diagrams from decontextualized oral discourse.

Source: TESOL (2006, p. 84)

Table 11.5 The Performance Indicators Differentiate Speaking Skill Levels for Language Proficiency While Maintaining Similar Social Studies Content

Domain	Topic	Level 1	Level 2	Level 3	Level 4	Level 5
Speaking	Rights and responsibilities Freedom and democracy Slavery	Respond to questions with words or phrases related to illustrated historical scenes.	Make general statements about illustrated historical scenes (e.g., "Women do vote now. Women did not vote in 1900.").	Describe or enact historical scenes based on illustrations or historical cartoons.	State a stance or position using conditional language (e.g., "If I lived in the 1850s. . .") from visually supported historical scenarios.	Evaluate or imagine different historical scenarios and their impact or consequences (e.g., "Imagine if we could not vote.").

Source: TESOL (2006, p. 86)

Many teachers like to begin the planning phase of their lessons with a brainstorming process. Some teachers prefer to brainstorm ideas using a semantic web; it helps them to expand their thinking visually and in several directions. Brainstorming ideas come from the content curriculum, the language arts curriculum, literature resources, personal interests of the teacher, ideas from colleagues and, most importantly, ideas from the students themselves (Figure 11.4).

Student brainstorming is an important part of the planning phase of a thematic instructional unit. Teachers who use thematic instruction believe that student choice empowers and involves students from the beginning of the unit. It is a powerful motivating force for learning. We ask students to give us ideas about what they think is important or interesting to learn about a particular topic. This web then becomes a road map that we and the students can follow for the rest of the unit. We like to use semantic webs on large pieces of chart paper when brainstorming ideas for a unit. We use various colors of magic markers to identify the categories of ideas and then keep the charts posted as the unit progresses so that students can see which areas we have worked on and others that will come later.

Figure 11.5 shows an example of a brainstorming web that middle-school students created for a unit on circulation. The teacher has written down all of the students' ideas and then chosen one of these categories to expand into a K-W-L chart (see Table 11.6). In the chart activity, students have the opportunity to rephrase their ideas as questions that ask more specifically what they want to know.

From the list of topics and questions generated by the teacher and students, it is then possible to start thinking about the content and language objectives for each phase of the unit. We have often used checklists of goals and objectives to ensure that we are focusing on all important areas and adhering to the content standards. In addition, writing objectives into our daily plans helps us to be more explicit about what we want students to know and be able to do during that lesson, and how we will differentiate the content, language, process, and assessment to meet our learners' needs. This explicitness enables us to communicate that information to our students as well. Objectives that are explicitly embedded into thematic activities communicate to parents, colleagues, and administrators that our instructional units

Figure 11.4 The Components of a Thematic Unit Can Come from Multiple Sources

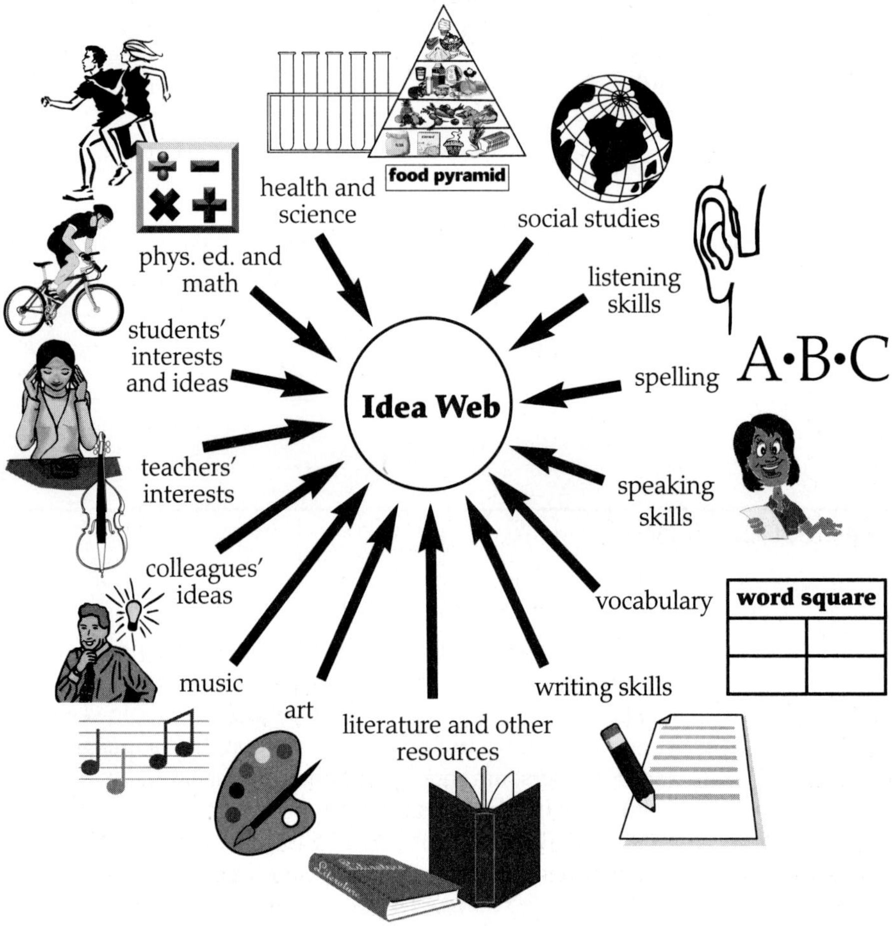

are based upon a set of standards that the school community has agreed upon. Objectives are meaningless, however, unless we can specify what successful learning will look like. How will students demonstrate that they have learned the big ideas of the content unit? How will they demonstrate ability to understand and communicate using the academic language of the topic? What kinds of products will they

Table 11.6 K-W-L Chart on the Functions of the Heart

What I *Know*	What I *Want* to Know	What I *Learned*
The heart has muscles and blood.	What are the parts of the heart?	
The heart pumps blood.	How does the heart pump blood?	
The heart keeps us alive.	Why does it stop pumping?	
	Where does the blood go?	

Figure 11.5 Middle School Students Brainstormed to Create a Semantic Web on the Topic of Circulation

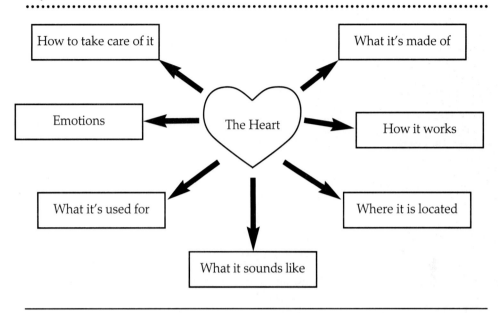

produce to demonstrate competency and success? Even at this "big picture" stage of planning, it's helpful to know what student learning will look like and to specify those products and tasks.

Learning activities necessary to produce successful products and teach essential skills need to be determined next. As mentioned earlier, the Bloom cue words suggest a variety of activities that can be adapted to the needs of the learners. If we want ELLs to "report" for example (comprehension level), we need to think about whether students need to become capable in oral or written reporting or both. We also need to determine ways to scaffold the reporting through student groupings and graphic organizers that assist organization of information. Finally, we need to provide an appropriate audience for the report and determine how we will assess it.

Donna Norman's unit on the American Southwest incorporated content objectives based upon the social studies standards from her state. The standards provided guidelines for her content but Donna needed to create objectives for her class that were more specific. She included research objectives in preparation for the research paper the students would write the following year. She emphasized oral and written language objectives because of the ELLs in the class. Finally, she added objectives that stretched the thinking skills of the students and helped them to develop learning strategies. A sampling of Donna's objectives include:

1. *State Standard:* Students will demonstrate their understanding of major themes, ideas, and turning points in the history of the Southwest. *Donna's Objectives:*

   - Read or listen to selected books and modified texts about the Navajo or Apache culture. Use highlighting with teacher support for finding specific information on the geography and peoples of the southwestern region in the 1800s.
   - Select information about one tribe to include in an illustrated report supported by a note-taking chart.

Video Exercise

Planning for a Thematic Unit

Go to MyEducationLab, select the topic **Sheltered Content Instruction,** and watch the video entitled **"Planning for a Thematic Unit"** to observe two teachers planning a unit on civilization. Complete the questions that accompany it. You may print your work or have it transmitted to your professor as necessary.

2. *State Standard:* Students will demonstrate their understanding of the geography of the interdependent world of the Southwest—including the distribution of people, places, and environments. *Donna's Objectives:*

   - Locate tribe settlement areas on a map of the U.S.
   - Determine the yearly rainfall for the southwestern settlement areas from a graphic.
   - Research the crops that can be grown in the Southwest in buddy pairs.

3. *State Standard:* Students will demonstrate their understanding of how societies develop economic systems to allocate scarce resources. *Donna's Objectives:*

   - Compare and contrast the traditional food gathering practices of the Navajo and Apache using a graphic organizer.

Assessment of a thematic unit occurs before, during, and after learning. Before beginning the unit, activating activities give teachers information on student prior learning or misconceptions and learning gaps. While presenting and working on the unit, teachers observe and record student performance for each objective. The final assessment is usually a part of the final culminating activity of the unit. This approach provides the teacher with an assessment that informs teaching at each phase of the unit. A framework for constructing a thematic unit is suggested in Table 11.7.

Organizing Language Curriculum in a Thematic Unit

Each content subject is communicated in language that differs in its grammar and vocabulary, thus making different demands on the language learner. In addition to grammar and vocabulary, ELLs must master the core knowledge of facts and ideas **(declarative knowledge)** as well as the skills and operations related to the subject **(procedural knowledge).** In general, students must be able to have a basic ability to read about the content, construct meaning, understand and participate in classroom discussions, make inferences, cite examples of major constructs, and determine cause and effect relationships (August & Hakuta, 1998). These generalized similarities are critical for all content subjects.

There are major differences in the language skills needed for individual content subjects, however. This is probably most obvious for subjects such as math that have specific notational systems. But the language of science and social studies differs in more than vocabulary. The verb tenses, sentence structures, and grammatical forms of these subjects are distinct. The language of science is the language of description and process. Social studies texts use specific past tense forms (uncommon in oral language) and complex, embedded sentence structures.

Because of the language demands of each of the content subjects, it is important to provide instruction for learners that will help their language skills grow and develop. The human costs of not addressing the needs of ELLs are devastating. Dropout rates for immigrant adolescents approach 50 percent in major city high schools (Toppo, 2006). It is time to acknowledge that language is essential to the teaching and learning of every content subject and that every teacher is a language teacher.

We have already discussed how language skills and knowledge can be integrated into the content curriculum in a way that permits ELLs to understand and communicate about the content while also expanding the range of language and vocabulary at their command. Scaffolding is one way that teachers can accomplish

Table 11.7 Unit Design for Thematic Instruction

Steps for Constructing Thematic Unit	Planning Guidelines
Step 1: Identify and Prioritize the Content Objectives.	1. What state or content standards underlie this unit? 2. What are the key ideas, operating principles, major concepts, or themes that are essential to the unit? 3. What language skills will students need to learn this content successfully? 4. What learning strategies will students need to be successful with this content? 5. How can I prioritize the knowledge and skills in this unit to ensure that all students will learn the most important elements?
Step 2: Determine What Student Success Will Look Like (Progress Indicators).	1. What skills and behaviors will students demonstrate to show that they have been successful? 2. What products will students create to demonstrate mastery of the learning?
Step 3: Create Scaffolded Learning Activities and Locate a Variety of Materials and Resources at Differing Proficiency Levels.	1. Create a variety of differentiated activities for each learning objective. 2. Collaborate with colleagues to locate materials and resources to facilitate student understanding at varying language proficiency levels. 3. Determine which activities will best meet the needs of which learners.
Step 4: Assess Student Learning.	1. Before beginning the unit, activate student learning and determine what students already know about the topic. 2. For each activity, observe, and record student strengths as well as areas where they need more instructional support. Select follow-up activities to meet needs and fill gaps revealed by assessment. 3. Create a culminating activity that will provide an overall assessment of the important objectives of the entire unit.

this goal. The sequencing of the language is also critical to student learning. Just as content learning is sequenced from the specific to the general, the practical to the theoretical, language skills need to be sequenced from practical to theoretical discourse. This sequencing principle happens naturally as we plan language-learning activities that increase the distance from the speaker to the hearer (Mohan, 1986). For example, the language used for Show and Tell and informal conversations occurs in a "here and now" context with limited distance from the speaker to the hearer. Gestures and situational context add meaning to the language. Giving a report or narrating a story requires greater distance from the speaker to the hearer and tends toward a more abstract use of language. Writing an essay or a research report requires even greater generalization, abstract language, and distance from speaker to hearer. As the distance increases, language must be more precise as there is limited context to support meaning. Ideally, each phase of the thematic unit will lead ELLs into greater abstraction and require more specific academic language use.

How Can Learning Strategies Be Incorporated into Thematic Instruction?

Learning strategies are an important part of thematic unit preparation for all of our students. For ELLs, they are particularly important. ELLs need to use these strategies to help them compensate for their limited language proficiencies. Strategies (mentioned in chapter 9) include generic learning strategies such as:

- Organizing main ideas
- Planning how to complete a learning task
- Listening to information selectively
- Self-checking aural and reading comprehension,
- Planning when, where, what, and how to study
- Using reference materials
- Taking notes
- Summarizing
- Relating new learning to prior learning
- Predicting and inferring meanings
- Asking questions of teachers and peers
- Working with others in a group

Learning strategies are most effectively taught within an integrated framework of content and language learning rather than as separate or incidental learning experiences. Teachers need to create objectives for including explicit instruction of certain strategies into their thematic units. Since most students can profit from this kind of explicit skill instruction, all learners in the class will benefit.

Second, learning strategies must be taught explicitly to ELLs using the modified teaching tools that are effective with them. We must model, demonstrate, develop needed language, and provide structured practice and independent practice. We must teach the strategies needed for understanding, remembering, and applying content learning. This means that teachers identify essential skills for the learning task, create an objective, name the skill, model its use, and provide abundant practice of the skill in a variety of situations. At a later date, when introducing tasks where the skill could be used again, students can be asked to review their lists of learned strategies (these are in student notebooks or on large charts on the wall) and decide which skills are most useful in completing the task successfully.

Third, ELLs should be asked to reflect upon their learning and self-assess what they have learned, how well they have learned, and what strategies were most useful in helping them learn. Even very young students can engage in simplified forms of self-assessment. The internal reflection helps to cement the use of the skill and ensure that it will be carried over into similar learning experiences without explicit reference from the teacher. The kinds of questions that can be used for self-assessment include the following:

- What have I learned today (this week, in this unit)?
- How can I use this learning in the future? How are this knowledge and these skills important in the world outside of school?
- In what areas am I making progress?
- What do I need to improve?
- What is my goal for tomorrow (next week, the next unit)?
- What did I enjoy the most today (this week, in this unit)?

ELLs need to learn strategies that help them become better learners, such as:

- Organizing main ideas
- Planning how to complete a learning task
- Listening to information selectively
- Checking their own comprehension
- Planning when, where, and what to study

Learners also need to know how to

- Use reference materials
- Take notes
- Summarize
- Relate new learning to prior learning
- Predict and infer meanings

During class, they need to be able to

- Ask questions of the teacher and their peers
- Work with others in a group

We cannot assume ELLs have learned these essential strategies from prior educational experiences. If we want learners to use learning strategies to achieve, we have to plan for their use.

Rona Wilson begins each year with her seventh grade students by concentrating on social learning strategies of questioning, encouraging, participating, and cooperating. She plans lessons where she defines the social skill, models the skill, and then sets up situations that require her students to practice each of the skills. Rona supports the ELLs in her class by writing the language necessary to the skill on large charts that she keeps hanging on the wall.

- For stating a personal opinion she writes sentence frames on the board and encourages learners to practice specific comments: "In my opinion . . ." "It seems to me . . ." "Let's consider . . ." "My idea is . . ."
- For disagreeing agreeably, sentence frames might include: "That may be true but consider . . ." "I have a different idea . . ." "I see the problem differently . . ."

After a while, students no longer need the wall charts as they incorporate the language into their growing language systems.

There is probably nothing that we do in the classroom that is as important as challenging our students cognitively, and teaching them to learn effectively and to think clearly. These are the skills that will enable all of our students to compete successfully in school and in the world. ELLs must be included in this essential skill learning as early as possible in their language development.

A Last Word

Teaching thematically at first glance appears to be a challenging endeavor. It is at second glance as well. The level of teaching skills required to teach in this way are weighty, and we don't learn them in our first year of teaching. It is important, however, to begin to learn them early on. The way that we learned was by reading, talking to colleagues, implementing and evaluating units, asking questions when we didn't know the answers, and sharing the successes and challenges that came about as we experimented with our students.

Our first attempt at thematic teaching resulted in a file folder of notes, materials, graphic organizers, and student products. That unit was pulled out the next year and adapted to the new crop of students in the classroom. As years went by, we were able to share our materials with colleagues and expand our repertoire of units—improving them constantly. In this way, we implemented what we believe is a very valuable teaching practice with a minimum of repeated effort on our part.

At the end of this book are examples of thematic units at two different grade levels. In addition, there are many Web resources available for thematic instruction for you to explore, some of which are listed here.

We know that you have teaching days filled with expectations, and that adding this challenge to others may appear daunting. But imbedding the standards and goals that are expected into meaningful, purposeful, and interesting learning experiences will pay off powerfully for your students.

Questions for Reflection

1. Thematic units generally flow from concrete experience to visual representation and finally, to abstract learning. Consider the reasons given for this progression in the chapter.

   - Do you agree that this progression is helpful for long-term student learning?
   - Do you find this progression to be prevalent in most K to 8 classrooms that you have observed or been a part of? Why or why not?
   - Give examples of recent lessons you have seen or taught where this progression was utilized.

2. Thematic instruction in the elementary and middle school grades is similar to interdisciplinary instruction in high schools. In what ways are they the same and different? Are the benefits equal at both stages of learning?

3. This chapter suggests a variety of different organizational structures that can be used to organize a thematic unit. What about state and content standards? Are they useful tools for organizing content thematically? Why or why not?

Activities for Further Learning

1. Visit the Techtrekers web site (http://www.techtrekers.com/Thematic.htm) and locate their "10 Key Reasons" for using thematic units. Working with a partner, prioritize these reasons from the most relevant for your situation to the least relevant. Next, identify reasons that are not included on the list and add them in order of priority. Write an explanation for the top three reasons on your list.

   - Why did you choose these three?
   - Why are they important?
   - Would these reasons compel your colleagues to begin to write their own thematic units?

2. Observe several lessons in classrooms with English language learners. Were there elements of these lessons that were concrete, visual, and abstract? What were the language requirements of learners for each of these lesson phases?

   - What did students have to listen to, say, read, or write during the concrete experience phase of the lesson?

- What did students listen to, say, read, or write during the visual representation phase of the lesson?
- What did students listen to, say, read, or write during the abstract learning phase of the lesson?
- Did the language increase in grammatical complexity? Semantic complexity? Give examples.
- Did the level of vocabulary become more specific? Give examples.

3. Review the two models described for the structure of a thematic unit: Bloom's hierarchy and Mohan's knowledge framework. Compare and contrast the two models for the following:

- Progression from concrete to visual to abstract
- Progression of language from contextualized to decontextualized
- Progression of thinking skills from simple to complex
- Which model appeals to you? Why?
- What problems do you anticipate in using either of these models?

4. Choose one of the two thematic units presented at the end of this book and categorize the activities and language usage included there according to Bloom's and Mohan's models. In what ways could you improve or modify the unit?
5. Using the same thematic unit, indicate additional methods for scaffolding the learning for ELLs at a lower level of language proficiency.
6. Create a graphic organizer that structures language and content topics for a thematic unit based on language arts and social studies. Choose a grade level from PreK to 8.
7. Create a graphic organizer that structures science and math topics for a thematic unit based on language arts and social studies. Choose a grade level from PreK to 8.
8. Review the learning strategies listed in this chapter.

- Which of these strategies do you habitually use when attending this class?
- Which strategies do you use when working with colleagues?
- Which strategies are most useful for students at the grade level you teach?
- Which strategies have you taught? Which ones have you never taught?

9. Create a thematic unit. Choose one grade level and a general theme or organizing principle that will integrate content from social studies, science, math, and language arts. Use the standards of your state or district to guide you. Be sure to include scaffolding for language learners and lessons targeted to their various language needs. Determine how you will assess your students.

PEARSON
myeducationlab *Where the Classroom Comes to Life* is a collection of online tools for your success in this course, your licensure exams, and your teaching career. Go to www.myeducationlab .com to utilize these extensive resources including videos from real classrooms, Praxis and licensure preparation, a lesson plan builder, and materials to help you in your teaching career.

Suggested Reading
....

Enright, D. S. & McCloskey, M. L. (1988). *Integrating English: Developing English language and literacy in the multicultural classroom.* Reading, MA: Addison-Wesley. This book has an extensive chapter of the development of thematic units. There are also two units provided in the back of the book in specific detail and at different grade levels.

Freeman, Y. S. & Freeman, D. E. (1998). *ESL/EFL teaching: Principles for success.* Portsmouth, NH: Heinemann. The Freemans relate the theory behind thematic teaching and learning, describe whole to part teaching, learner-centered education, and meaningful, purposeful, and social literacy learning. Includes a section on thematic unit organization and offers lesson plans to show how thematic planning is accomplished.

Freeman, Y. S., Freeman, D. E., & Mercuri, S. (2002). *Closing the achievement gap: How to reach limited-formal-schooling and long-term English learners.* Portsmouth, NH: Heinemann. This more recent book contains an entire chapter dedicated to thematic units.

Morales-Jones, C. A. (2002). Curriculum design and day-to-day ESOL instruction. In H. Zainuddin, N. Yahya, C. A. Morales-Jones, and E. N. Ariza. *Fundamentals of teaching English to speakers of other languages in K–12 mainstream classrooms*, (pp. 136–170). Dubuque, IO: Kendall-Hunt. Chapter 13 provides a thorough discussion of interdisciplinary content-based thematic instruction and illustrates a variety of ways to develop these units.

Richard-Amato, P. (2003). *Making it happen: Interaction in the second language classroom from theory to practice* (3rd ed.). NY: Longman. There is a short discussion of theme cycles and a more extensive section on thematic curriculum. Four large webs are provided showing how content is related in thematic curricula in K through grade three.

Web Sites for Further Learning

A to Z Themes and Thematic Units. There is a wealth of material to explore at this site—both units and links to other resources. Retrieved May 20, 2008.

http://www.atozteacherstuff.com/themes/

CEC Lesson Plans. This site (Columbia Education Center) provides lesson plans (created by teachers) that are grouped by subject and grade level. Links are available to other resources. Retrieved May 20, 2008.

http://www.col-ed.org/cur/

School Express.Com/Home. There are over 200 thematic units offered here. Although most of them are for sale for a low fee, there are six offered free for downloading. Retrieved May 20, 2008.

http://www.schoolexpress.com/

The TeachersCorner.Net. Ignore the advertisements that are sprinkled throughout the web site, and you will find links to lesson plans, thematic units, and other teacher resources. Retrieved May 20, 2008.

www.theteacherscorner.net

Thematic Units. Some of the units found here are specifically for bilingual or ESL learners. Retrieved May 20, 2008.

http://education.wsu.edu/graduate/specializations/ell/docs

Using the Net to Create Thematic Units. This site gives definitions of thematic units, reasons for using them, a structural outline, site links for creating units, and over two pages of annotated links for locating units. You'll also find a rubric for assessing a teacher-created thematic unit. Retrieved May 20, 2008.

http://www.techtrekers.com/Thematic.htm

Web Toolboxes for Educators. This site contains many links to tools that are useful in developing lesson plans and thematic units. Retrieved May 20, 2008.

http://www.ed.sc.edu/caw/toolboxthematicunits.html

References

Agor, B. (2000). Understanding our past: The middle ages. In S. Irujo (Ed.), *Integrating the ESL standards into classroom practice: Grades 6–8.* Alexandria, VA: TESOL.

August, D. & Hakuta, K. (Eds.). (1998). *Educating language-minority children.* Washington, DC: National Academy Press.

Bloom, B., Englehart, M., Furst, E., Hill, W., & Krathwohl, D. (Eds.). (1956). *Taxonomy of educational objectives: The classification of educational goals. Handbook I: Cognitive domain.* NY: David McKay.

Dewey, J. (1916). *Democracy and education.* NY: Macmillan.

Enright, D. S. & McCloskey, M. L. (1988). *Integrating English: Developing English language and literacy in the multilingual classroom.* Reading, MA: Addison-Wesley.

Gianelli, M. (1991). Thematic units: Creating an environment for learning. *TESOL Journal, 1*(1), 13–15.

Jenkins, E. (1998). *Teaching with the brain in mind.* Alexandria, VA: Association of Supervision and Curriculum Development.

Kagan, S. (1994). *Cooperative learning.* San Clemente, CA: Kagan Cooperative Learning.

Levine, L. N. (1995). Outline of topics and skills covered in teaching ESL K–12. In *English as a second language teacher resource handbook: A practical guide for K–12 ESL programs* (2nd printing) (pp. 61–83). Thousand Oaks, CA: Corwin Press.

Mohan, B. (1986). *Language and content.* Reading, MA: Addison-Wesley.

Peregoy, S. & Boyle, O. (2001). *Reading, writing, and learning in ESL: A resource book for K–12 teachers.* NY: Addison-Wesley Longman.

Richard-Amato, P. (2003). *Making it happen: Interaction in the second language classroom from theory to practice* (3rd ed.). NY: Longman.

Ritter, N. (1999). *Teaching interdisciplinary thematic units in language arts.* Bloomington, IN: ERIC Clearinghouse on Reading English and Communication. (ERIC Identifier No. ED436003).

Robinett, R. F., Bell, P. W., Rojas, P. M., & Goldstein, N. (1970). *White horse. Miami Linguistic Readers Level 13.* Lexington, MA: D. C. Heath.

Sylvester, R. (1995). *A celebration of neurons: An educator's guide to the human brain.* Alexandria, VA: Association for Supervision and Curriculum Development.

Teachers of English to Speakers of Other Languages, Inc. (1997). *ESL standards for pre-K–12 students.* Alexandria, VA: TESOL.

Teachers of English to Speakers of Other Languages, Inc. (2006). *PreK–12 English language proficiency standards.* Alexandria, VA: TESOL.

Toppo, G. (2006, June 20). Big-city schools struggle with graduation rates. *USA Today.* http://www.usatoday.com/news/education/2006-06-20-dropout-rates_x.htm.

Willis, J. (2006). *Research-based strategies to ignite student learning.* Alexandria, VA: Association for Supervision and Curriculum Development.

Wolfe, P. (2001). *Brain matters: Translating research into classroom practice.* Alexandria, VA: Association for Supervision and Curriculum Development.

● ●

Fairy Tales: A Thematic Unit for Grades K Through 3

The Fairy Tale unit is designed for students between grades Pre-K and 3. There are a variety of standards and activities that span this grade range, and teachers can pick and choose the activities that match the needs and levels of students in their classes.

The standards included here on Table A.1 (Content Curriculum Standards: Fairy Tales, Grades K–3) may not be the same as the ones in your state's curriculum. They have been gathered from various state and national standards, and from Mid-continent Research for Education and Learning (McREL). They are typical of standards that occur in the primary elementary school levels. In a topic as general as fairy tales, there are many other subject areas that could be pursued; our choices are suggestive and related to the development of literacy and language arts.

It is hoped that teachers will use this unit as a starting point for their own development of thematic units. Many of the activities can be adapted to other topics and adjusted for language and grade levels.

Unit Summary

Fairy Tales is a content-integrated unit focusing on the development of language and literacy in young children. Of special importance in the unit is the underlying focus on good citizenship and analysis of character traits of good citizens. Another focus is the understanding of the fairy tale genre, and the elements of good literature. Additional content learning in math and science are also integrated within the unit. The Fairy Tale unit consists of ten lessons, six of which are included in this appendix. To access the rest of the unit—Lessons 7 through 10—go to MyEducationLab and select the topic *Sheltered Content Instruction*.

Focus Questions
● ●

- What are the elements of a fairy tale? How do plot, characterization, and setting contribute to literature?
- What are the characteristics of good citizens? How does the rule of law contribute to a society?

Fairy Tales Web

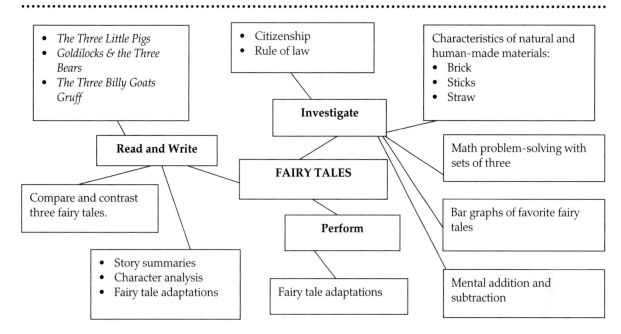

Unit References

Mid-continent Research for Education and Learning, Aurora, CO. (McREL)

http://www.mcrel.org

Fairy Tale Lesson Plan Resources

EDSITEment: Fairy Tales from Around the World. This site presents a detailed unit plan on fairy tales and lists Web resources. Retrieved May 27, 2008.

http://edsitement.neh.gov/view_lesson_plan.asp?id=387

Fairy Tale Links. Another site filled with links to lesson plans, units, and activities related to fairy tales. Some of these links will read the fairy tales aloud to students. Retrieved May 27, 2008.

http://www.manning.k12.ia.us/Elementary/onlineprojects/fairytales02/ftlinks.htm

Fairy Tale Unit. This site has many links to fairy tale lesson plans and writing activities. Retrieved May 27, 2008.

http://www.tooter4kids.com/classroom/FairyTaleUnit.htm

Fairy Tales Lesson Plans and Links K–3. The site has many fairy tale links and also ones related to folk tales. Retrieved May 27, 2008.

http://www.k-3learningpages.net/web%20fairy%20tales%20lesson%20plans.htm

Read Write Think: Fairy Tales from Life. The site presents a detailed fairy tale unit with many Web links to resource materials. Retrieved May 27, 2008.

http://www.readwritethink.org/lessons/lesson_view.asp?id=42

Welcome to Classic Fairy Tales. The site features Andersen and Grimm fairy tales as well as others from around the world. There are multiple versions of Cinderella and a wealth of Web links. Retrieved May 27, 2008.

http://webtech.kennesaw.edu/jcheek3/fairytales.htm

Table A.1 Content Curriculum Standards: Fairy Tales, Grades K–3

Content Areas	Curriculum Standards and Benchmarks

For Language Arts	• Students will use general reading strategies and skills of the reading process.
	  • Make predictions about story actions, events, and characters using prior knowledge, pictures, story structure, and topic, title, and cover.
	  • Use basic elements of phonetic analysis to decode unknown words (e.g., word families, consonant blends, digraphs, and long and short vowel patterns).
	  • Understand level-appropriate sight words and vocabulary.
	• Students will use reading skills and strategies to understand and interpret a variety of literary texts.
	  • Identify similarities in plot, setting, and character among a group of fiction works.
	  • Identify the structure and conventions of the fairy tale genre.
	  • Relate themes in works of fiction to personal experience.
	  • Distinguish cause from effect.
	• Students will use listening and speaking skills, and strategies for different purposes.
	  • Retell a main event from a story read or heard.
	  • Retell a story's beginning, middle, and end from a story read or heard.
	  • Make oral presentations that demonstrate appropriate consideration of audience, purpose, and the information to be conveyed.
	• Students will use the general skills and strategies of the writing process.
	  • Prewriting: Use strategies to plan written work (e.g., picture drawing, discussions with peers).
	  • Drafting and Revising: Use strategies to draft and revise written work (e.g., reread with a peer, rearrange elements to clarify meaning, add descriptive words).
	  • Edit and Publish: Use strategies to edit and publish (e.g., proofread with a peer, edit for punctuation and capitalization, illustrate, if appropriate).
	  • Evaluate writing (e.g., ask questions and make comments about writing, help peers to apply mechanical conventions).
	  • Write or dictate a story with a clear focus and coherent organization (e.g., beginning, middle, and end).
	• Students will use grammatical and mechanical conventions in written compositions.
	  • Write or copy a story using correct, standard English mechanics (e.g., legible printing, spaces between words, capitalization of names, beginning sentences, and appropriate end marks, such as periods and question marks).

For English as a Second Language	• Students will use English to achieve academically in all content areas.
	  • Participate in full class, group, and pair discussions.
	  • Ask and answer questions.
	  • Understand and produce technical vocabulary and text features according to content area.
	  • Use appropriate degree of formality with different audiences and settings.
	  • Use appropriate learning strategies to construct and apply academic knowledge.

For Science and Technology

- Students will demonstrate skills of scientific inquiry.
  - Ask questions based on observations of objects and events in the environment.
  - Make predictions based on observed patterns.
  - Discuss observations with others.
- Students will understand that materials both natural and human-made have specific characteristics that determine how they will be used.
  - Identify and describe characteristics of natural materials (e.g., wood, straw, and bricks).

For Social Studies/Civics

- Students will understand how character traits enhance a citizen's ability to fulfill personal responsibilities.
  - Give examples that show the meaning of the following words: fairness (justice), responsibility, rights, honesty, courage.
  - Give examples of fictional characters who are good citizens and describe the qualities that make them admirable (e.g., honesty, courage, trustworthiness).
- Students will understand the sources, functions, and purposes of law, and the importance of the rule of law for the protection of individual rights and the common good.
  - Know that a good rule or law solves a problem and is fair (promotes justice).

For Math

- Students will understand how to perform the processes of computation.
  - Add and subtract whole numbers.
  - Solve problems involving addition and subtraction of whole numbers.
- Students will represent math problems graphically, numerically, and verbally.
  - Draw pictures to represent problems.
  - Use discussions with teachers and peers to understand problems.
  - Understand whole number relationships (e.g., 3 is less than 6, 40 is 4 tens).
- Students will understand and apply concepts of data analysis.
  - Collect and represent information in simple graphs.

327

Table A.2 A Content-Integrated Unit for Grades K–3: Fairy Tales

Content Area	Lesson Phase	Activities	Scaffolds	Assessment
Language Arts	Activate Prior Knowledge	**What would you do if you came home and found a stranger in your house?** 1. Write the question on chart paper followed by the sentence starter "I would . . ." List student responses encouraging the use of "I would" through repetition and modeling. 2. Show the cover page of *Goldilocks and the Three Bears*. Ask students to predict the identity of the owners of the house and the intrusive stranger through prior knowledge, picture identification, and story title.	1. Small- and large-group brainstorming with a sentence-starter and teacher modeling. 2. Buddy talk prior to predictions.	1. Teacher observation.
Language Arts	Read and Write 1	*Goldilocks and the Three Bears* 1. Read the story making use of pictures to aid comprehension. Provide copies of the story for the children to follow along; use a big book edition or a copy on an overhead projector. 2. Compare student predictions to story events to determine accuracy. Ask questions, such as "Did Goldilocks enter the bears' house?" "Did Goldilocks eat their porridge?" "Did Goldilocks break their chairs?" "Did Goldilocks sleep in their beds?" etc. Model and encourage choral responses: "Yes, she did." 3. For beginning-level students, provide play opportunities to re-enact the story using realia and paper masks or name cards. 4. Display a pocket chart. Write the three events of the story on sentence strips. Read the strips in order and place in the pocket chart identified as the "first, second, and third" event. 5. Place students into groups of three and give each child a sentence strip. Children write one of the three events on a strip and read the strip within the small group. Next, groups place strips in the correct order in the pocket chart, responding to "What is the first event? Second event?" etc. Students read their strips aloud to the large group. 6. Literate students can write a summary of the story in their journals.	1. Point to appropriate characters and objects in pictures to increase comprehension. Provide realia, such as miniature furniture, tableware, etc. to focus and increase comprehension in story events. Encourage children to follow the print with their fingers if they are beginning literate. 2. Write and point to target questions and pictures as needed. Write and model group responses. 3. Small-group play-acting with props. 4. Ask children to retell the three events in Buddy pairs. 5. Small-group work with buddy reading and teacher prompting. 6. Pocket chart sentences provide support for journal writing.	1. Teacher observation. 2. Teacher observation. 3. Teacher observation. 4. Teacher observation. 5. Teacher observation and pocket chart responses. 6. Writing journals.

Read and Write 2	*Goldilocks and the Three Bears*	
	1. Read the story again with the children participating orally in choral responses, such as "too hot/cold/big/hard/soft/just right." Write these responses on a chart and point to them as prompts when needed.	1. Teacher observation.
	2. Model intonation, loudness, and body gestures for the three characters' stating: "Someone's been eating/sitting/sleeping in my porridge/chair/bed." Write these statements on a chart and practice with the large group and smaller groups.	2. Teacher observation.
	3. Ask WH questions for choral responses from the class: "Why didn't Goldilocks eat Papa Bear's porridge/sit in Papa Bear's chair/sleep in Papa Bear's bed?" Point to the chart and model their choral responses: "Because it was too hot/big/hard, etc." Continue for all characters.	3. Teacher observation.
	4. Display sight words "hot/cold/big/hard/soft" and teach word family and consonant blends using these five words. Use a variety of techniques, such as: • word cards manipulated by students • picture drawings of target vocabulary • word sorts of word families and rhymes • word sorts of initial and final consonant blends • masking of final or initial letters in a word • changing target consonants and blends to produce errors that can be corrected by students Expand instruction to the verbs "eating/sitting/sleeping."	4. Teacher observation of word grouping and rhyming tasks.
	5. Provide pairs of students with oak tag responses "Too hot/cold/hard/soft/big." Ask the WH questions again and tell students with the correct response to hold up their card. Continue with cards stating "Someone's been eating/sitting/sleeping, etc."	5. Teacher observation of word card responses.
	6. As a class activity, make puppets of the four main characters (toilet paper roll puppets, paper bag puppets, stick puppets, etc.). Each child can then use these puppets to call out the dialogue as the story is read to them. Later, divide students into groups of four and use the puppets to act out the story. Provide opportunities for students to watch each other perform.	6. Teacher observation of oral language structures used.

(Continued)

Table A.2 A Content-Integrated Unit for Grades K–3: Fairy Tales *(Continued)*

Content Area	Lesson Phase	Activities	Scaffolds	Assessment
	Read and Write 3	*Goldilocks and the Three Bears*		
		1. Display a graphic organizer of cause and effect. Place a picture of a rainstorm in the left side box followed by an arrow to a box on the right. Tell the students that you were in the rain yesterday. Ask "What happened as a result of standing in the rain?" Write the word "wet" in the right side box after student input. Continue with other examples and questions: "Because of the . . .?" "Due to the . . .?" Indicate that the cause of an action leads to an effect. Label the boxes "Cause" and "Effect."	1. Pictures, gestures, etc. that aid comprehension.	1. Teacher observation.
		2. Refer to the story of Goldilocks. Read the section where Goldilocks sees the bowls of porridge. Ask students to listen for the reason why she ate Baby Bear's porridge. Students talk in buddy pairs to determine the cause of Goldilocks' action. The story indicates that she was hungry. Write "hungry" in the cause box and ask students to talk about the effect of her hunger. Write "ate the porridge all up" in the effect box. Expand these boxes into complete statements, such as: "Goldilocks was hungry so she ate Baby Bear's porridge." Encourage students to tell each other the complete statement. Write the key sentence frame on the chart: "Goldilocks was _____ so she _____." Continue in this way to elicit information on the other two events in the story (tired/sat, very tired/slept). If students are at an intermediate level of language, introduce other cause and effect structures such as: "Because Goldilocks was _____ she _____" and "Goldilocks _____ because she was so _____." Students can write three of these sentences in their journals. Encourage more advanced learners to write other examples from the story.	2. Graphic organizer, buddy pairs, teacher modeling, key sentence frame, and oral language practice.	2. Teacher observation, oral language responses, and journal writing.
Civics/ Language Arts	**Investigate**	1. Use the story of Goldilocks to teach the character traits of good citizens. Reread the story of Goldilocks, asking students to listen and determine which character was breaking the law in the story. Give examples of breaking the law to aid comprehension. Ask students to talk in buddy pairs to find the answer to the question. Accept answers and encourage students to tell why they believe the character was a law breaker. Introduce the word "intruder" and define it. Ask which character in the story is an intruder. Encourage buddy talk where students decide what they would do if they found an intruder in their house.	1. Teacher examples, buddy pairs, connections to personal experience.	1. Teacher observation.

2. List the following vocabulary on a chart:

- polite
- rights
- honest
- fair

Give examples of each trait from a child's point of view. Provide pictures and play acting to aid comprehension and to relate each of the traits to the character of Goldilocks. Provide yes/no notecards or use hand signals to enable students to respond to WH questions, such as:

- Was Goldilocks polite when she entered the Bears' house?
- Was Goldilocks honest when she ate the porridge?
- Was Goldilocks being fair when she broke Baby Bear's chair?
- Did the Bears have rights that should protect them from intruders? etc.

2. Teacher examples, connections to children's lives, play acting, symbol responses, chart writing, Numbered Heads Together.

2. Teacher observation and Numbered Heads responses.

3. Remind the students of the meaning of "law" by referring to rules of the classroom and comparing those to rules in the community; e.g., laws against stealing, laws against intruding into people's homes, etc. Encourage buddy talk and list other laws that students can think of.

3. Buddy talk, connections to students' lives.

3. Teacher observation of chart responses.

4. Determine if Goldilocks was a good citizen or a bad citizen by soliciting ideas about good citizenship and listing them on a chart. Use buddy pairs or Numbered Heads Together for eliciting ideas. For example:

Good Citizen	Bad Citizen
Knocks before entering.	Intrudes.
Asks before taking things.	Steals.
Asks for permission.	Does not ask.
Obeys the law.	Does not obey.

Next, list the things that Goldilocks did to show she was a bad citizen and how she did not obey the law. Allow students opportunities to talk in buddy groups or use Numbered Heads Together to elicit ideas from small groups.

Ask students to complete the sentence frame in their journals: "I am a good citizen because_____." Provide chart paper lists to assist the writing.

4. Chart paper lists and vocabulary.

4. Journal entries.

5. Chart paper lists.

5. Journal writing.

(Continued)

Table A.2 A Content-Integrated Unit for Grades K–3: Fairy Tales   *(Continued)*

Content Area	Lesson Phase	Activities	Scaffolds	Assessment
Language Arts	Read and Write 4	1. Reinforce student knowledge of the writing process by supporting the writing of a summary of the Goldilocks story with a clear Beginning, Middle, and End. Depending on the level of the student, provide scaffolding of the following types: • Cloze summaries of a three-paragraph story that eliminate the names of the characters and some of the target vocabulary. • Outlines of the story with key sentence frames intact. • Question guidelines that lead to the chronological story structure. • Story web graphic organizer that corresponds to the appropriate number of main events in the story and provides signal words of chronology.	1. Cloze summaries, outlines, guided questions, graphic organizer, and key sentence frames.	1. Teacher observation of student literacy level.
		2. Assist students in the Prewriting phase by suggesting that they draw pictures of the events in the story and confer with buddy pairs. More limited students may need to have pictures provided for them, with word balloons filled in with target language. Other students will benefit from completing a graphic organizer together with the teacher, reinforcing the target language and signal words orally.	2. Pictures, word bubbles, buddy pairs, teacher-led completion of a graphic organizer.	2. Teacher observation.
		3. The Drafting, Revising, and Editing phases of the writing process can be done in buddy pairs or done one on one with the teacher. Other students may choose to work in small groups, reading their pieces aloud and editing with assistance from the group. Teach targeted mechanics (capitalization of names and beginning sentences, appropriate end marks, spaces between words, and legible printing) using visual clues if necessary, e.g., stop sign for periods and a red marker for capital letters.	3. Teacher assistance, buddy pairs or small groups, visual clues for targeted mechanics.	3. Teacher observation and checklist of targeted mechanics.
		4. Publishing the stories on the class Fairy Tale bulletin board or reading with another class will complete the phases of the writing process.	4. Bulletin board display or peer reading.	4. Final written summaries.

Math/ Language Arts	**Investigate**	1. Use the story of Goldilocks to reinforce addition and subtraction of sets of three. Use Cuisenaire rods or other manipulatives to direct students to add: • Three bears and three more bears, etc.	1. Cuisenaire rods or other manipulatives.	1. Teacher observation.
		2. Show students how to count the total number of bears. Show on the OHP how to represent the problem in numerals. Provide other directed problems using vocabulary from the story (bowls of porridge, chairs, beds, etc.). Encourage more advanced students to give directions to the class or to small groups.	2. Counting objects, OHP.	2. Math addition sheet.
		3. Next, direct students to count three bowls of porridge and take away the one that Goldilocks ate. Show how to represent numerically on the OHP. Use signal words of addition and subtraction throughout the activities.	3. Counting objects, OHP.	3. Math subtraction sheet.
		4. Provide word problems on large chart paper or the OHP that use the same language used in the addition/subtraction practice. For example: • The Bear family had three bowls of porridge. Goldilocks ate one bowl. How many bowls did they have left? • The Bear family had three chairs. Goldilocks broke one. How many more chairs did the Bears need to buy? • The Bear family had three chairs and three beds. How many pieces of furniture did they have in all? Use picture clues or realia if necessary to aid in comprehension. Encourage students to draw pictures of the problems to help in understanding the solution. Lastly, show how to represent the problems numerically.	4. Written problems, pictures or realia, drawings, OHP.	4. Three Bears problem sheet.
		5. Encourage more advanced learners to work together to create other problems for the class.	5. Small-group or buddy-pair work.	5. Student-generated problems.
Language Arts	**Activate Prior Knowledge**	**What can the goats do when the troll threatens their life?** 1. Introduce a second fairy tale, *The Three Billy Goats Gruff*. Show pictures on the cover and inside the book to identify the four major characters. Identify the troll as a monster who is threatening the goats' lives. Refer to the motivational question on the board. Ask students to talk in buddy pairs to determine an answer and list these on the chart.	1. Pictures, buddy talk.	1. Teacher observation of charted responses.

(Continued)

Table A.2 A Content-Integrated Unit for Grades K–3: Fairy Tales *(Continued)*

Content Area	Lesson Phase	Activities	Scaffolds	Assessment
	Read and Write 5	*The Three Billy Goats Gruff*		
		1. Read the story, making use of pictures to aid comprehension. Provide copies of the story for the children to follow along, use a big book edition, or show a copy on an overhead projector.	1. Pictures, guided reading copies of the story.	1. Teacher observation.
		2. Compare student predictions to story events to determine accuracy. Ask questions such as "Did the troll eat the youngest Billy Goat Gruff?" "Did the troll eat the second Billy Goat Gruff?" "Did the troll eat the biggest Billy Goat Gruff?" Model and encourage choral responses: "No, he didn't."	2. Key phrase written on chart.	2. Teacher observation.
		3. For beginning-level students, provide play opportunities to re-enact the story using realia and paper masks or name cards.	3. Play acting with realia.	3. Teacher observation.
		4. Display pictures of the three goats sized from smallest to largest in a pocket chart. Number the goats "no. 1," "no. 2," and "no. 3." Ask students to signal which is the smallest, middle-sized, and largest goat.	4. Pictures, signal responses, target vocabulary written on the board.	4. Teacher observation of signal and auditory responses.
		5. Next ask students to signal which is the youngest, middle-aged, and oldest goat.	5. Pictures, signal responses, target vocabulary written on the board.	5. Teacher observation of signal and auditory responses.
		6. Write the three events of the story on sentence strips. Read the strips in order and place in the pocket chart identified as the "first, second, and third" event. Read the events as a class.	6. Sentence strips and large-group reading.	6. Teacher observation.
		7. Place students into groups of three and give each child a sentence strip. Children write one of the three events on a strip and read the strip within the small group. Next, groups place strips in the correct order in the pocket chart, responding to "What is the first event? Second event? etc." Students read their strips aloud to the large group.	7. Small-group work, pocket chart model.	7. Teacher observation of placement of strips and reading of strips.
		8. Literate students can write a summary of the story in their journals. Non-literate students can draw pictures of the three events with the sentence strip labels beneath.	8. Pocket chart strips, pictures.	8. Student journals.

Read and Write 6	1. Read the story again with the children participating orally in choral responses, such as "It is I, the smallest/middle-sized/biggest Billy Goat Gruff." Write these responses on a chart and point to them as prompts when needed. Model intonation and volume of the three goats so that volume increases with size and age.	1. Large-group responses prompted by pointing to writing on a chart.	1. Teacher observation.
	2. Model intonation, loudness, and body gestures for the three characters' dialogue: "Who's that tripping over my bridge? I'm going to gobble you up." and "Don't eat me, I'm too little. Wait until the second/third Billy Goat Gruff comes. He's much bigger." Write these statements on a chart next to the appropriate pictures and practice with the large group and smaller groups.	2. Teacher modeling, chart writing, pictures, and small- and large-group practice.	2. Teacher observation.
	3. Ask WH questions for choral responses from the class: "Why didn't the troll eat the smallest/youngest/middle-sized, largest/middle-aged/oldest Billy Goat Gruff?" Point to the chart and model their choral responses: "Because he was too small/large, etc." Continue for all the characters.	3. Group choral response, chart-writing and teacher-modeling.	3. Teacher observation.
	4. Display sight words "troll/bridge/goat/small/big/large" and teach word family, vowel and consonant blends using these five words. Use a variety of techniques, such as: • word cards manipulated by students • picture drawings of target vocabulary • word sorts of word families and rhymes • word sorts of initial and final consonant blends • masking of final or initial letters in a word • changing target consonants and blends to produce errors that can be corrected by students Expand instruction to the verbs "tripping, coming, crossing."	4. Pictures, drawings, word cards, small-group and buddy-pair analysis.	4. Teacher observation of word-grouping and rhyming tasks.
	5. Provide pairs of students with oak tag responses: "too small/young/old/big/large." Ask the WH questions again and tell students with the correct response to hold up their cards.	5. Buddy pairs, written responses.	5. Teacher observation of word card responses.
	6. Next, assign roles to buddy-pair groups. Each pair is given a card identifying them as one of the goats or the troll. Display pocket card strips with dialogue such as: "Who's that tripping over my bridge?" and "It is only I, the smallest/middle-sized/biggest Billy Goat Gruff." As you display (and read) the dialogue, students who have that character's card should signal the character talking. More literate students can take over the role of reading the pocket chart dialogues.	6. Pocket card sentences and character cards, perhaps with pictures, buddy pairs.	6. Teacher observation of signal responses.

(Continued)

Table A.2 A Content-Integrated Unit for Grades K–3: Fairy Tales *(Continued)*

Content Area	Lesson Phase	Activities	Scaffolds	Assessment
		7. As a class activity, make puppets of the four main characters (using toilet paper roll puppets, paper bag puppets, stick puppets, etc.). Each child can then use these puppets to call out the dialogue as the story is read to them. Later, divide students into groups of four and use the puppets to act out the story. Provide opportunities for students to watch each other perform.	7. Puppets and small-group play-acting.	7. Teacher observation of oral language structures used.
Civics/ Language Arts	Investigate	1. Recall the story of Goldilocks and ask if Goldilocks was a good citizen in the story. Students may signal their responses as "thumbs up/down." Use buddy talk to determine why she was not a good citizen. Write comments on a chart, modeling and repeating to promote grammatical responses.	1. Signal responses, buddy talk, teacher prompting, and charting.	1. Teacher observation.
		2. Isolate any comments using the target vocabulary "fair" and "rights." Model these words within the context of the story. "It wasn't fair for Goldilocks to break Baby Bear's chair." "The Bear family has the right to keep out intruders."	2. Teacher modeling and repetition.	2. Teacher observation.
		3. Return to the story of the Billy Goats Gruff and ask if the goats have rights? Students can signal with thumbs up/down. Ask for buddy talk to determine if the troll was fair in threatening to eat the goats. Record responses as above.	3. Signals, buddy talk, teacher prompting, and charting.	3. Teacher observation.
		4. Refer to the list of characteristics of a Good Citizen and add the word "courage." Give examples of courage from a child's point of view. Show pictures of community members known for courage (police officers, firefighters, soldiers, etc.) Talk in buddy groups as to why these people show courage. Choose one character or community member in each buddy team. Draw a picture and write a sentence showing the person has courage.	4. Teacher examples, pictures, buddy pairs, drawings.	4. Teacher observation of buddy talk and final drawings.
		5. Determine which characters in Billy Goats Gruff show courage by a show of hands.	5. Group response.	5. Teacher observation.

Ocean Connections: A Thematic Unit for Grades 4 Through 8

The Oceans unit is designed for students between grades 4 and 8 (Table B2: A Content Integrated Unit for Grades 4–8 Ocean Connections). There are a variety of objectives and activities that span this grade range; teachers can pick and choose the activities that match the needs and levels of students in their classes.

The standards mentioned here (Table B1: Content Curriculum Standards, Ocean Connections Grades 4–8) may not be the same as the ones in your state curriculum. They have been gathered from various state and national standards and from McREL (Mid-continent Research for Education and Learning). They are typical of ones that occur in the intermediate and middle school levels. In a topic as general as Oceans, there are many other subject areas that could be pursued; our choices are suggestive and related to the theme of connections.

It is hoped that teachers will use this unit as a starting point for their own development of thematic units. Many of the activities can be adapted to other topics and adjusted for language and grade levels.

Unit Summary

Exploring the Oceans is a study of the dynamic interactions of living and non-living things in relation to the oceans. Of special importance in the unit are the various ocean ecosystems, their populations, interrelationships, and diversity. Another focus is the usefulness of oceans and the connections of humans to oceans for exploration and survival.

Focus Questions

- How do oceans contribute to human life? What connections exist between human activity and the oceans?
- What is an ecosystem? What are the interactions between biotic and abiotic elements in an ecosystem? How do these interactions support ocean survival?

Ocean Connections Web
....

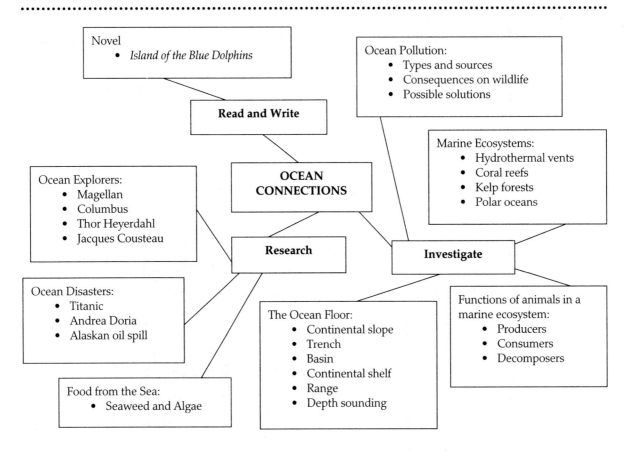

Novel
- *Island of the Blue Dolphins*

Read and Write

Ocean Pollution:
- Types and sources
- Consequences on wildlife
- Possible solutions

Marine Ecosystems:
- Hydrothermal vents
- Coral reefs
- Kelp forests
- Polar oceans

OCEAN CONNECTIONS

Ocean Explorers:
- Magellan
- Columbus
- Thor Heyerdahl
- Jacques Cousteau

Research

Investigate

Ocean Disasters:
- Titanic
- Andrea Doria
- Alaskan oil spill

The Ocean Floor:
- Continental slope
- Trench
- Basin
- Continental shelf
- Range
- Depth sounding

Functions of animals in a marine ecosystem:
- Producers
- Consumers
- Decomposers

Food from the Sea:
- Seaweed and Algae

Table B.1 Content Curriculum Standards: Ocean Connections, Grades 4–8

Content Areas	Curriculum Standards and Benchmarks

For Language Arts	• Students will use listening and speaking strategies for different purposes.
	  • Make oral presentations to the class (e.g., use notes and outlines; use organizational schema; include introduction, body, transitions, conclusions; use evidence to support opinions; use visual media).
	• Students will use general reading strategies and skills of the reading process.
	  • Use a variety of strategies to extend reading vocabulary (e.g., use definition, restatement, example, compare and contrast to verify word meanings).
	  • Use specific strategies to clear up confusing parts of a text (e.g., pause, reread the text, represent abstract information as mental pictures, draw upon background knowledge, explain concepts to a peer).
	• Students will use reading skills and strategies to understand and interpret a variety of informational texts, reference materials, electronic databases, and web sites.
	  • Summarize and paraphrase information in texts (e.g., arrange information in chronological or sequential order; convey main ideas, critical details, and underlying meaning).
	• Students will use reading skills and strategies to understand and interpret a variety of literary texts.
	  • Make inferences and draw conclusions about story elements (e.g., main and subordinate events; setting; theme; missing details).
	• Students will use the general skills and strategies of the writing process.
	  • Prewriting: Use a variety of prewriting strategies (e.g., make outlines, use published models, brainstorm, build background knowledge).
	  • Drafting and Revising: Use a variety of strategies to draft and revise written work (e.g., use an organizational scheme, rethink and rewrite for different audiences and purposes).
	  • Write expository compositions (e.g., state a purpose, present information that demonstrates knowledge about the topic of the report, organize and present information in a logical manner, use common expository features such as compare-contrast or problem-solution).
	  • Write in response to literature (e.g., respond to significant issues in a log or journal, ask questions, make connections).

For ESL Goals and Standards	• Students will use English to achieve academically in all content areas.
	  • To interact in the classroom.
	  • To obtain, process, construct, and provide subject matter information in spoken and written form.
	  • To use appropriate learning strategies to construct and apply academic knowledge.

For Science and Technology	• Students will demonstrate an ability to pursue science as inquiry.
	  • Use appropriate tools and techniques to gather, analyze, and interpret data.
	  • Think critically and logically to make the relationships between evidence and explanation.
	  • Communicate scientific procedures and explanations.
	• Students will demonstrate understanding of the diversity of organisms in an ecosystem.
	  • Explore a natural setting to locate diverse elements.
	• Adaptation and diversity occur as naturally occurring variations in populations.
	  • Draw inferences from investigations and confirm predictions through reading.

For Social Studies	• Students will demonstrate an understanding of the aims, obstacles, and accomplishments of early ocean explorers. • Interview an explorer to learn about his/her contributions to our knowledge of oceans.

For Math	• Students will represent situations numerically, verbally, and graphically.
	  • Determine volume of a rectangular solid.
	  • Create word problems related to the population of an ecosystem.
	  • Create scale models of organisms.
	• Students will develop graphs to describe situations.
	  • Create a graph to replicate the ocean floor.

Table B.2 A Content Integrated Unit for Grades 4–8: Ocean Connections

Unit		Activities	Scaffolds	Assessment
Science/ Math	Activate Prior Knowledge	**What Is an Ecosystem?** 1. Prepare the classroom with books, pictures, and other resources. Students browse among the materials for 15 minutes. 2. Display pictures of 4 *biomes*: coral reef, polar ocean, kelp forest, and hydrothermal vent. Each of these is an *ecosystem*. Brainstorm the meaning of ecosystem within small groups. 3. Report small-group findings. 4. Introduce notion of ecosystem as a *community* containing specific *populations* of organisms.	1. Provide many colorful pictures. 2. Small-group brainstorming with roles assigned. 3. Make analogies to human communities and populations. 4. Pair talk: students define the new vocabulary orally, then write a definition in journals.	1. Teacher observation. 2. Brainstorm maps. 3. Students give examples of *ecosystem, community,* and *population* from classroom pictures. 4. Journal definitions.
Science/ Language Arts	Investigate	**In What Ways Do Diversity and Adaptation Affect an Ecosystem?** 1. Take students for a walk through an unmanaged area of the school or local woodland. Students are to collect as many different kinds of leaves as possible. They should also take note of wildlife and sketch insect life. 2. Students sort the leaves into separate groupings and report on the numbers of different leaves found (*diversity* occurs when an ecosystem is composed of many different organisms). 3. Students return to the same area and each student collects one leaf of the most commonly occurring species. Compare the leaves and note the differences that occur within the species (*adaptation* occurs when ecosystems display diversity within a species) (Herzog, 2003). 4. Students predict reasons why ecosystems flourish with diversity and adaptation within species. Report to large group. Provide a textbook reading to support or discount students predictions.	1. Pair students to ensure that all understand directions. 2. Suggest categories for sorting and supply examples: size, color, texture, notches, etc. Ask various students to describe orally each of the different leaf groupings using these categories. 3. Use small groups for the sorting and comparison tasks. Comparisons may require a key sentence frame: "The ___ leaf is ___er than the ___ leaf." "The ___ leaf is the ___est." 4. Use reciprocal reading techniques in small groups.	1. Teacher observation. 2. Journal descriptions of various species. 3. Journal comparison sentences. 4. Homework in journals: How do diversity and adaptation help an ecosystem flourish?

Investigate	**How Do Organisms Within an Ecosystem Find Food?**		
		1. Remind students of the park ecosystem they have explored. List all of the food available in that ecosystem. Create a chart and sort the food under one of three columns: "producer," "consumer," and "decomposer." Provide examples of each of the three terms in other ecosystems including human ones.	1. Encourage students to create the three-column chart in their journals. Challenge students to describe an organism named by the teacher as one of the three categories. Tell why. Students add new vocabulary to journals, perhaps with pictures and native language equivalents of examples.
			1. Comprehension questioning of many/all students' journals.
		2. All organisms within an ecosystem are connected in *food chains* or *webs.* Pair students and direct them to create a food web for the following: "cat, caterpillar, corn, bacteria, cow, crow, deer, hawk, human, lettuce, mouse, fox, grass, and rabbit." Pairs share their food webs with other students explaining their choices (BC Education).	2. Create a sample food chain for students to use as a model.
			2. Student-made food chains.
		3. Students predict which group will be found in greatest numbers in an ecosystem: "producers," "consumers," or "decomposers." Give reasons why.	3. Provide time for Pair Talk and then use pinpoint questioning to help students explain their reasoning.
			3. Teacher observation.
Science/ Math/ Language Arts	**Investigate**	**What Can We Learn About the Ecosystems in the Ocean?**	
		1. Students are assigned to four groups. Each group will work on the following simulation activity (RAFT): "Your team has been appointed by the museum curator to prepare an exhibit for the museum about an ocean ecosystem. The exhibit you prepare will be presented by your team to invited guests at the end of the unit. Your exhibit will include: • An illustration or model of the ecosystem • Biotic and abiotic elements • A food chain showing relationships • A description of how humans impact the ecosystem • A chart listing important information such as location of the ecosystem, water temperatures, amount of sunlight, and population density • A five-minute talk by each team member describing important elements of one organism in the ecosystem	1. Create heterogeneous groups and assign roles to each group member so that there is positive interdependence in each group. Use cooperative learning strategies to prevent one student from dominating the group (Talking Chips, Talking Tokens, etc.). Teach cooperative language, e.g., how to make suggestions, agree, disagree, and praise.
			1. Provide a group dynamics self-assessment scale for each team on a daily basis. Teacher observation. Provide a rubric for students to self-assess their exhibit at the beginning of the project.

(Continued)

Table B.2 A Content Integrated Unit for Grades 4–8: Ocean Connections   *(Continued)*

Unit	Activities	Scaffolds	Assessment
	2. Help students to locate the four ecosystems on a map or globe: • Coral reef (Great Barrier Reef, Australia) • Polar ocean (the Weddell Sea, Antarctica) • Kelp Forest (Monterey Bay, CA, U.S.) • Hydrothermal Vent (Mid-Atlantic Ridge)	2. Drawing maps and color-coding them will help students achieve a sense of the geography of the ocean regions.	2. Student maps.
	3. Help the class to think about what they already know about these ecosystems. Use a K-W-L chart to collect known information about each ecosystem. Next, each group creates questions for the W column on the chart ("What I Want to Know"). These questions can guide the group's research.	3. Provide students with one-page K-W-L charts so they can create individualized charts.	3. Completed K-W-L questions.
	4. Play the card game (from Sea Connections at the Ocean Planet web site) to help students identify species and explain their connections in a food web. The game also provides clues as to how humans affect ocean ecosystems.	4. Teach card game rules with printed directions. Model one game with three selected students. Monitor the play to determine if students are cooperating and using the target language.	4. Self-assessment on game playing.
Science/ Math/ Language Arts	**Investigate** 1. Provide resource materials (pictures, texts, web sites, newspaper articles, magazines, etc.) to help students begin to locate the organisms in their ecosystem. Identify each as *producers, consumers,* or *decomposers* (some will have multiple roles).	1. View films of the ecosystems if possible. Resource materials need to be available for many different reading levels.	1. Journals with notes.
	2. Teach students to write a five-minute description of an organism including: introduction, body, transition words, conclusions, and evidence to support opinions.	2. Work with learners who need help on locating individual species. Identify an appropriate graphic organizer to assist in note-taking and summary description.	2. Completed graphic organizers and/or written summaries.
	3. Encourage student groups to create an aquarium model of their ecosystem using shoe boxes or other cardboard boxes. Students may also want to use acrylic sheets to simulate a glass aquarium. Determine the appropriate animals to include.	3. The aquarium project will generate useful language. Identify step-by-step procedures on a chart or graphic organizer. Assign specific roles for the project. Teach measurement terms (inch, foot, yard, etc.) for students used to metric measurement.	3. Self-assessment scale for project work.

Science/ Math **Investigate**

4. Teach students to calculate the volume of their aquariums and apply Spotte's rule for population density—no more than one linear inch of animal for every 6 gallons of water (Spotte, 1979). If volume calculation is new for the class, help students generate word problems based upon the topic and aquariums. Share these problems with other group members to solve.

5. Teach students to draw fish to scale for their aquariums using rulers and graph paper.

6. Provide poster boards and space in the classroom to assemble the museum exhibit and teach students to write letters inviting other classes, parents, and teachers to the final exhibition.

7. Teach standards for oral presentations. Practice the use of supporting devices: notes and outlines; organizational schema; and visual supports.

8. Inviting parents will help them to feel included in the classroom community. Provide simple snacks to create a community atmosphere.

How Can We See the Ocean Floor?

1. Use an illustration of a side-view of the ocean floor. Copy onto large chart paper or OHP and label the various elevations: "continental shelf," "continental slope," "basin," "trench," and "range."

2. Ask students to brainstorm answers to the focus question: How can we see the ocean floor? Write the answers on a web.

3. Explain that another method of "seeing" the ocean floor is through *depth sounding* measurement. Students will replicate the ocean floor in shoe boxes with paper maché land forms (Nevison, 1999). Pair students and tell them to use their journal drawings to create a similar ocean floor. When the paper maché is almost dry tell students to punch eight holes evenly spaced down the length of the shoebox. Replace the lid on the box.

---

4. Provide a prototype of a word problem for language learners to use as a model.

5. Use manipulatives to demo the concept of scale. Model the activity, practice sample drawing with the entire class, working in pairs before individual drawings.

6. Help students use a formal letter format and language for the invitations.

7. Pair students to practice their speeches before final presentation.

1. Students create their own drawings in their journals and label them. Check understanding of vocabulary at a later date with a semantic gradient. Students arrange the five terms from Shallow to Deep.

2. Explicate/illustrate unknown terminology (sonar, submarine, etc.)

3. Provide printed step-by-step directions and a model for students to replicate.

---

4. Word problems.

5. Scaled drawings.

6. Letters of invitation.

7. Rubric assessment of oral presentations.

1. Journals.

2. Student responses.

3. Teacher observation and completed shoe boxes.

(Continued)

343

Table B.2 A Content Integrated Unit for Grades 4–8: Ocean Connections *(Continued)*

Unit	Activities	Scaffolds	Assessment
	4. Using graph paper, students number the horizontal axis from 1 to 8. The vertical axis is numbered from 1 to 25 (measurements in cm). Provide dowels for students to insert in the eight holes until they hit the bottom of the paper maché land form. Mark the dowel, measure it, and mark the graph with a dot to indicate the depth. Continue with all eight holes and connect the dots to show a visual of the slope of the ocean floor. Label the parts of the graph.	4. Demonstrate the method for creating a graph. Use appropriate terminology throughout (*axis, horizontal, vertical,* etc.).	4. Completed graphs.
	5. The best use of this experiment is teaching a student from another class about the ocean floor without opening the shoe box to see it. Students help grade-mates to measure with dowels and create graphs in the same way that oceanographers create "soundings" of the ocean floor.	5. Practice giving directions before helping a grade-mate to measure your ocean floor shoebox.	5. Provide a rubric for assessing the activity before you begin. Observe students working in small groups. Ask questions requiring use of the new vocabulary.
Science/ Language Arts	**What Are the Causes and Consequences of Ocean Pollution?** (A lesson adapted from the web sites Ocean Planet: Pollution Solution and Howard, 2008)		
Investigate	1. Pair students to brainstorm answers to the focus question. Set a requirement of four causes per pair. Collect responses on a chart paper web. Indicate that some of the answers are correct, some are not correct, and some answers are missing.	1. Float around the room offering suggestions when students are "stuck." Model causation language: "Pollution is caused by___ is due to __, results in __."	1. Teacher observation.
	2. Give students a reading explaining the causes and a two-column chart labeled: "Pollution Causes" and "Pollution Cleaners." Students are to read the text to determine causes and cleaning agents for oil pollution. (See Pollution Solution at the Ocean Planet web site for a two-page reading.) Report results to the class and complete the chart on OHP.	2. Suggest that student pairs read aloud in quiet voices to assist limited readers. Provide highlighters to identify answers in the text. Both students highlight and record answers on charts. Individual students correct and complete charts for their journals. Provide key sentence frames for causation language on chalkboard. Encourage all students to use this grammar.	2. Completed charts.

3. Conduct an experiment to analyze the results of oil spills. (See Pollution Solution Lesson Plan, Step 2, for an alternate plan.) Pairs of students are supplied with an aluminum pie pan, medicine dropper of used motor oil, cotton balls, nylon, string, paper towels, liquid detergent, and feathers.

- Provide a lab sheet for students to record "What I Did," "What I Saw," and "What I Learned." Tell each team to place five drops of oil in the "ocean" (pan half filled with water).
- Observe the spill. Loop a piece of string around the spill and measure the length of string. Wait a minute and repeat. Record observations.
- Blow on the oil spill. Observe and record results.
- Shake the pan to create wave action. Observe and record results.
- Predict which material will clean up the spill the best. Use each and record the results.
- Dip a feather in the oil. Try to clean the feather at the sink with detergent. Record results.
- Add five drops of liquid detergent (*dispersant*) to the oil. Observe and record results.

4. In a follow-up discussion, ask student pairs to summarize their findings. Ask about implications for ocean clean-up, and the resulting damage to animal and human populations. Students summarize the results of this discussion in journals.

---

3. Model the experiment procedures and the recording of results on the lab sheet. Indicate whether recording of results is to be in complete sentences. If so, model possible "results" language on the chalkboard, e.g.,

- "The oil spill (increased, decreased) in size from ___ in. to ___ in. after one minute."
- "Wind action (increased, decreased) spread of the oil."
- "Liquid detergent was (not) successful in cleaning the feathers."
- "Liquid detergent was (successful, unsuccessful) in cleaning up the oil."

4. Students can use lab reports to help summarize their findings.

When talking about implications for the future, model "If . . . , then . . ." language forms. "If oil pollutes the ocean waters, then damage to marine life will occur." "If marine life is killed, then . . ." "If fish die off, then . . ." Provide a key sentence frame if you ask students to summarize this discussion in their journals.

---

3. Completed lab sheets.

4. Journal summaries.

(Continued)

Table B.2 A Content Integrated Unit for Grades 4–8: Ocean Connections *(Continued)*

Unit	Activities	Scaffolds	Assessment
Science/ Language Arts Research	**How Does the Ocean Contribute to the Human Diet?** (A lesson adapted from Ocean Planet: There Are Algae in Your House! web site.) 1. Students working in small groups create semantic webs indicating all of the food products that come from the oceans. Report back to the class to determine a listing. 2. Tell students they have left some important products off the list: cheese, chocolate milk, peanut butter, pudding, frozen desserts, fruit drinks. Ask if anyone can tell what all these products have in common. Tell students they all contain *sea weed*, a *marine algae* found in coastal waters. 3. Provide a text reading (You can use the background page on the Ocean Planet web site.) that describes the three kinds of algae: *alginate* (brown), *carrageenan* (red), and *beta carotene* (green). Give students a graphic organizer (web) to collect information while reading on three kinds of algae and how they are used in food products (as *stabilizers*, *thickeners*, and *colorants*). 4. Students will conduct a scavenger hunt for food products in their homes to find products containing the three forms of algae. Give each student a worksheet listing possible foods containing algae (see listing in Ocean Planet lesson plan no.1: There Are Algae in Your House). Show students how to find the information on the nutrition label of each product.	1. For more individual involvement, require each student to complete a web while brainstorming in a small group. 2. Produce pictures of these foods or actual products for clearer communication. Also, find pictures of red, brown, and green algae; or find examples of dried, edible seaweed sold in Asian markets. 3. The reading in Ocean Planet is filled with technical language. You can read this aloud and ask students to highlight the important facts. After reading, ask students to work in pairs to place the facts on the organizer. 4. Some of the food names may be unknown to students. They can search boxes and containers in their homes—foods with which they are familiar. Another option is to bring empty food containers into the classroom and help students to find the algae on the food cartons in class.	1. Completed webs. 2. Pinpoint questioning will help students to communicate their understanding that seaweed can be found in common food products. 3. Graphic organizer. Use the Paired Verbal Fluency structure to help students summarize the information orally. Teacher observation. 4. Completed worksheets.
Social Studies/ Language Arts Research	**How Did Ocean Explorers of the Past Use the Ocean to Contribute to Human Life?** 1. Draw an enlarged version of a world map on the bulletin board. If students have not already done so, involve them in coloring and labeling the five oceans. Use this map to refer to when discussing ocean explorers and tracing exploration routes.	1. Refer students to small maps to help with location and labeling.	1. Completed map.

		2. Use a K-W-L chart to help activate what students already know about ocean explorers. Magellan and Columbus should be part of their knowledge base but perhaps Thor Heyerdahl and Jacques Cousteau, among others, are not. Encourage students to choose any four ocean explorers to determine the answer to the focus question.	2. Provide small K-W-L charts where students can copy the information from the large class version.	2. K-W-L chart stapled into journal.
		3. Divide students into four heterogeneous groups and present them with the following task (RAFT): "You are a TV news crew about to interview a famous explorer. Your job requires you to research important facts about the explorer, prepare questions to ask him, and conduct an 'on camera' interview. After the interview, you will turn in your question list and the 5W charts with your collected research." If video cameras are available, ask each group to assign a camera person to record the interviews and present these on Parent's Night.	3. Assign roles to each group (researchers, questioners, TV news-persons, the explorer, camera operator, prop coordinator, prompter, etc.). Each student will need a 5W chart labeled "Who, What, When, Where, and Why" above each column. Provide models of the kinds of questions the teams can ask. Involve all students in question formation and assign many newspersons to ask the questions.	3. Provide students with a rubric prior to the assignment. The rubric should assess the information gathered as well as oral presentation skills and question quality.
			4. Prior to the discussion, pair students and ask them to write down at least four kinds of contributions. Use these lists to help all students participate in the discussion.	
		4. After the News Program, conduct a follow-up discussion on how the oceans contributed to human knowledge, skills, and wealth.		4. Participation in group discussion.
Social Studies/ Language Arts	Research	**In What Ways Has the Ocean Contributed to Human Disasters?** 1. Use this focus question to determine prior knowledge of students. Record their responses on a 5W chart. Students should be familiar with the Titanic sinking but may be unfamiliar with the sinking of the Andrea Doria, the 1989 Exxon Valdez oil spill in Prince Edward Sound, Hurricane Andrew in 1992 in Florida, attacks by great white sharks off the California coast, and many others.	1. Provide students with blank 5W charts with which to copy information from the class chart. Use Think-Pair-Share to generate student thought and increase contributions.	1. Completed 5W charts.

(Continued)

347

Table B.2 A Content Integrated Unit for Grades 4–8: Ocean Connections *(Continued)*

Unit		Activities	Scaffolds	Assessment
		2. Pair students and tell them to use their 5W questions to create a newspaper story about one disaster. If students are unfamiliar with the structure of a news story, use this opportunity to teach them that the 5W questions are answered in the first paragraph; the following paragraphs supply supplemental information in diminishing order of importance and interest.	2. Both partners research the same disaster and complete their charts together. Encourage students to use many sources at varying levels of readability as well as online sources. Provide students with a model newspaper story and an outline structure to use when organizing the story. Language learners can tell their stories to classmates as preparation for writing. Encourage groups to involve all students in the project, either as writers, artists, or presenters.	2. Completed outlines, stories, and 5W charts.
		3. After completing the stories, ask students to conduct a discussion in small groups. They are to list the benefits of oceans to human knowledge and survival. Next, students are to prioritize the Top Ten Ocean Benefits and present their lists in chart form to the class.	3. If students do not have the social skills to prioritize, teach/model a technique for coming to agreement (raising hands, taking a vote, etc.).	3. Provide a rubric for the cooperative effort during the group work and for the final presentation.
Language Arts	Read and Write	*Island of the Blue Dolphins*, by Scott O'Dell, is a classic novel of historical fiction. There are many opportunities for extending the novel into content-area learning: history of the Chumash Indians, history of the Aleuts, and history of the early Spanish missions. Themes that teachers have used to explore the text include: the role of women, the topic of loneliness, culture clash, and survival. At the end of this unit are references to many lesson plans and units that describe a variety of ways to teach the book. In this unit, we will explore the connections that exist between Karana, the 12-year-old Indian girl isolated on San Nicholas Island in the mid-1800s and the ecology of the marine environment surrounding the island. Students will be asked to explore the connections in the marine ecosystem and the connections with the humans who are in contact with that environment. The setting of the novel (time and place) is the focus of this unit.		

Activate Prior Knowledge	**How Could You Survive?**	
	1. Place students into small groups and ask them to imagine that they have been abandoned on a small island in the middle of the ocean. They need to find ways to survive for many years all alone. Ask students to list the top ten items that they will search for on the island to help them survive. They have come to this place with no equipment at all.	1. Provide a worksheet divided into two parts: (a) survival needs, and (b) sources. All students in the group agree on what to include on the list. Place a chart on the wall with "agreement language" and practice using this language before group work begins: • *"I'd like to add . . ."* • *"How about . . ."* • *"Good idea. Here's another suggestion . . ."* • *"Is that the most important . . .?"* • *"I don't agree. My thinking is . . ."*
		1. Top ten lists.
	2. After the group work, ask group members to report back and make one large class list. Help students to prioritize the list and offer supporting evidence for their choices.	
Read and Research	**Picture This: San Nicholas Island**	
	1. Pair students to do research on San Nicholas Island. Provide a variety of materials including web sites. Students will create a large chart picture of the island with size drawn to scale. The water surrounding the island is an important part of the novel. Students should include drawings of the habitats and animals that are found surrounding the island.	1. There is a great deal of information about this island available, but some students may not be able to access or read the information. Pair students carefully to be sure that one of the students is able to read and interpret the information. Preview the rubric with the class so that all students understand exactly what is required of the project. Show examples to illustrate your requirements more clearly. Give both good and bad examples.
		1. Create a rubric for this assignment indicating the specific kind/ amount of research required and the quality of the presentation (neatness, creativity, etc.).

(Continued)

Table B.2 A Content Integrated Unit for Grades 4–8: Ocean Connections   *(Continued)*

Unit	Activities	Scaffolds	Assessment
Read and Write	**Reading Together** 1. There are a variety of different ways to read the novel in a diversified classroom (see Chapters 6 and 7 for more specific suggestions). It is important to keep students involved in the excitement of the story so, if you have time and opportunity, you may want to read aloud to the class. The advantage of the read-aloud technique is that you can keep the book moving quickly with all students on the same page. Brief stops for discussion or Think Pair Share will clear up confusions.	1. Read aloud one short section at a time. Provide a question to focus the reading for that section. Give all students highlighters to mark the text when they find the answer or when they come across unknown words (use pencils if students cannot permanently mark the texts). Suggest a page number to find the answer to the target question if students are floundering.	1. Student responses to teacher question.
	2. Instead of creating questions for the students to answer, ask each student to create one question of their own based upon the short reading. These questions can be asked to the class as a whole, to a partner, given to the teacher for anonymous answers, or simply written into journals and answered for homework.	2. Provide examples of the kinds of questions you want students to write. Questions in the past tense are difficult for language learners. You may want to provide key question frames on the chalkboard to help them get started: • "Why did Karana . . . ?" • "Why didn't Karana . . . ?" • "Did you . . . ?" • "Who . . . _ed . . . ?" • "Was/Were . . . ?" Instead of factual recall questions, encourage students to write questions that connect the characters to their own lives. Float around the room assessing student questions and asking pinpoint questions to help students who are "stuck."	2. Student questions
	3. As the novel proceeds, ask students to keep track of the important *biotic* and *abiotic* elements in the ecosystem surrounding the island. A simple two-column chart in journals will suffice. These lists can later be used to create a food web for Karana.	3. Demonstrate how to draw the food webs using a flowchart graphic organizer. Recall the terms used in the ecosystem lessons: *consumer, decomposer, producer.*	3. Journal lists. Food web.

4. There will be a great deal of new vocabulary in the novel. All students should increase their vocabularies through a process of comprehension and use of the new language. In addition to asking students to highlight unknown vocabulary, require students to keep a vocabulary section in their journals. Select ten to twelve words daily (both new words and recycled ones from past lessons) and list them. Students can copy these words and self-assess their understanding of them ("I Know It," "I Kinda Know It," "I Don't Have a Clue").

4. If students check a column indicating that they know a word, ask them to demonstrate their understanding (write or orally explain the meaning). Encourage students to use pictures as clues, native language equivalents, examples, or comparisons to develop deeper layers of meaning. When assigning written work, ask students to use their vocabulary lists and reward those who do so.

4. Journal vocabulary lists and student self-assessment.

Read and Write

What happened today?

1. Require students to keep a diary writing in the first person as if they were Karana. The diary should be written in the past tense and tell of the important things that have happened during the day.

1. Before students begin to write, provide samples of diary entries as a motivation. Use the Paired Verbal Fluency strategy to help students generate what they are going to say in their diaries for that day. As an added support, post the important past-tense verbs from that day's reading on the board to assist in recall of events and provide grammar support. Students may also go back into the text to help with their diary writing.

1. Daily diary entries.

Read and Research

How Did Karana Manage to Survive?

1. Halfway through the book, return to the Top Ten Survival Lists and determine how Karana was able to survive on the island. After students have completed their research, ask students to contribute to a class chart listing as many of her survival strategies as students can provide. Students may copy those items that are missing to make their research more complete.

1. Provide examples of two or three of the items before asking students to work in pairs searching for the answers in the text:

   - "Food: Karana fished for, gathered, collected, etc. . . ."
   - "Clothing: Karana made . . ."
   - "Shelter: Karana built . . ."

1. Research charts.

(Continued)

351

Table B.2 A Content Integrated Unit for Grades 4–8: Ocean Connections *(Continued)*

Unit	Activities	Scaffolds	Assessment
	2. Write a summary paragraph for homework on one of the survival categories describing how Karana coped with survival.	2. Provide a graphic organizer with important word elements and chronology for students who will have difficulty writing a paragraph.	2. Summary paragraphs.
Read, Write, and Discuss	**What Impact Did Karana Have on the Ecosystem?**		
	1. Choose one incident in the novel (perhaps the hunting of sea otters by the Aleuts) and discuss the impact of this activity on the ecosystem of the island. Recall target vocabulary: *consumers, decomposers, producers,* and introduce *predator* and *prey.*	1. List important points on the OHP as the discussion continues. Help students to be prepared to answer by providing Think-Pair-Share time before the discussion begins. Wait time will be important in this discussion as well.	1. Student participation.
	2. Place students into small groups and ask each group to identify another incident in the novel that affected the ecosystem of the island. The group should list the effects of the incident.	2. If students have difficulty identifying incidents, prepare them for the task by listing the incidents on a chart and asking questions to identify one or two consequences.	2. Small group lists.
	3. Allow time to compare the incidents in a large-group discussion.	3. Ask students who have not yet responded to use their lists to respond in this discussion.	3. Student participation.
Write, Write, Write	1. As a culmination to the novel, teach students to write reviews of the book accompanied by pictures created on the computer. Students will need to learn how to write outlines—this is best done as a whole-class assignment where students suggest major events in the book. Write these events on the OHP with an outline graphic organizer (use the traditional outline form or any other that you have taught your students). Show students how to write important supporting facts under each major event. Include an introduction and a conclusion.	1. Using the completed outlines, pair students and provide them with time to tell a partner what they are going to write. Use the Paired Verbal Fluency structure so that students alternate and don't interrupt each other. Float around the room listening and offering help.	1. Teacher observation.

2. While some students are creating their artwork on the computer, work with pairs of students to help develop their written book reviews (see Chapter 8 for specific suggestions).

3. These book reviews can be shared with another class that has not yet read the book. Pair students and ask the writer to read his/her book review to a partner. The partner should be prepared to ask three questions about the book.

2. Language-learning students may benefit from a model book review or from a structured book review where specific information has been eliminated (as in a cloze text).
Model structures such as:
- "I admired . . ."
- "I was surprised that . . ."
- "I wondered why . . ."
- "I enjoyed . . ."
- "I would recommend . . ."

2. Written book reports.

3. Teacher observation. Lists of questions.

Unit References

∙∙∙

BC Education Grade 7 Life Science: Ecology. Retrieved May 27, 2008.
> http://www.royalbcmuseum.bc.ca/School_Programs/end_species/pdf/grade7final1.pdf

Herzog, R. M. (2003). Ecosystems—Plants lesson plan. Retrieved May 27, 2008.
> http://school.discovery.com/lessonplans/programs/yosemite/

Howard, J. Slick Sea Spills. Retrieved May 27, 2008.
> http://sln.fi.edu/tfi/activity/earth/earth-2.html

Mid-continent Research for Education and Learning, Aurora, CO. (McREL) Retrieved May 27, 2008.
> http://www.mcrel.org

Nevison, J. (1999). The Ocean Floor. Retrieved May 27, 2008.
> http://atozteacherstuff.com/pages/492.shtml

Ocean Planet: Pollution Solution. Retrieved May 27, 2008.
> http://www.smithsonianeducation.org/educators/lesson_plans/ocean/main.html

Ocean Planet: Sea Connections. Retrieved May 27, 2008.
> http://www.smithsonianeducation.org/educators/lesson_plans/ocean/main.html

Ocean Planet: There Are Algae in Your House! Retrieved May 27, 2008.
> http://seawifs.gsfc.nasa.gov/ocean_planet.html

Spotte, S. (1979). *Seawater aquariums: The captive environment.* Toronto, NY: Wiley-Interscience.

Science Lesson Plans

∙∙∙

Blue Planet: Coral Seas. Each of the Blue Planet lessons identifies objectives, procedures, vocabulary, research web sites, and an evaluation rubric. Joy Brewster is the author. Retrieved May 27, 2008.
> http://school.discovery.com/lessonplans/programs/BP_coralseas/

Blue Planet: Frozen Seas. Retrieved May 27, 2008.
> http://school.discovery.com/lessonplans/programs/BP_frozenseas/

Blue Planet: Open Ocean. Retrieved May 27, 2008.
> http://school.discovery.com/lessonplans/programs/BP_openocean/

Blue Planet: Seasonal Seas. Retrieved May 27, 2008.
> http://school.discovery.com/lessonplans/programs/BP_seasonalseas/

Cusick, E. N. and Pearce, P. (2000). Ecosystems. An AskERIC Lesson Plan. Retrieved May 27, 2008.
> http://www.eduref.org/cgi-bin/printlessons.cgi/Virtual/Lessons/Science/Ecology/ECL0200.html

Discovery School. Water to the Last Drop. This series of lessons focuses on the water cycle, ecosystems, and exploration of oceans. The Discovery School web site (http://www .discoveryschool.com) has an extensive listing of lesson plans organized by grade level and subject. Retrieved May 27, 2008.
> http://school.discovery.com/lessonplans/programs/water/

Science Resources

∙∙∙

Aquatic Network. Oceanography topics abound at this site: Jacques Cousteau, coastal zones, the deep sea, coral reefs, marine mammals, and plankton, to name a few. Retrieved May 27, 2008.
> http://www.aquanet.com

Broad, W. J. (2003, September 9). Deep under the sea, boiling founts of life itself. *The New York Times*, pp. D1, D4. This article summarizes the latest discoveries relative to underwater vents. Photos and maps are included.

Sea World. This site contains online materials related to diversity in oceans. Objectives, target vocabulary, and reference lists are included. Topics include arctic animals (with pictures, a map, and information regarding a food web), penguins, seals, sea lions, walruses, sharks, and whales. Retrieved May 27, 2008.

http://www.seaworld.org/just-for-teachers/guides/

Shedd Aquarium. An excellent site that will give students a look at the marine creatures they are studying. Retrieved May 27, 2008.

http://www.sheddaquarium.org/sea/

Temperate Oceans: Ocean Light Zones. Specific information related to the effect of light zones on marine life. Retrieved May 27, 2008.

http://mbgnet.mobot.org/salt/oceans/zone.htm

Temperate Oceans: Zonation. A helpful diagram of light zones is provided here. Retrieved May 27, 2008.

http://mbgnet.mobot.org/salt/oceans/zones.htm

Waikiki Aquarium. This site provides a virtual tour of exhibits, live camera views of various aquariums, and marine life profiles of a long list of species. Retrieved May 27, 2008.

http://www.aquarium.org

Island of the Blue Dolphin Resources

Channel Islands National Marine Sanctuary. This site is an excellent research tool for students. There is information related to the Intertidal Life of the islands (both habitats and species), the Subtidal Invertebrates, fish and kelp forest habitats (listings of all species in various habitats), Cetaceans, and Pinnipeds. There are underwater slides of many fish and invertebrates, and charts of marine mammal migrations by month. Under the Education tab, select "Cool Stuff" to find video clips, slides, word searches, and an Encyclopedia of the National Marine Sanctuaries where students can find the habitats, food sources, endangerment status, and other interesting facts about the marine species in the Channel Islands. Retrieved May 27, 2008.

http://www.cinms.nos.noaa.gov/seasons/jan.html

Island of the Blue Dolphins. Jacob Wismer's site contains many links to marine animals and literature connections. May 27, 2008

http://www.beavton.k12.or.us/jacob_wismer/resources/books/island.htm

Island of the Blue Dolphins Study Guide. This PDF format study guide from McGraw-Hill provides 22 pages of activities and student worksheets for the novel. Retrieved May 27, 2008.

http://www.glencoe.com/sec/literature/litlibrary/pdf/island_blue_dolphins.pdf

Literature Learning Ladders. This site is dedicated to *Island of the Blue Dolphins*. There are links to author information and many links to lesson plans, units, and research sites involving literature learning, marine life connections, information, and lessons related to Native Americans and to the Spanish missions. Retrieved May 27, 2008.

http://www.eduscapes.com/newbery/61a.html

The Solution Site. This site contains hundreds of thematic units organized by subject and grade level. Search here for the unit on *Island of the Blue Dolphins*. Retrieved May 27, 2008.

http://www.thesolutionsite.com

Schools of California Online Resources for Educators (SCORE). This is an extensive site created to supplement the teaching of the novel. There are lesson plans and connections for exploring the California Indians, missions, marine animal life, and literature study. Retrieved May 27, 2008.

http://www.sdcoe.k12.ca.us/score/blue/bluetg.html

Glossary

ABC summary: A summarizing technique for content learning. Students are required to summarize all that they have learned by structuring information alphabetically. Thus, in a lesson on reptiles and mammals, students might begin "Alligators are reptiles. Bears are mammals . . ." and so on.

Acquisition: Developing ability in a language by using it in natural communicative situations.

Activator: Any endeavor that helps bring to mind students' current or prior knowledge.

Active engagement: A principle of language teaching and learning in which learners play enjoyable, engaging, and active roles in the learning experience.

Activity-based communicative teaching and learning (The ABC Model): The research-based model of teaching upon which this book is based, including nine principles of teaching and learning.

Activity-based teaching and learning: One of the two dimensions of the ABC Model, which focuses on what learners bring with them to the classroom and the active role they plan in the language acquisition process.

Affective filter: A device that is raised or lowered depending on the motivation and self-esteem of the learner. A low filter allows the learner to interact easily with native speakers and receive increasingly larger amounts of comprehensible input.

Alphabetic language system: A language system in which one symbol generally represents one sound, for example, Latin, Vietnamese, English, most European languages, and many African languages.

Analytical learner: This type of learner prefers individual work and sequential learning.

Anticipation guide: A pre-post reading activity in which a reader responds to the content of a reading before reading, then compares the answers with the text after reading.

BICS (Basic Interpersonal Communication Skills): Language that occurs within a context-embedded social environment.

Bilingual education: A program model where two languages are used within a classroom for the purpose of instruction by both the teacher and the students. Bilingual education takes many forms in the U.S., including transitional, developmental, or two-way bilingual education.

Bio poem: A writing support structure that provides partially completed sentences in a poem format. Students insert their individual characteristics in the blank slots of the poem.

Bottom-up approaches: Approaches to reading in which the focus is placed on developing the building blocks of reading in sequence, which may include the ability to hear sounds, decoding skills, vocabulary and word study skills, fluency, and comprehension.

CALLA (Cognitive Academic Language Learning Approach): An instructional approach that integrates academic language development with content-area instruction and learning strategies.

CALP (Cognitive Academic Language Proficiency): The coded, reduced language of a textbook or a test.

Carousel brainstorming: An activator requiring small groups of students to respond in writing to prompts written on large sheets of poster paper that are taped on the walls of the room.

Choral reading: A reading strategy in which students each have their own copies of a text and all read together. Often the teacher or a student stands in front of the class to lead the oral reading.

Clarity: Teacher language has clarity when it is easy to hear, comprehensible and specific; avoids idiomatic expressions, jargon, and slang; and utilizes repetition, gestures, and word stress.

Cloze: A reading task where every fifth word (or so) is deleted. The structure of the text remains intact while teachers eliminate random words, target vocabulary, or nonessential vocabulary. Cloze can be used as a frame for writing or as an assessment of content learning.

Cognitively demanding: Cognitively demanding communication tasks require cognitive involvement on the part of the ELL for acquiring meaning.

Cognitively undemanding: Cognitively undemanding communication tasks are automatized or mastered by the learner and require little mental challenge for meaning to be communicated.

Communicative competence: The ability to use language to achieve a communicative purpose.

Communicative teaching and learning: One of the two dimensions of the ABC Model, which focuses on the importance of authentic, comprehensible communication in the learning of language.

Comprehensible input: Language directed to the learner that is understood by the learner.

Content standards: Statements that clearly state what students should know or be able to do in any specific content area. They include the knowledge, skills, and understanding that schools need to teach students in order for those students to reach a predetermined level of competency.

Context-embedded: Context-embedded communication tasks or activities are made more comprehensible for ELLs because they include background information, pictures, graphic information, or other context surrounding the communication act.

Context-reduced: Context-reduced language is decontextualized and abstract, with few if any context clues to support spoken or written words to help make the language comprehensible.

Cooperative learning: A specific kind of group work in which learners collaborate for the purpose of content learning, language learning, and social-skills building.

Corners: An activator (or summarizer) whereby students choose one of four corners designated by different choices relating to an opinion, a decision, or a preference. Students move to their chosen corner and talk to other students there about why they have made their choice.

Cultural mediator: Translator of culture; guide to the patterns and norms of behavior within a culture.

Cultural relevance: One of the principles of the ABC Model, in which classrooms respect and incorporate the cultures of learners in the classroom while helping them to understand the new culture of the community, the school, and the classroom.

Culture: The values, traditions, social and political relationships, and world view shared by a group of people bound together by a combination of factors that can include a common history, geographic location, language, social class, and/or religion.

Declarative knowledge: The facts and ideas that make up the knowledge load of a content unit.

Differentiated instruction: Teachers vary their instructional practices, both processes and procedures, to accommodate the needs of varied learners.

Differentiation: In this principle of the ABC Model, learning activities accommodate different language, literacy, and cognitive levels and incorporate many dimensions of learning: different learning styles, intelligences, and preferences.

Dipsticking: A form of checking for understanding where all students are checked, frequently, on the same topic throughout the lesson.

Discourse: Verbal expression in speech or writing.

Display questions: Questions asked even though the answer is well known to the questioner, typical of "school" questions.

Draw a picture/diagram: A lesson summarizer that requires students to present their learning in a picture or diagram format.

Dual language: A program model of bilingual education that uses two or more languages in content areas.

Early fluency: The third of four literacy levels. Learners begin to use multiple clues to make meaning from text and are able to understand the main ideas of texts as well as their emotional impact.

Early literacy: The second of four literacy levels. Learners at this level understand that books have messages that do not change and that there are certain conventions regarding how print is presented.

Emergent literacy: The first of four literacy levels. Learners at this level understand that print can carry meaningful messages, but are still learning to encode, decode, and understand these messages.

English as a second language (ESL): A field of study dedicated to teaching English as an additional language; often taught in an English language setting.

English language development (ELD): Courses or classes dedicated to teaching English as an additional language.

English language learners (ELL): Students at the beginning to advanced level of acquiring English who are identified as needing special instruction in English.

English language proficiency test: A test specifically designed to assess language development of ELLs, often used to assess learners' and schools' progress toward meeting standards.

English to speakers of other languages (ESOL): A course in which the content is the study of English for speakers of other languages. This acronym is sometimes used in place of English as a Second Language (ESL) or English as a Foreign Language (EFL).

ESL pull-out: A type of program model in which ELLs are taken out of their classrooms for specialized English language instruction. This model is most often used at the elementary level or in districts where there is a low incidence of ELLs.

ESL push-in: A type of program model in which a second-language specialist (ESL or ELD teacher) comes into classrooms to team-teach or turn-teach with the mainstream classroom teacher for the benefit of the ELLs in the classroom.

Explanatory devices: Any teaching aids that support student comprehension of the content learning.

Feature analysis: A strategy in which learners use a matrix to explore how terms and concepts are related to one another and to make distinctions between them.

Field independent: A learning style where learners perceive discrete items as separate from the organized field.

Field sensitive: A learning style where learners tend to perceive the organization of the field as a whole rather than its parts.

Fluency: At this fourth literacy level, learners are becoming mature readers. They make sense of longer and more complex texts approaching or at the level of their native-speaking peers; they use a variety of strategies flexibly to accomplish their reading purposes.

Formative assessment: Classroom-based assessment consisting of the multiple and various ways that teachers gather information about their students' learning throughout the instructional process.

Fossilization: Grammatical errors that persist and remain impervious to change.

Global learner: A learner who has a preference for learning which focuses on the whole rather than the parts.

Graphic organizers: Pictures, designs, or diagrams with graphical elements used by teachers and learners as visual clues to meaning to outline text and to illustrate principles within a text.

Graphophonemic aspects of language: The connection between sound patterns of words and word parts with spelling patterns.

Guided reading: In this reading approach, teachers work with small groups with similar reading processes using progressively leveled readers. Teachers select and introduce new books, teach reading skills and strategies, and support children as they read the text to themselves.

Holistic measures of reading: Reading assessments that give an overall view of a learners' ability. They may have sub-scores for specific skills.

Informal reading inventories: An individually administered reading assessment in which learners read aloud and teachers use evaluation codes and questions to evaluate the reading. It is designed to help teachers determine students' reading instructional needs (see Reading inventory).

Inside-outside circles: A cooperative learning structure that requires students to form two circles, with one circle inside the other and students in both circles facing each other. Pairs answer teacher questions, solve problems, or review for a test. One circle rotates to provide new partners.

Instructional conversation: Developing learners' language and thinking through assisted performance, which may include modeling, feeding back, contingency managing, directing, questioning, explaining, and task structuring.

Intensive reading: Students are directed to read a duplicated text several times, each time for a different purpose, each time marking their discoveries in the text in different ways (underlining, highlighting, annotating, etc.).

Interaction: Student-to-student communication regarding content learning or language learning.

Interference: The transference of elements of one language to another at various levels including phonological (letters and sounds), grammatical (structures and word order), lexical (words and word meaning), and orthographical (writing system).

Jigsaw: A cooperative learning technique whereby a text or content information is divided among a small group of learners. Each learner becomes an "expert" in one part of the learning experience and then teaches that part to other learners in their group.

Key sentence frames: Model sentences containing grammatical structures to be learned. Students use these models to create their own sentences.

K-W-L chart: A chart containing three columns labeled "What I Know," "What I Want to Know," and "What I Learned." The chart is used both to activate and to summarize content information.

Language experience approach: After a discussion of a shared or recalled experience, students dictate a narrative as the teacher writes it on a chart, projected computer screen, or transparency. Teacher and students revise and edit the text together and use it for learning about reading.

Learning: Developing conscious knowledge of language elements to increase language proficiency.

Learning logs: Notebooks in which students write brief summaries of content learning on a frequent or daily basis.

Learning strategies: Cognitive tools used by learners to enhance their learning and develop their language competence. These strategies can be observable behaviors, steps, or techniques, or non-observable thoughts or mental practices, such as visualization or positive thinking.

Lexical aspects of language: Aspects related to words and meaning.

Lexicon: The vocabulary of the language.

Limited English proficient (LEP): A term used by the U.S. government to designate English Language Learners. Most ESL/ELD professionals prefer not to use this term because of its negative connotations.

Line-ups: An instructional strategy whereby learners stand in two lines facing each other and respond to their partners based on a teacher's questioning. Line-up order criteria can be determined by criteria such as alphabetical order or birth month or date.

Linguistic competence: The ability of a speaker to control pronunciation, morphology, syntax, and social uses of a language.

Literacy: When students learn to construct and convey meaning from their own written texts and the texts of others. It includes all four modes of language: reading, writing, listening, and speaking.

Logographic language: A system in which one symbol represents the meaning of a concept, individual word, or part of a word. Arabic numerals and mathematical symbols are examples of logographic symbols. Chinese and Japanese (Kanji) are examples of logographic languages.

Minimal pairs: Pairs of words that differ in only one speech sound such as *fin* and *thin*.

Miscue analysis: An examination of learner reading errors or substitutions as the basis for determining learner strengths and weaknesses in reading.

Modeling: Explicitly showing students how to perform processes or create products that are the result of classroom instruction.

Monitor: An internal grammatical editor that is called into play as students learn the formal structure and requirements of a language.

Morpheme: A word or part of a word that conveys a grammatical or lexical meaning (such as the *-ed* ending that turns a present tense verb into the past tense).

Morphology: The linguistic system dealing with meaningful units of language and how they are combined to form words (e.g., want, wanted, wanting, unwanted).

Multiple intelligences: A framework for teaching/learning based upon eight different kinds of learning aptitudes and preferences.

Numbered heads together: A cooperative learning strategy whereby students in small groups each receive a number. Teachers then ask a question of the class. Students in each group put their heads together to confirm the correct answer. The teacher then spins a dial, tosses dice, or pulls a number card to find a student with that number to answer the question.

One-question quiz: A summarizer whereby the teacher asks a summarizing question and students respond in written form.

Overgeneralization: A communication strategy whereby ELLs perceive patterns of language usage, generate a rule from many examples heard in the environment, and apply the rule in a speaker-listener conversation where the rule is not usually used (e.g., "He goed outsider").

Performance-based assessment: A form of assessment involving a "performance" in which the learner constructs a response: for example, responses to questions, story telling, oral presentations, role plays, writing pieces, captioned artwork, media products, and so on. Performance-based assessment generally falls into three types: products, performances, and process-oriented assessments.

Phonemes: The smallest unit of speech sounds that can make a difference in meaning (such as the vowel sounds in pin/pen).

Phonemic awareness: A critical precursor to a child's ability to read. It is defined as the understanding that spoken language is composed of a series of discrete sounds that may be broken down, combined, and manipulated in a variety of ways.

Phonics: A method of teaching elementary reading and spelling based on the phonetic interpretation of ordinary spelling.

Phonology: Rules governing the sound system of English, including sound-symbol relationships, intonational variations, stress, pitch, and juncture.

Picture walk: A strategy to help activate ELLs' prior knowledge and set the stage for reading. The teacher "reads" the pages of a picture book without reading the words; pointing out, and having students point out key characters, aspects of the setting, events, and/or ideas; and having them ask questions and make guesses about the content of the book.

Point of view: A reading comprehension technique whereby students take on the role of characters in a fiction or nonfiction text, and work to understand the motivation behind the actions of characters from a story.

Portfolio assessment: A form of assessment that uses multiple pieces of writing, encourages reflection and self-assessment on the part of the student, and provides for increasing development of skills over a long period of time.

Positive transference: Learners use aspects of their first language to help them develop skills in a second language, e.g., writing, speaking, and reading.

Pragmatics: The conversational rules guiding the use of language in a social situation. These rules change as a variety of social factors change: context, age, purpose, etc.

Prior knowledge: One of the principles of the ABC Model, in which teachers help learners use their prior knowledge of language, content, and the world to develop new language and increase learning.

Problem-based learning: A teaching/learning structure which provides meaningful learning for students by basing the curriculum on solving real-life problems facing the community and the world.

Procedural knowledge: The skills and operations consistent with a content area, for example, reading for comprehension and solving a word problem.

Process grade: An assessment of process learning such as essay writing or delivering an oral report.

Product grade: An assessment of the amount of content knowledge learning displayed by the learner.

Progress indicator: Description of observable behaviors that indicate students are showing progress in meeting a learning standard.

Project learning: One form of content learning that embeds the content into a multi-step task that is engaging to learners.

Pull-out: An organizational model of instruction whereby the ESL teacher teaches students in a classroom separate from the mainstream class.

Push-in: An organizational model of instruction whereby the ESL teacher teaches students within the mainstream classroom, either in a separate group or integrated within the mainstream class.

Question-Answer-Response (QAR): Learners learn to ask different types of questions and to locate answers in a text. Teachers, model, teach, and help learners practice the four levels of questions of QAR: "right there" questions, "think and search" questions, "author and you" questions, and "on your own" questions.

RAFT: A type of role play. The teacher creates a scenario about the content being studied defining the Role, Audience, Form, and Time of the scenario.

Reading inventory: A form of holistic assessment of reading. The inventory is administered individually, using progressively more difficult texts. Teachers assess oral reading fluency and then ask targeted questions to determine reading comprehension.

Reciprocal teaching/reading: A strategy in which teachers model and explain four types of questioning strategies: summarizing, clarifying, question-generating, and predicting. Then learners read passages to one another, taking turns in the "teacher" role, asking their partners the four kinds of questions about the reading.

Register: In linguistics, a register is a subset of a language used for a particular purpose or in a particular social setting Register is dependent on the context of language use, the topic, the relationship of speaker and hearer, and the channel of communication.

Reliability: Occurs when there is consistency and dependability in assessment results that occur over a period of time and when scored by different raters.

Role plays: These learning activities are dramatic skits scripted by the teacher or by the students and often based upon content learning concepts or situations.

Rubric: A scoring scale using numbers or letters that identify specific criteria used to evaluate a product or presentation, often at several levels of performance.

Running record: An informal reading assessment tool in which teachers ask learners to read texts at appropriate levels and use a coding system to record what learners read, including repetitions, corrections, mispronunciations, and so on. Teachers also ask for a retelling to assess comprehension. The resulting data is then analyzed to determine a number of sub-scores in learners' reading used for diagnostic teaching.

Scaffolding: Assistance and contextual support provided by teachers, parents, and knowledgeable peers to help learners comprehend and achieve at higher levels.

Scaffolds: Various types of support provided to learners, including language adaptations, contextual cues such as graphics, visuals, and interactive peer activities that add support to the language and content learning.

Schema: A cognitive framework or concept that helps organize and interpret information. Schema developed in one language may be transferred to another language.

Second language learners: Students learning English as an additional language.

Self-assessment: A form of assessment that helps learners to process their own skill development, take responsibility for their own learning, and acquire the kinds of study skills, attitudes, and practices that will lead to greater learning achievement.

Semantic gradient: A vocabulary activity whereby words are arranged in order on a specified scale: e.g., greater-lesser, longer-shorter, older-younger, etc.

Semantic mapping: Sometimes called "spider mapping," this graphic organizer accumulates attributes arranged like the spokes of a wheel around a central concept.

Semantics: The scientific study of meaning in language.

Shared reading: Teachers and learners read together using enlarged texts (such as big books, charts, or projected texts), which all learners can easily see. Teachers use a pointer to direct students to look at the text being read as they engage learners in experiencing reading. Teachers and students use the text in many ways to explore and learn about language.

Shared-to-guided reading: In this bridging strategy, designed for ELLs, teachers first "walk" learners through the text,

using picture cues to develop vocabulary. Then teachers set the scene, read and reread the text aloud, and help students recall and discuss the content. Students read the book independently or with partners and follow up on reading with recall, skill development, and expressive responses to the literature.

Shared writing: Teachers use the shared writing strategy to model writing, and to encourage a rich academic conversation as they guide learners through the writing process using text generated by the learners.

Sheltered instruction: An approach for teaching content to English language learners in strategic ways that make the subject matter concepts comprehensible while promoting the students' English language development.

Sheltered Instruction Observational Protocol (SIOP): An observational form and a model of instruction for teaching language learners about content and language.

Signals: Student responses to teacher questions that are nonverbal codes: they may use hands or other objects to show responses.

Signal words: Words that show a text's organizational structure. Sets of signal words are used for different types of texts, for example, chronological sequence (first, second, next, last . . .), comparison/contrast (but, on the other hand, although . . .), or description (above, outside of, appears to be . . .).

Silent period: A period of time when language learners resists speaking the target language while listening to, learning from, and analyzing comprehensible input.

Simplification: A communication strategy whereby ELLs avoid speaking about complex topics, avoid using full grammatical utterances, or avoid using word forms that they do not yet know.

Simulations: Dramatic activity, more structured than a role play, that is an imitation of some real thing, state of affairs, or process. The teacher structures the learning concretely for the students and often encourages them to develop scripts.

Slates: Individual writing boards used for practice and assessment of student comprehension during a lesson.

Sociolinguistic aspects of language: Aspects of language related to social and cultural contexts, for example, the way one's speech changes with people of different status in a society or in different social settings.

Sort tasks: Students choose categories and sort vocabulary to further their comprehension and recall of the words.

Specially Designed Academic Instruction in English (SDAIE): A model for sheltered instruction designed to promote cognitively challenging content and language learning.

SQ3R (Survey, Question, Read, Recite, Review): A reading comprehension strategy technique that includes strategies for before, during, and after reading. The "S" asks students to survey the text they are about to read (e.g., preview headings, illustration, and boldface terms.) Then students create questions (the "Q") they expect will be answered in the text. The 3 "Rs" stand for "read," "recite"

groups in response to a teacher's signal, carry out a conversation task, and then, at another signal from the teacher, prepare to discuss or respond in a new group.

Summarizer: An activity at the end of a learning period to help students and teacher assess and organize the day's learning.

Summative assessment: The process of evaluating the learning of students at a point in time. Formal summative assessment is administered in order to evaluate programs, curriculum, and/or district or state education performance. Summative assessment may be accomplished by district-wide standardized testing.

Syllabic language: A language system, such as Japanese or Korean, in which one symbol represents a syllable, or consonant-vowel combination.

Syntactic aspects of language: Aspects of language related to language patterns and grammar.

Syntax: The study of the rules by which words or other elements of sentence structure are combined to form grammatical sentences.

Thematic instruction: Sequenced learning activities revolving around many aspects of a central topic or theme, offering students opportunities to visit the learning objectives of the unit through a variety of activities using many modes of learning.

Think-aloud strategy: A strategy in which the teacher states thought processes and steps in a learning sequence out loud, helping learners to acquire them.

Think-pair-share (TPS): An interactional routine whereby students think about a response to a teacher's question, pair themselves with another student to discuss their responses, and finally share their responses with another group or the full class.

3-2-1 summary: A summarizing structure whereby students list three important elements, then two important elements, then one most critical piece of information in response to the teacher's questions.

Thumbs up/Thumbs down: A way for students to signal their answers by turning their thumb up (true) or down (false).

Ticket to leave: A structure whereby students are asked summary questions that they must answer correctly, orally or in writing, before leaving class.

Top-down approaches: Approaches to reading that focus on getting meaning from text, and teach skills in the context of meaning.

Total physical response (TPR): A language teaching method in which learners perform actions in response to a series of commands. It is based upon the research indicating that language can be learned through kinesthetic responses to auditory commands.

Transfer: A communication strategy whereby learners apply aspects of a language they know to a new language. They use native language rules and concepts to understand and speak the new language. In addition, generic literacy concepts and skills are also thought to transfer from the L1 to the L2. Transfer can be positive, helping learners with the new language, or negative, interfering with learning the new language.

Validity: Occurs when assessment instruments measure what they were designed to measure.

Wait time: The teacher waits approximately 3 to 5 seconds after asking a comprehension question before calling on a student. This longer than usual wait time increases the quality and quantity of student responses.

WebQuest: An inquiry-oriented lesson format in which most or all the information that learners work with comes from the Web. The teacher provides the links necessary to complete the quest so students can focus on the materials rather than spending time looking for them. One version of the WebQuest has five parts: Introduction, Task, Process, Evaluation, and Conclusion.

Wordsplash: A selection of vocabulary words that are splashed across a sheet of chart paper or on an overhead transparency. The content topic is centered on the paper. Students are asked to make predictions about how the words are related to the content concept by generating sentences. The wordsplash is usually used prior to instruction or prior to reading the content information.

Word square: A vocabulary learning technique whereby a note card is divided into four quadrants. The target word is placed in one of the quadrants. The other three quadrants require students to create a definition, write a native language equivalent, find a synonym or antonym, write a dictionary definition, locate the part of speech, draw a picture, or copy a sentence from the text.

Word wall: A systematically organized collection of words displayed in a classroom; a tool to give students access to vocabulary.

Writing portfolio assessment: A form of assessment that uses multiple pieces of writing, encourages reflection and self-assessment of the part of the student, and provides for increasing development of skills over a long period of time.

Writing process: This approach to teaching writing uses step-by-step phases that guide a learner through the selection of a topic, understanding the purpose of the writing, collecting and organizing ideas, drafting, editing, revising, and "publication" of a finished work.

Writers' workshop: A process approach to writing that allows students to write in class frequently, choosing their own topics, evaluating their writing, and growing as writers.

Zone of proximal development (ZPD): A concept developed by Lev Vygotsky, through which he described the ideal place where learning and development meet, as the ideal focus of classroom instruction. In the ZPD, teachers (and peers) can enable learners to achieve learning just beyond their current developmental level.

Index

Aaronson, E., 185
ABC summary, 275
About Me blank worksheet, 86
Abstract learning, 303–305
Abstract to concrete, continuum of, 303–305
Academic achievement, cooperative learning and, 233
Academic language
  defined, 94
  learning, 94–97
  literacy development in, 168
  versus social language, 15, 18
Academic proficiency tests, 265
Academic registers, 14
ACCESS test (Assessing Comprehension and Communication in English State-to-State for English Language learners), 194, 276
Acculturation, 51
Acquisition, defined, 9
Acquisition-learning hypothesis, 9–10
Activator, 249
Active engagement, 27, 42
Activity-Based Communicative Teaching and Learning Model (ABC Model), 26–27, 68
  principles of, 26, 27–29, 39, 299
Activity-based teaching and learning, 26–30, 39
Adolescents, 67
Affective environment, 13
Affective filter hypothesis, 10
After-school programs, 52
Age
  appropriate materials and, 193
  differences due to, 15–16, 18
  placement by, 15
Agor, Barbara, 249, 251, 301
Algorithms, 137
Alphabetic language systems, 177–178
American Sign Language, 4
Amphibian Observation Rubric, 286
Amygdala, 8
Analysis, level of thinking, 238
Analytical learners, 70–71, 72
Angelou, Maya, 29
Anstrom, A., 132–133
Anticipation Guide, 179, 180
Application, level of thinking, 238
Application activities, 132
Argumentation, 255
Asher, James, 149

Assessment(s)
  accommodations for ELLs, 263, 265, 266–278
  areas of, techniques for, 272–273
  authentic, 278–286
  in bilingual classrooms, 264
  categories of, 264–265
  classroom-based, 264, 277
  content, 273
  critical factors affecting, 273–278
  defined, 264
  from ELD programs, 194
  of English language proficiency, 193, 197, 276
  fair, reliable, and valid, 266–268
  formative, 257, 258, 273–277, 278
  holistic measures of, 194–195
  to improve learning, 268–270
  to inform teaching, 268–270
  of language proficiency, 276
  in lesson phases, 257–258, 274–275
  in literacy development, 193–197
  in math, 135
  multiple, 39
  of older learners, 192
  ongoing informal, 192, 257, 258
  of oral language development, 119–122, 266, 272
  performance-based, 193, 197, 278–286
  portfolio, 270
  process-oriented, 282
  product, 280–281
  publisher-made, 196
  in reading, 196–197, 263, 272
  rubrics for, 269
  scaffolding for, 270, 271
  self- (see Self-assessment)
  of specific literacy skills, 194
  standardized, 194, 264
  standards effect on, 286–293
  summative, 257, 258, 273–276
  teacher-made, 194, 196, 278
  of thematic units, 316
  types, purposes, and formats of, 265
  using familiar instructional techniques in, 270–273
  using multiple sources of information, 270
  in writing, 218–225, 272 (see also Tests)
Ausubel, D. P., 242
Authentic assessment, 278–286
Author's Chair, 221

Background knowledge. (see Prior knowledge)

Basic Interpersonal Communication Skills (BICS), 14
Bias
  negative, 18
  in testing, 277, 278
BICS (Basic Interpersonal Communication Skills), 14
Bigelow, M., 11
Bilingual classrooms
  assessment in, 264
  math, 136
Bilingual education, 86, 136
Billows, F., 254, 255
Bio poem, 281
Bloom, B., 237, 238, 256, 305, 307
Bodily-kinesthetic intelligence, 36
Books
  finding appropriate, 181
  picture, 128
  reviews of, 213 (see also Textbooks)
Bottom-up approach, 162–163, 164–165
Brainstorming, 242, 245, 313, 315
  carousel, 245
  in writing, 203
Brown, H. D., 17
Brown, K., 232
Bruner, J., 113, 173
Bulletin boards, 64, 65, 210

California English Language Development Test (CELDT), 193, 194, 276
CALLA (Cognitive Academic Language Learning Approach), 74–76, 239–240
CALP (Cognitive Academic Language Proficiency), 74–76, 239–240
Carle, Eric, 181
Carousel brainstorming, 82
Carousel Reports, 82
Center for Equity and Excellence in Education (CEEE), 276
Center for Research on Education Diversity and Excellence (CREDE), principles of, 47
Center for Research on Evaluation, Standards, and Student Testing (CRESST), 276
Chalkboard (whiteboard), 64, 65, 69
Challenge, 47
Chambers, Tyler, 179
Chants, 144
Choice Independent Reading, 179–180

Chomsky, Noam, 4, 9
Choral reading, 182
Circle stories, 128
Clarity, 109, 249
Clarity tools, 106–108
Classification, 307
Class participation, 28
Classroom arrangement, 63–66
Classroom-based assessment, 264, 277
    principles of, 266–273
Classroom environment, 12, 18
    physical, 63–66
    positive, 19–22
    social, 67–72
Classroom management, 60–86
    getting information, 61
    theoretical frameworks for instruction, 73–87
Classroom placement, 278
Classroom presentations, 112
Classrooms
    community building in, 67
    private space in, 65–66
    public areas in, 64–65
Clay, Marie, 195
Clear speech, 106–108
Cloze, 266, 271, 273
Cognition, individual differences in, 15–16, 18
Cognitive Academic Language Learning Approach (CALLA), 74–76, 239–240
    classroom example of, 74–76
    lesson phases of, 74–76
Cognitive Academic Language Proficiency (CALP), 14, 94
Cognitive empathy, 109
Cognitive levels, low to high, 305
Cognitively demanding, 73, 74
Cognitively undemanding, 73, 74
Cognitive psychology, 234–235
Cognitive strategies, 18
Collaboration, 29–30, 39, 299–300
Collaborative dialogues, 118–119
Collaborative reading strategy (CRS), 11
Collier, V. P., 104
Communication, goals of, 239
Communication strategies, 18
Communicative Teaching and Learning, 26, 27, 39
Community
    collaborating with, 55
    competence, 310
    supporting education of ELLs, 52–56
Community building, 67
Competence
    communicative, 310, 311,
    linguistic, 113
Complex grammar, 19
Comprehensible input, 10, 20, 300
    of oral language, 33
    with scaffolding, 30–32, 39
    of written language, 33
Comprehension
    assessment of, 195

checking devices, 252–253
    level of thinking, 238
    in SOLOM matrix, 120
Comprehension questions, 252
Computer reformulation, 220
Concrete to abstract, continuum of, 303–305
Content
    appropriate, 233
    assessment of, 273
    interesting, 20
Content-based units. (*see* Thematic units)
Content classrooms, 127–144
Content goals, 35
Content information, 240
Content integration, 34–35, 39, 305
Content learning, 127–144
    language issues and, 278
    and oral language development, 127–144
Content learning log, 212
Content objectives, defining, 235–237
Content standards, 308–312
Content teachers, 232
Context embedded, 14
Context reduced, 14
Contextualized language, 6
Contextual support, range of, 73–74
Contexualization, 47
Conversation, instructional, 47, 119, 185, 254, 255
Cooper, Elisha, 181
Cooperation, versus individualism, 70
Cooperative learning, 74, 78, 79–83
    achievement and, 233
    basic principles of, 79, 80–81, 112
    creating will to cooperate, 81
    management in, 81–82
    teambuilding in, 80–81
Cooperative learning environment, 46
Cooperative learning structures, examples of, 81, 82, 88
Corners, 244–245
Corrective feedback, 234
Correspondence, 254, 255
Criterion-referenced tests, 265, 266
Cultural context, 170
Cultural differences, 15–16, 18
    in the classroom, 45
    in language patterns, 96–97
Cultural experiences, drawing upon, 45
Cultural illiteracy, 46
Culturally relevant classroom, 29
Cultural mediator, 45
    defined, 46
    techniques of, 46–47
Cultural organizers, 46
Cultural perspective, 45
Cultural relevance, 28–29, 39, 68, 193, 299
Culture, 45, 46
    background, 62
    classroom, 45
    family, 62

Culture shock, 17–18, 51
Cummins, J., 14, 94, 232
Curriculum
    academically challenging, 233
    in thematic units, 312–316
Customizing, of language, 7
Cycle graphic organizer, 215
Cyclical stories, 129
Cyrillic alphabet, 178

Debates, 282
Declarative knowledge, 316
Demonstrations, 282
Description, 305, 308
Desks, 66
Dewey, John, 37, 298
Dialogue journals, 210
Dialogues, 134
    collaborative, 118–119
    reading, 182
    in social studies, 134
    with students, 112
DIBELS (Dynamic Indicators of Basic Early Literacy Skills), 195
Dictionary, personal, 31, 32, 33
Differentiated Instruction (DI), 74, 85–86
    classroom example of, 87
    implementing, 85–86
    modification of, 85–86
Differentiation, 37–38, 39, 300
    and learning styles, 36
    in practice, 36, 39
Dioramas, 280
Dipsticking, 252, 273
Directions, giving, 109
Direct performance tests, 265
Discourse, 14
Display questions, 97
Diversity, accommodations for, 46
Dixon, J. K., 232
Dodge, Bernie, 148
Drafting, 214, 219
Drafts
    reviewing, 219
    sharing and reviewing, 214–215
Drama, 255
Draw a picture/diagram, 257
Dual language classrooms, 264
Dynamic Indicators of Basic Early Literacy Skills (DIBELS), 195

Early fluency, 173, 182
Early literacy, 173, 181–182
Early production stage, 100, 102–104, 280, 281, 282
Editing, 215, 220, 221
    checklist, 223
ELD (English Language Development), 34, 72, 194, 196, 268
    teachers, 72
ELA (English Language Arts) standards, 309
ELLs (English language learners), 2
    older, 190–193

Emergent literacy, 173, 181–182
Emotionally positive environment, 20
Encourage, Question, Suggest (EQS), 215, 219
English as a Second Language (ESL), 9, 35
English Language Arts (ELA) standards, 309
English Language Development (ELD), 34, 72, 194, 196, 268
English language learners (ELLs), 2
   older, 190–193
English language proficiency
   standards, 40–41
   tests, 193, 194
English to Speakers of Other Languages (ESOL), 160, 276, 309
Environment
   cooperative learning, 46
   language-learning, 13
   role in language acquisition, 20
EQS (Encourage, Question, Suggest), 215, 219
Equal participation, 80
Error correction, 16–17, 18
ESL (English as a Second Language), 9, 35
   class, 46
   pull-out, 264
   push-in, 264
   Standards, 310–311
ESOL (English to Speakers of Other Languages), 160, 276, 309
Evaluation, 238, 307, 308
Experiments, designing and implementing, 143
Explanatory devices, 108–109, 249
Explicit phonics, 179
Exposition, 255

Fables, 230–231
Fairy tales, thematic unit on, 324–336
Family-school relationships, 51, 53–55
Feature analysis, 182, 183
Feedback, 300
   consistent, 37–39
   corrective, 234
   goals and, 37–39
Field independent style, 70–71, 72
Field sensitive style, 70–71, 72
Fitzgerald, J., 167
Fluency
   assessment of, 195
   early, 173, 182
   rubric for, 154
   in SOLOM matrix, 120
Fluency level, choosing texts for, 182
Formal operations, 7
Formative assessment, 257, 258, 273–278
Fossilize, 16
Fountas, I. C., 164, 181, 182, 184, 186
Fractions, 140, 141
Freeman, Y., 182
Frontal lobe, 8
Fuchs, D., 285

Fuchs, L., 285
Furniture arrangement, instruction goals and, 63–64

Garcia, E., 193
Gardner, Howard, 36
Generalization, 18
Geographic referents, 131
Gibbons, P., 94, 113
Gifted students, 278
Global learners, 70–72
Goals
   clear, appropriate, 37–39, 300
   content, 37
   in ESL standards, 310–311
   language, 37
Goodman, Kenneth, 163, 195
Gower, R., 109
Grades, product and process, 267, 268
Grammar, 170
   early, 5
   rubric for, 154
   in second language acquisition, 9
   in SOLOM matrix, 121
Graphic organizers, 183, 281
   for math operations, 138
   for outlining texts, 183
   sample, 108, 184
   for story elements, 128, 130
   for thinking concepts, 108
   word squares, 30, 190
   for writing, 203, 215, 219
Graphophonemic aspects of language, 168–170
Grid Format Activity, 152
Group discussions, 282
Grouping, 230
   cultural determinants for, 68
   for different purposes, 63
   heterogeneous, 232–233
Group work
   strategies for, 69
   successful, 69
Group work chart, 312
Guided practice, 250–253
Guided reading, 161, 163, 164, 184, 186

Hadaway, N. L., 213
Harklau, L., 232
Heath, S. B., 96, 97, 166
Heterogeneous grouping, 232–233
Historical referents, 131
Holdaway, Don, 163
Holistic measures of reading, 194–195
Holt, J., 4
Home-school connections, 53, 170, 185
Homework, 54
How Children Fail (Holt), 4
Human Languages Website, The (Chambers), 179

Idea Web, 314
Igoa, Christine, 18

Illiteracy, cultural, 46
Illustrations, 280
Imitation, 4
Immersion, 6
Immigrants, 62
Immigration, 132
Improving America's Schools Act of 1994, 277
Independent practice, 254–256
Independent reading, 179–180
Indirect performance tests, 265
Individual accountability, 80
Individualism, 70
Induction, 98
Inference, 18
Informal language, 95
Informal reading inventories, 195
Information, basic, 62
Innate language, 4
Innatist theory, 9, 11–12
Input hypothesis, 10
Inquiry-based learning, 302
Instruction
   adapting for learning styles, 45
   clear, 106
   culturally mediated, 46
   designing for older learners, 193
   high level of, 233
   interaction model of, 232
   location in the classroom, 233
   organizing, 72–87
   theoretical approaches to, 74
Instructional conversation, 47, 119, 185
Integrated language
   principles of, 26–42
   teaching and learning, 26
Integrated Literacy Approach, 171–172
Intelligences, multiple, 36, 83–85
Intensive reading, 185
Interactionist position, 11–12
Interaction
   between learners, 249
   opportunities for, 13
Interactional structures, 112–113, 114–116
Interaction model of instruction, 232
Interactive approach, 20
Interactive journals, 210, 212
Interference, 207
Intermediate fluency stage, 101–102, 104–105, 280, 281, 282
Interpersonal intelligence, 36, 84
Interviews, 281
   oral histories and, 134
   practicing, 134
   recording, 134
Intonation, 19
Intrapersonal intelligence, 84
Izumi, S, 11

Jigsaw, 80, 81, 185, 250
Joint productive activity, 47
Journals, 281
   dialogue, 210

interactive, 210, 212
literary, 212–213

Kagan, S., 79, 80, 116
Karl, Linda, 85
Key sentence frames, 251
Kinesthetic intelligence, 83
Klingner, J. K., 11
Knowledge
 declarative, 316
 level of thinking, 238
 prior (*see* Prior knowledge)
 procedural, 316
Krashen, S. D., 9–10, 11, 19, 30, 98,
  166, 279
Kropp, Ray, 85
K-W-L Chart, 242–243, 244, 249, 313

Language
 common components of, 4
 cultural differences in, 96–97
 graphophonemic aspects of, 168–170
 level of instruction and, 233–234
 lexical aspects of, 168
 sociolinguistic aspects of, 170
 syntactic aspects of, 170
Language acquisition
 complexity of, 14–15
 environment for, 13, 5–9
 factors affecting, 12–18
 first language, 3–5, 6–9
 grammatical knowledge for, 9
 as integrated learning experience, 8–9
 natural aspect of, 3–4
 during play, 4, 5
 second language, 9–12
 social, 7
 strategies used in, 17–18
 topics for, 7
 universal aspect of, 3 (*see also* Oral
  language development)
Language acquisition device (LAD), 4
Language and content input, 248–250
Language Arts
 oral language development in, 127–130
 Reader's Theater, 130
 storytelling, 127–130
Language Assessment Battery (LAB), 276
Language Assessment Scales (LAS),
  194, 276
Language context, 13
Language development
 factors affecting, 18
 setting objectives in, 47
Language experience approach, 186
Language forms, 99
Language functions, 240
Language goals, 37
Language input, 18
 environment and, 13
Language/Literacy Matrix, 172–173
Language load, 13–14, 18
Language output, environment and, 13
Language proficiency levels, 280–282, 313

Language proficiency tests, 265
Language transfer, 18–19
Learners
 differences in, 36
 goals for, 37–39
Learning
 conversational elements of, 119
 at home, 54
 instructional elements of, 119
 problem-based, 81–83
 social nature of, 119
 through multiple modalities, 68–69
Learning Buddies, 114
Learning logs, 257, 281, 282
Learning strategies, 18, 29, 39, 300
 objectives, 239–240
 in practice, 30
 rubric for, 289
 in SI, 77
Learning styles, 37
 characteristics of, 71
 culturally determined, 70
 field independent, 70, 72
 field sensitive, 70–71, 72
 matching, 68–72
 teaching suggestions for various, 72
Learning supports, 241
Leki, I., 207
Lesson planning
 activating prior knowledge, 236,
  242–245
 for assessment, 236, 257–258
 beyond phase, 254–258
 characteristics that support learning
  and, 231–234
 defining content objectives, 235–237
 format for integrated learning,
  234–235
 guided practice, 236, 250–253
 independent practice, 254–256
 into phase, 235–245
 language and content input and, 236,
  248–250
 language objectives, 236, 237–239
 learning strategy objectives, 236,
  239–240
 lesson components, 236
 lesson phases in, 236
 performance indicators, 240–241
 summarizing and, 236, 256–257
 through phase, 245–253
 through the lesson, 245–253
 vocabulary learning and, 236, 245–248
Letter sounds. (*see* Phonemic awareness)
Lexical aspects of language, 168
Lexicon, 14
Likert-scale rubric, 285–286
Limited English proficient (LEP), 277
Limited language input, 12
Lindholm-Leary, K. J., 232
Line-ups, 82
Linguistic intelligence, 36
Listening
 to parents, 49

in pre-production stage, 149–155
 skills assessment in, 152, 155
 for understanding, 151–155
Literacy
 defined, 162–165, 196
 early, 173, 181–182
 emergent, 173, 181–182
Literacy development
 in academic language, 168
 comparing to oral language
  development, 171–173
 dimensions of, 196
 holistic measures of, 194–195
 levels of, 172
 in native language, 165–168
 of older learners, 190–193, 196
 in social language, 168
 strategies for, 163, 173–190
 through reading, 160–197
 through writing, 203–225
 transfer from native to second
  language, 166–168
 unique characteristics of ELLs in,
  165–172
 using reading to develop, 162
Literary journals, 212–213
Logical-mathematical intelligence, 36
Logical-sequential intelligence, 84
Logographic language, 177
Low anxiety classroom, 11

Macaulay, David, 29
Mailboxes, 210
Marzano, R., 285
Materials supports, 241
Math, 134–140
 assessment in, 135
 bilingual programs in, 136
 computations in, 136
 factors affecting achievement in,
  135–136
 function words, 65
 hands-on methods in, 60–61
 instructional techniques for, 136–140
 language of, 65
 oral language development in, 134
 use of manipulatives in, 138
 use of visuals in, 139
 vocabulary of, 135
 word problems in, 136–138
Math rubric, 38
Mayer, R. E., 235
Memorization, 18
Memory, visual components of, 69
Merchant, P., 233, 244
Message boards, 210
Migrants, 62
Migrant schools, 52
Minimal pairs, 150
Miscue analysis, 195
Modeling, of processes and products,
  249
Mohan, Bernard, 255, 298, 303, 305, 307
Monitor, 11

Monitor hypothesis, 11
Morpheme, 14
Morphology, 14
Multiculturalism, 45
Multidimensional Fluency Scales, 195
Multilanguage communities, 4
Multiple intelligences, 36, 83–85
Music, 144
My Painted house, My Friendly Chicken, and Me (Angelou), 29

Narrative, 255
National Council of Teachers of Mathematics (NCTM), 134–135, 138
National Literacy Panel, 164
National Reading Panel, 164
National Research Council (NRC), 141
National Science Education Standards (NSES), 141
Native speakers (NS), 11
Naturalist intelligence, 36, 84
Natural order hypothesis, 10
Negative bias, 18
Negotiation of meaning, 11, 12
Neighborhood environment, effect on academic achievement, 52
New York State English as a Second Language Achievement Test, 194
No Child Left Behind Act (NCLB), 164, 194, 265, 275, 276
Nonsense Word Fluency (NWF), 195
Norm-referenced tests, 265
Note cards, 252
Numbered Heads Together, 78, 80, 82

Ocean connections, thematic unit for, 337–355
Older learners, 15–16, 17, 190–193
    assessment of, 192
    literacy development of, 196
    recommendations for teaching, 192–193, 196
Olivier, R., 234
Olmedo, I. M., 133
One-question quiz, 252
Open-ended questions, 11, 49, 117
Oral Fluency Assessment from Scholastic, 195
Oral history, 132–134
Oral interviews, 129
Oral language development
    academic language, 94–97
    assessment, rubric for, 119–122, 154, 272
    classroom conditions for, 126–155
    comparing to literacy development, 171–173
    comprehensible input and, 33
    conditions for learning, 93–94
    in content areas, 127–144
    scaffolding, 113–118
    stages of, 98–105
    strategies for, 92–122
    teacher tools for, 105–119

TESOL language levels of, 98–99, 102–105
    through listening, 149–155
    through music and poetry, 144–146
    through role plays, 147
    through WebQuests, 148
Oral language proficiency, as a prerequisite, 164
Oral presentations, 281
Oral traditions, 96–97
Overgeneralization, 18

Paired Verbal Fluency (P-V-F), 115–116
Palinscar, A. S., 188
Paraphrase Passport, 116
Parental involvement, 28
    and children's success, 48–49
    in decision making, 55
    in low-income communities, 48
    non-traditional roles and, 51
    research on, 51
    types of, 51
    volunteering, 54
Parent Resource Center, 56
Parents
    listening to, 49
    stages of adjustment for, 51
Parent-teacher conference, 49
Peabody Picture Vocabulary Test-4, 195
Peer groups, 67
Performance-based assessment (PBA), 193, 278–286
Performance indicators, 240–241
Personal dictionary, 31, 32, 33
Persuasive essays, rubric for, 224
Phonemes, 14, 163
Phonemic awareness, 149, 169, 179, 195
Phonics
    adapting for ELLs, 174–179
    assessment of, 195
    developing concepts of, 169
    explicit, 179
Phonology, 14
Physical activity, 20
Physical environment, organizing, 63–66
Piaget, Jean, 6
Picture books, 128
Picture walk, 186
Pinnell, G. S., 164, 181, 182, 184, 186
Placement
    age level, 15
    classroom, 278
    of gifted students, 278
    reading group, 278
    special education, 278
Place value chart, 139
Pocketful of Opossums, A, (Almada, et al.), 128–129, 161
Poetry, 144
Point of view, 186–187
Portfolios, 280
Positive interdependence, 80
Positive transference, 207

Poster board presentations, 280
Pragmatics, 14
Predisposition, 4
Pre-production stage, 99–102, 280
    importance of listening in, 149–155
Presentation formats, 67–68
Pre-writing stage, 214, 219
Prior knowledge
    activating, 131, 142, 242–245, 300
    as key to comprehension, 32–34, 39
    in literacy, 167
    in practice, 35
Private space, 65–66
Problem-based learning, 74, 81–83
Problem solving, hands-on, 60–61
Procedural knowledge, 316
Process grade, 267, 268
Process-oriented assessment, 282
Product grade, 267, 268
Program evaluation, 264–265
Progress indicators, 309
Project learning, 74, 83–85
Projects, 280
Pronunciation, 19
    rubric for, 154
    in SOLOM matrix, 120
Prosody, 195
Provisioning, 61
Public areas, 64–65
Publication, 254, 255
Publisher-made reading assessments, 196
Publishing, 215, 221
Pull-out, 264
Purposeful use, language for, 6, 20
Push-in, 264
Pyramid (Macaulay), 29

Question-answer-response (QAR), 187
Questioning techniques, 105
Question-response patterns, 110–113
    interactional structures, 112–113
    wait time and, 111–112
Questions
    comprehension, 252
    display, 97
    open-ended, 117
Quickwrite, 219

RAFT (Role Audience Form Time), 147, 148
Ramey, D. R., 110
Ramirez, J. D., 110
Rap, 144
Rap chants, 99
Reader's Theatre, 130
Reading
    assessment in, 263, 272
    using to develop literacy, 162 (*see also* Literacy)
Reading aloud, 187–188, 219
Reading behavior, 284
Reading development, strategies to support, 174–190

Reading instruction
    bottom-up approach to, 162, 163–164
    integrated approaches to, 164–165
    top-down approach to, 162, 163–164
Reading inventories, 195
Reading levels, 173
Reading Recovery, 195
Reading skills tests, 195–197
Reading transfer, language to language, 15
Reciprocal interaction model of
    instruction, 232
Reciprocal teaching/reading, 188
Recitation limits, 110
Referents, 106
Reflection, 254, 255
Refugees, 62
Register, 14, 170
    shifts in, 94–95
Reliability, test, 264, 266
Remedial programs, selection of, 278
Reviewing, 219
Review journals, 181
Revising, 221
    sentences, 204
    in writing process, 215, 216, 220
Rhythmic intelligence, 84
Ritter, N., 302
Role plays, 134, 147, 255, 281
Roman alphabet, 177–178
Round Robin or Roundtable, 82
Round the Clock Learning Buddies,
    114–115
Rubrics, 269
    four-column, 285
    for learning strategies, 289
    for listening and speaking skills, 155
    math, 38
    for oral language assessment, 154
    persuasive essays, 224
    for product assessment, 284–286
    for writing, 285, 286, 287
Running record, 195

Samway, K. D., 209
Saphier, J., 109
Sarcasm, 106
Sayers, D., 232
Scaffolding, 20, 113
    for assessment, 270, 271
    in communication, 240
    comprehensible input with, 30–32,
        39, 300
    during guided practice, 251
    of instructional language, 33
    for literacy development, 173–174, 175
    in science, 141
    for science experiment, 117
    in writing, 214–221
Scaffolds, 31, 32, 128, 130, 155, 240, 251,
    282, 292
Schema, 26, 207, 254
School community, 51
School-community relationships, 53
School events, participation in, 50

School language, 21
School records, previous, 62
Schools, comparing Latin American and
    U.S., 50
Science
    factors affecting achievement in,
        141–142
    instructional techniques for, 142–144
    oral language development in,
        140–144
    oral language skills needed for,
        142–143
    writing in, 203
Science experiment, scaffolding for, 117
Scientific method, 143
SDAIE (Specifically Designed Academic
    Instruction in English), 74, 76
Second language acquisition
    compared to first language
        acquisition, 9–12
    strategies for, 76
Second language learners, 11, 309
Self-assessment, 122, 196, 279–283
    active learning behavior and, 284
    content unit and, 283
    good reading behavior and, 284
    learning strategies and, 288
    listening and speaking and, 283
    for math, 290
Self-reliance, 70
Semantic gradient, 140
Semantic mapping, 242, 243
    graphic organizers, 184, 219
    for new vocabulary, 247
Semantics, 14, 163
Semantic Web, 315
Sensory-motor stage, 7
Sentences
    combining, 204, 220
    revising, 204
    sequence of, 205
Sequence of events, 307, 308
Service learning, 255–256
Shared reading, 189
Shared-to-guided reading, 189
Shared writing, 216–218
Sheltered Instruction Observation
    Protocol (SIOP), 74, 76–78, 85
Sheltered instruction (SI)
    classroom example of, 78
    review and assessment in, 78–79
Signal words, 216, 217
Signals, 19, 33, 39, 49, 81, 85, 95, 116,
    216, 217, 220, 252, 272, 274
Sign language, 4
Silent period, 10
Simplification, 18
Simulations, 147–148
Simultaneous interaction, 80
SIOP (Sheltered Instruction
    Observation Protocol), 74, 76–78,
    85
Slates, 253
Small groups, 68, 139, 232, 234

Social context, 170
Social differences, 15–16, 18
Social environment, 14
    components of, 67
    organizing, 67–72
Social integration, 71
Social language, 192
    versus academic language, 14–15, 18
    literacy development in, 168
Social studies
    content learning in, 130
    oral language development in,
        130–134
    textbooks and, 131–132
    writing standards for, 222
Social supports, 241
Sociolinguistic aspects of language, 170
SOLOM, (Student Oral Language
    Observation Matrix), 119–122
    as an assessment tool, 121
    chart, 120–121, 285
Songs, 144
Sort tasks, 73, 143, 274
Sound discrimination, 149–151
Sound patterns, 168
Sound-symbol transfer, 178
Sound-Symbol Transfer Issues, 177, 178
Spatial intelligence, 36
Speaking skills, assessment of, 155
Special education placement, 278
Special education teacher, 87
Specifically Designed Academic
    Instruction in English (SDAIE), 74,
    76
Speech emergence, 100–102, 104, 280,
    281, 282
Spellchecker, 221
Spelling, 168
Spider Mapping, 242
SQ3R (Survey, Question, Read, Recite,
    Review), 29
Stack, L., 225
Stand and Deliver, 82
Standardized testing, 264, 265
Standardized tests, 194, 270, 275–276,
    277
    for reading achievement, 193, 194, 197
Standards, in thematic units, 308–312,
    315, 316
Stanford Diagnostic Reading Test, 277
Stir the Class, 116
Story elements, 128
    graphic organizers for, 128, 130
Story plot, 130
Story setting, 128
Storytelling, 127–130
Student Oral Language Observation
    Matrix (SOLOM), 119–122
    as an assessment tool, 121
    chart, 120–121, 285
Subject referents, 131
Summarizing, 256–257
Summative assessment, 257, 258,
    273–276

Sunshine State Standards of Florida, 290, 291
Supported practice, 234
Support services, online, 62
Syllabic language, 177
Syntactic aspects of language, 170
Syntax, 14, 163
Synthesis, level of thinking, 238

Talking Chips, 116, 312
Talking Tokens, 116
Taxonomy, 305, 307
Teacher-directed instruction, 231–232
Teacher language, 96, 108, 233–234
    aspects of effective, 106
Teachers
    connection to families, 48–51
    content, 232
    as cultural mediators, 45–48
    multicultural, 45
Teachers of English to Speakers of Other Languages (TESOL), 38–39, 98, 222, 286–288, 309, 312
Teaching styles, 72
Teach the Text Backward, 131–132
Technology, using for learning, 232
10-2 structure, 112
Terrell, T. D., 9–10, 11, 19, 98, 279
TESOL (Teachers of English to Speakers of Other Languages), 38–39, 98, 222, 286–288, 309, 312
Testing
    bias in, 277, 278
    cultural issues in, 277–278
    formative, 273, 276–277
    standardized, 264, 265
    summative, 273–276
Testing corporations, 277
Tests
    academic proficiency, 265
    criterion-referenced, 265, 266
    direct performance, 265
    formative, 273, 276–277
    indirect performance, 265
    language proficiency, 265
    norm-referenced, 265
    reliability in, 266
    standardized, 194, 270, 275–276, 277
    summative, 273–276
    validity in, 266, 267 (see also Assessment(s))
Texas English Language Proficiency Assessment System (TELPAS), 194
Textbook graphics, 131
Textbooks, 131–132
    choosing and adapting, 180–182
    oral language learning and, 131
Thematic instruction
    challenge of, 319–320
    criteria for, 299–301
    defined, 298–301
    incorporating learning strategies in, 318–319

memory enhancement and, 302
planning phases of, 313
sequencing curricula with, 302
structuring of, 298 (see also Thematic units)
Thematic units, 298
    assessment of, 316
    components of, 314
    as connections, 301–303
    examples of, 324–336, 337–355
    organizing content curriculum in, 312–316
    organizing information in, 307
    organizing language curriculum in, 316–317
    skill development within, 305
    standards in, 308–312
    steps for constructing, 317
    structure of, 303–308 (see also Thematic instruction)
Think-aloud strategy, 189, 281
Thinking levels, 305
    and activities for, 306
    Bloom's taxonomy of, 238
Think-Pair-Share (T-P-S), 115
Thomas, W. D., 104
3-2-1 summary, 256
Thumbs up/thumbs down, 252
Ticket to leave, 256
Timed-Pair-Share, 80, 81
Titles, 205
Top-down approaches, 162, 163–164
Topic selection, 13
Total Physical Response (TPR), 35, 99, 149
Transfer, 18–19, 166–167
Translators
    availability of, 62
    using children as, 49
Tutoring, 135, 137

Unclear language, 107–108
Understanding skills, 45
Universal grammar, 4

Validity, 264, 267
Vaughn, S., 11
Venn Diagram, 216, 217
Verbal/linguistic intelligence, 84
Visual intelligence, 84
Visual learners, 71
Visuals, in math, 139
Vocabulary
    assessment of, 195
    content-specific, 107, 246
    lesson planning for, 245–248
    math, 135
    rubric for, 154
    in sentence context, 247
    in SOLOM matrix, 120
    student self-assessment and drawings, 247–248
    test of receptive, 195–196

Vocabulary load, 19
Volunteering, 55
Vygotsky, L., 19, 30, 113, 119

Wait time, 32, 111–112
WebQuest, 148
Welcoming classroom, 61
Whole Language philosophy, 163
Wolfe, P., 84
Wong Fillmore, L., 233, 234
Woodcock-Muñoz, 276
Word meanings, in literacy development, 168
Word order, in other languages, 267
Word problems, 136–138, 232
Wordsplash, 243–244
Word square, 30, 190, 247
Words read correctly per minute (WCPM) rate, 195
Word wall, 65, 210, 211
Workshops, parent/community, 52
World-class Instructional Design and Assessment (WIDA), 194, 214, 222
Writer's workshop, 176
Writing
    assessment of, 218–225, 272–273
    challenges of teaching, 209
    checklists for, 221–222, 225
    comprehensible input and, 33
    and comprehension, 207
    content-based, 207
    determining goals in, 222–225
    interactive, 209–213
    and language development, 207–208
    portfolio assessment, 270
    process, 214–218
    purpose of teaching to ELLs, 206, 207–208
    rubrics for, 285, 286, 287
    scientific, 203–204
    self-assessment, 223
    standards for ELLs, 222–225
Writing conferences, 221
Writing development
    aspects of, 208
    with ELLs, 206–207
    environment for, 209
    stages of, 206
Writing process, 214–218
    shared, 216–218
    steps in, 214–216
Writing software, 221

Young, L., 233, 244
Young, T. A., 213
Yuen, S., 110

Zone of proximal development (ZPD), 19, 113